T0211152

Lecture Notes in Artificial Intelligence 12882

Subseries of Lecture Notes in Computer Science

More information about this subseries at http://www.springer.com/series/1244

Enrique Alba · Gabriel Luque ·
Francisco Chicano · Carlos Cotta ·
David Camacho · Manuel Ojeda-Aciego ·
Susana Montes · Alicia Troncoso ·
José Riquelme · Rodrigo Gil-Merino (Eds.)

Advances in Artificial Intelligence

19th Conference of the Spanish Association
for Artificial Intelligence, CAEPIA 2020/2021
Málaga, Spain, September 22–24, 2021
Proceedings

 Springer

Editors
Enrique Alba
University of Malaga
Málaga, Spain

Gabriel Luque
University of Malaga
Málaga, Spain

Francisco Chicano
University of Malaga
Málaga, Spain

Carlos Cotta
University of Malaga
Málaga, Spain

David Camacho
Technical University of Madrid
Madrid, Spain

Manuel Ojeda-Aciego
University of Malaga
Málaga, Spain

Susana Montes
University of Oviedo
Oviedo, Spain

Alicia Troncoso
Pablo de Olavide University
Seville, Spain

José Riquelme
University of Seville
Seville, Spain

Rodrigo Gil-Merino
University of Malaga
Málaga, Spain

ISSN 0302-9743   ISSN 1611-3349 (electronic)
Lecture Notes in Artificial Intelligence
ISBN 978-3-030-85712-7   ISBN 978-3-030-85713-4 (eBook)
https://doi.org/10.1007/978-3-030-85713-4

LNCS Sublibrary: SL7 – Artificial Intelligence

This Springer imprint is published by the registered company Springer Nature Switzerland AG
The registered company address is: Gewerbestrasse 11, 6330 Cham, Switzerland

Preface

This volume contains a selected and peer-reviewed set of papers explicitly submitted to CAEPIA 20/21, the XIX Conference of the Spanish Association for Artificial Intelligence, held in Málaga, Spain, during September 22–24, 2021. This series of conferences is a well-established biennial Spanish event on Artificial Intelligence (AI) that started back in 1985. Previous editions took place in Alicante, Málaga, Murcia, Gijón, San Sebastián, Santiago de Compostela, Sevilla, La Laguna, Madrid, Albacete, Salamanca, and Granada.

CAEPIA is a national forum open to researchers from all over the world to present and discuss their latest scientific and technological advances in AI. Authors were kindly requested to submit unpublished original papers describing relevant achievements on AI topics for evaluation to appear in this volume. The conference welcomed theoretical, methodological, technical, and applied research.

Several federated congresses and workshops related to relevant AI tracks took place within CAEPIA: XX Spanish Congress on Fuzzy Logic and Technologies (ESTYLF); XIV Spanish Congress on Metaheuristics, Evolutionary and Bioinspired Algorithms (MAEB); X Symposium of Theory and Applications of Data Mining (TAMIDA); and six workshops.

Within CAEPIA 20/21 we also had a Doctoral Consortium (DC) for students. This is a forum for doctoral students to interact with other researchers by discussing their PhD advances and working plans. As an additional AI activity, we ran the 4th Competition on Mobile Apps with AI Techniques, side by side with a new edition of the AI Dissemination Videos Competition.

All the above activities endorse AI, and we strove to reach a high quality in the scientific papers, the DC, and the competitions. The scientific program of CAEPIA 20/21 also offered a track to disseminate outstanding recently published papers (Key Works: KW) appearing in renowned journals and fora. CAEPIA has always aimed to be recognized as a flagship conference in AI, and thus the peer reviewed papers, especially for this LNAI volume, went through a strict evaluation process. The total number of submissions to CAEPIA 20/21 was 186 (neither DC nor competitions nor KW submissions (83 additional contributions) were included in this number, since they went through a different evaluation process). Only 25 outstanding manuscripts were selected for this volume after a thorough double-blind review process that involved at least three reviews per submission, for which we are grateful to the area experts and the Program Committee. The reviewers judged the overall quality of the submitted manuscripts, together with the quality of the methodology employed, the soundness of the conclusions, the significance of the topic, the clarity, and the organization, among other evaluation criteria. On the basis of these reviews, the area experts proposed a final number of articles that were analyzed and approved by the editors of this LNAI volume.

CAEPIA 20/21 invited two internationally renowned researchers for a plenary talk. Our conference was held as a big event within the still larger Spanish Conference on Computer Science (CEDI), itself having very interesting plenary talks too. Our two plenary speakers were Óscar Cordón (Artificial Intelligence for Forensic Anthropology and Human Identification) and Yaochu Jin (Data-Driven Evolutionary Optimization).

AEPIA and the organizers of CAEPIA 20/21 recognized the best PhD theses and all the original articles in federated events written by both, seniors and students. CAEPIA 20/21 also aimed to promote the presence of women in AI research. As in previous editions, the Frances Allen award recognized the two best PhD theses defended by a woman during the last two years.

The editors of this volume would like to thank the many people that contributed to the success of CAEPIA 20/21: authors, members of the Scientific and Program Committees, invited speakers, event organizers, electronic media managers, etc. We would like to especially thank the tireless work of the Organizing Committee, our sponsors (like VRAIN in Valencia), the Springer team, and AEPIA for their support.

Last but not least, on behalf of the CAEPIA 20/21 participants, Enrique Alba (General Chair), and Gabriel Luque (LNAI volume responsible) really thank the University of Malaga (local premises for the conference) and the whole Spanish community working in AI (and their many foreign collaborators) for making this event a real success.

July 2021

Enrique Alba
Gabriel Luque
Francisco Chicano
Carlos Cotta
David Camacho
Manuel Ojeda-Aciego
Susana Montes
Alicia Troncoso
José Riquelme
Rodrigo Gil-Merino

Organization

General Chair

Enrique Alba   University of Malaga, Spain

Awards Committee Chair

Eva Onaindia   Polytechnic University of Valencia, Spain

Tutorials and Workshops Chairs

Rodrigo Gil-Merino   University of Malaga, Spain
Araceli Sanchís   University Carlos III of Madrid, Spain

General Session Chair

Francisco Chicano   University of Malaga, Spain

Competitions Chairs

Alberto Bugarín   University of Santiago de Compostela, Spain
José Antonio Gámez   University of Castilla-La Mancha, Spain

Responsible for the LNAI Proceedings of CAEPIA

Gabriel Luque   University of Malaga, Spain

Doctoral Consortium Chairs

José Riquelme   Universidad de Sevilla, Spain
María José Del Jesús Díaz   Universidad de Jaén, Spain

Conferences and Workshop Chairs

XX ESTYLF

Manuel Ojeda-Aciego   University of Malaga, Spain
Susana Montes   University of Oviedo, Spain

XIV MAEB

Carlos Cotta	University of Malaga, Spain
David Camacho	Technical University of Madrid, Spain

X TAMIDA

Alicia Troncoso	Universidad Pablo de Olavide, Spain
José C. Riquelme	Universidad de Sevilla, Spain

IABiomed 20/21

Mar Marcos	Universitat Jaume I, Spain
David Riaño	Universitat Rovira i Virgili, Spain
José M. Juárez	Universidad de Murcia, Spain

IA-SIT 20/21

Paz Sesmero	University Carlos III of Madrid, Spain
Pablo Marín	University Carlos III of Madrid, Spain
Juan Pedro Llerena	University Carlos III of Madrid, Spain

AI4D 20/21

Agapito Ledezma Espino	University Carlos III of Madrid, Spain
José Antonio Iglesias Martínez	University Carlos III of Madrid, Spain
David Camilo Corrales Muñoz	Institut national de la recherche agronomique (INRA), France
Elias Said Hung	International University of La Rioja, Spain

QUARTI 20/21

Javier Echanobe	University of the Basque Country, Spain
Enrique Alba	University of Malaga, Spain

AGM 20/21

Carlos González Val	AIMEN Technological Center, Spain
Juan Manuel Fernández Montenegro	AIMEN Technological Center, Spain
Andrea Fenández Martinez	AIMEN Technological Center, Spain
Santiago Muiños Landin	AIMEN Technological Center, Spain
Omar A. Mures	University of A Coruña (UDC), Spain
José A. Iglesias-Guitián	University of A Coruña (UDC), CITIC - Centre for ICT Research, Spain

SCAI 20/21

Jamal Toutouh	University of Malaga, Spain
Enrique Alba	University of Malaga, Spain

Organizing Committee

Publicity

Rubén Saborido	University of Malaga, Spain

Visual Concepts

Christian Cintrano	University of Malaga, Spain
José Ángel Morell	University of Malaga, Spain

Web

José Ángel Morell	University of Malaga, Spain

IT Hybrid Format

Francisco Chicano	University of Malaga, Spain
Andrés Camero	German Aerospace Center, Germany

Area Chairpersons

Óscar Corcho	Universidad Politécnica de Madrid, Spain
Javier del Ser	Tecnalia, Spain
Juan Manuel Fernández Luna	University of Granada, Spain
Jesús García Herrero	Universidad Carlos III de Madrid, Spain
Pedro Larrañaga	Universidad Politécnica de Madrid, Spain
Patricio Martínez Barco	Universidad de Alicante, Spain
Miguel Molina Solana	University of Granada, Spain
Serafín Moral Callejón	University of Granada, Spain
Eva Onaindia	Polytechnic University of Valencia, Spain
Juan Pavón Mestras	Universidad Complutense de Madrid, Spain
David Pearce	Universidad Politécnica de Madrid, Spain
José Luis Pérez de la Cruz Molina	University of Malaga, Spain
Petia Radeva	Universitat de Barcelona and Computer Vision Center, Spain

Program Committee

Maedeh Aghaei	Universitat de Barcelona, Spain
Amparo Alonso-Betanzos	University of A Coruña, Spain
Jaume Bacardit	Newcastle University, UK
Antonio Bahamonde	Universidad de Oviedo at Gijon, Spain
Javier Bajo	Universidad Politécnica de Madrid, Spain
Emili Balaguer-Ballester	Bournemouth University, UK
Ana M. Barbancho	University of Malaga, Spain
Álvaro Barreiro	University of A Coruña, Spain
Edurne Barrenechea	Public University of Navarra, Spain
Senén Barro	University of Santiago de Compostela, Spain
José Ángel Bañares	University of Zaragoza, Spain
Ana M. Bernardos	Universidad Politécnica de Madrid, Spain
Concha Bielza Lozoya	Universidad Politécnica de Madrid, Spain
Daniel Borrajo	JPMorgan & Chase AI Research Lab, Spain
Juan Botia	King's College London, UK
Vicent Botti	Universitat Politècnica de València, Spain
Humberto Bustince	UPNA, Spain
Pedro Cabalar	University of A Coruña, Spain
José M. Cadenas	Universidad de Murcia, Spain
Zoraida Callejas	University of Granada, Spain
Iván Cantador	Universidad Autónoma de Madrid, Spain
Robert Castelo	Universitat Pompeu Fabra, Spain
Francisco Chicano	University of Malaga, Spain
Óscar Corcho	Universidad Politécnica de Madrid, Spain
Rafael Corchuelo	University of Seville, Spain
Carlos Cotta	University of Malaga, Spain
Zakaria Abdelmoiz Dahi	University of Malaga, Spain
Sergio Damas	University of Granada, Spain
Luis M. de Campos	University of Granada, Spain
André de Carvalho	University of Sao Paulo, Brazil
Luis De La Ossa	University of Castilla-La Mancha, Spain
Juan José Del Coz	University of Oviedo at Gijón, Spain
Javier del Ser	Tecnalia, Spain
Natalia Díaz-Rodríguez	ENSTA Paris, Institut Polytechnique de Paris, France
José Dorronsoro	Universidad Autónoma de Madrid, Spain
Jorge Fandinno	Potsdam University, Germany
Juan Manuel Fernández Luna	Universidad de Granada, Spain
Mariano Fernández López	Universidad San Pablo CEU, Brazil
Antonio Fernández-Caballero	Universidad de Castilla-La Mancha, Spain
Francesc J. Ferri	University of Valencia, Spain
José Manuel Galán	Universidad de Burgos, Spain
José Gámez	University of Castilla-La Mancha, Spain
Jesús García Herrero	University Carlos III of Madrid, Spain

Raúl García-Castro	Universidad Politécnica de Madrid, Spain
Rafael M. Gasca	University of Seville, Spain
Lluis Godo	IIIA - CSIC, Spain
Juan Gómez Romero	University of Granada, Spain
Antonio González	University of Granada, Spain
Manuel Graña	University of the Basque Country, Spain
Carlos Gómez-Rodríguez	Universidade da Coruña, Spain
César Hervás	University of Córdoba, Spain
Iñaki Inza	University of the Basque Country, Spain
Luis Jiménez Linares	University of Castilla-La Mancha, Spain
Kaisar Kushibar	University of Barcelona, Spain
Pedro Larrañaga	Universidad Politécnica de Madrid, Spain
Jordi Levy	IIIA - CSIC, Spain
Adolfo López	INSISOC - University of Valladolid, Spain
Gabriel Luque	University of Malaga, Spain
Victoria López	CUNEF University, Spain
Lawrence Mandow	University of Malaga, Spain
Felip Manya	IIIA - CSIC, Spain
Eugenio Martínez-Cámara	University of Granada, Spain
Luis Martínez	University of Jaén, Spain
Patricio Martínez Barco	Universidad de Alicante, Spain
José Massa	Universidad de Buenos Aires, Argentina
Rafael Medina-Carnicer	University of Córdoba, Spain
Marcos Mejía	Universitat de Barcelona, Spain
Belén Melián	Universidad de La Laguna, Spain
Pedro Meseguer	IIIA - CSIC, Spain
Eva Millán	University of Malaga, Spain
José M. Molina	Universidad Carlos III de Madrid, Spain
Miguel Molina Solana	University of Granada, Spain
Susana Montes	University of Oviedo, Spain
Serafín Moral Callejón	Universidad de Granada, Spain
Rafael Morales-Bueno	University of Malaga, Spain
Bhalaji Nagarajan	Universitat de Barcelona, Spain
José Fernando Núñez	Universitat de Barcelona, Spain
Manuel Ojeda-Aciego	University of Malaga, Spain
José Ángel Olivas	UCLM, Spain
Eva Onaindia	Polytechnic University of Valencia, Spain
Sascha Ossowski	University Rey Juan Carlos, Spain
Francisco Parreño	Universidad de Castilla-La Mancha, Spain
Miguel Ángel Patricio	Universidad Carlos III de Madrid, Spain
Juan Pavón Mestras	Universidad Complutense de Madrid, Spain
David Pearce	Universidad Politécnica de Madrid, Spain
Antonio Peregrín	University of Huelva, Spain
Giuseppe Pezzano	Universitat de Barcelona, Spain
Filiberto Pla	University Jaume I, Spain
Héctor Pomares	University of Granada, Spain

Contents

Optimization and Search

Real-World Applications

Machine Learning

Prediction of Epiretinal Membrane from Retinal Fundus Images Using Deep Learning

Ángela Casado-García[1], Manuel García-Domínguez[1], Jónathan Heras[1(✉)], Adrián Inés[1], Didac Royo[2], and Miguel Ángel Zapata[2,3]

[1] Department of Mathematics and Computer Science, Universidad de La Rioja, Logrono, Spain
{angela.casado,manuel.garciad,jonathan.heras,adrian.ines}@unirioja.es
[2] Optretina, Barcelona, Spain
{didac,mazapata}@optretina.com
[3] Hospital Vall Hebron, Passeig Roser 126, Sant Cugat del Vallès, 08195 Barcelona, Spain

Abstract. An epiretinal membrane (ERM) is an eye disease that can lead to visual distortion and, in some cases, to loss of vision. Screening retinal fundus images allows ophthalmologists to early detect and diagnose this disease; however, the manual interpretation of images is a time-consuming task. In spite of the existence of several computer vision tools for analysing retinal fundus images, they are mainly focused on the diagnosis of diabetic retinopathy and glaucoma. In this work, we have conducted a thorough study of several deep learning architectures, and a variety of techniques to train them, in order to build a model for automatically diagnosing ERM. As a result, we have built several models that can be ensembled to achieve a F1-score of 86.82%. The lessons learned in this work can serve as a basis for the construction of deep learning models for diagnosing other eye diseases.

Keywords: Epiretinal membrane · Fundus · Image classification · Deep learning · Ensemble.

1 Introduction

An expert observation of retinal fundus features not only provides information about eye diseases, but also might indicate long-term conditions, such as diabetes, hypertension, or cardiovascular diseases [12]. Therefore, screening eyes, together with a timely consultation and treatment, is instrumental for early detection and diagnosis of ocular pathologies and systemic issues that need attention. Unfortunately, the manual interpretation of images is a time-consuming

This work was partially supported by Ministerio de Economía y Competitividad [MTM2017-88804-P].

E. Alba et al. (Eds.): CAEPIA 2021, LNAI 12882, pp. 3–13, 2021.
https://doi.org/10.1007/978-3-030-85713-4_1

task for ophthalmologists, and this has led to the development of computer-aided diagnosis systems based on computer vision techniques [3].

As in many other medical fields, deep learning techniques have revolutionised the automatic analysis of fundus images, and these methods have achieved a performance that is comparable with the assessment of ophthalmologists [6]. Most deep learning models in this area have focused on the diagnosis of diabetic retinopathy [6], glaucoma [16], and age-related macular degeneration [26]; but, patients may also suffer from other pathologies, and, hence, it is instrumental the development of techniques and methods for automatically diagnosing other diseases such as epiretinal membrane.

An epiretinal membrane (ERM) is a fibrocellular tissue found on the inner surface of the retina that is associated with loss of central vision and decreased visual acuity [5]. In spite of being one of the main causes for vitreoretinal surgery and having a high prevalence [27], it does not exist a screening procedure for diagnosing epiretinal membranes. Currently, the gold standard for diagnosing ERM is based on the exploration of the fundus by an ophthalmologist, and the confirmation via the analysis of optical coherence tomography images (OCT) [10,17]. However, acquiring OCT images is an expensive procedure that is not available for all patients. On the contrary, acquiring fundus images is cheaper, and most medical centres have the resources to acquire them. In this work, we have focused on building a classification model for diagnosing ERM in retinal fundus images; this can be seen as a first step towards designing a screening procedure for diagnosing this disease.

The main contribution of this paper is a thorough study of deep learning architectures for detecting ERM from fundus images using the dataset presented in Sect. 2—the study was approved by a institutional ethics review board. In such a study, we have tested several approaches for training deep learning architectures (see Sect. 3) including data augmentation using Generative Adversial Networks, transfer learning from two different datasets, or ensemble methods. The results presented in Sect. 4 show that the best approach to tackle the diagnosis of ERM consists in ensembling a variety of models (both convolutional and transformer-based) that were pre-trained on a multi-disease detection dataset for fundus images [14], and then fine-tuned in our ERM dataset. Such an approach achieved a F1-score of 86.82%. Finally, we demonstrate, see Sect. 5, the usage of occlusion based attribution to interpret the outputs produced by our models.

2   Dataset

The ERM dataset employed in this work was created from retinal images of a private database, a nationwide database that collected retinal information from patients attending to optometrists. Images of the database were acquired using different non-mydriatic fundus cameras, all of them approved by the National Health Service for Diabetic Screening in the UK [2]. Optometrists were instructed to perform posterior pole retinal photography, centred on the macula and including the optic disc and vascular arcades [28]. The patients' information from the images was anonymised before sending them to the reading centre where 12 retina specialists characterised the images for changes in the macula, retina, and optic disc.

The ERM dataset consists of 4081 images (2108 positive samples, and 1973 negative samples) with a size of 299 × 299, and it was randomly split using an 80% of the images for training, and a 20% for testing. Furthermore, a 10% of the training dataset was employed for validation in order to adjust the hyperparameters of the models. This dataset has been employed to train several deep learning architectures using different approaches presented in the following section.

3 Training Procedures

We have conducted a thorough study of several families of deep learning architectures for diagnosing ERM—all the necessary code and models to run our experiments is available at https://github.com/CoVUR/ERM. The studied architectures, summarised in Table 1, included 3 manually designed convolutional neural networks (namely, ResNet [7], ResNeSt [32] and HRnet [25]), 2 architectures found by neural architecture search (EfficientNet [22] and NasNet [35]); and 2 transformer-based architectures that are ViT [4], and its training efficient version, Deit [24]. All the networks used in our experiments were implemented in Pytorch [15], and have been trained thanks to the functionality of the Fastai library [8] using a GPU Nvidia RTX 2080 Ti, and using the cross entropy loss function. In order to train the different models, we considered 4 approaches: baseline models, CycleGAN augmentation, state-of-the-art bag of tricks, and transfer learning from a close domain.

First of all, and in order to establish a baseline for our models, we have used the transfer-learning method presented in [8]. This is a two-stage procedure that starts from a model pretrained in the ImageNet challenge, and can be summarised as follows. In the first stage, we replaced the head of the model (that is, the layers that give us the classification of the images), with a new head adapted to the number of classes of each particular dataset. Then, we trained these new layers (the rest of the layers stayed frozen) with the data of each particular dataset for two epochs. In the second stage, we unfreezed the whole model and retrained all the layers of the model with the new data for 50 epochs. In order to find a suitable learning rate for both the first and second stage, we used cyclical learning rates for optimisation [20]. Moreover, we employed early stopping based on monitoring the validation loss, and data augmentation [18] (using vertical and horizontal flips, rotations from –180° to 180°, zooms and lighting transformations) to prevent overfitting.

In addition to the classical data augmentation techniques employed for training our baseline models, we have also studied an approach that consists in using a Generative Adversarial Network (GAN) to synthesise new retinal images [23]. In particular, we trained a CycleGAN model [34] that allowed us to synthesise ERM images from healthy images and viceversa (1652 healthy images, and 1622 ERM images were generated using this procedure). The CycleGAN model was

Table 1. Architectures and backbones employed in our study

Architecture	Backbones
Resnet	34, 50, 101
Resnest	26, 50, 50_4s2x40, 101
EfficientNet	B0–B3
ViT	ViT-B/16-244, ViT-B/16-R50-384
Deit	ViT-B/16-384
NasNet	050
HRnet	w32, w40, w44, w48, w64

trained using the UPIT library[1] for 15 epochs and using the learning rate suggested by the algorithm presented in [20]. The generated images were combined with the original dataset and used for training the models by employing the same procedure presented in the previous paragraph.

In the third set of experiments, we employed a bag of "tricks" that have been successfully employed in the literature to improve the performance of deep classification models. First of all, we replaced the Adam optimisation algorithm, the by-default optimiser used in Fastai, with the Ranger algorithm, which combines ideas from the RAdam optimisation algorithm [9] and the Lookahead optimiser [33]. Moreover, we used two regularisation techniques that are Label Smoothing [21] and MixUp [31]. Finally, we applied the cyclical learning rate policy for convergence proposed in [11]. In order to identify the benefits provided by each trick, an ablation study was conducted.

The last approach that we explored to train our models was based on the fact that transfer learning produces better results when there is a close relation between the source and target task. Hence, we started by training the models with the RIADD dataset [13] (a dataset of 8289 images for multi-disease detection on retinal images); and, subsequently, we fine-tuned the models for our ERM dataset. It is worth mentioning that the models trained for the RIADD dataset did not aim to detect the multiple diseases, but we simplified the problem to determine whether the retinal images were healthy. The RIADD's models were trained using the procedure presented for the baseline approach.

Finally, and in order to further improve the performance of our models, we employed ensemble methods. Namely, we tested the ensemble of several models [30] (that is, given an image, we averaged the predictions produced by multiple models to obtain a final output), the application of test-time augmentation [19] (that is, given an image, we created random modifications of such an image, performed predictions on them using a model, and, finally, returned the average of those predictions), and the combination of these two techniques. As we will show in the following section, these ensemble techniques considerably improved the performance of individual models.

---

[1] https://github.com/tmabraham/UPIT.

4   Results and Discussion

The models trained with the different approaches presented throughout the previous section were evaluated on the testing set using the F1-score as metric, see Table 2 for a summary of the results. The rest of this section is devoted to discuss the advantages and disadvantages of each training approach.

Table 2. F1-score achieved by the studied architectures using the baseline procedure, the CycleGAN dataset, the bag-of-tricks, and transfer learning from a close domain. Moreover, we include the results obtained by applying test-time augmentation (TTA) to the models fine-tuned from a close domain, and the results for the RIADD dataset. In italics the best model for each approach, and in bold face the best overall model without TTA.

Architecture	Baseline	CycleGAN	Tricks	Transfer	TTA	RIADD
Resnet-34	55.22	55.18	72.21	59.09	65.69	75.04
Resnet-50	49.53	58.04	75.23	72.18	72.63	73.93
Resnet-101	53.04	46.53	71.85	72.20	72.20	68.38
Resnest-26	55.18	53.59	73.62	62.68	66.36	75.57
Resnest-50	56.02	56.22	76.72	49.22	55.57	75.76
Resnest50d_4s2x40d	56.12	61.99	78.36	63.38	68.10	73.05
Resnest101	59.03	49.63	76.31	56.92	64.00	76.07
EfficientNet-B0	51.16	60.47	73.83	67.43	65.05	78.87
EfficientNet-B1	48.62	47.26	70.14	66.09	71.16	79.05
EfficientNet-B2	60.20	49.94	71.98	61.82	65.30	79.19
EfficientNet-B3	56.68	50.20	73.41	66.96	65.67	79.45
VIT-B/16-244	69.41	62.80	72.21	73.13	76.25	83.01
ViT-B/16-R50-384	*81.29*	62.91	67.39	83.86	84.23	87.44
Deit-B/16-384	74.85	72.11	*81.52*	76.46	76.77	87.01
Nasnet-050	55.55	49.76	71.30	55.23	50.66	52.65
HRNet-w32	73.74	67.15	80.50	79.22	81.17	*87.98*
HRNet-w40	71.09	52.53	70.76	**84.00**	*85.52*	87.30
HRNet-w44	72.33	60.79	71.30	82.61	83.27	87.50
HRNet-w48	70.60	*76.12*	73.95	82.17	84.59	86.32
HRNet-w64	73.78	50.27	77.88	83.70	84.35	87.59

We start by analysing the baseline models. As we can notice from the first column of Table 2, the F1-score of most models is under 70%. The exceptions are the family of HRNet models, and the two transformer-based architectures. The most plausible explanation for those results is the high-resolution representation learned by those models in the ImageNet dataset, which is better transferred

Table 3. Ablation study of the bag of tricks using F1-score as metric. Each column represents a technique (B: baseline, R: Ranger optimiser, F: Flat cosine annealing, L: Label Smoothing, M: MixUp; and the rest of columns are combinations of the previous techniques). Each row represents an architecture (R: Resnet, RS: ResNeSt, E: EfficientNet, ViT: ViT, Deit: Deit, N: Nasnet, H: HRNet).

	B	R	F	L	M	RF	RM	FM	RL	FL	LM	RFL	RFM	RFLM
R-34	55.22	59.54	72.21	59.92	66.02	66.96	58.27	0.00	57.04	71.30	65.33	60.02	54.29	61.03
R-50	49.53	60.86	1.29	75.23	74.55	52.83	59.57	72.21	48.59	11.62	74.09	59.85	67.97	65.35
R-101	53.04	57.30	49.82	68.10	54.48	54.42	51.42	33.06	50.82	0.00	71.85	67.35	43.18	45.60
RS-26	55.18	58.54	0.42	66.67	64.85	72.43	62.60	72.21	57.52	72.21	71.48	73.62	60.92	72.17
RS-50	56.02	62.01	71.81	76.72	73.59	54.81	47.53	72.21	57.65	0.00	74.19	60.40	65.61	59.68
RS-50d	56.12	61.67	1.30	75.81	78.36	65.10	67.13	0.00	65.44	72.19	69.90	64.06	69.31	70.49
RS-101	59.03	60.64	39.11	74.35	76.31	58.37	49.34	2.98	59.93	7.49	70.49	59.68	68.33	62.07
E-0	51.16	55.89	0.00	72.10	69.60	68.81	62.65	68.25	55.60	25.54	67.27	66.75	73.83	73.83
E-1	48.62	55.84	56.43	69.03	67.28	66.67	55.13	0.00	63.96	0.00	68.41	70.14	66.49	66.58
E-2	60.20	63.49	71.98	67.42	66.92	69.21	55.93	58.75	58.69	0.00	65.82	71.14	70.49	65.59
E-3	56.68	61.20	71.22	72.81	57.55	68.91	57.52	69.22	60.09	64.04	67.88	73.41	64.65	68.26
ViT-244	69.41	68.40	0.00	72.21	70.92	0.00	67.20	72.21	72.21	72.21	72.21	0.00	72.21	0.00
ViT-384	81.29	67.39	67.74	60.84	59.74	2.17	38.07	62.15	57.28	66.21	66.13	66.27		
Deit-384	74.85	70.73	72.21	80.39	81.52	63.86	76.94	72.21	72.21	72.18	77.77	72.66	77.51	76.40
N-050	55.55	59.72	27.19	58.63	50.18	54.38	52.55	71.30	54.45	70.60	54.17	52.73	52.22	52.96
H-32	73.74	55.23	77.51	77.51	80.50	79.82	53.81	78.27	76.74	70.34	74.27	79.26	54.30	50.75
H-40	71.09	54.00	58.89	69.76	70.76	58.93	60.99	24.38	61.92	70.11	65.04	64.56	66.59	62.06
H-44	72.33	55.33	62.57	63.85	69.96	67.32	66.16	70.28	71.30	64.17	70.46	69.59	68.29	67.33
H-48	70.60	49.42	70.53	73.95	73.49	72.34	73.90	67.68	67.74	67.69	69.58	72.26	73.55	72.86
H-64	73.78	55.02	71.24	76.56	77.88	61.89	72.01	0.00	0.85	69.60	70.34	66.75	72.70	74.47

F1-score colour scale: 0   18   36   54   72   90

to this particular context of diagnosing ERM. It is specially remarkable the ViT-B/16-R50-384 model that achieved a F1-score of 81.29%.

We focus now on the results achieved when training the models with the dataset augmented with the images generated with the CycleGAN model. As we can notice from Table 2, the results highly vary among models ranging from an improvement of 9% in the Efficientnet-B1 model, to a 23% decay in the HRNet-w64 model. In general, in most models, augmenting the dataset with the images generated by the CycleGAN had a negative impact. This might occur due to the challenge of producing realistic images with the GAN models [1]; therefore, this approach needs further investigation to be successfully applied.

On the contrary to the results achieved with the augmented CycleGAN dataset, a clear benefit is obtained with the bag of tricks. Thanks to the set of applied tricks, all the architectures were able to achieve a performance over 70%—the exception is the ViT-B/16-R50-384 architecture whose performance considerably decayed from the baseline models. From the ablation study, see Table 3, we can notice that there is not a single technique, or combination of techniques, that always produce the best results. However, the usage of Label Smoothing and MixUp as regularisation techniques consistently produced good results. It is also worth mentioning that the benefits obtained with each individual technique did not stack when combined with other techniques. This hinders the applicability of this bag of tricks since lots of experiments must be conducted to find which methods should be applied to produce the best result for each architecture.

An approach that served to improve most base models, and did not require so many experiments as the bag of tricks, is the application of transfer learning from the RIADD dataset. Pretraining the models with such a dataset, and then fine-tuning them for the ERM dataset achieved a mean improvement of 7.57%. There were only 3 models which performance decayed using this approach, and some models improved more than a 20%. The architectures that took more advantage of this approach were those from the HRNet family, since all of them reached a performance close or even higher than 80%. In fact, the best overall individual model was obtained with the HRNet-w40 architecture with a F1-score of 84%.

We also analysed how the performance of the individual models could be improved thanks to the application of ensemble methods. The ensemble of the 5 best models achieved a F1-score of 84.76%; that is an improvement of 0.76% regarding the best individual model. Since, 4 out of 5 of the best models belonged to the same family, we also tested the ensemble of the best individual model of each family; however, the F1-score obtained by such an ensemble was 81.01%, worse than the best individual model. Moreover, we analysed the impact of test-time-augmentation. This technique was applied to each individual model built using the close transfer approach, and, as we can notice in Table 2, the majority of models improved thanks to it (namely, a mean improvement of 3%, and only the performance of 3 models decayed). The best result was again obtained with the HRNet-w40 model with an improvement of 1.52%. Finally, we combined the ensemble of the output produced by the test-time augmentation of the 5 best models, and this produced a F1-score of 86.82%, the best overall result.

As a summary of this section, we can conclude that transformer based architectures (that is, ViT and Deit) are a sensible alternative to convolutional neural networks when applying transfer-learning from natural images to retinal fundus images. Moreover, the performance of most models can be boost by applying techniques like LabelSmoothing or MixUp, but this requires the conduction of lots of experiments. A similar enhancement, but that does not require so many adjustments, can be achieved by applying transfer learning from the RIADD dataset, and, therefore, this is a sensible approach when the amount of computational resources is limited. Last but not least, the performance of models can be further improved thanks to the application of ensemble techniques.

Up to now, we have mainly focused on producing the best possible performance model, in the next section, we try to shed light on how those models take their decisions.

5   Interpretability Considerations

One of the main drawbacks of deep classification models is their black-box nature, which hinders the usage and trust of these models. An approach to tackle this issue is the application of model interpretability techniques. Among the available techniques, we employed the occlusion-based attribution algorithm [29] supported by the Captum library[2]. Using this algorithm, we estimated which

---

[2] https://captum.ai.

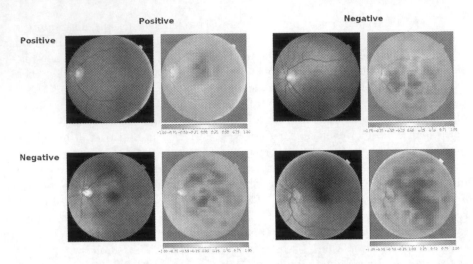

Fig. 1. Sample of occlusion-based attribution confusion matrix on the HRNet-w40 model. The red pixels in the heatmap indicate a negative attribution region (areas whose absence increases the score), whereas the green pixels indicate a positive attribution region (areas whose presence increase the prediction score)

areas of the image were critical for the classifiers' decision by occluding them and quantifying how the decision changed. We run a sliding window of size 15×15 with a stride of 8 along both image dimensions; and, at each location, we occluded the image with a baseline value of 0 which corresponds to a grey patch.

In Fig. 1, we have depicted the result of applying the occlusion-based attribution algorithm to a true positive, a true negative, a false positive, and a false negative. It is worth noting that in the correct predictions, positive attribution regions (areas whose presence increase the prediction score) clearly surpass negative attribution regions (areas whose absence increase the score); whereas in those images where the model fails, there is a considerable mix of positive and negative attribution regions. Moreover, it is also worth mentioning that the

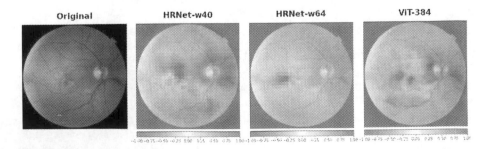

Fig. 2. Occlusion-based attribution heatmaps for the three best individual models

relevant regions are not the same for all the models, see Fig. 2. This gives an interpretation to the boost provided by ensemble methods, since different models take into account different features, and their combination can be the key for outputting the correct result.

6   Conclusions and Further Work

In this paper, we have thoroughly studied several approaches to build deep learning models for diagnosing epiretinal membrane. The best results, with a F1-score of 86.82%, was achieved by using the HRNet and transformer-based architectures, and combining 3 techniques (transfer learning from the RIADD dataset, test-time augmentation and model ensemble). As further work, we plan to extend our work to other retinal diseases, and improve the quality of images generated by GAN models since this can be helpful when images of a disease are scarce.

References

1. Arjovsky, M., Bottou, L.: Towards principled methods for training generative adversarial networks. In: International Conference on Learning Representations (2017)
2. Authors not listed: Diabetic eye screening: guidance on camera approval (2020), https://www.gov.uk/government/publications/diabetic-eye-screening-approved-cameras-and-settings/diabetic-eye-screening-guidance-on-camera-approval
3. Balakrishnan, U., et al.: A hybrid pso-defs based feature selection for the identification of diabetic retinopathy. Curr. Diabet. Rev. **11**(3), 182–190 (2015)
4. Dosovitskiy, A., et al.: An image is worth 16x16 words: transformers for image recognition at scale. In: International Conference on Learning Representations (2021)
5. Foos, R.Y.: Vitreoretinal juncture — simple epiretinal membranes. Albrecht von Graefes Archiv für klinische und experimentelle Ophthalmologie **189**, 231–250 (1974)
6. Gulshan, V., et al.: Development and validation of a deep learning algorithm for detection of diabetic retinopathy in retinal fundus photographs. JAMA **316**(22), 2402–2410 (2016)
7. He, K., Zhang, X., Ren, S., Sun, J.: Deep residual learning for image recognition. In: IEEE Conference on Computer Vision and Pattern Recognition, pp. 770–778 (2016)
8. Howard, J., Gugger, S.: Fastai: a layered API for deep learning. Information **11**, 108 (2020)
9. Liu, L., et al.: On the variance of the adaptive learning rate and beyond. In: International Conference on Learning Representations (2020)
10. Lo, Y.C., et al.: Epiretinal membrane detection at the ophthalmologist level using deep learning of optical coherence tomography. Sci. Rep. **10**, 8424 (2020)
11. Loshchilov, I., Hutter, F.: Sgdr: Stochastic gradient descent with warm restarts. In: International Conference on Learning Representations (2017)

12. MacGillivray, T., et al.: Retinal imaging as a source of biomarkers for diagnosis, characterization and prognosis of chronic illness or long-term conditions. Br. J. Radiol **87**(1040), 20130832 (2014)

13. Pachade, S., et al.: Retinal fundus multi-disease image dataset (rfmid): a dataset for multi-disease detection research. Data **6**(2), 14 (2021)

14. Pachade, S., et al.: Retinal fundus multi-disease image dataset (rfmid): a dataset for multi-disease detection research. Data **6**(2) (2021). https://doi.org/10.3390/data6020014

15. Paszke, A., et al.: Pytorch: an imperative style, high-performance deep learning library. In: Advances in Neural Information Processing Systems 32, pp. 8024–8035. Curran Associates, Inc. (2019)

16. Ran, A.R., et al.: Deep learning in glaucoma with optical coherence tomography: a review. Eye **35**, 188–201 (2021)

17. Reintragulchai, S., et al.: Predicting chance of success on epiretinal membrane surgery using deep learning. In: 14th International Joint Symposium on Artificial Intelligence and Natural Language Processing (2019)

18. Simard, P., Steinkraus, D., Platt, J.C.: Best practices for convolutional neural networks applied to visual document analysis. In: 12th International Conference on Document Analysis and Recognition, vol. 2, pp. 958–964 (2003)

19. Simonyan, K., Zisserman, A.: Very deep convolutional networks for large-scale image recognition. In: International Conference on Learning Representations (2015)

20. Smith, L.: Cyclical learning rates for training neural networks. In: IEEE Winter Conference on Applications of Computer Vision, pp. 464–472 (2017)

21. Szegedy, C., et al.: Rethinking the inception architecture for computer vision. In: IEEE Conference on Computer Vision and Pattern Recognition, pp. 2818–2826 (2016)

22. Tan, M., Le, Q.V.: Efficientnet: rethinking model scaling for convolutional neural networks. Int. Conf. Mach. Learn. **97**, 6105–6114 (2019)

23. Tavakkoli, A., et al.: A novel deep learning conditional generative adversarial network for producing angiography images from retinal fundus photographs. Sci. Rep. **10**(21580) (2020)

24. Touvron, H., et al.: Training data-efficient image transformers & distillation through attention (2021). https://arxiv.org/abs/2012.12877

25. Wang, J., et al.: Deep high-resolution representation learning for visual recognition. IEEE Transactions on Pattern Analysis and Machine Intelligence (2020)

26. Yan, Q., et al.: Deep-learning-based prediction of late age-related macular degeneration progression. Nat. Mach. Intell. **2**, 188–201 (2020)

27. Zapata, M., et al.: Prevalence of vitreoretinal interface abnormalities on spectral-domain oct in healthy participants over 45 years of age. Ophthalmol. Retina **1**(3), 249–254 (2017)

28. Zapata, M., et al.: Telemedicine for a general screening of retinal disease using nonmydriatic fundus cameras in optometry centers: Three-year results. Telemed. e-Health **23**(1), 30–36 (2017)

29. Zeiler, M.D., Fergus, R.: Visualizing and understanding convolutional networks. Eur. Conf. Comput. Vis. LNCS **8689**, 818–833 (2014)

30. Zhang, C., Ma, Y. (eds.): Ensemble Machine Learning: Methods and Applications. Springer, NewYork (2012)

31. Zhang, H., et al.: mixup: beyond empirical risk minimization. In: International Conference on Learning Representations (2018)

32. Zhang, H., et al.: Resnest: Split-attention networks (2020). https://arxiv.org/abs/2004.08955
33. Zhang, M., et al.: Lookahead optimizer: k steps forward, 1 step back. In: Advances in Neural Information Processing Systems, vol. 32. Curran Associates, Inc. (2019)
34. Zhu, J.Y., et al.: Unpaired image-to-image translation using cycle-consistent adversarial networks. In: International Conference on Computer Vision, pp. 2242–2251 (2017)
35. Zoph, B., et al.: Learning transferable architectures for scalable image recognition. In: IEEE/CVF Conference on Computer Vision and Pattern Recognition, pp. 8697–8710 (2018)

LabelDetection: Simplifying the Use and Construction of Deep Detection Models

Ángela Casado-García and Jónathan Heras[✉]

Department of Mathematics and Computer Science, Universidad de La Rioja,
Logrono, Spain
{angela.casado,jonathan.heras}@unirioja.es

Abstract. Deep learning algorithms for object detection on images have
been successfully applied in several fields; however, non-expert users
might find difficult to adopt these techniques due to several reasons.
First of all, using detection models requires some knowledge about the
library employed to built them; and, in general, it is not usually possible to interact with the predictions produced by the models. In addition,
training custom models is also challenging because there are several algorithms implemented in different libraries, and each of them uses its own
annotation format, and is configured in a particular way. In this paper,
we face all those challenges by developing LabelDetection, a graphical
tool that allows non-expert users to employ models trained with different algorithms and libraries. Moreover, LabelDetection is an end-to-end
application that provides the necessary features to annotate a dataset of
images, and train a variety of object detection models. Finally, LabelDetection simplifies the use of advance techniques like test-time augmentation, that improves the accuracy of detection models; and data distillation, that reduces the number of images that must be annotated to
train a model. LabelDetection is freely available at https://github.com/
ancasag/LabelDetection.

Keywords: Deep learning · Object detection · Test time
augmentation · Data distillation

1   Introduction

Object detection is a fundamental task in computer vision since it is a key
step in many real-world applications such as security [2], satellite imagery [11]
or healthcare [21]. Over the last few years, a lot of progress has been made
in this field thanks to the use of deep convolutional neural networks [32], and
deep detectors have achieved impressive results in large datasets such as Pascal
VOC [12] and MS COCO [17].

This work was partially supported by Ministerio de Economía y Competitividad
[MTM2017-88804-P].

© Springer Nature Switzerland AG 2021
E. Alba et al. (Eds.): CAEPIA 2021, LNAI 12882, pp. 14–22, 2021.
https://doi.org/10.1007/978-3-030-85713-4_2

However, the process of creating and using detection models poses several challenges. First of all, for both the creation and use of those models, it is necessary to have some programming skills, and know how to use the detection algorithms and the libraries that implement them. Another problem that arises when building detection models is that they need a large number of annotated images, and this is a tedious and time-consuming task that may require expert knowledge [14]. Moreover, the use of detection models is not trivial since most of them can only be used within the library where they were built; and, therefore, it is necessary to have the necessary dependencies installed in the users computers, and know how the specific library works. Finally, it is usually not possible to interact with model predictions due to the lack of a simple and intuitive graphical interface designed for that purpose.

In this work, we address the aforementioned problems with the development of LabelDetection, a graphical application that guides the user in the process of building object detection models, facilitates the use of those models to detect objects in new images, and also allows the interaction with the generated predictions. Specifically, the main features of LabelDetection are:

- LabelDetection is a graphical tool that helps the user in all the steps required to train a variety of object detection algorithms based on deep learning techniques. This is achieved by wrapping several libraries and frameworks that provide different object detection architectures.
- LabelDetection can be used as the interface for a wide variety of object detection models trained using different libraries. In addition, this interface allows users to interact with the predictions generated by them.
- LabelDetection can be employed to train object detection models not only from fully annotated datasets but also from partially annotated datasets thanks to a semi-supervised technique known as data distillation.
- LabelDetection users can improve the accuracy of their models thanks to a technique known as test-time augmentation, and without writing a single line of code.

The rest of the paper is organised as follows. First, we provide the necessary background to contextualise our work. Subsequently, we introduce the main features of LabelDetection and apply it to the detection of wheat heads to show the feasibility and benefits of using our tool. We end the paper with some conclusions and further work. LabelDetection is an open-source tool that can be downloaded from https://github.com/ancasag/LabelDetection.

2   Background

In this section, we briefly introduce object detection libraries, their limitations, and two techniques that, in general, improve object detection models and are not directly included in any existing object detection library.

2.1 Object Detection Libraries

Deep learning for object detection is a growing field where new architectures and algorithms are publicly released [15]. However, in their initial form, most new architectures are released as research artefacts that are not prepared for using them in custom datasets. This problem has been solved with the development of several object detection libraries, see Table 1, that provide a common pipeline to train different detection models. The outstanding work conducted by the developers of object detection libraries might be enhanced by including two features that are missed in all those libraries.

The first feature that is missing is a simple way of producing the input dataset that will be used for training the algorithms. Each library requires images annotated in a particular format (being Pascal VOC and COCO the most common formats), and structured in a particular way (split of training and test set, and configuration files). This hinders the usage of the libraries since the task of annotating the images must be conducted in an external tool, such as LabelImg[1] or YOLO mark[2]; and the output produced by those tools must be manually organised, and in some cases transformed to the correct format.

The second issue with object detection libraries is the lack of an interface to interact with the predictions produced by the trained models. Object detection models can only be employed within the library that was used for producing them and, hence, require some programming skills. Moreover, the predictions produced by the models in a given image are usually drawn on the image; and, hence, it is not possible to interact with them (that is, add, remove or edit the predicted bounding boxes), a task that is necessary when using the detection models for analysing images.

Table 1. General features of libraries for object detection

library	Language	Year	Underlying library
Darknet detection [24]	C++	2018	Darknet
Detectron [31]	Python	2019	PyTorch
IceVision [29]	Python	2020	PyTorch
MaskRCNN-benchmark [19]	Python	2018	PyTorch
MXNet Detection [7]	Python	2019	MXNet
MMDetection [5]	Python	2019	PyTorch
SimpleDet [8]	Python	2019	MXNet
Tensorflow Detection API [13]	Python	2019	Tensorflow
Tensorpack [30]	Python	2019	Tensorflow

---

[1] https://github.com/tzutalin/labelImg.
[2] https://github.com/AlexeyAB/Yolo_mark.

In addition to these usability features, developers of object detection models might improve the performance of their models by applying two techniques that have been successfully used in the literature, but that are not directly supported by any library: test-time augmentation and data-distillation.

2.2   Test-Time Augmentation

Data augmentation [25] is a technique widely employed to train deep learning models. This technique consists in generating new training samples from the original training dataset by applying transformations that do not alter the class of the data. There is a variant of data augmentation for the test dataset known as *test-time augmentation* [26]. This technique creates random modifications of the test images, performs predictions on them, and, finally, returns an ensemble of those predictions. This technique is widely employed in the context of image classification [26]; and, even if it can be applied for object detectors, some transformations, like flips or rotations, change the position of the objects in the image and this issue must be taken into account when ensembling the predictions. A procedure to tackle this issue was presented in [4]. Test-Time augmentation is the basis for a semi-supervised learning technique known as data-distillation that allows us to train detection models using both labelled and unlabelled data.

2.3   Data Distillation

Deep learning methods are data demanding, and acquiring and annotating the necessary amount of images for constructing object detection models is a tedious and time-consuming process that might require specialised knowledge [14]. This has led to the development of semi-supervised learning techniques [34], a suite of methods that use unlabelled data to improve the performance of models trained with small dataset of annotated images. Data distillation [20] is a semi-supervised learning procedure that applies a trained model on manually labelled data to multiple transformations of unlabelled data, ensembles the multiple predictions, and, finally, retrains the model on the union of manually and automatically labelled data.

In this section, we have presented some features that can facilitate the construction and use of deep detection models, and also improve their performance. In this work, instead of proposing a new library that incorporates the aforementioned features, we have developed a wrapper that can be adapted for any existing object detection library; and, hence, it can take advantage of the efforts of different communities bringing to the table the best of each of them.

3   LabelDetection

LabelDetection is a graphical tool implemented in Python, and developed using, as a basis, LabelImg, a widely used image annotation application. LabelDetection helps non-expert users in the annotation of datasets, the process to train a model, and the use of such a trained model. The functionality to annotate datasets included in LabelDetection is provided by LabelImg, so we will focus on presenting the features included in LabelDetection for training and using different detection models.

3.1 LabelDetection for Training Models

The annotation produced by LabelDetection follows the PascalVOC format, that can be employed to train most object detection algorithms. In order to use an annotated dataset to train an algorithm, the dataset must be split into a training and testing set; however, the algorithms are sensitive to the folder structure containing the training and testing files, and such an organisation depends on the concrete algorithm and library. Moreover, object detection algorithms require several configuration files, that also depend on the particular algorithm and library implementing it. LabelDetection solves these issues by generating a zip file containing the dataset annotated with the structure and format required by different algorithms and also the necessary configuration files. In addition, LabelDetection generates a Jupyter notebook [16] that configures the environment, installs the necessary libraries, trains a model with the training set using transfer learning [22], and finally evaluates the model against the testing set—the Jupyter notebooks generated by LabelDetection can be run either locally, provided the users have a GPU, or using cloud services like Google Colaboratory [9].

LabelDetection can currently generate Jupyter notebooks for the following algorithms and libraries: several versions of the YOLO algorithm [24], based on the Darknet library [23]; SSD [18], using the MxNet library [6]; and several algorithms implemented in Keras, namely, Mask R-CNN [1], EfficientDet [27], FSAF [33] and FCOS [28]. In addition, LabelDetection has been designed to easily include this functionality for other algorithms and object detection libraries. LabelDetection also offers the possibility of including the data distillation procedure in the Jupyter notebooks. To this aim, the user must have a set of images that are not annotated, and select the transformation techniques that will be applied to the images for data distillation, see Fig. 1.

3.2 LabelDetection for Object Detection

LabelDetection can be employed not only to train object detection models, but also use them—this facilitates the dissemination of such models and avoids the development of new graphical interfaces for each new model, a task that is almost an art [3]. LabelDetection can apply models trained with any of the previously mentioned algorithms (as in the case of model creation, this functionality can be easily extended to other algorithms and libraries), and it only requires the weights and configuration files of those models; that is, users do not need to install any additional library or write a single line of code. In addition, LabelDetection allows users to apply test-time augmentation to all the supported models in order to improve their accuracy by selecting the set of transformations to

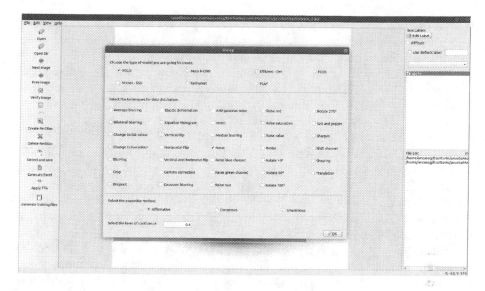

Fig. 1. LabelDetection interface

apply. Finally, the bounding boxes produced by a model can be visualised and modified from the LabelDetection interface; and, a summary of the detected objects can be exported to an Excel file.

In the next section, we illustrate the feasibility of using LabelDetection for training different models, and the benefits of applying both data distillation and test-time augmentation to those models.

4   Case Study

In this section, we employ the different algorithms and methods included in LabeDetection for creating models for detecting wheat heads. To this aim, we have used the Global WHEAT Dataset [10], a large-scale dataset for wheat head detection from field optical images. This dataset includes very large range of cultivars. All images share a common format of 1024×1024 px with a resolution of 0.1–0.3 mm per pixel. The dataset contains 4700 high-resolution RGB images (4578 were used for training, and 422 for testing) and 190000 labelled wheat heads collected from several countries around the world at different growth stages with a wide range of genotypes.

Using LabelDetection, we have built detection models for this dataset in the Google Colaboratory environment[3]. Namely, we have trained the models using only the labelled data, and also applying data distillation. Moreover, we studied the impact of applying test-time augmentation in all the models. The results, in terms of precision, recall and F1-score, of our study are presented in Table 2,

---

[3] https://colab.research.google.com.

that is divided into three blocks. The first block contains the results obtained from the models trained using only the labelled data, the second block contains the results obtained by applying test-time augmentation, and in the last block we include the results of the models trained using data distillation. Using the labelled data, we have trained the v3, v4, and csresnet versions of the YOLO algorithm; and FSAF, FCOS, and EfficientDet algorithms. All the models were trained for 50 epochs and using the default parameters of each algorithm. The model that offers best trade-off between precision and recall is the v4 version of the YOLO algorithm, and the other 2 versions of the YOLO algorithm also achieve a F1-score over 0.80. This is also the case for the FSAF algorithm, whereas FCOS achieves a F1-score of 0.6 and EfficientDet is the worse model.

The performance of all the aforementioned models, but FSAF and the v4 version of YOLO, can be improved thanks to the application of the test-time augmentation. As transformations, we applied both vertical and horizontal flips, a rotation of 90°, gamma correction, and histogram normalisation. Moreover, we considered the predictions on the images without transforming them. Using this approach, we achieved an improvement ranging from 1% (in the v3 version of YOLO) to 50% (in the EfficientDet model).

Finally, we applied data distillation by using 1578 unlabelled images that were pseudo labelled by transforming them (using vertical and horizontal flips) and ensembling the predictions obtained by each model. All architectures but the v4 version of YOLO an FSAF improved their performance between a 3% and a 51%.

This case study allows us to illustrate that LabelDetection can be employed to construct a variety of detection models and easily compare them without having experience working on deep learning. Moreover, those models can be considerably improved thanks to data distillation and test-time augmentation. The advantage of the former technique is that it is faster in inference time, but it takes longer to train the models.

Table 2. Results for the Global Wheat dataset using the different networks and methods available in LabelDetection

	Normal			TTA			Data distillation		
Algorithm	Precision	Recall	F1-score	Precision	Recall	F1-score	Precision	Recall	F1-score
Csresnet	0.94	0.69	0.80	0.93	0.73	0.82	0.93	0.76	0.84
EfficientDet	0.40	0.31	0.35	0.93	0.79	0.85	0.93	0.80	0.86
FCOS	0.67	0.54	0.60	0.89	0.80	0.84	0.92	0.85	0.89
FSAF	0.93	0.85	0.89	0.81	0.81	0.81	0.83	0.87	0.85
YOLO v3	0.95	0.79	0.86	0.91	0.83	0.87	0.92	0.87	0.89
YOLO v4	0.89	0.92	0.91	0.90	0.81	0.90	0.90	0.91	0.91

5   Conclusions and Further Work

LabelDetection is an end-to-end graphical application that aims to facilitate the construction and usage of robust object detection models by providing access to state-of-the-art detection algorithms, and also simplifying the application of advance techniques like data distillation and test-time augmentation. In the future, we plan to extend LabelDetection with new object detection algorithms and libraries. Moreover, and since it is possible to train different models with LabelDetection, we will explore how to include the functionality to ensemble those models.

References

1. Abdulla, W.: Mask R-CNN for object detection and instance segmentation on Keras and TensorFlow. https://github.com/matterport/Mask_RCNN (2017)
2. Akcay, S., et al.: Using deep convolutional neural network architectures for object classification and detection within X-ray baggage security imagery. IEEE Trans. Inf. Fosics Secur. **13**(9), 2203–2215 (2018)
3. Anderson, J., McRee, J., Wilson, R.: Effective UI: The Art of Building Great User Experience in Software. O'Reilly Media (2010)
4. Casado-García, A., Heras, J.: Ensemble methods for object detection. In: Proceedings of the 24th European Conference on Artificial Intelligence (ECAI 2020) (2020)
5. Chen, K., et al.: MMDetection: open MMLab detection toolbox and benchmark. CoRR **abs/1906.07155** (2019), http://arxiv.org/abs/1906.07155
6. Chen, T., Li, M., Li, Y., et al.: MxNet: A Flexible and Efficient Machine Learning Library for Heterogeneous Distributed Systems. CoRR **abs/1512.01274** (2015)
7. Chen, T., Li, M., Li, Y., et al.: Mxnet object detection. https://gluon-cv.mxnet.io/build/examples_detection/index.html (2019)
8. Chen, Y., Han, C., Li, Y., et al.: Simpledet: a simple and versatile distributed framework for object detection and instance recognition. CoRR **abs/1903.05831** (2019), http://arxiv.org/abs/1903.05831
9. Colaboratory team: Google colaboratory (2017). https://colab.research.google.com
10. David, E., et al.: Global Wheat Head Detection (GWHD) dataset: a large and diverse dataset of high-resolution RGB-Labelled images to develop and benchmark wheat head detection methods. Plant Phenom. 3521852 (2020)
11. Etten, A.V.: You only look twice: rapid multi-scale object detection in satellite imagery. CoRR **abs/1805.09512** (2018)
12. Everingham, M., Gool, L.V., Williams, C.K.I., et al.: The Pascal visual object classes (VOC) challenge. Int. J. Comput. Vis. **88**(2), 303–338 (2010)
13. Huang, J., Rathod, V., Sun, C., et al.: Speed/accuracy trade-offs for modern convolutional object detectors. In: IEEE Conference on Computer Vision and Pattern Recognition (CVPR 2017), pp. 3296–3305 (2017)
14. Irvin, J., Rajpurkar, P., Ko, M., et al.: Chexpert: A large chest radiograph dataset with uncertainty labels and expert comparison. In: The Thirty-Third AAAI Conference on Artificial Intelligence (AAAI 2019) **33**, 590–597 (2019)
15. Jiao, L., Zhang, F., Liu, F., et al.: A survey of deep learning-based object detection. IEEE Access **7**, 128837–128868 (2019)

16. Kluyver, T., Ragan-Kelley, B., Perez, F., et al.: Jupyter notebooks—a publishing format for reproducible computational workflows. In: Proceedings of the 20th International Conference on Electronic Publishing, pp. 87–90. IOS Press, Amsterdam (2016)

17. Lin, T.Y., Maire, M., Belongie, S., et al.: Microsoft COCO: common objects in context. In: Proceedings of the European Conference on Computer Vision (ECCV 2014), vol. 8693, pp. 740–755 (2014)

18. Liu, W., Anguelov, D., Erhan, D., et al.: Ssd: single shot multibox detector. In: Proceedings of the European Conference on Computer Vision (ECCV 2016), vol. 9905, pp. 21–37 (2016)

19. Massa, F., Girshick, R.: maskrcnn-benchmark: Fast, modular reference implementation of Instance Segmentation and Object Detection algorithms in PyTorch. https://github.com/facebookresearch/maskrcnn-benchmark (2018)

20. Radosavovic, I., Dollár, P., Girshick, R., et al.: Data Distillation: Towards Omni-Supervised Learning. In: Proceedings of the IEEE Conference on Computer Vision and Pattern Recognition. pp. 4119–4128. CVPR'18 (2018)

21. Ramachandran, S., George, J., Skaria, S., et al.: Using YOLO based deep learning network for real time detection and localization of lung nodules from low dose CT scans. In: Proceedings of Medical Imaging 2018: Computer-Aided Diagnosis, p. 53 (2018)

22. Razavian, A.S., Azizpour, H., Sullivan, J., et al.: CNN features off-the-shelf: an astounding baseline for recognition. In: Conference on Computer Vision and Pattern Recognition Workshops (CVPRW 2014), pp. 512–519 (2014)

23. Redmon, J.: Darknet: Open Source Neural Networks in C (2016). http://pjreddie.com/darknet/

24. Redmon, J., Farhadi, A.: Yolov3: an incremental improvement (2018). CoRR **abs/1804.02767**

25. Simard, P., Steinkraus, D., Platt, J.C.: Best practices for convolutional neural networks applied to visual document analysis. In: Proceedings of the International Conference on Document Analysis and Recognition (ICDAR 2003), vol. 2, pp. 958–964 (2003)

26. Simonyan, K., Zisserman, A.: Very deep convolutional networks for large-scale image recognition. In: Proceedings of the 3rd International Conference on Learning Representations (ICLR 2015) (2015). http://arxiv.org/abs/1409.1556

27. Tan, M., Pang, R., Le, Q.V.: EfficientDet: scalable and efficient object detection (2019). CoRR **abs/1911.09070**

28. Tian, Z., Shen, C., Chen, H., et al.: Fcos: fully convolutional one-stage object detection (2019). CoRR **abs/1904.01355**

29. Track, A.F.: Icevision: an agnostic object detection framework (2020). https://github.com/airctic/icevision

30. Wu, Y.: Tensorpack (2016). https://github.com/tensorpack/

31. Wu, Y., Kirillov, A., Massa, F., et al.: Detectron2 (2019). https://github.com/facebookresearch/detectron2

32. Zhao, Z.Q., Zheng, P., Xu, S., et al.: Object detection with deep learning: a review. In: IEEE Trans. Neural Netw. Learn. Syst. **30**, 1–21 (2019). https://doi.org/10.1109/TNNLS.2018.2876865

33. Zhu, C., He, Y., Savvides, M.: Feature selective anchor-free module for single-shot object detection (2019). CoRR **abs/1903.00621**

34. Zhu, X., Goldberg, A.B. (eds.): Introduction to Semi-Supervised Learning. Morgan & Claypool Publishers, San Rafael (2009)

A Proposal to Integrate Deep Q-Learning with Automated Planning to Improve the Performance of a Planning-Based Agent

Carlos Núñez-Molina, Ignacio Vellido, Vladislav Nikolov-Vasilev, Raúl Pérez🆔,
and Juan Fdez-Olivares$^{(\boxtimes)}$ 🆔

Department of Computer Science and AI, University of Granada, Granada, Spain
{ccaarlos,ignaciove}@correo.ugr.es,
{fgr,faro}@decsai.ugr.es

Abstract. In this work we propose an architecture which learns to select subgoals with Deep Q-Learning in order to decrease the load of a planner when faced with scenarios with tight time restrictions, such as online execution systems. We have trained this architecture on a video game environment used as a standard testbed for intelligent systems applications. We experiment with different values of the discount rate γ and show the importance of long-term thinking when selecting subgoals. We also compare our approach against a classical planner and show how it is able to greatly reduce time requirements, although obtaining plans with 25% more actions on average. We conclude our approach is competitive with a classical planner and presents better generalization properties than most Reinforcement Learning algorithms when applied to new levels of the same game.

Keywords: Automated planning · Goal reasoning · Deep Q-learning

1 Introduction

Automated Planning [4] is a subfield of Artificial Intelligence devoted to providing goal-oriented, deliberative behaviour to both physical and virtual agents, e.g., robots or video game automated players. An automated planner takes as input a planning domain, an initial state and a goal and searches for a plan (sequence of actions) which allows the agent to reach the goal from the initial state. Despite great advances in the integration of Automated Planning into online execution systems [11,12], real-time requirements still hinder the generalized adoption of Automated Planning in such scenarios. One main issue is that in most real-world problems the search space grows exponentially with problem size so, even with heuristics, finding a suitable plan can take very long.

This work has been partially supported by Spanish Government Project MINECO RTI2018-098460-B-I00 and UE FEDER.

E. Alba et al. (Eds.): CAEPIA 2021, LNAI 12882, pp. 23–32, 2021.
https://doi.org/10.1007/978-3-030-85713-4_3

Regarding online execution, architectures which rely on Machine Learning (ML) and Reinforcement Learning (RL) present some advantages over planning: they usually require very little prior knowledge (they do not need a planning domain) and, once trained, they act quickly. Nevertheless, they also present some drawbacks. Firstly, they are very sample inefficient and require a lot of data to learn [17]. Secondly, they usually present bad generalization properties when applied to new levels of the same game they have been trained on [20].

Since both Automated Planning and Reinforcement Learning have their own pros and cons, it seems natural to try to combine them as part of the same agent architecture, which would ideally possess the best of both worlds. Aligned with that purpose, the main contribution of this paper is the proposal of a Goal Selection Module based on Deep Q-Learning [9] and its integration into a planning and acting architecture to control the behaviour of an agent, in a real-time environment. We have tested our approach on the tile-based video game known as Boulder Dash, present in the GVGAI video game framework [13], training and testing on different levels of the same game to measure its generalization abilities. We conduct experiments to show that, when training on enough data, a Deep Q-Learning model which carries out long-term thinking when selecting subgoals performs better than one which does not. We also compare the performance of a planning and acting architecture endowed with our Goal Selection Module against a classical planner, and show that selecting goals with Deep Q-Learning drastically improves time performance, although obtaining plans with a 25% decrease in quality (measured as plan length). Moreover, we also show that in several cases, the planning and acting architecture can efficiently solve problems that cannot be addressed with a classical planner alone.

In the following sections we explain the GVGAI framework and provide a background on both the language to represent planning knowledge (PDDL) and Deep Q-Learning. We then present an overview of the architecture and show how the Goal Selection Module learns. After that, we present the results of our empirical study. We then compare our approach with related work, and finish by presenting our conclusions and future work.

2   Background

GVGAI. To test our planning and acting architecture we have used the General Video Game AI (GVGAI) Framework [13]. This framework provides a game environment with a large quantity of tile-based games which are also very different in kind. For example, it comprises purely reactive games, such as *Space Invaders*, and also games which require long-term planning in order to be solved successfully, such as *Sokoban*. In this work we have used a deterministic version of the GVGAI game known as Boulder Dash, which is shown in Fig. 1. In our version, the agent must traverse the level (up, down, right or left, one tile at a time), collect nine gems (by simply getting to tiles containing them) and then go to the exit, all of this while minimizing the number of actions used. The agent can't pass through walls and needs two turns to pass through a boulder (the first one to break it and the second one to walk through). This game is used to extract the episodes of planning and acting our Goal Selection Module is trained on. We have chosen GVGAI because game levels are represented as simple text files (known as level description files), enabling us to quickly create many levels to train and test our architecture on.

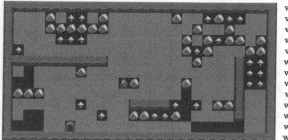

Fig. 1. A snapshot of a level of *Boulder Dash* (left) and the content of its level description file (right). This file is written in the Video Game Description Language, VGDL [13], where each type of object has a different ASCII character associated (e.g., *w* for walls).

PDDL. To encode the inputs for our Planner Module, we have used PDDL [3], the standard language used in Automated Planning for representing planning domains and problems. A PDDL *domain file* contains a description of both, the predicates used to represent a problem state, and the preconditions and effects of every action an agent can execute. A PDDL *problem file* contains a representation of the problem: its initial state and the goal to achieve. A planner receives as inputs these two files and returns a plan, which is constituted by an ordered sequence of instantiated PDDL actions. Given a GVGAI game, we can create its associated planning domain by encoding in PDDL the different objects of the game and their dynamics. Each game level will have a different planning problem associated, representing its initial state and the goal to achieve. For instance, in Boulder Dash a goal corresponds to getting a gem present at the level.

Deep Q-Learning. Q-Learning [19] is one of the most widely used techniques in Reinforcement Learning [15]. As every RL technique, it learns a policy π that, in every state s, selects the best action a from the set of available actions A in order to maximize the expected cumulative reward R. It does so by associating a value to each (s, a) pair, known as the Q-value $Q(s, a)$. This value represents the expected cumulative reward R associated with executing action a in state s, i.e., how good a is when applied in s. One of the main problems Q-Learning has is that it needs to learn the Q-value for each of the (s, a) pairs independently, which together constitute the Q-table. If the action or state space are too large, the Q-table grows and the learning problem becomes intractable. Deep Q-Learning [9] solves this problem, since it makes use of a Deep Neural Network to approximate the Q-values. For this reason, we use Deep Q-Learning in pursuit of the good generalization abilities shown in [9].

3   The Planning and Acting Architecture

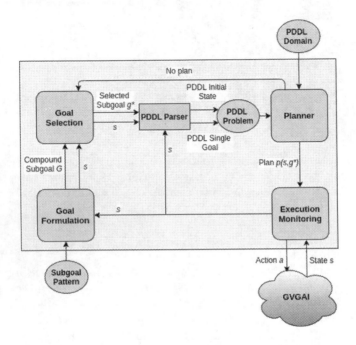

Fig. 2. An overview of the planning and acting architecture.

An overview of the planning and acting architecture can be seen on Fig. 2. The **Execution Monitoring** Module communicates with the GVGAI environment, receiving the current state s of the game. It also supervises the state of the current plan. If it is not empty, it returns the next action a. If it is empty, the architecture needs to find a new plan. The **Goal Formulation** Module receives s and generates the compound subgoal G, which is a list of single subgoals $\{g_1, g_2, ..., g_n\}$. The **Subgoal Pattern** contains the prior information about the domain needed to automatically generate G given s. We have limited the scope of this work to subgoals of the type (*goto tileX*). In Boulder Dash each $g \in G$ corresponds to either getting one of the available gems in s or getting to the exit of the level (this is the final goal g_f of the game). The **Goal Selection** Module receives G and selects the best subgoal $\hat{g} \in G$ given s. The **PDDL Parser** encodes $\hat{g}$ as a PDDL Single Goal, i.e., (*goto tile13*), and s as a PDDL Initial State, which together constitute the PDDL Problem. The **Planner** Module receives the PDDL Problem along with the PDDL Domain, provided by a human expert, and generates a plan $p(s, \hat{g})$ which achieves $\hat{g}$ starting from s. In case $\hat{g}$ cannot be reached from s (in Boulder Dash this happens when $\hat{g} = g_f$ and the agent has not got nine gems or more), the Planner Module returns an empty plan and the Goal Selection Module must select a new subgoal. This situation corresponds to a prediction mistake by the Goal Selection Module. Finally, the Execution Monitoring Module receives $p(s, \hat{g})$ and the cycle completes.

4   Goal Selection Learning

In order to select the best subgoal $\hat{g} \in G$ for a given s, the Goal Selection Module iterates over every $g \in G$ and predicts the length $l_{P(s,g)}$ of its associated plan $P(s, g)$, selecting the subgoal $\hat{g}$ with the plan of minimum length. This length $l_{P(s,g)}$ corresponds to the length $l_{p(s,g)}$ of the plan $p(s, g)$ which achieves g starting from s plus the length of the plan which, after obtaining g, reaches the final goal g_f by achieving the required subgoals in the order predicted as optimal by the Goal Selection Module. This way, the Goal Selection Module conducts long-term thinking and selects subgoals in a non-greedy way.

The Goal Selection Module uses a Convolutional Neural Network (CNN) [8] that receives s and a $g \in G$ and outputs the predicted plan length $l_{P(s,g)}$. The state s is represented as a *one-hot matrix*, i.e., a matrix where each cell contains a one-hot vector associated with a tile of the level, which encodes the objects present in that tile. Each position of the one-hot vector correponds to a different type of object. The subgoal g is also encoded in the one-hot vector of its corresponding tile. The CNN does not receive any information about s or g in addition to this one-hot matrix. This type of representation allows us to encode both s and g in the same data structure, which is suitable for applying convolutions on.

The architecture of the CNN is heavily inspired by the one used in the original DQN paper [9]. It is constituted by three convolutional layers, the first one with 32 filters and the other two with 64 filters each, and one fully-connected layer with 128 units. We have applied Batch Normalization after each convolutional layer and before the first one. In order to train the CNN, we have decided to apply the methodology followed by Deep Q-Learning [9]. To do so, we establish a correspondence between our problem and Reinforcement Learning (RL), but considering that our objective is to minimize the length $l_{P(s,g)}$ of the entire plan $P(s, g)$. An action a in RL corresponds in our work to achieving a subgoal g, the reward r obtained by executing a at s corresponds to $-l_{p(s,g)}$ (the negative length of the plan $p(s, g)$ that starts at s and achieves a subgoal g), the expected cumulative reward R associated with (s, a) corresponds to $-l_{P(s,g)}$, and maximizing R corresponds to maximizing $-l_{P(s,g)}$ (i.e. minimizing $l_{P(s,g)}$). Table 1 shows this correspondence.

The CNN of the Goal Selection Module predicts $l_{P(s,g)}$, which in Deep Q-Learning corresponds to the Q-value $Q(s, a)$. Since its correct value $Q^*(s, a)$ is unknown, we need to utilize the Bellman Equation, which recursively defines the optimal Q-values using other Q-values $Q(s', a')$. The loss L function incorporates this to define the error to be minimized:

Table 1. Correspondence between RL and our problem.

RL	Our work
Action a	Subgoal g
Reward r	$-l_{p(s,g)}$
Cumulative reward R	$-l_{P(s,g)}$
Maximize R	Maximize $-l_{P(s,g)}$ = Minimize $l_{P(s,g)}$

$$L = (Q(s,a) - Q^*(s,a))^2 = (Q(s,a) - (r + \gamma \min_{a' \in A'} Q(s',a')))^2 \quad (1)$$

where s' is the next state (after applying a in s), A' is the set of applicable actions in s' and γ is the *discount factor*.

We train the CNN on static datasets, using one dataset per level. Every sample $(s, \hat{g}, r, s')$ in a dataset is obtained by running a planning episode that starts at a state s (representing a state of the corresponding game level), achieves one single goal $\hat{g}$, returns a plan $p(s, \hat{g})$ of length r and reaches a final state s'. The planning domain for all the episodes is a representation of the player's actions in the Boulder Dash game. The datasets are populated by performing random exploration on the training levels, i.e., by selecting the subgoal $\hat{g}$ at random, collecting a maximum of 500 distinct samples per level.

5   Experiments and Analysis of Results

We have chosen the Fast-Forward (FF) Planning System [5] for our Planner Module because it is compatible with PDDL2.1 features such as conditional effects and PDDL functions, which are expressive enough to represent domains such as those of video games. FF carries out a best-first search and in our experiments we have observed it is unable to find the shortest plan for all the game levels. Nevertheless, it is able to find plans of sub-optimal length, so we have used the evaluation function $f = g + 5 * h$, where g is the current plan length and h is an estimation of the plan length.

In our first experiment we tried to compare the performance of our model for differents values of the discount factor γ. We tested different values and obtained the best results for $\gamma = 0.7$. We then trained our model using $\gamma = 0.7$ (the best value) and $\gamma = 0$ (which corresponds to the extreme case where the Q-value is equal to $l_{p(s,g)}$) on datasets of different sizes and evaluated the trained models on 11 test levels, averaging the results obtained across 5 repetitions. The training and test levels are different in order to measure the generalization ability of our model. All the levels used, for both train and test, share the same size and can be further grouped into *easy* and *hard* levels. Hard levels are simply those FF needs a lot of time to solve. For instance, we found that in Boulder Dash this happens with levels that contain a lot of boulders. We trained each model for 100000 iterations (using a batch size of 32) independently of the dataset size, which translated into a training time of approximately one hour per model on a machine with a Ryzen 5 3600X CPU and a RTX 2060 GPU. For each model we obtained its *action coefficient*, calculated as the geometric mean of the quotients between the length of the plan obtained by the model for each level and the one obtained by a baseline model, which we call the Random Model. This model selects subgoals $g \in G$ completely at random, so it represents a way of selecting subgoals without making use of the information present at the state of the game. Figure 3 shows the results obtained.

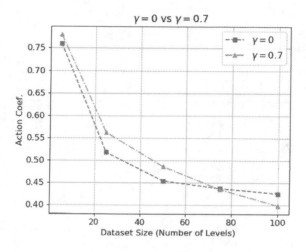

Fig. 3. A plot comparing the performance of our model for two different values of γ. The X axis represents the size of the training dataset: 5, 25, 50, 75 and 100 levels. The Y axis represents the action coefficient of each model (lower is better).

When the discount rate γ is 0, the Q-value is equal to $l_{p(s,g)}$ and, thus, the model does not consider the total plan $P(s,g)$ but only the first section of it $(p(s,g))$, i.e., it selects subgoals in a greedy way. This model is simpler than the one with $\gamma = 0.7$ so, for small datasets (5, 25 and 50 levels), it obtains better results since it is able to generalize better to new levels. However, for bigger datasets (75 and 100 levels), the model with $\gamma = 0.7$ performs better. This shows that, when trained on enough data, a model which conducts long-term thinking when selecting subgoals is superior to one which does not.

In our second experiment we evaluated our model (with $\gamma = 0.7$) against the Random Model and a classical planner (the same one we use for our Planner Module) which solves the levels *directly*, i.e., without performing any goal selection. We trained our model on 100 training levels (again using 100000 training iterations) and evaluated it on 11 test levels (5 easy levels and 6 hard levels), obtaining the average time spent and plan length for each level. The results of our experiment can be seen in Table 2.

Table 2. Results of the executions of our model (GS), the Random Model (RM) and a classical planner (CP) on 11 test levels. We used 15 repetitions for our Goal Selection Model and the Random Model and one repetition for the classical planner (since it is deterministic). A value of − means the corresponding model could not solve the level after 1 h of execution (timeout). Each cell shows the average number of actions/time spent and the standard deviation.

Models	Plan length (Number of actions)										
	Easy levels					Hard levels					
	0	1	2	3	4	5	6	7	8	9	10
GS	85 ± 5	62 ± 20	66 ± 10	93 ± 19	71 ± 16	100 ± 21	128 ± 15	156 ± 28	112 ± 22	88 ± 17	103 ± 25
RM	207 ± 47	188 ± 59	144 ± 32	177 ± 45	190 ± 46	214 ± 67	302 ± 90	456 ± 101	235 ± 91	239 ± 55	262 ± 74
CP	80	51	42	74	41	−	−	−	−	−	114

Models	Time (seconds)										
	Easy levels					Hard levels					
	0	1	2	3	4	5	6	7	8	9	10
GS	1.3 ± 0.08	0.53 ± 0.1	1.23 ± 0.07	0.59 ± 0.09	1.22 ± 0.07	0.66 ± 0.12	1.33 ± 0.05	0.99 ± 0.19	1.46 ± 0.17	0.6 ± 0.09	1.32 ± 0.11
RM	0.47 ± 0.1	0.43 ± 0.12	0.32 ± 0.06	0.39 ± 0.1	0.45 ± 0.1	0.55 ± 0.12	0.61 ± 0.16	0.97 ± 0.2	0.58 ± 0.2	0.53 ± 0.11	0.52 ± 0.12
CP	92.44	0.41	0.04	279.76	0.05	−	−	−	−	−	54.55

If we compare the lengths of the plans obtained we can observe that the Goal Selection Model finds plans which, on (geometric) average, contain 59% fewer actions than the ones obtained by the Random Model but 25% more actions than the ones obtained by the classical planner. If we now compare the times of each model, we can see that the fastest one is the Random Model. This was to be expected since the Random Model does not spend time selecting subgoals (it selects them at random). Then, the Goal Selection Model spends, on (geometric) average, 30% of the time the classical planner needs. This time accounts for both goal selection and planning times. In addition, it has 100% coverage, whereas the classical planner can only solve one out of the six hard levels before the one-hour timeout. Even for those levels it can solve, the planner spends more than 50 s in three of them, while the Goal Selection Module is able to solve all the 11 levels under 1.5 s, with no significant difference in time between the easy and hard levels. Therefore, we can conclude that, although our model obtains plans which are 25% worse (longer) than those obtained by a classical planner, it greatly reduces time requirements and can quickly solve levels of any complexity, even those the classical planner cannot solve.

6   Related Work

The use of Neural Networks (NN) in Automated Planning has been a topic of great interest in recent years. Some works have applied Deep Q-Learning to solve planning and scheduling problems as a substitute for online search algorithms

[10,14]. In our work, we also employ Deep Q-Learning but, instead of using it as a substitute for classical planning, we integrate it along with planning into our planning and acting architecture, which we hypothesize it is generalizable across a wide range of game domains.

Other works train a NN so that it learns to perform an *explicit planning process* [16,18], showing better generalization abilities than most RL algorithms. [16] argues that this happens because, in order to generalize well, NNs need to learn an explicit planning process, which most RL techniques do not. Although our architecture does not learn to plan it does incorporate an off-the-shelf planner which performs explicit planning. We believe this is why our approach shows good generalization abilities.

There exist several works which incorporate Goal Selection into planning and acting architectures, such as [7] and [2]. Jaidee et al. propose a Goal Reasoning architecture which combines Case-Based Reasoning with Q-Learning [6]. In our work, we have focused on learning to select subgoals, using Deep Q-Learning instead of traditional Q-Learning in order to give our architecture the ability to generalize to new states. [1] makes use of a CNN which learns to select subgoals from images. Unlike our work, the CNN is trained by a hard-coded expert procedure in a supervised fashion and the set of eligible subgoals is always the same, regardless of the state of the game.

7 Conclusions and Future Work

We have proposed an architecture which learns to select goals with Deep Q-Learning in order to interleave planning and acting. We have tested our architecture on the GVGAI game known as Boulder Dash, using different levels for training and testing in order to measure its generalization abilities. We have observed how, for big datasets (more than 35000 samples), the model with $\gamma = 0.7$ outperforms the one with $\gamma = 0$, showing the importance of long-term thinking when selecting goals.

Our approach is competitive with a classical planner. Although it obtains plans which are 25% longer on average, it greatly reduces time requirements and can quickly solve levels of any complexity, even those the classical planner cannot tackle. In addition, our approach presents better generalization properties than most RL algorithms when applied to new levels of the same game [20], but requires more domain-specific knowledge. In future work, we intend to conduct experiments on different GVGAI games and apply our architecture to non-deterministic environments, making use of Deep Q-Learning to manage uncertainty.

References

1. Bonanno, D., Roberts, M., Smith, L., Aha, D.W.: Selecting subgoals using deep learning in minecraft: a preliminary report. In: IJCAI Workshop on Deep Learning for Artificial Intelligence (2016)

2. Cox, M.T.: Perpetual self-aware cognitive agents. AI Mag. **28**(1), 32–45 (2007)
3. Fox, M., Long, D.: PDDL2: 1: an extension to PDDL for expressing temporal planning domains. J. Artif. Intell. Res. **20**, 61–124 (2003)
4. Ghallab, M., Nau, D., Traverso, P.: Automated Planning and Acting. Cambridge University Press, New York (2016)
5. Hoffmann, J.: FF: the fast-forward planning system. AI Mag. **22**(3), 57 (2001)
6. Jaidee, U., Muñoz-Avila, H., Aha, D.W.: Learning and reusing goal-specific policies for goal-driven autonomy. In: Agudo, B.D., Watson, I. (eds.) ICCBR 2012. LNCS (LNAI), vol. 7466, pp. 182–195. Springer, Heidelberg (2012). https://doi.org/10.1007/978-3-642-32986-9_15
7. Klenk, M., Molineaux, M., Aha, D.W.: Goal-driven autonomy for responding to unexpected events in strategy simulations. Comput. Intell. **29**(2), 187–206 (2013)
8. Krizhevsky, A., Sutskever, I., Hinton, G.E.: ImageNet classification with deep convolutional neural networks. In: Advances in Neural Information Processing Systems, pp. 1097–1105 (2012)
9. Mnih, V., et al.: Playing Atari with deep reinforcement learning. arXiv preprint arXiv:1312.5602 (2013)
10. Mukadam, M., Cosgun, A., Nakhaei, A., Fujimura, K.: Tactical decision making for lane changing with deep reinforcement learning (2017)
11. Niemueller, T., Hofmann, T., Lakemeyer, G.: Goal reasoning in the clips executive for integrated planning and execution. In: Proceedings of the International Conference on Automated Planning and Scheduling, vol. 29, pp. 754–763 (2019)
12. Patra, S., Ghallab, M., Nau, D., Traverso, P.: Acting and planning using operational models. In: Proceedings of the AAAI Conference on Artificial Intelligence, vol. 33, pp. 7691–7698 (2019)
13. Perez-Liebana, D., et al.: The 2014 general video game playing competition. IEEE Trans. Comput. Intell. AI Games **8**(3), 229–243 (2015)
14. Shen, Y., Zhao, N., Xia, M., Du, X.: A deep q-learning network for ship stowage planning problem. Pol. Marit. Res. **24**(s3), 102–109 (2017)
15. Sutton, R.S., Barto, A.G.: Reinforcement Learning: An Introduction. MIT Press, Cambridge (2018)
16. Tamar, A., Wu, Y., Thomas, G., Levine, S., Abbeel, P.: Value iteration networks. In: Advances in Neural Information Processing Systems, pp. 2154–2162 (2016)
17. Torrado, R.R., Bontrager, P., Togelius, J., Liu, J., Perez-Liebana, D.: Deep reinforcement learning for general video game AI. In: 2018 IEEE Conference on Computational Intelligence and Games (CIG), pp. 1–8. IEEE (2018)
18. Toyer, S., Trevizan, F., Thiébaux, S., Xie, L.: Action schema networks: generalised policies with deep learning. In: Thirty-Second AAAI Conference on Artificial Intelligence (2018)
19. Watkins, C.J.C.H.: Learning from delayed rewards (1989)
20. Zhang, C., Vinyals, O., Munos, R., Bengio, S.: A study on overfitting in deep reinforcement learning (2018). arXiv preprint arXiv:1804.06893

ReLU-Based Activations: Analysis and Experimental Study for Deep Learning

Víctor Manuel Vargas[ID], David Guijo-Rubio[✉][ID], Pedro Antonio Gutiérrez[ID], and César Hervás-Martínez[ID]

Universidad de Córdoba, Córdoba, Spain
{vvargas,dguijo,pagutierrez,chervas}@uco.es
https://www.uco.es/ayrna

Abstract. Activation functions are used in neural networks as a tool to introduce non-linear transformations into the model and, thus, enhance its representation capabilities. They also determine the output range of the hidden layers and the final output. Traditionally, artificial neural networks mainly used the sigmoid activation function as the depth of the network was limited. Nevertheless, this function tends to saturate the gradients when the number of hidden layers increases. For that reason, in the last years, most of the works published related to deep learning and convolutional networks use the Rectified Linear Unit (ReLU), given that it provides good convergence properties and speeds up the training process thanks to the simplicity of its derivative. However, this function has some known drawbacks that gave rise to new proposals of alternatives activation functions based on ReLU. In this work, we describe, analyse and compare different recently proposed alternatives to test whether these functions improve the performance of deep learning models regarding the standard ReLU.

Keywords: Activation functions · Deep learning · Convolutional neural networks

1 Introduction

In the last decade, the number of works that propose to use models based on deep learning methods have significantly increased. Deep learning models can learn high level representations of complex problems related to multiple areas

This work has been subsidised by "Ministerio de Economía y Competitividad del Gobierno de España y Fondos FEDER" (grant reference: TIN2017-85887-C2-1-P), by "Consejería de Salud y Familia de la Junta de Andalucía" (grant reference: PS-2020-780) and by "Consejería de Economía, Conocimiento, Empresas y Universidad de la Junta de Andalucía" (grant reference: UCO-1261651). Víctor Manuel Vargas's research has been subsidised by the FPU Predoctoral Program of the Spanish Ministry of Science, Innovation and Universities (MCIU), grant reference FPU18/00358.

© Springer Nature Switzerland AG 2021
E. Alba et al. (Eds.): CAEPIA 2021, LNAI 12882, pp. 33–43, 2021.
https://doi.org/10.1007/978-3-030-85713-4_4

like supervised learning (classification or regression) [5], object localization [11], or image retrieval [2], among others. In most cases, these kind of models are used when the datasets that we want to learn from are composed of images or sequences. For the latter case, the Recurrent Neural Networks (RNN) or Long Short Term Memory Networks (LSTM) have demonstrated to obtain good performance. On the other hand, for image data, the most common alternative is to use Convolutional Neural Networks (CNN) as they can convert the low level features (image pixels) to high level abstract features (lines or shapes), which then can be used to train a traditional artificial neural network model.

The CNNs are commonly formed up of several parts or steps: (1) Convolutional layers operate over the pixels of the images using a convolution operation with a given kernel shape in order to extract higher level features from that image. Each element of that kernel is a parameter of the model and must be learned from the training data. (2) Batch normalisation layers were proposed [8] as a tool to improve the convergence speed of the model and mitigate training stagnation problems by normalising the outputs of the convolutional layer. (3) The activation function introduces non-linearities in the model in order to achieve more complex representations and defines the output range for any given input. The traditional activation functions used in shallow artificial neural networks have been replaced by simpler alternatives on deep learning models. (4) Pooling layers are used to reduce the dimensionality of the features extracted by the convolutional layers. This operation is done by taking the minimum, maximum or average value of groups of adjacent features.

Regarding activation functions, recently, multiple alternatives have been proposed. The traditional sigmoid function was discarded as it was proved that using this kind of exponential functions with deep models does not lead to a good convergence, saturating the gradients easily. That is the main reason why some simple activation functions were proposed. Nowadays, the most commonly used activation function for deep networks is the Rectified Linear Unit (ReLU) [14]. The root cause of this popularity relies on its simplicity and the simplicity of its first derivative, which enhances the training process by allowing faster gradients computation and suppressing problems related to gradients saturation. However, as it is described in Sect. 2, some problems related to the negative part of this activation arises in some cases, and, therefore, some recent works proposed different alternatives to solve these issues while taking profit of the good properties of the ReLU function.

In this work, we analyse the ReLU function together with some recently proposed alternatives and perform an experimental and statistical analysis of the performance of all these functions to check whether they provide a significant improvement concerning the original proposal. The rest of this paper is organised as follows: in Sect. 2, the ReLU function and its alternatives are described, in Sect. 3 we describe the experimental design and the datasets used as benchmark to evaluate the activation functions, in Sect. 4 we present and analyse the results from a descriptive point of view and from a statistical view, and, finally, in Sect. 5 we present the conclusions of this work.

2   ReLU-Based Activation Functions

The Rectified Linear Unit (ReLU) has been widely used as activation function for deep learning models since it was proposed for the first time in [14]. It was presented as an alternative to the sigmoid function, which is commonly used on shallow neural networks. The ReLU function is easily implemented by thresholding an activation map at zero [1]. Also, its gradients are computed in a straight-forward way, as it is the unit when the input value is positive and zero in the rest of the domain. Therefore, only a subset of neurons will be active for a given input, thus improving the computational cost as the output is a linear function of the input. This linearity causes the successive gradients to be calculated in a faster way, since it is not necessary to calculate an exponential function such as the one required by the sigmoid. The function is defined as:

$$f_{\mathrm{ReLU}}(x) = \max(0, x). \tag{1}$$

The ReLU activation has demonstrated to accelerate the convergence of stochastic gradient descent compared to previous alternatives used in shallow networks. In this way, multiple recent works [4] used this function for deep learning.

Nevertheless, the sparsity introduced by having zero values in the negative part can reduce the predictive performance, reducing the generalisation capability of the model. Also, the fact that the output of the function is zero when the input is negative can hinder learning negative values [6].

Following these limitations of the ReLU activation, many recents works have proposed alternatives that try to exploit the good characteristics of the ReLU at the same time that they fix the flaws of this function. In most cases, they are non-saturating nonlinear functions which are parametrics extensions thereof. In the rest of this Section, some of these alternatives are described.

2.1   Leaky Rectified Linear Unit

The Leaky ReLU function (LReLU) [12] is a parametric alternative of the ReLU that was proposed with the purpose of alleviating the problems caused by the hard zero activation of the ReLU. It is defined as:

$$f_{\mathrm{LReLU}}(x) = \begin{cases} x, & x > 0, \\ \alpha x, & x \leq 0, \end{cases} \tag{2}$$

where the α fixed parameter defines the slope of the negative part and is often pre-assigned with a small value like 0.01.

2.2   Parametric Rectified Linear Unit

The Parametric Rectified Linear Unit (PReLU) [6] was proposed as another generalisation of the ReLU function. The main idea behind this function is similar to the one described in the LReLU activation. However, in this case, the slope of the negative part, i.e. the α value, is a free parameter learned from data. The authors of that work stated that the PReLU improves model fitting with nearly zero extra computational cost. The function is defined as:

$$f_{\text{PReLU}}(x) = \begin{cases} x, & x > 0, \\ \alpha x, & x \leq 0, \end{cases} \tag{3}$$

where α represents a channel-shared or channel-wise free parameter. Channel-shared parameters have only one value for all the channels while channel-wise parameters have one value for each channel.

2.3   Elastic Rectified Linear Unit

The Elastic Rectified Linear Unit (EReLU) function [9] only modifies the positive part of the function and does not include any extra parameters. The negative part remains as zero, then it does not correct one of the main drawbacks of the original ReLU function, which is the one caused by the hard zero activation. The function was defined in its original work as Eq. 4.

$$f_{\text{EReLU}}(x) = \begin{cases} kx, & x > 0, \\ 0, & x \leq 0, \end{cases} \tag{4} \qquad f_{\text{EPReLU}}(x) = \begin{cases} kx, & x > 0, \\ \beta x, & x \leq 0, \end{cases} \tag{5}$$

In Eq. 4 k is a coefficient randomly selected from a uniform distribution for each element of the feature maps, $k \sim U(1 - \alpha, 1 + \alpha)$, with $\alpha \in (0, 1)$. α is a parameter representing the degree of response fluctuation. The value of k changes in each iteration of the training stage when using the stochastic gradient descent algorithm. At test time, this parameter is replaced with $\mathbb{E}[k] = 1$ (the expectation of k). Thus, at test time, EReLU behaves exactly like ReLU.

The authors of [9], also proposed the parametric form of the function described. The Elastic Parametric Rectified Linear Unit (EPReLU) joins EReLU and PReLU activations and fixes the issue of the zero output in the negative part by treating the positive and negative domain separately. The function is defined as Eq. 5. In this equation, k is the same parameter introduced in EReLU, and β is a free parameter which needs to be learned from training data. Each parameter controls the slope of the positive and negative domain respectively.

2.4   Randomised Leaky Rectified Linear Unit

The Randomised Leaky Rectified Linear Unit (RReLU) [19] introduces a random component in the negative part of the function by sampling its slope from a uniform distribution instead of using a constant value or learning it from the data. The function can be defined as:

$$f_{\text{RReLU}}(x) = \begin{cases} x, & x > 0, \\ \alpha x, & x \leq 0, \end{cases} \tag{6}$$

where α is a channel-wise parameter, $\alpha \sim U(a, b)$ and $a, b \in [0, 1]$, $a < b$.

When evaluating, the slope (α) is set to its expectation to achieve deterministic results. Therefore, $\hat{\alpha} = \mathbb{E}[\alpha] = \frac{a+b}{2}$ during the test phase.

2.5 Sloped Rectified Linear Unit

The Sloped ReLU [15] is another alternative to the standard ReLU function that introduces a learnable parameter that modifies the slope of the positive part. However, it does not change the negative part, thus it preserves the same problem caused by the zero activation. The Sloped ReLU is defined as:

$$f_{\text{SlopedReLU}}(x) = \max(0, \alpha x), \tag{7}$$

where α denotes a trainable slope parameter ($\alpha > 0$).

2.6 Paired Rectified Linear Unit

The Paired ReLUs [17] tries to correct the problem caused by the zero activation by concatenating two ReLU-like functions. The first has a non-zero activation when the inputs are in the positive domain while the second one is active when the input is negative. In this way, the function always takes values different from zero, but the main drawback of this function is that it converts an input of shape S to $2S$, which leads to a higher computational cost and use of memory. The activation scheme is defined as:

$$f_{\text{Paired}}(x) = (\max(sx - \theta, 0), \max(s_p x - \theta_p, 0)), \tag{8}$$

where s and s_p are two scale parameters that are initialised to 0.5 and -0.5, respectively, and θ and θ_p are a pair of trainable parameters. Hence, $f_{\text{Paired}}(x)$ represents the concatenation of the output of two parts of the function.

2.7 Randomly Translational Rectified Linear Unit

The Randomly Translational Rectified Linear Unit (RTReLU) [3] introduces a random term a in the positive part. The authors stated that it compensates the jitter of the input. The negative part remains unchanged, and, therefore, the problems related to having no activation for the negative part are still present. The function expression is shown in Eq. 9.

$$f_{\text{RTReLU}}(x) = \begin{cases} x + a, & x + a > 0, \\ 0, & x + a \leq 0, \end{cases} \quad (9) \qquad f_{\text{RTPReLU}}(x) = \begin{cases} x + a, & x + a > 0, \\ k(x + a), & x + a \leq 0, \end{cases} \quad (10)$$

In Eq. 9, a is a channel-wise parameter sampled from a Gaussian distribution, that defines the offset on the horizontal axis.

This transformation which was applied to the standard ReLU function, can be applied to other functions like the PReLU. In this way, in the same work, the authors proposed the Randomly Translation PReLU (RTPReLU) too. The expression of this function is obtained in a similar way and is defined in Eq. 10. In this equation, a is the same parameter described in the previous alternative and k is a channel-wise parameter that denotes the slope of the negative part.

3   Design of the Experiments

In this Section, the design of the experiments along with the datasets considered and the validation scheme are described.

3.1   Datasets

The activation functions described in Sect. 2 were mainly proposed to be used on CNNs which are intended to be used with images. Therefore, to evaluate and compare the performance of these functions, we are using three well-known benchmark image datasets: CIFAR-10, CIFAR-100 and Fashion-MNIST.

CIFAR-10 and CIFAR-100. The CIFAR-10 dataset is composed of a training set with 50,000 images and a test set with 10,000 images. Each image is categorised in one of ten different classes. All of them are RGB images rescaled to 32 × 32. The partitions described along with that image size are standard and used to evaluate the performance of multiple proposals in the literature [7,10]. Some images extracted from the training set are shown in Fig. 1.

The CIFAR-100 dataset is similar to the aforementioned CIFAR-10 dataset as it has the same number of samples and train/test partitions. However, in this case, the samples are separated into 100 different classes, which are grouped into 20 superclasses. This class hierarchy gives birth to a fine label or real class and a coarse label associated with the superclass. In this work, we used the fine labels.

Fig. 1. CIFAR-10 images belonging to the training set.

Fashion-MNIST. Fashion-MNIST is a dataset composed of images of different types of clothes products and accessories obtained from Zalando. The training set is composed of 60,000 grayscale images and the test set contains 10,000. These images are associated with one of 10 labels and resized to 28 × 28.

3.2   Model and Training Process

The model proposed to be used along with the datasets described is a CNN with the VGG16 architecture [16], that has demonstrated to achieve good performance in several classification problems including large datasets like ImageNet [10]. The model contains around 15.0M parameters. The standard model uses ReLU activations after every convolutional block. In our case, we have modified the activation to use each of the functions described in Sect. 2. At the output of the network, we added a dense layer with 512 units and, after that, another dense layer with $N - 1$ units, being N the number of classes, followed by the softmax function that determines the probability for each class.

The model described could be improved depending on the problem considered but, as we will focus on comparing each of the activation functions considered, we used the same architecture for all the experiments.

Concerning the training process and the validation scheme, the model described was trained with each of the datasets detailed in this Section. A validation set was obtained from the training set by randomly extracting 5% of the samples. The loss of the validation set was used as a metric for the early stopping strategy, in a way that we can stop the training process when the best stage has been reached. In order to mitigate the random effects, the experiments have been repeated five times with five different seeds.

The Stochastic Gradient Descent (SGD) algorithm with decay and Nesterov momentum has been used to optimise the model. The loss function considered was the standard categorical cross-entropy, which is the standard loss function for classification problems. The initial learning rate (η_0) of the optimiser was set to 0.1, the decay factor to 10^{-6} and the Nesterov momentum to 0.9. Moreover, the actual learning rate is determined by the initial learning rate and the epoch number following the expression: $\eta = \eta_0 \cdot 0.5^{\frac{epoch}{20}}$. These parameters were validated using a 5-fold cross-validation scheme.

4   Results and Analysis

This Section presents the results of the experiments that were described in Sect. 3. Table 1 shows the mean accuracy score of the five executions for each of the activation functions and datasets as well as the mean accuracy for each of the functions across all the datasets. The best result is in bold font.

As can be deduced from the results presented in Table 1, the Parametric ReLU obtained the best average results. However, it is necessary to do an statistical analysis in order to demonstrate that the differences in average accuracy are statistically significant. In this way, we first performed a Kolmogorov-Smirnov test to check whether the accuracy values follow a normal distribution. Then, an ANOVA II test [13] taking as factors the activation function and the dataset was done to check if these factors have a significant impact on the accuracy. The results of this statistical test are shown in Table 2. This table shows, for each factor or interaction, the sum of the squares (SS), the degrees of freedom (DF),

Table 1. Accuracy mean results for test set.

Activation	VGG-16 accuracy			
	CIFAR-10	CIFAR-100	Fashion	Mean
ReLU	0.91768	0.64586	0.94022	0.83459
LReLU	0.91766	**0.66278**	0.93912	0.83985
PReLU	**0.91920**	0.66122	0.94108	**0.84050**
EReLU	0.91126	0.64478	0.94016	0.83207
EPReLU	0.90586	0.62896	0.93742	0.82408
RReLU	0.89708	0.58316	0.93508	0.80511
SlopedReLU	0.91852	0.65628	0.94000	0.83827
Paired	0.91168	0.61634	0.93420	0.82074
RTReLU	0.91506	0.65808	**0.94126**	0.83813
RTPReLU	0.91634	0.65898	0.93570	0.83701

the mean of the squares (MS), the value of the F statistic and its significance level (p-value). If the latter is smaller than 0.05, then the factor is statistically significant. These results show that both factors, the dataset and the activation function have a significant impact on the accuracy obtained (p-values < 0.001) and, also, there is an interaction between them (p-value < 0.001). This latter statement means that an activation function can achieve good performance on some datasets while the accuracy obtained for others can be poor.

Table 2. ANOVA II results.

Source	SS	DF	MS	F-ratio	p-value
Model	106.331	30	3.544	92957.142	<0.001
Dataset factor	106.299	3	35.433	929293.289	<0.001
Activation factor	0.017	9	0.002	50.094	<0.001
Dataset × Activation	0.015	18	0.001	21.308	<0.001
Error	0.005	120	0.0004		
Total	106.335	150			

In order to complete the statistical analysis and given that there are significant differences depending on both factors, a posthoc Tukey's HSD test [18] has been performed to compare the different activation functions. The results of the aforementioned test, which are shown in Table 3, divided the activation functions in four different groups, meaning that the functions that belong to the same group have no significant differences between them while the functions in different groups are significantly different in terms of accuracy. Also, the groups are denoted in ascending order of accuracy. In this way, the RReLU obtained the worst performance as it is alone in the first group. The Paired ReLU and the EPReLU are in the second group, thus, they have the second worst results. In group 4, we can find most of the functions, including the ReLU. The main conclusion that we can extract from these results is that the functions derived from the standard ReLU, did not improve the performance in terms of accuracy. Most of the alternatives are similar to the standard ReLU and some others obtain worst average results than ReLU.

Table 3. Post-hoc HSD Tukey's Test for accuracy metric (15 samples for each function)

Activation	Subsets			
	1	2	3	4
RReLU	0.80511			
PairedReLU		0.82074		
EPReLU		0.82408		
EReLU			0.83207	
ReLU			0.83459	0.83459
RTPReLU			0.83701	0.83701
RTReLU			0.83813	0.83813
SlopedReLU			0.83827	0.83827
LReLU				0.83985
PReLU				0.84050
p-values	1.000	0.897	0.166	0.219

5   Conclusions

In this work, we have described and analysed the Rectified Linear Unit together with nine alternatives that were proposed in the recent years based on it. We performed an experimental comparison between all of them using a convolutional neural network model and three separate benchmark datasets. The results of this experimental analysis regarding the accuracy metric were shown, and the functions were compared in a descriptive form as well as in a statistical form. The results of the statistical tests performed reported that the activation function is a significant factor affecting the accuracy obtained. Also, the posthoc test shown that there are some functions based on the ReLU that perform worse than the original proposal, but there is not any ReLU alternative that performs significantly better than the base function. Given these results, we can conclude that the alternatives presented to mitigate the problems of the ReLU were not the ideal alternative and, in some cases, they came with an increased computational cost that is not justified. In this way, future research works focused on improving the activation functions for deep learning, should try to explore different alternatives not based on the ReLU function, having activation in the negative part as well as in the positive domain.

References

1. Andrearczyk, V., Whelan, P.F.: Convolutional neural network on three orthogonal planes for dynamic texture classification. Pattern Recogn. **76**, 36–49 (2018). https://doi.org/10.1016/j.patcog.2017.10.030
2. Bai, C., Huang, L., Pan, X., Zheng, J., Chen, S.: Optimization of deep convolutional neural network for large scale image retrieval. Neurocomputing **303**, 60–67 (2018). https://doi.org/10.1016/j.neucom.2018.04.034
3. Cao, J., Pang, Y., Li, X., Liang, J.: Randomly translational activation inspired by the input distributions of ReLU. Neurocomputing **275**, 859–868 (2018). https://doi.org/10.1016/j.neucom.2017.09.031
4. Diaz-Pinto, A., Colomer, A., Naranjo, V., Morales, S., Xu, Y., Frangi, A.F.: Retinal image synthesis for glaucoma assessment using DCGAN and VAE models. In: Yin, H., Camacho, D., Novais, P., Tallón-Ballesteros, A.J. (eds.) IDEAL 2018. LNCS, vol. 11314, pp. 224–232. Springer, Cham (2018). https://doi.org/10.1007/978-3-030-03493-1_24
5. Fang, L., Zhang, H., Zhou, J., Wang, X.: Image classification with an RGB-channel nonsubsampled contourlet transform and a convolutional neural network. Neurocomputing, 1–12 (2019). https://doi.org/10.1016/j.neucom.2018.10.094
6. He, K., Zhang, X., Ren, S., Sun, J.: Delving deep into rectifiers: surpassing human-level performance on ImageNet classification. In: Proceedings of the IEEE International Conference on Computer Vision, pp. 1026–1034 (2015). https://doi.org/10.1109/iccv.2015.123
7. Ide, H., Kurita, T.: Improvement of learning for CNN with ReLU activation by sparse regularization. In: 2017 International Joint Conference on Neural Networks (IJCNN), pp. 2684–2691. IEEE (2017). https://doi.org/10.1109/ijcnn.2017.7966185
8. Ioffe, S., Szegedy, C.: Batch normalization: accelerating deep network training by reducing internal covariate shift. In: Proceedings of the 32nd International Conference on Machine Learning, vol. 37, pp. 448–456 (2015)
9. Jiang, X., Pang, Y., Li, X., Pan, J., Xie, Y.: Deep neural networks with elastic rectified linear units for object recognition. Neurocomputing **275**, 1132–1139 (2018). https://doi.org/10.1016/j.neucom.2017.09.056
10. Krizhevsky, A., Sutskever, I., Hinton, G.E.: ImageNet classification with deep convolutional neural networks. In: Advances in Neural Information Processing Systems, pp. 1097–1105 (2012). https://doi.org/10.1145/3065386
11. Kudo, Y., Aoki, Y.: Dilated convolutions for image classification and object localization. In: 2017 Fifteenth IAPR International Conference on Machine Vision Applications (MVA), pp. 452–455. IEEE (2017). https://doi.org/10.23919/mva.2017.7986898
12. Maas, A.L., Hannun, A.Y., Ng, A.Y.: Rectifier nonlinearities improve neural network acoustic models. In: Proceedings of the ICML, vol. 30, p. 3 (2013)
13. Miller, R.G., Jr.: Beyond ANOVA: Basics of Applied Statistics. Chapman and Hall/CRC (1997). https://doi.org/10.1201/b15236
14. Nair, V., Hinton, G.E.: Rectified linear units improve restricted Boltzmann machines. In: Proceedings of the 27th International Conference on Machine Learning, pp. 807–814 (2010)
15. Seo, J., Lee, J., Kim, K.: Activation functions of deep neural networks for polar decoding applications. In: 28th Annual International Symposium on Personal, Indoor, and Mobile Radio Communications (PIMRC), pp. 1–5. IEEE (2017). https://doi.org/10.1109/pimrc.2017.8292678

16. Simonyan, K., Zisserman, A.: Very deep convolutional networks for large-scale image recognition. arXiv preprint arXiv:1409.1556 (2014)
17. Tang, Z., Luo, L., Peng, H., Li, S.: A joint residual network with paired ReLUs activation for image super-resolution. Neurocomputing **273**, 37–46 (2018)
18. Tukey, J.W.: Comparing individual means in the analysis of variance. Biometrics **5**(2), 99–114 (1949). https://doi.org/10.2307/3001913
19. Xu, B., Wang, N., Chen, T., Li, M.: Empirical evaluation of rectified activations in convolutional network. arXiv preprint arXiv:1505.00853, pp. 1–5 (2015)

Studying the Effect of Different L_p Norms in the Context of Time Series Ordinal Classification

David Guijo-Rubio[ID], Víctor Manuel Vargas[✉][ID], Pedro Antonio Gutiérrez[ID], and César Hervás-Martínez[ID]

Department of Computer Science and Numerical Analysis,
University of Córdoba, Córdoba, Spain
{dguijo,vvargas,pagutierrez,chervas}@uco.es

Abstract. Time Series Ordinal Classification (TSOC) is yet an unexplored field of machine learning consisting in the classification of time series whose labels follow a natural order relationship between them. In this context, a well-known approach for time series nominal classification was previously used: the Shapelet Transform (ST). The exploitation of the ordinal information was included in two steps of the ST algorithm: 1) by using the Pearson's determination coefficient (R^2) for computing the quality of the shapelets, which favours shapelets with better ordering, and 2) by applying an ordinal classifier instead of a nominal one to the transformed dataset. For this, the distance between labels was represented by the absolute value of the difference between the corresponding ranks, i.e. by the L_1 norm. In this paper, we study the behaviour of different L_p norms for representing class distances in ordinal regression, evaluating 9 different L_p norms with 7 ordinal time series datasets from the UEA-UCR time series classification repository and 10 different ordinal classifiers. The results achieved demonstrate that the Pearson's determination coefficient using the $L_{1.9}$ norm in the computation of the difference between the shapelet and the time series labels achieves a significantly better performance when compared to the rest of the approaches, in terms of both Correct Classification Rate (CCR) and Average Mean Absolute Error (AMAE).

Keywords: Time series · Ordinal classification · L_p norm · Shapelet quality measures

This work has been subsidised by "Ministerio de Economía y Competitividad del Gobierno de España y Fondos FEDER" (grant reference: TIN2017-85887-C2-1-P), by "Consejería de Salud y Familia de la Junta de Andalucía" (grant reference: PS-2020-780) and by "Consejería de Economía, Conocimiento, Empresas y Universidad de la Junta de Andalucía" (grant reference: UCO-1261651). Víctor Manuel Vargas's research has been subsidised by the FPU Predoctoral Program of the Spanish Ministry of Science, Innovation and Universities (MCIU), grant reference FPU18/00358.

© Springer Nature Switzerland AG 2021
E. Alba et al. (Eds.): CAEPIA 2021, LNAI 12882, pp. 44–53, 2021.
https://doi.org/10.1007/978-3-030-85713-4_5

1   Introduction

Time Series Ordinal Classification (TSOC) is the machine learning field focusing on the classification of time series in which the associated discrete target values present a natural order relationship between them [9]. An example of this type of problems could be classifying people's heart rate by the age's group they belong, in which the labels could be *baby*, *child*, *teenager*, *adult* or *elderly*. Note that severe misclassification errors, such as classifying a *baby* as *adult*, should be far more penalised than misclassifying a *baby* as *child*. More examples of these problems could be found in the meteorological field [7] or in wave height prediction [8], among others.

There are three main ways to tackle these problems: 1) as nominal classification problems, nevertheless, it ignores the natural order between the labels; 2) as regression problems, implying the assignment of a numerical value to each label (assuming a distance between labels that can hinder the performance of the regressor); and 3) considering them as ordinal classification problems, which is the most appropriate approach given that it takes the natural order between the labels into account and does not assume a distance between values. This third strategy is the one we are considering for this study.

On the other hand, one of the most common techniques for time series nominal classification is the use of shapelets [24] in several ways. Shapelets are subsequences of the original time series that allow the comparison of similarity by considering shape. The first approach [24] considered the use of a decision tree with the Information Gain (IG) measure to assess the shapelet candidates and keep the best. Nowadays, there are a huge variety of methods using shapelets from different perspectives, among which the Shapelet Transform (ST) [13] is one of most powerful techniques. It builds a transform of the original dataset by computing the distances from the shapelets extracted to the original time series, in such a way that any classifier could be built on this transformed dataset.

The ordinal information of the labels can be exploited in two different steps of the ST as described in [9]: 1) in the computation of the shapelet quality measure and 2) by using an ordinal classifier over the transform. The results achieved in [9] demonstrated that the best shapelet quality measure when tackling ordinal time series datasets is the Pearson's determination coefficient (R^2), which outperformed the IG (the quality measure used by the original ST).

In this work, the main objective is to improve this shapelet quality measure by analysing the effect that the L_p norm has on the computation of the label distances. For this, we have considered the same set of ordinal time series datasets from the UEA-UCR time series classification repository as in [9], 10 ordinal classifiers and a wide range of p values for the L_p norm, where $1 \leq p \leq 2$.

The rest of the paper is organised as follows. Section 2 has a twofold objective: Sect. 2.1 details the fundamental notions regarding time series and shapelets, whereas Sect. 2.2 shows the study of the L_p norm behaviour when applied to the shapelet quality measure. Section 3 presents the experimental settings (Sect. 3.1) and the experimental results, statistical tests and discussion (Sect. 3.2). Finally, Sect. 4 closes the paper with the main conclusions of this work.

2   Background

This section includes the basic notions of time series, along with the idea of time series shapelets and the study of the effect produced by using different L_p norms in the shapelet quality measurement.

2.1   Time Series

Time series classification is defined as the task of building a classifier from a set of labelled training time series. A time series $\mathbf{x}_i$ is defined as a set of time-ordered values $\{x_{i1}, x_{i2}, \ldots, x_{im}\}$ of length m and can be assigned a label $\mathcal{C}_i$. Note that in this study we have focused on time series with the same number of observations (i.e. m is constant). In this sense, a time series classification dataset $\mathbf{D}$ is formally defined as $\mathbf{D} = \{\mathbf{t}_1, \mathbf{t}_2, \ldots, \mathbf{t}_n\}$, in such a way that $\mathbf{t}_i = \langle \mathbf{x}_i, \mathcal{C}_i \rangle$. Hence, the time series classification task mainly consists in learning an accurate mapping function from the set of input attributes $\mathbf{x}_i$ to the output $\mathcal{C}_i$.

Ordinal Time Series. When considering ordinal time series, the label associated to each time series, $\mathcal{C}_i$, belongs to a set of categories following an order relationship, i.e. $\mathcal{C}_i \in Y = \{\mathcal{C}_1, \mathcal{C}_2, \ldots, \mathcal{C}_q\}$, where q is the number of categories and $\{\mathcal{C}_1, \mathcal{C}_2, \ldots, \mathcal{C}_q\}$ are the ordinal labels satisfying the constraint $C_1 \prec C_2 \prec \ldots \prec C_q$ (note that the operator $\prec$ represents the order relationship). Focusing on the UEA-UCR time series classification repository [3], a subset of 7 ordinal time series datasets satisfying the previous constraint was identified in [9], where specific information regarding this set of ordinal time series datasets is detailed.

Shapelets. It is well known that time series commonly have subsequences with specific features that could characterise the time series and, therefore, could be representative not only of the time series from which they are extracted but also of the class to which the time series belongs. These subsequences are known as shapelets and were firstly proposed by Ye and Keogh in [24]. In this first approach, the shapelets were embedded into a decision tree in which the splits were performed according to a single shapelet and its quality, measured by means of the Information Gain (IG) [21]. Nevertheless, due to its outstanding merit on time series data mining, novel approaches have been proposed to the literature [6,10,13]. Most of them consider the creation of a transformation of the original time series dataset [13], known as Shapelet Transform (ST). The attributes of this new representation are the distances from the shapelets to the time series being evaluated. The main advantages of building this new representation are the possibility of applying any classifier and the lack of need of searching for shapelets sequentially at each node of the tree, which is computationally intensive.

More formally, a shapelet $\mathbf{s} = \{s_1, s_2, \ldots, s_l\}$ is a subsequence of a time series $\mathbf{t}_j = \langle \mathbf{x}_j, \mathcal{C}_j \rangle$ with $\mathbf{x}_j = \{x_{j1}, x_{j2}, \ldots, x_{jm}\}$, where $l \leq m$. Note that $\mathcal{C}_j$ is the class of both the shapelet $\mathbf{s}$ and the time series $\mathbf{t}_j$ due to the fact the shapelet $\mathbf{s}$ is an exact subsequence of $\mathbf{t}_j$. The procedure for extracting the shapelets is divided in three main steps [13], which are performed iteratively until all the shapelets have been extracted (which is known as enumerative search) or until satisfying a given time constraint (known as contracted search): 1) Candidate generation: from all possible subsequences satisfying the previous length constraint, one random shapelet is kept. 2) Similarity measurement: the similarity between the shapelet and all the time series is computed by means of the Euclidean distance. This distance is computed by keeping the minimum of all the distances between the shapelet and all the subsequences with the same length as the shapelet. 3) Shapelet quality measurement: depending on the previous similarity measurement and the strategy or metric followed, each shapelet is given a quality with the purpose of retaining only high quality shapelets.

As can be imagined, the number of shapelets that could be extracted from a time series dataset is extremely large depending on the length of the subsequences, the number of training time series and the search strategy considered (enumerative or contracted). In this sense, the use of a shapelet quality measure is required in order to retain only those shapelets with a high quality, this is, those which are more representative of a class and, thus, enable us to differentiate better between classes. So far, this task has been performed using the IG, which has been proved to be excellent and is used in one of the state-of-the-art techniques in time series nominal classification, the HIVE-COTE [2]. Nevertheless, given that we are focusing on TSOC, it is better to select the best shapelets exploiting the ordinal information present in them. For this, in a previous paper [9], several shapelet quality measures considering ordinal information of the dataset were compared against the standard IG, being the one based on the Pearson's determination coefficient (R^2), the one achieving the best results. This shapelet quality measure is based on the correlation between the distances obtained from the shapelet $\mathbf{s}$ to the time series $\mathbf{t}_i$ (here represented as $d_{\mathbf{s},\mathbf{t}_i}$) and the difference of the class indices (i.e. the label of the shapelet and the label of $\mathbf{t}_i$), which is the cost of misclassification associated to the pair of labels being compared (here represented as $c_{\mathbf{s},\mathbf{t}_i}$). In this way:

$$d_{\mathbf{s},\mathbf{t}_i} = \min \left\{ \sum_{j=1}^{l} (s_j - r_j)^2, \quad \forall \mathbf{r} \in \mathbf{t}_i \right\}, \tag{1}$$

where $\mathbf{r}$ is a subsequence of the time series $\mathbf{t}_i$ with the same length that the shapelet $\mathbf{s}$ (sliding window of l elements). On the other hand, the cost associated to the misclassification of two labels is defined as follows:

$$c_{\mathbf{s},\mathbf{t}_i} = |\mathcal{O}(\mathcal{C}_j) - \mathcal{O}(\mathcal{C}_i)|, \tag{2}$$

where $\mathcal{C}_i$ is the class of the time series $\mathbf{t}_i$ and $\mathcal{C}_j$ is the class of the time series $\mathbf{t}_j$ to which the shapelet $\mathbf{s}$ belongs to. Besides, $\mathcal{O}(\mathcal{C}_k) = k, \; k \in \{1, \ldots, q\}$, i.e.

$\mathcal{O}(\mathcal{C}_k)$ is the position of the category in the ordinal scale and $c_{\mathbf{s},\mathbf{t}_i}$ is the number of categories between $\mathcal{C}_i$ and $\mathcal{C}_j$.

The Pearson's determination coefficient (R^2) is expressed as:

$$R^2(\mathbf{s}) = \frac{S^2(d_{\mathbf{s},\mathbf{t}_i}, c_{\mathbf{s},\mathbf{t}_i})}{S^2_{d_{\mathbf{s},\mathbf{t}_i}} S^2_{c_{\mathbf{s},\mathbf{t}_i}}}, \tag{3}$$

where $S(d_{\mathbf{s},\mathbf{t}_i}, c_{\mathbf{s},\mathbf{t}_i})$ is the covariance between $d_{\mathbf{s},\mathbf{t}_i}$ and $c_{\mathbf{s},\mathbf{t}_i}$. $S^2_{d_{\mathbf{s},\mathbf{t}_i}}$ and $S^2_{c_{\mathbf{s},\mathbf{t}_i}}$ are the variances of $d_{\mathbf{s},\mathbf{t}_i}$ and $c_{\mathbf{s},\mathbf{t}_i}$, respectively.

The following section shows the effect of using different L_p norms when computing the difference between the class indices of the shapelet $\mathbf{s}$ and the time series $\mathbf{t}_i$, $c_{\mathbf{s},\mathbf{t}_i}$ (Eq. 2), which so far has been computed using the L_1 norm, i.e. the absolute value of the difference of the ranks.

2.2   Effect of the L_p Norm

The use of different L_p norms in optimisation algorithms has been a hot topic in several field, including binary classification [5] or feature selection [25], among others. Moreover, in [19], the L_p norms are used to provide a specific type of push. Depending on the value, the objective varies: e.g. setting a large p makes the objective to focus on the top of the ranked list. In [17], the authors demonstrated that L_2 norm methods tend to "expand" or "bleed out" over natural boundaries. Therefore, using a L_p norm where $1 < p < 2$ should provide a more appropriate alternative when able to be optimised efficiently. In [15], the authors present an L_p norm alternative to Least Squares Support Vector Machine (LSSVM) [22], paying special attention to their behaviour: 1) the edge points may be ignored by using the L_2 norm in the classification error measurement, whereas they could be the most important samples and special attention should be given to them (such is the case of anomaly detection [14]); 2) if the sample size is smaller than the number of features, it would be an ill condition or singularity, which means that LSSVM is not suitable for small sample size problems. The use of this type of generalized norms has drawn a huge attention in different applications, such as 3D medical image super-resolution [23].

In linear regression problems, calculating the coefficient of determination for the accuracy of the models and its prediction, using the mean and variance of the involved variables, is common and these statistics are typically based on the Euclidean norm (L_2 norm). However, for some of these tasks, the L_p norms have raised a huge attention. Bregman divergences is one of the standard tools for analysing online machine learning algorithms [16], allowing a generalisation of the least mean squared algorithm. In this sense, the loss bounds for these so-called L_p norm algorithms involve others than the standard L_2 norm [5].

Given the above considerations, in this work, the L_p norm with $1 \le p \le 2$ is proposed as an alternative to the distance between the classes of the shapelet $\mathbf{s}$ and the time series $\mathbf{t}_i$. In this sense, Eq. 2 is redefined as follows:

$$c^p_{\mathbf{s},\mathbf{t}_i} = |\mathcal{O}(\mathcal{C}_j) - \mathcal{O}(\mathcal{C}_i)|^p, \quad 1 \le p \le 2. \tag{4}$$

And therefore, the new Pearson's determination coefficient ($R_p^2(\mathbf{s})$, previously defined in Eq. 3) can be expressed as:

$$R_p^2(\mathbf{s}) = \frac{S^2(d_{\mathbf{s},\mathbf{t}_i}, c_{\mathbf{s},\mathbf{t}_i}^p)}{S_{d_{\mathbf{s},\mathbf{t}_i}}^2 S_{c_{\mathbf{s},\mathbf{t}_i}^p}^2}, \quad 1 \le p \le 2. \tag{5}$$

To give a visual idea of the effect of the L_p-norm, Fig. 1 shows an example of 6 values of p, specifically the 6 values resulting in the best performance in the experiments of Sect. 3. In Fig. 1, the x-axis represents class differences from -5 to 5, whereas the y-axis depicts the L_p norm values (Eq. 4).

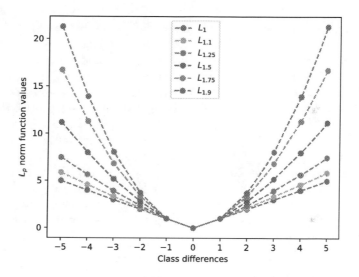

Fig. 1. Geometric interpretation of the best 6 L_p norms on one-dimensional vector.

3   Experimental Results and Discussion

This section includes the experimental settings for the 10 different ordinal classifiers chosen for this study, as well as a discussion of the results obtained[1].

3.1   Experimental Settings

The code for the Shapelet Transform (ST) has been obtained from the `sktime` toolkit [18][2]. As mentioned in Sect. 2.1, there are two types of search for the ST. In this paper, we focus on the contracted one, fixing the contracted time to one hour. The standard train and test splits given in the time series classification

---

[1] Code used in this paper and results achieved are available in the website https://github.com/dguijo/TSOC/releases/tag/1.0.1.

[2] Code is available in the website https://github.com/alan-turing-institute/sktime.

repository are used. Regarding the ordinal classifiers, in this work, the following 10 methods are used: SVR, SVC1VA, CSSVC, SVORIM, SVOREX, SVORIM-LIN, OPBE, HPOLD, ORBOOSTALL and KDLOR. Further details about these methods can be found in [12, 20][3]. All of them have been run once, given they are deterministic. The ordinal classifiers have been evaluated using the Correct Classification Rate (CCR) and the Average Mean Absolute Error (AMAE) [1]. The CCR is computed as the percentage of correctly classified patterns over the total number of patterns, whereas AMAE is defined as:

$$AMAE = \frac{1}{q} \sum_{i=1}^{q} \frac{1}{n_i} \sum_{j=1}^{n_i} |\mathcal{O}(\mathcal{C}_j) - \mathcal{O}(\hat{y}_j)|, \tag{6}$$

where n_i is the number of patterns belonging to class i. It is worthy of mention that CCR measures the global performance of the classifier, whereas AMAE measures the ordinal classification errors individually analised for each class. Due to the fact that this work is focused on ordinal time series, it is not advisable to rely only on CCR as it ignores order information. AMAE is better suited considering order information of the labels and assuring that all classes contribute to the final error.

Regarding the hyperparameters of the ordinal classifiers, a nested 10-fold cross-validation procedure with AMAE as the parameter selection criteria has been used. In this sense, the cost parameter and the kernel width are adjusted in the range $\{10^{-3}, 10^{-2}, \ldots, 10^{3}\}$. Besides, for KDLOR, the values $\{10^{-6}, 10^{-2}\}$ are used in order to avoid singularities in the covariance matrices, and, for SVR, the values $\{10^{-3}, 10^{0}\}$ are used for defining the margin of tolerance where no penalty is given to errors.

3.2   Experimental Results

The results achieved by the 10 ordinal classifiers, applied to the 7 ordinal time series datasets using the 9 different L_p norms when computing the Pearson's determination coefficient (R_p^2) are summarised in Table 1, where the mean ranking results for both performance metrics (AMAE and CCR) are included. For this, first of all, we have computed the average performance of each ordinal classifier over the different datasets. After that, the ranks in terms of AMAE and CCR are computed, in such a way that, for each classifier, a ranking of 1 is given to the best method (based on the average of the 7 datasets) and a 9 is given to the worst one. As can be seen, using the $L_{1.9}$ norm ($R_{1.9}^2$) achieves the best results, not only in terms of AMAE, but also in terms of CCR, with a huge difference with the nearest methods, $R_{1.0}^2$ and $R_{1.5}^2$, respectively. In this way, our results show that $p = 2$ involves an excessive penalisation of errors, whereas $p = 1$ behaves quite good for AMAE (note that the L_1 norm is implicit in the

---

[3] These classifiers are available in the website https://github.com/ayrna/orca.

Table 1. Mean ranking results in AMAE and CCR obtained by computing the average of each ordinal classifier over the 7 datasets.

Ranking	$R_{1.0}^2$	$R_{1.1}^2$	$R_{1.25}^2$	$R_{1.4}^2$	$R_{1.5}^2$	$R_{1.6}^2$	$R_{1.75}^2$	$R_{1.9}^2$	$R_{2.0}^2$
AMAE	*3.60*	5.35	4.05	7.25	4.75	6.45	6.05	**1.15**	6.35
CCR	4.75	6.10	4.65	7.65	*3.85*	6.05	4.80	**1.60**	5.55

The best result is in bold face and the second one in italics.

definition of this metric) but is not able to obtain so good results for CCR. An intermediate value ($p = 1.5$) leads to good accuracy but worse AMAE values, concluding that the best balance is obtained by $p = 1.9$.

Table 2. Results of the Holm's test using $R_{1.9}^2$ shapelet quality measure as control method: corrected α values, compared method and p-values, ordered by the number of comparison, i.

Control alg.: $R_{1.9}^2$	AMAE		CCR	
i $\alpha_{0.05}^*$	Method	p_i	Method	p_i
1 0.00625	$R_{1.4}^2$	0.00000_+	$R_{1.4}^2$	0.00000_+
2 0.00714	$R_{1.6}^2$	0.00002_+	$R_{1.1}^2$	0.00024_+
3 0.00833	$R_{2.0}^2$	0.00002_+	$R_{1.6}^2$	0.00028_+
4 0.01000	$R_{1.75}^2$	0.00006_+	$R_{2.0}^2$	0.00126_+
5 0.01250	$R_{1.1}^2$	0.00061_+	$R_{1.75}^2$	0.00898_+
6 0.01667	$R_{1.5}^2$	0.00329_+	$R_{1.0}^2$	0.01011_+
7 0.02500	$R_{1.25}^2$	0.01789_+	$R_{1.25}^2$	0.01276_+
8 0.05000	$R_{1.0}^2$	0.04546_+	$R_{1.5}^2$	0.06619

Subscript $+$ represents a statistical significant win for $\alpha = 0.05$.

In order to determine whether the previous differences are achieved by chance, a set of non-parametric statistical tests have been applied. First of all, the Friedman's test has been applied to the AMAE and CCR evaluation metrics, with a significance level of $\alpha = 0.05$, where the confidence interval is $C_0 = (0, F_{\alpha=0.05} = 2.070)$. The null-hypothesis (all the algorithms perform similarly in mean ranking) is rejected for both performance metrics, given that $F\text{-val.}_{\text{AMAE}} = 7.854 \notin C_0$ and $F\text{-val.}_{\text{CCR}} = 5.495 \notin C_0$. Moreover, following the guidelines in [4] and given that the null-hypothesis in Friedman's test is rejected, the Holm's test has been carried out using the approach with the shapelet quality measure $R_{1.9}^2$ as control method, as it achieved the best mean ranks in Table 1. In this way, Table 2 shows the results of the Holm's test. As can be seen, using the $L_{1.9}$ norm significantly outperforms the rest of methods in terms of AMAE. Regarding CCR, $R_{1.9}^2$ also finds significant differences with respect to all of the norms except $R_{1.5}^2$.

4   Conclusions

This paper presents an analysis of the effect of using different L_p norms for the computation of the shapelet quality measure in the Shapelet Transform (ST) when applied to Time Series Ordinal Classification (TSOC). For this, 9 different L_p norms with $1 \leq p \leq 2$ have been evaluated to be used along with the Pearson's determination coefficient (R^2) for the computation of the shapelet quality. An experimental comparison of these 9 values for the L_p norm has been performed using 7 ordinal datasets and 10 ordinal classifiers. The results obtained and the statistical tests carried out demonstrated that $R^2_{1.9}$ (i.e. R^2 using the $L_{1.9}$ norm for computing the difference between the shapelet and the time series labels) achieves significantly better results than the rest of the L_p norms in terms of both AMAE and CCR (for the latter, all the differences were significant except against $R^2_{1.5}$). Nevertheless, due to CCR does not bear in mind the ordinal scale, lower attention should be drawn. The results obtained in this work outperform a previous study [11], where the L_1 was used.

As future work, it would be interesting to include an updated comparison against the state-of-the-art techniques in time series nominal classification, in order to demonstrate that, when dealing with ordinal time series datasets, the use of a specific L_p norm can further improve the results of [11].

References

1. Baccianella, S., Esuli, A., Sebastiani, F.: Evaluation measures for ordinal regression. In: Ninth International Conference on Intelligent Systems Design and Applications, ISDA 2009, pp. 283–287. IEEE (2009)
2. Bagnall, A., Lines, J., Bostrom, A., Large, J., Keogh, E.: The great time series classification bake off: a review and experimental evaluation of recent algorithmic advances. Data Min. Knowl. Disc. **31**(3), 606–660 (2017)
3. Bagnall, A., Lines, J., Keogh, E.: The UEA UCR time series classification archive (2018). http://timeseriesclassification.com
4. Demšar, J.: Statistical comparisons of classifiers over multiple data sets. J. Mach. Learn. Res. **7**, 1–30 (2006)
5. Gentile, C.: The robustness of the p-norm algorithms. Mach. Learn. **53**(3), 265–299 (2003)
6. Grabocka, J., Schilling, N., Wistuba, M., Schmidt-Thieme, L.: Learning time-series shapelets. In: Proceedings of the 20th ACM SIGKDD International Conference on Knowledge Discovery and Data Mining (2014)
7. Guijo-Rubio, D., et al.: Ordinal regression algorithms for the analysis of convective situations over Madrid-Barajas airport. Atmos. Res. **236**, 104798 (2020)
8. Guijo-Rubio, D., Durán-Rosal, A.M., Gómez-Orellana, A.M., Gutiérrez, P.A., Hervás-Martínez, C.: Distribution-based discretisation and ordinal classification applied to wave height prediction. In: Yin, H., Camacho, D., Novais, P., Tallón-Ballesteros, A.J. (eds.) IDEAL 2018, pp. 171–179. Springer, Cham (2018). https://doi.org/10.1007/978-3-030-03496-2
9. Guijo-Rubio, D., Gutiérrez, P.A., Bagnall, A., Hervás-Martínez, C.: Time series ordinal classification via shapelets. In: 2020 International Joint Conference on Neural Networks (IJCNN), pp. 1–8. IEEE (2020)

10. Guijo-Rubio, D., Gutiérrez, P.A., Tavenard, R., Bagnall, A.: A hybrid approach to time series classification with shapelets. In: Yin, H., Camacho, D., Tino, P., Tallón-Ballesteros, A.J., Menezes, R., Allmendinger, R. (eds.) IDEAL 2019. LNCS, vol. 11871, pp. 137–144. Springer, Cham (2019). https://doi.org/10.1007/978-3-030-33607-3_16

11. Guijo-Rubio, D., Gutiérrez, P.A., Bagnall, A., Hervás-Martínez, C.: Ordinal versus nominal time series classification. In: Lemaire, V., Malinowski, S., Bagnall, A., Guyet, T., Tavenard, R., Ifrim, G. (eds.) AALTD 2020. LNCS (LNAI), vol. 12588, pp. 19–29. Springer, Cham (2020). https://doi.org/10.1007/978-3-030-65742-0_2

12. Gutiérrez, P.A., Pérez-Ortiz, M., Sánchez-Monedero, J., Fernandez-Navarro, F., Hervás-Martínez, C.: Ordinal regression methods: survey and experimental study. IEEE Trans. Knowl. Data Eng. **28**(1), 127–146 (2016)

13. Hills, J., Lines, J., Baranauskas, E., Mapp, J., Bagnall, A.: Classification of time series by shapelet transformation. Data Min. Knowl. Disc. **28**(4), 851–881 (2014)

14. Ju, H., Lee, D., Hwang, J., Namkung, J., Yu, H.: PUMAD: PU metric learning for anomaly detection. Inf. Sci. **523**, 167–183 (2020)

15. Ke, T., Zhang, L., Ge, X., Lv, H., Li, M.: Construct a robust least squares support vector machine based on LP-norm and l∞-norm. Eng. Appl. Artif. Intell. **99**, 104134 (2021)

16. Kivinen, J., Warmuth, M.K., Hassibi, B.: The p-norm generalization of the LMS algorithm for adaptive filtering. IEEE Trans. Signal Process. **54**(5), 1782–1793 (2006)

17. Liu, M., Gleich, D.F.: Strongly local p-norm-cut algorithms for semi-supervised learning and local graph clustering. arXiv preprint arXiv:2006.08569 (2020)

18. Löning, M., Bagnall, A., Ganesh, S., Kazakov, V., Lines, J., Király, F.J.: sktime: a unified interface for machine learning with time series. In: Workshop on Systems for ML at NeurIPS 2019 (2019)

19. Rudin, C.: The p-norm push: a simple convex ranking algorithm that concentrates at the top of the list (2009)

20. Sánchez-Monedero, J., Gutiérrez, P.A., Pérez-Ortiz, M.: ORCA: a Matlab/Octave toolbox for ordinal regression. J. Mach. Learn. Res. **20**(125), 1–5 (2019)

21. Shannon, C.E.: A mathematical theory of communication. ACM SIGMOBILE Mob. Comput. Commun. Rev. **5**(1), 3–55 (2001)

22. Suykens, J.A., Vandewalle, J.: Least squares support vector machine classifiers. Neural Process. Lett. **9**(3), 293–300 (1999)

23. Thurnhofer-Hemsi, K., López-Rubio, E., Roe-Vellve, N., Molina-Cabello, M.A.: Multiobjective optimization of deep neural networks with combinations of LP-norm cost functions for 3d medical image super-resolution. Integrated Computer-Aided Engineering (Preprint), 1–19 (2020)

24. Ye, L., Keogh, E.: Time series shapelets: a new primitive for data mining. In: Proceedings of the 15th ACM SIGKDD International Conference on Knowledge Discovery and Data Mining, pp. 947–956. ACM (2009)

25. Ye, Y.F., Shao, Y.H., Deng, N.Y., Li, C.N., Hua, X.Y.: Robust LP-norm least squares support vector regression with feature selection. Appl. Math. Comput. **305**, 32–52 (2017)

STree: A Single Multi-class Oblique Decision Tree Based on Support Vector Machines

Ricardo Montañana$^{(\boxtimes)}$ (ID), Jose A. Gámez (ID), and Jose M. Puerta (ID)

Computing Systems Department, University of Castilla-La Mancha, Albacete, Spain
Ricardo.Montanana@alu.uclm.es, {Jose.Gamez,Jose.Puerta}@uclm.es

Abstract. We propose a new oblique decision tree algorithm based on support vector machines. Our algorithm produces a single model for a multi-class target variable. On the contrary to previous works that manage the multi-class problem by using clustering at each split, we test all the one-vs-rest labels at each split, choosing the one which minimizes an impurity measure. The experimental evaluation carried out over 49 datasets shows that our algorithm is ranked before those used for comparison, and significantly outperforms all of them when the SVM hyperparameters are carefully tuned.

Keywords: Oblique decision trees · Supervised classification · SVM

1 Introduction

Decision trees (DT) [12] are one of the most used classification models in data mining, with recent success stories such as its use by Microsoft Kinect for real-time human pose estimation [19]. This is due, among other advantages, to their high performance and structural simplicity, which make them easily understandable by humans, increasing in this way the confidence to use them in real world applications.

In this work we focus on supervised classification, where the goal is to induce a function or *classifier* $f : X_1 \times \cdots \times X_n \to Y$, where $X_1, \ldots, X_n$ are the predictive attributes that define the object to be classified and Y is the target variable or *class*, which takes values in a set of finite and disjoint categories (or *labels*), $Y = \{y_1, \ldots, y_k\}$. When a DT is used as classification function (f), it is a tree-shaped data structure where each leaf node is labeled with a value of Y and the inner nodes contain *tests* related to the predictive attributes. Branches coming out from an inner node represent the different answers to its associated test. An object (instance) is classified by following the path from the root to a leaf, using its attribute values to answer the tests at inner nodes. The object is classified with the label associated to the reached leaf.

The *standard* or most known model of DT is the one which uses univariate tests, usually by comparing the selected attribute with a threshold (e.g. $X_i \leq \theta$).

© Springer Nature Switzerland AG 2021
E. Alba et al. (Eds.): CAEPIA 2021, LNAI 12882, pp. 54–64, 2021.
https://doi.org/10.1007/978-3-030-85713-4_6

This type of DT is known as orthogonal or axis-parallel DT because of the partition of the input (attribute) space it generates. Due to the success of axis-parallel DTs there exists a plethora of machine learning algorithms to learn them from data, being C4.5 [17] and CART [5] two of the most used (both were included in the selection of the top ten algorithms in data mining [21]). However, this type of DTs cannot (directly) capture decision boundaries non parallel to the axes, having to *approximate* them by using several consecutive tests, which leads to complex (DT size) and, probably, less accurate models.

Oblique decision trees (ODT) [15] allow the use of multivariate tests in the inner nodes, obtaining in this way more compact models and, usually, better performance, at the expense of a higher time cost. Originally, a linear combination of (some of) the input variables was used as test function, $g(X_1, \ldots, X_n) \leq \theta$, but later more powerful machine learning techniques as support vector machines (SVM) or neural networks (NN) [3] have also been used.

In this work we focus on the use of SVM to obtain the test in the inner nodes, with the goal of producing an accurate single-model ODT able to manage multi-class $(k > 2)$ variables. Although DTs (ODTs) are successfully used as base classifiers to build ensembles, e.g. Random Forest [6], in this first attempt we limit our study to the base ODT classifier. Our main contributions are:

- We introduce *STree*, a new SVM-based ODT. The method is able to deal with a multi-class target variable by producing a single model. The main idea behind the method is to guide the splitting process by obtaining a partition which allows to properly classifying one of the class labels with respect to (all) the remaining labels.
- An extensive experimental evaluation is carried out over a benchmark which contains 49 datasets and 5 competing algorithms. In the experiments we tested two configurations for STree, one by using a default parameterization, whose results are clearly competitive with respect to the included competing approaches, and other, with fine-tuned hyperparameters, which significantly outperforms the tested algorithms.

Our study is organized in four sections apart from this introduction. In Sect. 2 we briefly review the closer proposals to our approach, which is described in detail in Sect. 3. Section 4 contains the extensive experimental evaluation carried out over a significant benchmark, as well as its analysis. Finally in Sect. 5 we present our concluding remarks and outline future research lines.

2   Related Work

Growing a DT from data is (usually) a recursive partitioning process that splits the data into several subsets according to the test selected at each inner node. The recursive partitioning method stops when the data received by a node (mostly) belongs to the same label, then, this node becomes a leaf. Therefore, the key point in the DT learning process is how to select the test or split for an inner node. In axis-parallel DTs, information or statistical measures have been considered to decide which test reduces most the uncertainty of the class variable. Shannon entropy (C4.5 [17]) or Gini index (CART [5]) are usual choices.

In *oblique* DTs more powerful multivariate tests are used, which leads to more compact and (usually) accurate models. However, deciding the test for a given inner node is also more computationally expensive. In most ODT algorithms the test is a linear combination of the input attributes, that is, $\beta_0 + \beta_1 X_1 + \cdots + \beta_n X_n > 0$. Then, the goal is to search for the β parameters which define the hyperplane producing the binary partition that most reduces the uncertainty of the class variable. In CART-LC [5] a coordinate descent method is used to optimize those parameters, while in OC1 [15] the method is improved by using multiple restarts and random perturbations to escape from local optima. Both, CART-LC and OC1 initialize the search with the best axis-parallel partition. In WODT [22] the optimization problem is transformed to consider the continuous and differentiable function of weighted information entropy as objective, thus, gradient descent can be used as optimization method. Furthermore, in WODT a random hyperplane is used as initialization. Metaheuristic algorithms have also been used to escape from local optima [18].

Apart from linear functions, more powerful machine learning models like neural networks or support vector machines have also been considered as split criteria [2,11], allowing in this way multivariate linear and non-linear tests. In this paper we focus on the use of support vector machines (SVM) [4,20] to build the test associated to inner nodes. The standard SVM algorithm looks for the optimal separating hyperplane which maximizes the margin of the training data regarding a binary class variable. To be able of doing this in non-linearly separable problems, we could transform the input vectors into a high dimensional feature space, where a linear classification problem is solved. These two steps can be joined in a direct computation method by using the so-called *kernel trick*, where different types of kernel can be used (linear, polynomial, etc.).

In the literature we can find several ODT approaches based on SVMs. Thus, standard SVMs with linear [2], radial-basis function [24] and polynomial [14] kernels have been used to learn the hyperplane at each inner node. More complex SVM algorithms like multisurface proximal SVM (MPSVM) are used in [13] and [23], while a twin bounded SVM (TBSVM) is used in [9]. Both, MPSVM and TBSVM learn two hyperplanes, each one being the closer to the data samples of one class and the farthest from the data samples of the other class; instances are then classified by using their distance to both hyperplanes.

The algorithms in [9,13,14,23] are able to manage multi-class problems. In [14] k, one per class, one vs rest binary problems are considered and so k SVM models learnt. Then, a vector of length k is built for each instance, where dimension i is its distance to the i-th hyperplane. Instances are then clustered in r groups by using the X-means algorithm [16]. The number of clusters, r, is determined by the X-means algorithm and is the number of branches coming out from that inner node. In [9] and [23], at each inner node, class labels are clustered into two groups by using the Bhattacharyya distance, then, these two groups are used to solve the binary classification problem by MPSVM and TBSVM respectively. Finally, in [13] at each inner node the multi-class problem is transformed into a binary one by facing the class label with more instances against the group formed by the rest of labels.

3   Proposed Method: STree

Our goal is to design a flexible SVM Oblique Decision Tree (STree) able to cope with a multi-class target variable, $Y = \{y_1, \ldots, y_k\}$, by producing a single DT. Different SVM-ODT algorithms have been presented previously in the literature (see Sect. 2), although most of them have been directly used as base classifiers for ensemble models, without testing them as individual classifiers. The main features of our algorithm are:

- A *binary* tree is obtained, as in [9,13,23], but on the contrary to [14].
- The binary split or classification problem set in each inner node is not obtained by using clustering as in [9,14,23], but facing one class label against the rest (as in [13]). However, instead of always selecting the majority class label, we try the k one vs rest cases and choose the best one according to an impurity score, being more flexible at the expense of extra computational cost.
- As there is no agreement about which kernel is better or worse for a specific domain, we allow the use of different kernels (linear, polynomial and Gaussian radial basis function).

Our method works recursively and at each (recursive) call the algorithm receives a set of instances T. Then, the method proceeds as follows:

1. If the stopping condition (max depth, almost only one class label, etc.) is met, a leaf node is created with *outcome* equals to the more frequent label in T.
2. Otherwise, we have to split T into two groups, T^+ and T^-, in order to create the two branches for this inner node. To do this, we have to transform the multi-class problem into a binary one. Let $k' \leq k$ the number of different class labels appearing in T (notice that as the tree grows in depth, not all the labels will be present in the received set T).
   - If $k' = 2$ we already have a binary classification problem. We apply the SVM algorithm to learn the maximum margin hyperplane H and split the instances of T in T^+ and T^- accordingly to its distance to H. The hyperplane H is stored in the node.
   - If $k' > 2$ we use the well known *one-vs-the-rest* (OVR) strategy [3, pg. 339] and define k' binary classification problems: $\{y_1\}$ vs $\{y_2, \ldots, y_{k'}\}$, $\{y_2\}$ vs $\{y_1, y_3, \ldots, y_{k'}\}$, etc. Let H_i be the hyperplane learnt by the SVM algorithm for the i-th binary classification problem, T_i^+ and T_i^- be the partition of T it generates, and $impurity(Y, T)$ be a measure which evaluates the impurity of the class variable Y in T. Then, we select the hyperplane H^* such that

$$H^* = \arg \min_{i=1,\ldots,k'} \frac{|T_i^+|}{|T|} impurity(Y, T_i^+) + \frac{|T_i^-|}{|T|} impurity(Y, T_i^-),$$

which is stored in the node.

3. Once the hyperplane and the corresponding partition (T^+, T^-) have been selected, two branches are created for this node: positive, for those instances having positive distance to the hyperplane, and, negative, for those instances having negative distance to the hyperplane. Two recursive calls are then launched with T^+ and T^- as set of input instances respectively.

In our implementation Shannon entropy has been used as impurity measure. No pruning stage has been already designed for STree, however a pre-pruning is allowed by setting a maximum depth for the tree.

Regarding inference, for a given instance the tree must be traversed from the root to a leaf node, whose associated label is returned as outcome. At each inner node the stored hyperplane H is used and the distance of the instance to it computed. If the obtained value is ≥ 0 then the instance goes on by following the *positive* branch, otherwise it goes on by following the *negative* one.

4   Experimental Evaluation

In this Section we describe the comprehensive experiments carried out to evaluate our proposal.

4.1   Benchmark

As benchmark we have selected the same 49 datasets used in [9]: 45 of them are from the UCI machine learning repository [8] while the other 4 correspond to a problem about fecundity estimation for fisheries (see [9] for the details). The first four columns of Table 1 report the name, number of instances, attributes and class labels for each dataset.

4.2   Algorithms

The following algorithms have been included in the comparison:

- STree*. Our proposal with a fine tuned parameterization, done by using a grid search method. As mentioned in Sect. 3 our goal is to design a flexible classifier, so different hyperparameters, most of them related to the SVM learning algorithm, can be varied. In particular, in this study we have tuned the following hyperparameters:
    - Kernel. Can be linear, polynomial or Gaussian radial basis function (RBF). Default is linear.
        * Kernel coefficient gamma is optimized for polynomial and RBF kernels. Default value is $\frac{1}{n \times data.variance}$.
        * Degree is optimized for polynomial kernel. Default is 3.
    - C. Regularization hyperparameter. Default is 1.
    - Max number of iterations for the SVM (optimization) learning algorithm. Default is 10^5.

- Max features. Number of features used to build the hyperplane. Default is all.

  In https://git.io/JYpff we show the hyperparameter values used for each dataset. When empty, the default value is selected.
  - STree-default. Our proposal without fine-tuning, i.e. using the default parameterization for the SVM algorithm: kernel=linear, $C = 1.0$, max iterations $= 10^5$, and max features = all.
  - TBSVM-ODT[1]. Algorithm to learn a multi-class oblique DTs by using Bhattacharyya distance-based clustering and Twin Bounded SVMs [9].
  - J48SVM-ODT(See Footnote 1). Algorithm to learn a multi-class oblique DTs by using X-means clustering and SVM algorithm [14].
  - WODT. Recent algorithm to learn oblique DTs based on using weighted entropy and continuous optimization [22].
  - OC1. Classical algorithm to learn oblique DTs [15].
  - CART. Classical algorithm to learn axis-parallel DTs [5].

In both STree* and STree-default entropy has been used as impurity measure and no maximum depth has been set, the tree grows until all the instances received in a node belong to the same class label or the hyperplane learnt by the SVM cannot separate the instances.

STree has been implemented in `python` as a `scikit-learn` classifier[2]. Publicly available versions of CART (`python/scikit-learn`) and OC1 (`C`) have been used. The code for WODT (`python`), J48SVM-ODT (`java/Weka`) and TBSVM-ODT (`Matlab`) have been provided by their authors. All the experiments have been run in a 3.8 GHz 8-core 10th-generation Intel Core i7 running macOS Big Sur operating system.

4.3 Results and Analysis

To evaluate the performance of each pair (algorithm, dataset), we have run a five fold cross validation 10 times (10×5cv). The same 10 seeds have been used in all the pairs to randomize the data before the cross validation. As no severe imbalance is presented in any dataset (see [9, Table A1]), accuracy is used to compare the tested algorithms performance. The mean and standard deviation over the 50 runs of the 10×5cv are reported in Table 1.

To properly analyze the results we have carried out a standard machine learning statistical analysis procedure [7,10] using the `exreport` tool [1]. First, a Friedman test ($\alpha = 0.05$) is performed to decide if all the algorithms are equivalent. If this hypothesis is rejected, a post hoc test is performed by using Holm's procedure ($\alpha = 0.05$) by using as control the algorithm ranked first by Friedman test.

---

[1] In [9] and [14] ensemble methods are proposed. In this paper we compare against the proposed base ODT classifiers.

[2] The code can be found in https://git.io/J3jkQ.

Table 1. Accuracy results (mean ± std) for all the algorithms and datasets.

#	Dataset	#S	#F	#L	STree*	STree default	WODT	J48SVM-ODT	OC1	CART	TBSVM-ODT
1	balance-scale	625	4	3	**0.9706 ± 0.015**	0.9107 ± 0.025	0.9213 ± 0.031	0.9402 ± 0.022	0.9192 ± 0.023	0.7821 ± 0.036	0.7067 ± 0.231
2	balloons	16	4	2	**0.8600 ± 0.285**	0.6533 ± 0.263	0.6783 ± 0.253	0.5950 ± 0.188	0.6200 ± 0.261	0.6833 ± 0.270	0.6050 ± 0.230
3	breast-cancer-wisc-diag	569	30	2	**0.9728 ± 0.017**	0.9689 ± 0.018	0.9659 ± 0.014	0.9518 ± 0.025	0.9335 ± 0.026	0.9239 ± 0.023	0.9657 ± 0.014
4	breast-cancer-wisc-prog	198	33	2	**0.8111 ± 0.058**	0.8021 ± 0.054	0.7076 ± 0.068	0.7240 ± 0.072	0.7100 ± 0.080	0.6915 ± 0.072	0.7449 ± 0.054
5	breast-cancer-wisc	699	9	2	0.9667 ± 0.014	0.9667 ± 0.014	0.9424 ± 0.018	**0.9672 ± 0.012**	0.9402 ± 0.021	0.9434 ± 0.021	0.9429 ± 0.017
6	breast-cancer	286	9	2	**0.7342 ± 0.048**	**0.7342 ± 0.048**	0.6632 ± 0.049	0.7074 ± 0.052	0.6497 ± 0.068	0.6363 ± 0.055	0.6564 ± 0.050
7	cardiotocography-10clases	2126	21	10	0.7915 ± 0.019	0.7915 ± 0.019	0.7793 ± 0.020	**0.8303 ± 0.017**	0.7955 ± 0.019	0.8109 ± 0.019	0.7748 ± 0.018
8	cardiotocography-3clases	2126	21	3	0.9006 ± 0.015	0.9006 ± 0.015	0.9014 ± 0.016	**0.9285 ± 0.012**	0.8998 ± 0.014	0.9205 ± 0.014	0.8967 ± 0.013
9	conn-bench-sonar-mines-rocks	208	60	2	0.7555 ± 0.068	0.7555 ± 0.068	**0.8041 ± 0.058**	0.7389 ± 0.064	0.7108 ± 0.072	0.7254 ± 0.069	0.7730 ± 0.055
10	cylinder-bands	512	35	2	0.7150 ± 0.037	0.7150 ± 0.037	0.7025 ± 0.037	**0.7265 ± 0.030**	0.6711 ± 0.042	0.7126 ± 0.046	0.6751 ± 0.036
11	dermatology	366	34	6	**0.9718 ± 0.021**	0.9661 ± 0.020	0.9642 ± 0.017	0.9571 ± 0.024	0.9161 ± 0.043	0.9396 ± 0.024	0.9707 ± 0.018
12	echocardiogram	131	10	2	**0.8148 ± 0.100**	0.8088 ± 0.070	0.7424 ± 0.080	0.8055 ± 0.084	0.7483 ± 0.083	0.7444 ± 0.083	0.7535 ± 0.072
13	fertility	100	9	2	**0.8800 ± 0.055**	0.8660 ± 0.062	0.8040 ± 0.068	0.8570 ± 0.071	0.7930 ± 0.084	0.7990 ± 0.084	0.7980 ± 0.079
14	haberman-survival	306	3	2	**0.7356 ± 0.043**	**0.7356 ± 0.043**	0.6640 ± 0.048	0.7150 ± 0.049	0.6516 ± 0.058	0.6405 ± 0.055	0.7201 ± 0.048
15	heart-hungarian	294	12	2	**0.8275 ± 0.051**	0.8177 ± 0.051	0.7619 ± 0.052	0.7850 ± 0.048	0.7583 ± 0.045	0.7506 ± 0.045	0.7798 ± 0.045
16	hepatitis	155	19	2	**0.8245 ± 0.074**	0.7961 ± 0.072	0.7684 ± 0.084	0.7619 ± 0.058	0.7568 ± 0.073	0.7658 ± 0.073	0.7737 ± 0.064
17	ilpd-indian-liver	583	9	2	**0.7235 ± 0.038**	**0.7235 ± 0.038**	0.6779 ± 0.036	0.6903 ± 0.042	0.6601 ± 0.050	0.6640 ± 0.038	0.6967 ± 0.036
18	ionosphere	351	33	2	**0.9533 ± 0.024**	0.8661 ± 0.037	0.8795 ± 0.039	0.8920 ± 0.034	0.8797 ± 0.041	0.8758 ± 0.038	0.8754 ± 0.034
19	iris	150	4	3	**0.9653 ± 0.032**	**0.9653 ± 0.032**	0.9467 ± 0.037	0.9460 ± 0.035	0.9480 ± 0.047	0.9387 ± 0.044	0.9534 ± 0.031
20	led-display	1000	7	10	0.7030 ± 0.029	0.7030 ± 0.029	0.7047 ± 0.029	**0.7209 ± 0.029**	0.6993 ± 0.031	0.7037 ± 0.030	0.7018 ± 0.024
21	libras	360	90	15	**0.7886 ± 0.052**	0.7478 ± 0.056	0.7756 ± 0.055	0.6597 ± 0.063	0.6450 ± 0.062	0.6550 ± 0.059	0.7267 ± 0.046
22	low-res-spect	531	100	9	**0.8838 ± 0.032**	0.8531 ± 0.034	0.8555 ± 0.032	0.8383 ± 0.039	0.8247 ± 0.034	0.8352 ± 0.031	0.7909 ± 0.034
23	lymphography	148	18	4	**0.8350 ± 0.059**	0.7738 ± 0.077	0.7800 ± 0.076	0.7786 ± 0.079	0.7346 ± 0.075	0.7683 ± 0.076	0.7616 ± 0.073
24	mammographic	961	5	2	0.8192 ± 0.022	0.8192 ± 0.022	0.7580 ± 0.025	**0.8215 ± 0.024**	0.7688 ± 0.021	0.7569 ± 0.021	0.7802 ± 0.026
25	molec-biol-promoter	106	57	2	0.7671 ± 0.091	0.7644 ± 0.083	**0.7789 ± 0.077**	0.7440 ± 0.091	0.7348 ± 0.079	0.7158 ± 0.079	0.6672 ± 0.089
26	musk-1	476	166	2	**0.9164 ± 0.028**	0.8435 ± 0.032	0.8412 ± 0.034	0.8269 ± 0.047	0.7764 ± 0.044	0.7769 ± 0.044	0.8340 ± 0.036
27	oocytes_merluccius_nucleus_4d	1022	41	2	**0.8351 ± 0.022**	0.8107 ± 0.025	0.7348 ± 0.026	0.7435 ± 0.034	0.7432 ± 0.039	0.7196 ± 0.031	0.7923 ± 0.024
28	oocytes_merluccius_states_2f	1022	25	3	**0.9154 ± 0.020**	**0.9154 ± 0.020**	0.9029 ± 0.022	0.9021 ± 0.022	0.8892 ± 0.022	0.8912 ± 0.025	0.9106 ± 0.018
29	oocytes_trisopterus_nucleus_2f	912	25	2	**0.8010 ± 0.022**	**0.8010 ± 0.022**	0.7491 ± 0.036	0.7540 ± 0.034	0.7477 ± 0.034	0.7258 ± 0.030	0.7619 ± 0.029
30	oocytes_trisopterus_states_5b	912	32	3	**0.9222 ± 0.018**	0.9167 ± 0.020	0.8888 ± 0.021	0.8984 ± 0.026	0.8639 ± 0.026	0.8703 ± 0.021	0.9221 ± 0.016

(continued)

Table 1. (*continued*)

#	Dataset	#S	#F	#L	STree*	STree default	WODT	J48SVM-ODT	OC1	CART	TBSVM-ODT
31	parkinsons	195	22	2	0.8821 ± 0.048	0.8821 ± 0.048	**0.9005 ± 0.051**	0.8446 ± 0.052	0.8656 ± 0.055	0.8559 ± 0.058	0.8792 ± 0.043
32	pima	768	8	2	**0.7667 ± 0.030**	0.7667 ± 0.030	0.6882 ± 0.035	0.7505 ± 0.027	0.6930 ± 0.035	0.7012 ± 0.031	0.6970 ± 0.033
33	pittsburg-bridges-MATERIAL	106	7	3	**0.8677 ± 0.071**	0.7913 ± 0.070	0.7995 ± 0.077	0.8503 ± 0.074	0.8103 ± 0.088	0.8006 ± 0.076	0.8114 ± 0.072
34	pittsburg-bridges-REL-L	103	7	3	0.6322 ± 0.101	0.6322 ± 0.101	0.6184 ± 0.085	**0.6450 ± 0.104**	0.6050 ± 0.121	0.6172 ± 0.102	0.6221 ± 0.084
35	pittsburg-bridges-SPAN	92	7	3	**0.6598 ± 0.117**	0.6302 ± 0.097	0.5872 ± 0.116	0.6149 ± 0.119	0.5793 ± 0.097	0.5575 ± 0.096	0.6302 ± 0.086
36	pittsburg-bridges-T-OR-D	102	7	2	**0.8616 ± 0.069**	0.8616 ± 0.069	0.8375 ± 0.074	0.8383 ± 0.078	0.8315 ± 0.083	0.8225 ± 0.089	0.8210 ± 0.072
37	planning	182	12	2	**0.7353 ± 0.067**	0.7046 ± 0.075	0.5683 ± 0.087	0.7114 ± 0.050	0.5670 ± 0.098	0.5740 ± 0.078	0.5906 ± 0.072
38	post-operative	90	8	3	**0.7111 ± 0.075**	0.6756 ± 0.090	0.5567 ± 0.106	0.7011 ± 0.087	0.5422 ± 0.128	0.5822 ± 0.106	0.5394 ± 0.103
39	seeds	210	7	3	**0.9529 ± 0.028**	0.9490 ± 0.037	0.9290 ± 0.042	0.9090 ± 0.049	0.9324 ± 0.037	0.9162 ± 0.042	0.9425 ± 0.029
40	statlog-australian-credit	690	14	2	0.6783 ± 0.039	0.6672 ± 0.039	0.5617 ± 0.038	0.6603 ± 0.036	0.5739 ± 0.058	0.5720 ± 0.041	**0.6783 ± 0.032**
41	statlog-german-credit	1000	24	2	**0.7625 ± 0.027**	0.7625 ± 0.027	0.6825 ± 0.021	0.7244 ± 0.028	0.6874 ± 0.038	0.6897 ± 0.025	0.6876 ± 0.029
42	statlog-heart	270	13	2	**0.8230 ± 0.044**	0.8230 ± 0.044	0.7778 ± 0.048	0.8096 ± 0.048	0.7493 ± 0.058	0.7344 ± 0.047	0.7476 ± 0.051
43	statlog-image	2310	18	7	0.9559 ± 0.010	0.9526 ± 0.008	0.9534 ± 0.011	**0.9676 ± 0.011**	0.9501 ± 0.009	0.9613 ± 0.009	0.9536 ± 0.043
44	statlog-vehicle	846	18	4	**0.7930 ± 0.030**	0.7930 ± 0.030	0.7297 ± 0.030	0.7323 ± 0.031	0.7085 ± 0.037	0.7064 ± 0.031	0.7896 ± 0.029
45	synthetic-control	600	60	6	0.9500 ± 0.025	0.9388 ± 0.030	**0.9785 ± 0.015**	0.9223 ± 0.031	0.8632 ± 0.037	0.9023 ± 0.025	0.9716 ± 0.015
46	tic-tac-toe	958	9	2	**0.9844 ± 0.008**	0.9833 ± 0.008	0.9423 ± 0.033	0.9833 ± 0.008	0.9185 ± 0.037	0.9523 ± 0.019	0.9749 ± 0.012
47	vertebral-column-2classes	310	6	2	0.8529 ± 0.041	0.8529 ± 0.041	0.8071 ± 0.056	0.8523 ± 0.045	0.8152 ± 0.047	0.7997 ± 0.042	0.8226 ± 0.040
48	wine	178	13	3	**0.9792 ± 0.022**	0.9758 ± 0.024	0.9679 ± 0.028	0.9786 ± 0.021	0.9162 ± 0.047	0.9016 ± 0.053	0.9775 ± 0.021
49	zoo	101	16	7	**0.9575 ± 0.045**	0.9476 ± 0.042	0.9514 ± 0.044	0.9238 ± 0.047	0.8910 ± 0.077	0.9556 ± 0.044	0.9363 ± 0.049

We carried out two statistical analysis, including or not algorithm STree*. When all the algorithms are included, Friedman test reports a p-value of 4.9919e−27, thus rejecting the null hypothesis that all the algorithms are equivalent. The results of the post hoc Holm's tests are shown in Table 2(a) by using STree* as control. The columns *rank* and p-value represent the ranking obtained by the Friedman test and the p-value adjusted by Holm's procedure, respectively. The columns *win*, *tie* and *loss* contain the number of times that the control algorithm wins, ties and loses with respect to the row-wise algorithm. The p-values for the non-rejected null hypothesis are boldfaced. As can be observed (finely tuned) STree* algorithm significantly outperforms the remaining algorithms. In order to compare our proposal without tuning the hyperparameters we have repeated the statistical analysis excluding STree*. Again Friedman test rejects the hypothesis of all the algorithms being equivalent (p-value 2.8244e−16). The post hoc analysis is shown in Table 2(b), where STree-default is taken as control, as it is now the algorithm ranked first by Friedman test. As we can observe, when the hyperparameters are not tuned for STree, STree-default significantly outperforms all the algorithms but J48SVM-ODT, there being no statistically significant difference in this case.

Table 2. Results of the post-hoc test for the mean accuracy of the algorithms.

Method	rank	p-value	win	tie	loss
STree*	1.65	–	–	–	–
STree_default	2.83	7.172e−03	28	21	0
J48SVM-ODT	3.49	5.142e−05	41	0	8
TBSVM-ODT	4.34	2.338e−09	46	1	2
WODT	4.37	1.999e−09	43	0	6
CART	5.45	1.696e−17	45	0	4
OC1	5.88	2.211e−21	48	0	1

(a) With STree*

Method	rank	p-value	win	tie	loss
STree_default	2.04	–	–	–	–
J48SVM-ODT	2.65	**1.053e−01**	34	0	15
TBSVM-ODT	3.39	7.314e−04	40	0	9
WODT	3.49	3.788e−04	34	0	15
CART	4.53	1.791e−10	41	0	8
OC1	4.90	2.026e−13	45	0	4

(b) Without STree*

Finally, we have also analyzed the complexity (size) of the obtained trees (see https://git.io/J3jI6) and also the training time of the different algorithms (see https://git.io/J3jI9). Table 3 shows the results on average over the 49 datasets once we normalize them by using STree-default as control. Regarding size we can observe that STree obtains the smallest trees, while J48SVM-ODT and WODT, which are the closer algorithms to STree, obtain trees with twice the nodes of STree-default. Regarding time, although this is not a fair comparison because of the different implementations, we can observe that apart from axis-parallel CART, STree algorithms are strongly competitive, with only TBSVM-ODT being faster than STree-default, but that algorithm is so far in accuracy.

Table 3. Datasets used during the experimentation

	STree*	STree-default	WODT	J48SVM-ODT	OC1	CART	TBSVM-ODT
Size	0.87	1.00	19.18	2.17	2.00	8.58	3.52
CPU time	0.85	1.00	7.96	3.61	7.13	0.09	0.88

5   Conclusion

A new algorithm to build oblique DT able to directly manage a multi-class target variable has been presented. The algorithm produces a binary DT that needs to learn several hyperplanes at each split, although only one is stored for inference. The experiments show that the proposal works well over a great range of domains (49 datasets) and its performance is remarkable when compared against 5 competing algorithms. We also observe that tuning the hyperparameters of the SVM algorithm for each dataset is key to obtain better results, leading to an STree version that significantly outperforms all the competing tested methods.

As future research we plan to work with sub-spaces (few variables) instead of considering all the features at each node of the ODT. These variables can be selected by using some univariate or multivariate filter feature selection algorithm, or randomly following the random-subspace principle [6]. Aggregating this weaker classifiers by using ensemble-based techniques is also of interest, as has been done in [9,14]. Finally, the advantage of a fine tuning of the SVM hyperparameters has revealed to be key in the performance of the proposed algorithm, at the expense of a high computational CPU time requirement. As future research we plan to study some type of light *auto-tuning* that can be carried out embedded in the STree algorithm.

Acknowledgements. We are indebted to the authors of [9,14] and [22] because of providing us with the code of their implementations. This work has been partially funded by FEDER funds, the JCCM Government and the Spanish Goverment through the projects SBPLY/17/180501/ 000493 and PID2019-106758GB-C33.

References

1. Arias, J., Cózar, J.: ExReport: fast, reliable and elegant reproducible research (2016). https://cran.r-project.org/web/packages/exreport/index.html. Accessed 04 Aug 2021
2. Bennett, K.P., Blue, J.A.: A support vector machine approach to decision trees. In: 1998 IEEE International Joint Conference on Neural Networks Proceedings, vol. 3, pp. 2396–2401 (1998)
3. Bishop, C.M.: Pattern Recognition and Machine Learning. Springer, New York (2006)
4. Boser, B.E., Guyon, I.M., Vapnik, V.N.: A training algorithm for optimal margin classifiers. In: Proceedings of the Fifth Annual Workshop on Computational Learning Theory, COLT 1992, pp. 144–152 (1992)

5. Breiman, L., Friedman, J.H., Olshen, R.A., Stone, C.J.: Classification and Regression Trees. Wadsworth and Brooks, Monterey (1984)
6. Breiman, L.: Random forests. Mach. Learn. **45**(1), 5–32 (2001). https://doi.org/10.1023/A:1010933404324
7. Demšar, J.: Statistical comparisons of classifiers over multiple data sets. J. Mach. Learn. Res. **7**, 1–30 (2006)
8. Dua, D., Graff, C.: UCI machine learning repository (2017). http://archive.ics.uci.edu/ml
9. Ganaie, M., Tanveer, M., Suganthan, P.: Oblique decision tree ensemble via twin bounded SVM. Expert Syst. Appl. **143**, 113072 (2020)
10. García, S., Herrera, F.: An extension on "statistical comparisons of classifiers over multiple data sets" for all pairwise comparisons. J. Mach. Learn. Res. **9**, 2677–2694 (2008)
11. Kontschieder, P., Fiterau, M., Criminisi, A., Bulò, S.R.: Deep neural decision forests (2015)
12. Kotsiantis, S.B.: Decision trees: a recent overview. Artif. Intell. Rev. **39**(4), 261–283 (2013). https://doi.org/10.1007/s10462-011-9272-4
13. Manwani, N., Sastry, P.S.: Geometric decision tree. IEEE Trans. Syst. Man Cybern. Part B **42**(1), 181–192 (2012)
14. Menkovski, V., Christou, I.T., Efremidis, S.: Oblique decision trees using embedded support vector machines in classifier ensembles (2008)
15. Murthy, S.K., Kasif, S., Salzberg, S.: A system for induction of oblique decision trees. J. Artif. Intell. Res. **2**(1), 1–32 (1994)
16. Pelleg, D., Moore, A.W.: X-means: extending k-means with efficient estimation of the number of clusters. In: Proceedings of the Seventeenth International Conference on Machine Learning (ICML 2000), pp. 727–734 (2000)
17. Quinlan, J.R.: C4.5: Programs for Machine Learning. Morgan Kaufmann Publishers Inc., San Francisco (1993)
18. Rivera-Lopez, R., Canul-Reich, J., Gámez, J.A., Puerta, J.M.: OC1-DE: a differential evolution based approach for inducing oblique decision trees. In: Rutkowski, L., Korytkowski, M., Scherer, R., Tadeusiewicz, R., Zadeh, L.A., Zurada, J.M. (eds.) ICAISC 2017. LNCS (LNAI), vol. 10245, pp. 427–438. Springer, Cham (2017). https://doi.org/10.1007/978-3-319-59063-9_38
19. Shotton, J., et al.: Efficient human pose estimation from single depth images. IEEE Trans. Pattern Anal. Mach. Intell. **35**(12), 2821–2840 (2013)
20. Vapnik, V.N.: The Nature of Statistical Learning Theory. Springer, Heidelberg (1995). https://doi.org/10.1007/978-1-4757-2440-0
21. Wu, X., et al.: Top 10 algorithms in data mining. Knowl. Inf. Syst. **14**(1), 1–37 (2007). https://doi.org/10.1007/s10115-007-0114-2
22. Yang, B.B., Shen, S.Q., Gao, W.: Weighted oblique decision trees. In: Proceedings of the AAAI Conference on Artificial Intelligence, vol. 33, pp. 5621–5627 (2019)
23. Zhang, L., Suganthan, P.N.: Oblique decision tree ensemble via multisurface proximal support vector machine. IEEE Trans. Cybern. **45**(10), 2165–2176 (2015)
24. Zhang, L., Zhou, W., Su, T., Jiao, L.: Decision tree support vector machine. Int. J. Artif. Intell. Tools **16**(1), 1–16 (2007)

Deep Reinforcement and Imitation Learning for Self-driving Tasks

Sergio Hernández-García$^{(\boxtimes)}$ (iD) and Alfredo Cuesta-Infante (iD)

Universidad Rey Juan Carlos, Móstoles, Spain
{sergio.hernandez,alfredo.cuesta}@urjc.es

Abstract. In this paper we train four different deep reinforcement and imitation learning agents on two self-driving tasks. The environment is a driving simulator in which the car is *virtually* equipped with a monocular RGB-D camera in the windshield, has a sensor in the speedometer and actuators in the brakes, accelerator and steering wheel. In the imitation learning framework, the human expert sees a photorealistic road and the speedometer, and acts with pedals and steering wheel. To be efficient, the state is a representation in the feature space extracted from the RGB images with a variational autoencoder, which is trained before running any simulation with a loss that attempts to reconstruct three images, the same RGB input, the depth image and the segmented image.

Keywords: Self-driving · Imitation learning · Reinforcement learning

1 Introduction

Self-driving cars are one of the medium/long-term goals attracting more attention from many different fields of research, ranging from artificial intelligence, to automation, sensing or traffic management, to mention only a few. According to the Society of Automotive Engineers (SAE) J3016 standard, there are five levels of automation in driving: 1) assisted driver, 2) partly automated, 3) highly automated, 4) fully automated, 5) driver-less [15]. Currently, level 2 is available to some extent in many commercial cars as lane keep assistant and automated parking; whereas level 3 can only be found in top-of-the-range cars. Companies such as Waymo, Uber, Tesla, Baidu, Wayve, BMW or Audi, among many others, are boosting and leading the research. Their prototypes include a battery of sensors, mainly cameras, but also proximity sensors, LIDAR, GPS, etc.; and proprietary algorithms. However, we, as human drivers, lack of all these data. Instead, we *only* see what we are looking at; moreover, according to findings in psychology, we are indeed only aware of the small *window* we are focusing on at a given time. We also have to learn driving taking lessons from a teacher. Ideally, then, the goal to attain should be a fully automated car equipped with

This work has been funded by the Spanish Government research fundings RTI2018-098743-B-I00 (MICINN/FEDER) and Y2018/EMT-5062 (Comunidad de Madrid).

E. Alba et al. (Eds.): CAEPIA 2021, LNAI 12882, pp. 65–74, 2021.
https://doi.org/10.1007/978-3-030-85713-4_7

one or more cameras providing it with stereoscopic vision (this requirement is not necessarily satisfied by all human drivers), and a learning method able to mimic the human expert.

The problem, stated in this way, fits into the reinforcement learning (RL) paradigm; in which an agent *learns* to make decisions in an environment that evolves according to a state machine. The agent gets a reward for positive actions and its goal is to accumulate as much, and as soon, as possible. Moreover, the idea of learning from an expert is better captured by Imitation learning methods. From that point of view, one option is Behaviour Cloning (BC), where we have a data set of situations paired with actions taken, and the agent is trained to match them, as in any supervised problem. The other option is Inverse Reinforcement Learning (IRL), where the goal is to get the reward function out of the expert actions and then use that reward function to train our RL agent.

In this paper, we present a comparison of four agents in order to assess different approaches to teach driving. Specifically we test a pure RL agent, an agent trained with Behaviour Cloning (BC) [12], a Vanilla Deep IRL [1] agent and a Generative Adversarial Imitation Learning (GAIL) [8] agent.

Since RL is intrinsically trial-and-error, we run all the experiments on the simulated environment CARLA (Car Learning to Act) [6], in which the only sensor is a single camera on the windshield aiming at the front. Notice that most of the self-driving algorithms make an internal virtual representation of its environment out of the sensed information, and it is in that representation where they plan their actions. Hence, using CARLA to train the decision making process does not make any difference with respect to running the same algorithm in a true testing car.

2   Background

In this section we briefly recap the most relevant facts about Reinforcement and Imitation Learning (RL and IL respectively).

The RL framework consists of three components: the **Agent** is the artificial intelligent that makes decisions and selects the actions a_t to take given the state s_t, the **Environment** is a finite state machine which states transition in time as the agent acts, and the **Reward function** that is shaped by the expert to lead the agent's learning process. Formally, it is expressed as a tuple $(S, A, P(s_t, a_t, s_{t+1}), R(s_t, a_t, s_{t+1}))$ where S is the set of possible states that can be observed by the agent, A is the set of actions the agent can take, $P(s_t, a_t, s_{t+1})$ is the probability function that models the transition from state $s_t \in S$ to state $s_{t+1} \in S$ given the action $a_t \in A$, and $R(s_t, a_t, s_{t+1})$ is the reward function that measures how good it was to take the action a_t in state s_t and move to the next state s_{t+1}. During the RL training, the objective of the agent is to learn a policy π that produces a trajectory of states $s_0, s_1, ..., s_{t-1} \in S$ such that the expected reward function is maximised.

On the other hand, Imitation Learning (IL) is an approach that explodes the knowledge from an expert in an specific task to teach the agent how to do that task, in some way it is very similar to how humans learn from a teacher. We split this approach in two main groups: 1) Behavioral Cloning (BC), which is a supervised learning approach to the problem, so we need a paired data set of states and actions; and 2) Inverse Reinforcement Learning (IRL), which aims to extract a reward function from the expert demonstrations to train a RL agent. Clearly, IRL framework includes the components of RL, and incorporates two: **Expert data** containing demonstrations of how the agent should solve in such a environment, and a **Discriminator** that is trained to distinguish between expert demonstrations and agent actions. The latter is a key component for obtaining the reward function.

Self-driving cars have been of interest to the RL community for long time. Early approaches are due to BC [12], and more recently using neural networks in PilotNet [3] and [4]. An RL approach based on real measures from different sensors like GPS, proximity sensors or speedometer was used in a RL solution in [13] and [9] uses a DDPG agent for mapping images directly into steering degrees. Within the framework of IRL, [2] aims at learning to predict the steering, acceleration and braking values of a self-driving car directly from the raw images. High level orders such as *go forward*, *turn right/left* and *stop* have been incorporated in [5,11] and [7].

In this paper we have selected a Proximal Policy Optimization (PPO) agent [14] that is used three times: as the pure RL and as the agent in an Imitation learning framework in two solutions. We also use a BC agent, which consists of a neural network for regression with tanh activation so the outputs are bounded to $[-1, 1]$. Additionally to the neural networks implemented in each agent, we have trained a Variational AutoEncoder (VAE) [10], which transforms RGB images to the feature space.

3 Setup

A common approach of many solutions for designing systems that must make decisions in real environments, such as self-driving cars, is to perceive the surroundings and make a representation in a virtual world where the next steps are simulated to plan the actions. This real-to-virtual transformation is out of the scope of this paper, as we focus on learning the decision-making process of steering, braking and accelerating to successfully travel from the start to the end of a road.

Since our goal is to use imitation learning to train the driver agent, it is necessary to have demonstrations of (*state*, *action*) pairs; but the state is an abstraction of what the human expert sees. For this reason, we use a photorealistic driving simulator in which the human can act as in the real world. In this section we present the virtual environment as well as what and how is sensed from it, what kind of demonstrations we produce with it and the type of agents we train.

Fig. 1. (Left) Scenario with two-lane road with traffic lines. (Right) Scenario with two-lane residential street without traffic lines.

3.1   Simulation and Sensors

We use two scenarios generated with CARLA, SCN1 and SCN2, described below, and each one can be travelled in both directions.

SCN1 consists of a two-lane road of 660 m approx., with well defined traffic lines and gentle combination of curves (Fig. 1, Left).
SCN2 consists of a residential street of 300 m approx., wide enough for two lanes, but without any traffic lanes except for the shoulders (Fig. 1, Right).

The car is controlled with the accelerator, the brake and the steering wheel. Thus, the actions taken at time t are given by the tuple $a_t = (A_t, B_t, S_t)$, where $A_t, B_t \in [0, 1]$ are how much the accelerator and brake are pushed, and $S_t \in [-1, 1]$ is a mapping of how many degrees the steering wheel has been turned, in the range $[-270, 270]$.

The sensors in the car are a speedometer and a RGB-D camera, with resolution 128×128, on the windshield aiming at the front that provides both image and depth information of the road ahead. This information is obviously obtained from the simulator and recorded as images to mimic what the human senses when recording the demonstrations. On the other hand, the human expert sees the road as if he was sitting behind the wheel and also sees a speedometer in the screen.

3.2   Computer Vision System

Images are not observed directly by the agent, as they are by the human expert. Instead, they are processed to extract a feature map in a much lower dimensionality space [9]. To this end, we use a Variational Auto-Encoder (VAE) [10]. The encoder is a convolutional network that transforms each image into vectors $\mu, \sigma \in \mathbb{R}^{128}$, where μ is the mean and σ is the elements of the diagonal covariance matrix of a multivariate normal (MVN) distribution. In other words, the encoder maps the RGB image, that the human expert can see in the screen, into a probability distribution of the feature space. During training, such a MVN is sampled to obtain a feature map that is decoded in three images: the same RGB input image, the depth image of the input and the segmented image of the input,

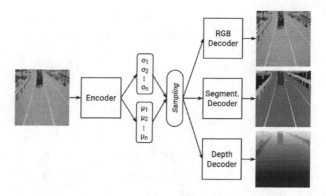

Fig. 2. Architecture of VAE trained for encoding the images from the embedded camera.

as depicted in Fig. 2. The loss of each decoder is the cross entropy, and the loss of the VAE is the sum of each decoder loss plus the Kullback-Leibler divergence between the MVN obtained and the standard MVN. Once trained, the feature map of an image is only the vector μ. Details of the VAE layers are given in Appendix.

The VAE is trained with 20,000 RGB images from the simulator, paired with its depth and segmentation images, before any driving learning; and then used to produce the feature map of each image as the car advances when the agent is commanding it.

3.3   Human Expert Demonstrations

Imitation learning algorithms need a data set of demonstrations of an expert performing the task that we want the agent to learn, in our experiments the expert is a human driver. For recording demonstrations we used a video game steering wheel with two pedals for accelerating and braking as input device. Each demonstration spans over 6,000 time steps, and in each one of them we store the feature map produced by the VAE out of each image, as well as the actions taken along with the speed of the car. These demonstrations will also serve as a reference for measuring the performance of each trained agent.

3.4   AI Agents

We have trained four agents. The first one is just a reinforcement agent trained via Proximal Policy Optimization (PPO). Then we use the same agent but trained with two different Inverse Reinforcement Learning (IRL) methods, namely Vanilla Deep IRL (DeepIRL) and Generative Adversarial Imitation Learning (GAIL). Finally, we use Behaviour Cloning (BC) to produce the last agent. A brief recap about each one of them is given below.

The state observed by the agent is a stack of 10 arrays, corresponding with the last 10 time steps. Each array consists of the feature map together with the speed and the action taken.

PPO. The agent trained with reinforcement learning via Proximal Policy Optimization consists of an *Actor* and a *Critic*; both being LSTM-based neural networks. The actor aims to select the actions to perform in each time step given an state. The critic evaluate how good is to be in the current state compared to the others. The reward will be +1 when the car is moving forward and less than 1.75 m away from the centre of the right lane of the road and −1 otherwise.

DeepIRL. We train the same PPO agent with the reward function obtained from a Vanilla Deep Inverse Reinforcement Learning algorithm given the set of demonstrations.

For learning the reward function this method uses a *Discriminator* network that is trained to distinguish between actions collected in the demonstrations and actions taken by the agent. Specifically, we implement the *Apprenticeship Learning* proposal in [1] replacing the original SVM with the Discriminator neural network. The algorithm mainly consist of a loop with three steps:

1. *Collecting agent experiences.* We let the agent to act on the environment in exploitation mode recording the (*state*, *action*) pairs. As a result we have a data set of agent experiences.
2. *Training the discriminator.* We merge in a single, labelled, data set agent experiences and the data set created by the expert and train the discriminator to predict a score of similarity.
3. *Running the agent on RL.* We let the agent to explore the environment using the reward function shaped by the score of the discriminator.

GAIL. As in the previous case, we use the same PPO agent, but now with the reward function obtained from Generative Adversarial Imitation Learning (GAIL). In this case the loop consists of four steps.

1. *Collecting agent experiences.* We let the agent to act exploring the environment. The states visited due to the actions taken are collected as experiences.
2. *Training the discriminator.* Just as in DeepIRL, the discriminator network is trained with a labelled data set created with the experiences from step 1 and from the expert.
3. *Update rewards.* We append a reward to each tuple (s_t, a_t, s_{t+a}) collected in step 1. This reward r_t is obtained with the discriminator trained in step 2.
4. *Train the agent.* Train the actor and critic networks in PPO agent with the tuples (s_t, a_t, s_{t+a}, r_t), i.e. with the experiences collected in step 1 and the corresponding rewards computed in step 3 for each one of them.

BC. Behaviour cloning is the agent trained by supervised learning on the expert experiences. Since this IL algorithm is not based on RL, it does not make any sense using a PPO agent. Instead, we use an unique neural network similar to the actor network used by the other algorithms. The loss function is the mean square error between the expert's actions and the output of the network.

4   Experiments

We carry out two experiments, with the following common elements in them. First, the goal in both is to finish the route keeping the car on the right lane or side, depending on the scenario, without going off the road or colliding; and the four agents are tested on both experiments. Second, the car is placed randomly within the right line or side of the road when starting a run. Third, agents PPO, DeepIRL and GAIL are trained for 150 episodes. We denote as an *episode* the learning process that starts when the agent begins to move the car from the start until it stops, which can occur when 1) the car reaches the end, 2) the car collides with the guardrail or another car, or 3) 60 s after beginning to move in the scenario 1 and 40 s in scenario 2 (about 50% of extra time with respect to the expert to reach the end). On the other hand, the BC agent is trained for 10 epochs, where an *epoch* is completed every time the training set is completely used. Finally, the metrics we collect on each episode are: **Path** is the total length travelled by the car, **Speed** is the average speed during the travel, **Off** is the number of times the car went off the right lane of the road and **Coll** (Collision) is the number of collisions that happened, these two last metrics have to be very low to be good. Notice that all the metrics are averaged across 20 episodes for each test.

4.1   Experiment 1

In this experiment we want the agent to learn to move forward on the right lane of scenario 1 and the right side of the road in scenario 2.

Table 1 shows the performance of the human expert in scenario 1 in terms of the metrics described above, both in absolute values and the increment with respect to the first row. BC agent is not able to reach the end. This leads us to think that the supervised approach for learning to drive is not appropriate. The purely reinforcement learning approach is not appropriate neither because the whole process depends on the reward shaping, which can barely capture the complexity of driving when it is done by humans. On the other hand, the two IRL approaches almost attain the whole route with a smooth driving. Moreover, the agent learns to take more risks as he drives faster but at the cost of driving off the road more often. The table also shows the ability to redirect the car when going off to avoid colliding. Thus, with BC and RL, every time the car goes off the lane, it crashes; while with DeepIRL and GAIL agents are able to adjust the direction, returning to the lane and avoid colliding.

Table 2 shows the results, on the same metrics with respect to the human, in scenario 2. The lack of traffic lanes apparently degrades the performance of DeepIRL and GAIL. Quantitatively, the Path increment is comparable to the same metric in the first scenario, about 8% of the total path length with GAIL and about 15% with DeepIRL, so rather than a degradation, the effect can be seen as an improvement on RL and BC agents. A reason for the improvement of BC is that its speed is slower than the expert and much slower than DeepIRL and GAIL. This conservative driving is less prone to make errors; in fact, the

Table 1. Results of experiment 1 on scenario 1. The horizontal bars represent the difference with respect to expert's performance.

Agent	Path	Δ Path	Speed	Δ Speed	Off	Coll
Expert	663.25		25.17		0	0
BC	316.29	-346.96	23.92	-1.25	1	1
RL	488.77	-174.48	28.64	3.47	0.4	0.4
DeepIRL	567.16	-96.09	30.28	5.11	3.95	0
GAIL	606.12	-57.13	30.34	5.17	1.6	0

Table 2. Results of experiment 1 on scenario 2. The horizontal bars represent the difference with respect to expert's performance

Agent	Path	Δ Path	Speed	Δ Speed	Off	Coll
Expert	305.25		19.68		0	0
BC	294.85	-10.4	19.06	-0.62	0	0
RL	278.35	-26.9	23.8	4.12	0.25	0.25
DeepIRL	255.5	-49.75	21.31	1.63	0.6	0
GAIL	279.41	-25.84	25.37	5.69	3.4	0.15

car never goes off. The improvement on RL may be due to the simplicity of the road. With no traffic lines, the reconstruction tasks on the VAE are simpler and the feature maps more expressive.

For the sake of clarity we include a visualization with bars of the difference with respect to the expert. Positive values have bars growing rightwards, and negative values leftwards.

4.2 Experiment 2

In this experiment we add an extra goal: to stop the car when an obstacle appears. We use the scenario 1, in which there are a few cars stopped on the left lane, and one car in our lane randomly located along the road within an interval around half-way. This makes this task more challenging since the agent needs to learn to discard all the cars in the opposite direction and take care only of the one in its way. We have tried several reward shapes for the RL agent, but none of them was satisfactory so it is not reported. The rest of results are shown in Table 3.

The most noticeable fact is the positive path increment with DeepIRL, which means that the agent manages to avoid the obstacle and keep on running until it goes off and collides. GAIL, on the contrary, performs much worse. We have noticed that this agent is continuously braking from the very beginning, which is also reflected in the drop of speed. In this case, BC performs reasonably well, probably because it focuses on stopping at the same distance than the expert does.

Table 3. Results of experiment 2. The horizontal bars represent the difference with respect to expert's performance

Agent	Path	Δ Path	Speed	Δ Speed	Off	Coll
Expert	176.16		14.91		0	0
BC	151.41	-24.75	15.8	0.89	0	0
DeepIRL	294.72	118.56	18.83	3.92	3.2	0.2
GAIL	15.4	-160.76	2.9	-12.01	0.2	0.2

5   Conclusions

In this paper we use a driving simulation as the digital representation that a self-driving car might produce from its surrounding by means of its sensors. Then we use a variational autoencoder that combines three losses for extracting a representation in the feature space. Finally, we have tested four algorithms for teaching a RL agent to carry out two self-driving tasks. We highlight that the reward shaping prevents from using purely RL agents because of the diversity of situations that it should model; while Imitation learning seems to be a better approach because all the agents tested under this paradigm have shown good performances.

Appendix

Here, we include additional information about the network architectures we have used for this paper.

Actor. An input layer of 256 LSTM neurons with hyperbolic-tangent activation, followed by three hidden dense layers of 1024, 1024 ans 128 neurons respectively, all of them with ReLU activation, and an output layer of 3 dense neurons with hyperbolic tangent activation function.

Critic. The same layer organization than the Actor but the output layer has a single neuron with linear activation function.

Discriminator. An input layer of 256 LSTM neurons with hyperbolic-tangent activation, followed by two hidden dense layers of 256 and 128 neurons respectively, both with ReLU activation, and an output layer of a single dense neuron with sigmoid activation.

VAE Encoder. The input layer simply admits the images. Then, there are four convolutional layers of 16, 16, 16 and 32 filters respectively, all of them of size 3×3 and stride of 2, followed by a dense layer of 2048 neurons with ReLU activation. There are two output headers that produce the mean and the standard deviation vectors, μ and σ, respectively. This layers have a single layer with 128 dense neurons and linear activation.

VAE Decoder. Recall that the VAE proposed has three decoders that reconstruct different representations of the input image. However, they all have the same architecture that begins with an input layer of 128 neurons, followed by a dense layer of 2048 dense neurons with ReLU activation, then four transposed convolutional layers of 32, 16, 16 and 16 filters respectively, all of them with size 3×3 and ReLU activation, and an output layer which is a transposed convolution with 3 filters of size 3×3 and sigmoid activation.

References

1. Abbeel, P., Ng, A.Y.: Apprenticeship learning via inverse reinforcement learning. In: Proceedings of the 21st International Conference on Machine Learning (ICML), p. 1 (2004)
2. Bewley, A., Rigley, J., Liu, Y., Hawke, J., et al.: Learning to drive from simulation without real world labels. In: International Conference on Robotics and Automation, pp. 4818–4824 (2019)
3. Bojarski, M., Del Testa, D., Dworakowski, D., Firner, B., et al.: End to end learning for self-driving cars. Preprint arXiv:1604.07316 (2016)
4. Bojarski, M., Yeres, P., Choromanska, A., Choromanski, K., et al.: Explaining how a deep neural network trained with end-to-end learning steers a car. Preprint arXiv:1704.07911 (2017)
5. Codevilla, F., Müller, M., López, A., Koltun, V., Dosovitskiy, A.: End-to-end driving via conditional imitation learning. In: International conference on Robotics and Automation (ICRA) (2018)
6. Dosovitskiy, A., Ros, G., Codevilla, F., Lopez, A., Koltun, V.: CARLA: an open urban driving simulator. In: Proceedings of the 1st Annual Conference on Robot Learning, pp. 1–16 (2017)
7. Hawke, J., Shen, R., Gurau, C., Sharma, S., et al.: Urban driving with conditional imitation learning. In: IEEE International Conference on Robotics and Automation (ICRA), pp. 251–257 (2020)
8. Ho, J., Ermon, S.: Generative adversarial imitation learning. In: Advances in Neural Information Processing Systems, vol. 29, pp. 4565–4573 (2016)
9. Kendall, A., Hawke, J., Janz, D., Mazur, P., et al.: Learning to drive in a day. In: 2019 International Conference on Robotics and Automation (ICRA), pp. 8248–8254 (2019)
10. Kingma, D.P., Welling, M.: Auto-encoding variational bayes. In: Bengio, Y., LeCun, Y. (eds.) 2nd International Conference on Learning Representations (ICLR) (2014)
11. Liang, X., Wang, T., Yang, L., Xing, E.: CIRL: controllable imitative reinforcement learning for vision-based self-driving. In: Proceedings of the European Conference on Computer Vision (ECCV), pp. 584–599 (2018)
12. Pomerleau, D.A.: ALVINN: an autonomous land vehicle in a neural network. In: Advances in Neural Information Processing Systems, vol. 1, pp. 305–313 (1989)
13. Riedmiller, M., Montemerlo, M., Dahlkamp, H.: Learning to drive a real car in 20 minutes. In: Frontiers in the Convergence of Bioscience and Information Technologies, pp. 645–650 (2007)
14. Schulman, J., Wolski, F., Dhariwal, P., Radford, A., Klimov, O.: Proximal policy optimization algorithms. Preprint arXiv:1707.06347 (2017)
15. Society of Automotive Engineers: Taxonomy and definitions for terms related to driving automation systems for on-road motor vehicles j3016_201806 (2018)

Human Activity Recognition with Capsule Networks

Laura Llopis-Ibor[✉] [iD], Alfredo Cuesta-Infante [iD], Cesar Beltran-Royo [iD],
and Juan José Pantrigo [iD]

Universidad Rey Juan Carlos, Móstoles, Spain
{laura.llopis,alfredo.cuesta,cesar.beltran,juanjose.pantrigo}@urjc.es

Abstract. Human activity recognition is a challenging problem, where deep learning methods are showing to be very efficient. In this paper we propose the use of capsule networks. This type of networks have proved to generalize better to novel viewpoints than convolutional neural networks. We show that the use of capsule networks into a straightforward architecture, between a convolutional preprocessing stage to extract visual features and a header for carrying out the task, is able to attain competitive results with spatio-temporal data without the use of any kind of recurrent neural network. Moreover, an analysis of the obtained results shows that our architecture is capable of learning the properties that encode the spatio-temporal dynamics of the movements that characterize each activity.

Keywords: Capsule network · Human Activity Recognition · Skeleton based action recognition · Image embedding

1 Introduction

Broadly speaking, Human Activity Recognition (HAR) is the task of assigning the correct activity label at the end of a sequence of video frames. Attaining a good HAR performance enables the development of many applications in Human-Computer Interaction (HCI) [7] such as industrial machinery operating without a dashboard, assisting elderly or people with disabilities in everyday tasks [5] as well as at work or developing natural and immersive interfaces.

HAR presents many challenges. If the video sequence has been taken from a single monocular camera it is frequent to have auto-occlusions, there is no direct information of the depth dimension, and obviously it is necessary to rely on computer vision techniques to extract the features out of each frame. On the other hand, when having multiple views another extra challenge is to match and

This work has been funded by the Spanish Government research fundings RTI2018-098743-B-I00 (MICINN/FEDER) and Y2018/EMT-5062 (Comunidad de Madrid). Dr. Beltran-Royo is funded by the Spanish Government research funding RTI2018-094269-B-I00.

© Springer Nature Switzerland AG 2021
E. Alba et al. (Eds.): CAEPIA 2021, LNAI 12882, pp. 75–85, 2021.
https://doi.org/10.1007/978-3-030-85713-4_8

fuse all the information collected. Some devices provide a sequence of *skeletons*, i.e. a tree representing a series of joints in the human body, in which each node represents 2D or 3D coordinates of the corresponding joint (depending on the device). In this case the challenge is to distinguish tasks that are similar when the information provided by the image is missing, such as combing and waving. Background information is usually irrelevant to the activity being performed. Using 3D skeletons results in more robust models because all the background information or illumination changes present in images are ignored. It is also a less ambiguous representation than its 2D counterpart.

In this paper we present a capsule network (Capsnet) for HAR based on 3D skeletons. As [17] claims, one of the drawbacks of capsule networks is that they try to model every entity found in an image; thus, working on skeletons we get over this problem. Specifically, we use Tree Structure Skeleton Image (TSSI) to convert a sequence of 3D joint arrays into an image. Then, this image is fed into the capsule network. Our hypothesis is that the benefits of capsule networks are able to extract and relate the time dependencies from the TSSI without using any kind of Recurrent Neural Network mechanisms such as Long-Short Term Memories (LSTM) or Gated Recurrent Units (GRU).

2   Related Work

HAR is a field of research that has attracted great interest over the last decade. Early approaches consist of hand-crafted features and classifiers trained to recognize the activities. Among the variety of hand-crafted features proposed are the camera motion corrected descriptors [21], saliency-aware matching kernels [14], simplified Fisher kernel representations [25] or part-based multiple features [11]. However, due to the decreasing price of motion-capture devices in recent years, and the rise of their availability [2], the accessibility to skeletal-based data has increased. Thus, research in the field has recently shifted towards fully automatic methods based on deep learning.

Skeleton-Based Deep Learning HAR. Early works focused on the use of recurrent neural networks (RNN) to model the long-term spatial and temporal relationship between joints. Wang *et al.* [22] propose a two-stream RNN architecture that analyzes both the contextual dependence in the time domain and the spatial configuration of the skeletons to then fuse the result for action recognition. Song *et al.* [20] employ a spatio-temporal attention model based on LSTM networks to focus on the most relevant frames and joints for a given action.

Given the success of convolutional neural networks in image-based tasks, they have also been used in the HAR domain. Wang *et al.* [23] propose a convolution-based architecture where they use *Joint Trajectory Maps* as encoding, representing the spatial configuration of the joints and their trajectory in three images through color coding. The resulting maps graphically represent the joint trajectory, motion direction, body parts and motion magnitude. Caetano *et al.* [4] propose an image encoding of the information regarding joint motion over time. Unlike previous works, Núñez *et al.* [15] do not use a graphical representation of the skeletons. In their work they apply a CNN directly on the 3D skeleton data and use the obtained features to feed a LSTM layer.

The most recent works focus on modeling skeletons as graphs. Following this representation, Yan *et al.* [24] applies a Graph Convolutional Neural Network (GCN). They extend this representation to the temporal domain by linking joints between consecutive skeletons. In this line, Huang *et al.* [9] presents a learnable approach to capture body parts information. Their work manages to highlight important body parts in the skeleton and combines this information with joint-level information for activity recognition. Si *et al.* [19] propose a LSTM unit that applies graph convolutions to work with graph-structured skeletal data. They state that their approach is able to learn the co-occurrence relationship between spatio-temporal features in addition to those features.

Capsule Networks for HAR. The idea of capsules was first proposed by Hinton *et al.* [8], however the breakthrough is due to Sabour et al. [17] with their trainable approach to these units. In their work they prove that capsule networks are more robust to affine transformations than convolutional counterparts.

Algamdi *et al.* [1] builds up on the work of Sabour et al. to adapt it to the HAR domain. To do so, they use a deeper CNN to create features from which the capsules are created. This enables the extraction of more complex patterns as the input of the model is a video sequence that includes unnecessary background information for action recognition. Moreover, they implement a weight pooling step on the previous features to reduce the number of created capsules. This results in a reduction of the computational cost of this model.

Jayasundara *et al.* [10] apply capsule networks to estimate the optical flow between pairs of images. They use three consecutive layers of capsules to calculate the motion features that are then fed to an autoencoder network to retrieve the final motion image, which is subsequently used for action recognition. The authors remark that capsules are capable of preserving the structure of entities and therefore they don't need to use a multi-scale approach nor other additional tools to estimate optical flow.

The previously discussed works apply capsule networks on RGB video frames from action sequences. We take advantage of the similarity between the capsule architecture and the CNNs and use an image representation of skeletal data as input to our network. To the best of our knowledge, we are the first approach to use capsule networks on image encoded skeletal data.

3   HAR Capsules

Capsule networks were proposed to solve the shortcomings of CNNs for image-based problem as described in Sect. 2. In this work, the human activities are defined by a sequence of joint positions. In order to apply a capsule network architecture we encode the data into images following the Tree Structure Skeleton Image (TSSI), introduced in [26].

3.1   Sequence Cutting

The input data of our model is a sequence composed of skeletons, one skeleton per video frame. Each skeleton consists of 25 joints where each joint is a position in a three-dimensional space. Since not all activities last the same time, the sequences will contain a variable number of skeletons. The first step to be carried out in the preprocessing stage is creating sequences of fixed length. To this end, we create sub-sequences form each sequence by selecting quasi-equally spaced skeletons.

We start by defining the number of sub-sequences that can be derived from a sequence as $b = \frac{|S|}{l}$; where $|S|$ is the length of a sequence of skeletons and l is the network input sequence length. Since the number of sub-sequences can be a real value, the last sub-sequence will contain repeated skeletons from the other sub-sequences.

The list of indices for each sub-sequence is the set $I = \{\lfloor s + i \cdot b \rfloor\}$; where $s \in \{1, \ldots, \lfloor b+1 \rfloor\}$, and $i \in \{0, \ldots, l-1\}$ for each s. Applying this list of indices I to a sequence S generates the set of sub-sequences $S' = \{J_i \mid i \in I, J_i \in S\}$.

3.2   Image Embedding

Capsule networks focus on extracting properties that represent entities from images and on putting them together to create the entities that represent the classes sought in a classification problem. The first two layers of our capsule architecture make use of convolutions for the aforementioned extraction. Therefore, to use this type networks it is necessary to convert the skeletal data into images. This problem has already been addressed in the HAR domain by approaches that have had this same issue, such as CNNs.

In order to convert the three-dimensional positions of the joints into an image representation we use the Tree Structure Skeleton Image codification [26]. It starts with an arrangement of the joints along the columns of an image and the skeletons along the rows. According to [26], this distribution ensures that a convolution operation will only establish relationships between connected or temporally adjacent joints. Since the position of each joint is three-dimensional, three grayscale images are obtained, which are used as the channels of an image representation of the sequence.

The arrangement that avoids unconnected joints in contiguous columns is obtained by traversing the graph; i.e. the skeleton tree where the root node is the spine joint. This ordering is applied to the joints of each skeleton in a sequence, as shown in Fig. 1.

Finally, values are normalized to the unit interval. Additionally, for this task we propose the use of a bone normalization and scaling process. First, we set the origin point of each joint to their parent joint. Next, we normalize the length of each bone. This process removes inter-subject variability from the data set and makes this representation rotation and translation invariant. In addition, it emphasizes the movement performed by a joint without depending on its predecessors. After this normalization, all the bones of the skeleton share the same motion range, a three-dimensional sphere.

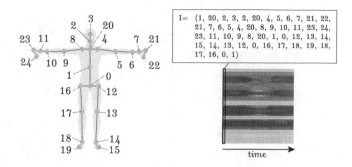

Fig. 1. TSSI encoding process. On the left, the skeleton graph where joints are the numbered nodes. On the right, the result of the depth-first search on the skeleton employed to encode the first column of the TSSI image. The color of each *pixel* is due to (x, y, z) coordinates used as RBG channels.

3.3   Capsule Network

The architecture used in this work is similar to the one proposed in [17], and depicted in Fig. 2. It can be divided in the following components:

Base Feature Extraction. The input image is first processed by a convolutional layer with 236 kernels of size 3×3 pixels, stride of 1 and ReLU activation. The output of this layer is a set of 236 feature maps of 21×47 pixels.

Low Level Capsules. The next layer applies 18 groups of 11 convolutional kernels of 13×13 pixels and stride 2 on the previous feature maps. The results are 18 groups of 11 feature maps of size 5×18 pixels. Each group is split along the rows and columns into 90 vectors of length 11, resulting a total of 1620 vectors in $\mathcal{R}^{11}$. Each one of those vectors d_i is then processed by the squash function to rescale its module to the unit interval in a non-linear fashion,

$$squash(d_i) = \frac{\|d_i\|^2}{1 + \|d_i\|^2} \frac{d_i}{\|d_i\|} \tag{1}$$

The result are denoted *low level* capsules $u_i \in [0, 1]^{11}$.

High Level Capsules. The 18 groups of low level capsules represent 18 patterns of motion throughout the image. In this architecture, those patterns are used to establish part-whole relationships with the *high level* capsules. In this work there is a high level capsule for each class in the data set.

First, the properties of each high level capsule are predicted from the low level ones. This is done by a transformation matrix $W_{i,j}$ of size 11×21 for each pair of low level capsules and high level capsules. As a result we obtain a *predicted* high-level capsule $\hat{u}_i$. There are $11 \times 21 \times 1620 \times C$ trainable parameters in this layer, where C is the number of classes of the data set.

After each capsule has been transformed we use the dynamic routing algorithm proposed in [17] to cluster together the predictions and to create higher

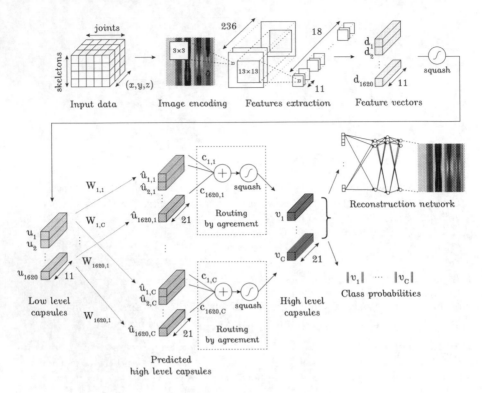

Fig. 2. Diagram illustrating the different phases that compose the capsule network presented in this work. First, a sequence of skeletons is encoded into a TSSI [26] image. Then feature vectors are extracted and squashed in order to obtain low level capsules. These capsules are transformed and clustered together to generate high level capsules. Finally, the encoded image is reconstructed and the probability for each class is obtained.

level capsule properties. This clustering is done iteratively based on the similarity between all the predictions for a high level capsule. The obtained values are then processed by the squash function (1) to generate each high level capsule, v_j. The module $\|v_j\|$ of each high level capsule is used as its class probability.

Reconstruction Network. To regularize the training of the capsule network we use a fully connected network to reconstruct the input image from the high level capsules, as suggested in [17]. Only the high level capsule corresponding to the true class is taken into account. This is done by setting all high level capsules to zeros except the one corresponding to the true class. This network has two hidden layers with sizes of 3072 and 6144, respectively.

Loss. The total loss of the architecture is computed from the loss of the capsule network and the reconstruction network, $\mathcal{L}_{cap}$ and $\mathcal{L}_{reco}$ respectively. For the capsule network, the margin loss proposed in [17] is used, with $m^+ = 0.7$, $m^- = 0.3$ and $\lambda = 2$. For the reconstruction network, the loss is the mean squared error between the input image and the reconstructed image. In order to balance these two losses we use two trainable coefficients s_{cap} and s_{reco}. These coefficients are also summed to the total loss to self-balance their influence as detailed in [16]:

$$\mathcal{L} = e^{-s_{cap}} \mathcal{L}_{cap} + s_{cap} + e^{-s_{reco}} \mathcal{L}_{reco} + s_{reco} \tag{2}$$

4   Experiments

In this section we describe the data sets used for the evaluation of our proposal and the setting of our experiments. We analyze the results obtained and perform a comparison against works from the state of the art in skeleton based HAR.

The experiments were conducted on a Intel Xeon E5-2698v4, 2.20 GHz CPU and a NVIDIA Tesla V100 GPU with 32 GB of RAM. We trained our network for 100 epochs with a learning rate of 10^{-5} using the Adam optimization algorithm and batch size of 36. At epoch 50 we decreased the learning rate by a factor of 0.1. All of the hyperparameters have been selected by a constrained random search that ensured the best network accuracy on the validation phase of the training.

4.1   Data Sets

The proposed architecture has been evaluated on two widely used activity recognition data sets. The first one, NTU RGB+D [18], is a data set composed of 56880 sequences representing 60 actions performed by 40 subjects and captured by Kinect V2 cameras from 80 viewpoints. The actions are captured simultaneously by 3 cameras. Each sequence is composed of a variable number of skeletons and each skeleton is composed of 25 joints. For actions involving two subjects we have only used the skeleton of the main actor, as described in [18]. The authors of this data set propose two evaluation protocols. In the first protocol, 20 subjects are used for training and another 20 for evaluation (Cross-Subject). The second protocol uses the sequences captured by camera 2 and 3 for training and those of camera 1 for evaluation (Cross-View). The second data set, NTU RGB+D 120 [12], is an extension of the previous set. The size of the data set increases to 114480 sequences representing 120 actions performed by 106 subjects and captured from 155 viewpoints. As before, the authors propose two evaluation protocols: Cross-Subject and Cross-Setup. For the Cross-Subject protocol, 53 specific subjects should be used for training and 53 for evaluation. On the other hand, for the Cross-Setup protocol, 16 setups are used for training and 16 setups for evaluation.

4.2   Results and Discussion

The results obtained for the above data sets using their evaluation protocols, together with state-of-the-art works are shown in Table 1. Our architecture is not using either recurrent neurons nor graph neural network, and yet our results

Table 1. Results of the proposed architecture and state-of-the-art works. The Cross-Subject (CS60) and Cross-View (CV60) protocols from the NTU RGB+D were used. For the NTU RGB+D 120 the Cross-Subject (CS120) and Cross-Setup (CST120) protocols were used. These results are reported by their respective authors. The results of the work marked with * are reported in [26].

Model	CS60 (%)	CV60 (%)	CS120 (%)	CST120 (%)
Deep RNN [18]	56.2	64.0	–	–
HBRNN* [6]	59.1	64.0	–	–
Deep P-LSTM [18]	62.9	70.2	–	–
Trust Gate LSTM [13]	69.2	77.7	–	–
TSSI [26]	73.1	76.5	–	–
TSRJI [3]	73.3	**80.3**	65.5	59.7
SkeleMotion [4]	**76.5**	84.7	**67.7**	**66.9**
Ours	74.2	77.1	63.2	64.6

are competitive with respect to the state of the art. The most similar proposal is TSSI [26], which consist of a ResNet-50. Moreover, our results also outperform works that include recurrent networks. We noticed a significant number of false positives between actions that have a similar spatial configuration. In addition, the network is also able to distinguish between actions where the subject performs the same movements in a different order. This leads us to think that our proposal is able to capture spatial-temporal relationships. However these similar activities degrade the overall performance of the classifier.

In the proposed architecture, a fully connected network is used to reconstruct the input image from the high level capsules generated by the capsule network. The output capsule generated by the network for an input sequence contains the properties that define the action performed in it. We can visualize its effect by modifying the values of these properties and depicting the reconstructed skeleton to see which characteristic of the subject's movement each one encodes. We do this modification by adding values from an interval $[-0.25, 0.25]$ with a 0.1 step. Figure 3 shows the result of modifying the values of one property of an output capsule. This modified property characterizes the right and left forearms movement. As the value of this property increases, the forearms movement becomes wider.

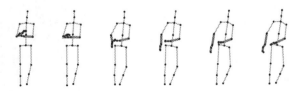

Fig. 3. Reconstructed input skeleton modifying the third high level capsule property of the action "take off jacket". Wider limbs are the most affected by the previous modification.

5   Conclusions

In the present work, a capsule network architecture for activity recognition based on skeletal data has been presented. The results of our proposal are better than other works employing methods based on CNNs. In the analysis performed using the reconstruction network, it can be observed that the capsule network is able to isolate the properties that define the motion of the human body. This suggests that this type of network has potential in the field of activity recognition and it's able to model spatio-temporal relationships between joints. To further our research we intend to develop a new routing algorithm that models human movement dynamics and to introduce attention mechanisms.

References

1. Algamdi, A.M., Sanchez, V., Li, C.: Learning temporal information from spatial information using CapsNets for human action recognition. In: IEEE International Conference on Acoustics, Speech and Signal Processing (ICASSP), pp. 3867–3871 (2019). https://doi.org/10.1109/ICASSP.2019.8683720
2. Altun, K., Barshan, B., Tunçel, O.: Comparative study on classifying human activities with miniature inertial and magnetic sensors. Pattern Recogn. **43**(10), 3605–3620 (2010). https://doi.org/10.1016/j.patcog.2010.04.019
3. Caetano, C., Brémond, F., Schwartz, W.R.: Skeleton image representation for 3D action recognition based on tree structure and reference joints. In: 32nd SIBGRAPI Conference on Graphics, Patterns and Images (SIBGRAPI), pp. 16–23 (2019). https://doi.org/10.1109/SIBGRAPI.2019.00011
4. Caetano, C., Sena, J., Brémond, F., Dos Santos, J.A., Schwartz, W.R.: SkeleMotion: a new representation of skeleton joint sequences based on motion information for 3D action recognition. In: 16th IEEE International Conference on Advanced Video and Signal Based Surveillance (AVSS), pp. 1–8 (2019). https://doi.org/10.1109/AVSS.2019.8909840
5. Chamroukhi, F., Mohammed, S., Trabelsi, D., Oukhellou, L., Amirat, Y.: Joint segmentation of multivariate time series with hidden process regression for human activity recognition. Neurocomputing **120**, 633–644 (2013). https://doi.org/10.1016/j.neucom.2013.04.003
6. Du, Y., Wang, W., Wang, L.: Hierarchical recurrent neural network for skeleton based action recognition. In: Proceedings of the IEEE Conference on Computer Vision and Pattern Recognition (CVPR) (2015). https://doi.org/10.1109/CVPR.2015.7298714
7. Erol, A., Bebis, G., Nicolescu, M., Boyle, R.D., Twombly, X.: Vision-based hand pose estimation: a review. Comput. Vis. Image Underst. **108**(1), 52–73 (2007). https://doi.org/10.1016/j.cviu.2006.10.012
8. Hinton, G.E., Krizhevsky, A., Wang, S.D.: Transforming auto-encoders. In: Honkela, T., Duch, W., Girolami, M., Kaski, S. (eds.) ICANN 2011. LNCS, vol. 6791, pp. 44–51. Springer, Heidelberg (2011). https://doi.org/10.1007/978-3-642-21735-7_6
9. Huang, L., Huang, Y., Ouyang, W., Wang, L.: Part-level graph convolutional network for skeleton-based action recognition. In: The 34th AAAI Conference on Artificial Intelligence, pp. 11045–11052 (2020). https://doi.org/10.1609/aaai.v34i07.6759

10. Jayasundara, V., Roy, D., Fernando, B.: FlowCaps: optical flow estimation with capsule networks for action recognition. In: Proceedings of the IEEE/CVF Winter Conference on Applications of Computer Vision (WACV), pp. 3409–3418 (2021)

11. Li, M., Leung, H., Shum, H.P.H.: Human action recognition via skeletal and depth based feature fusion. In: Proceedings of the 9th International Conference on Motion in Games, pp. 123–132 (2016). https://doi.org/10.1145/2994258.2994268

12. Liu, J., Shahroudy, A., Perez, M., Wang, G., Duan, L.Y., Kot, A.C.: NTU RGB+D 120: a large-scale benchmark for 3D human activity understanding. IEEE Trans. Pattern Anal. Mach. Intell. **42**(10), 2684–2701 (2020). https://doi.org/10.1109/TPAMI.2019.2916873

13. Liu, J., Shahroudy, A., Xu, D., Wang, G.: Spatio-temporal LSTM with trust gates for 3D human action recognition. In: Leibe, B., Matas, J., Sebe, N., Welling, M. (eds.) ECCV 2016. LNCS, vol. 9907, pp. 816–833. Springer, Cham (2016). https://doi.org/10.1007/978-3-319-46487-9_50

14. Nguyen, T.V., Song, Z., Yan, S.: STAP: spatial-temporal attention-aware pooling for action recognition. IEEE Trans. Circ. Syst. Video Technol. **25**(1), 77–86 (2015). https://doi.org/10.1109/TCSVT.2014.2333151

15. Núñez, J.C., Cabido, R., Pantrigo, J.J., Montemayor, A.S., Vélez, J.F.: Convolutional neural networks and long short-term memory for skeleton-based human activity and hand gesture recognition. Pattern Recogn. **76**, 80–94 (2018). https://doi.org/10.1016/j.patcog.2017.10.033

16. Ramírez, I., Cuesta-Infante, A., Schiavi, E., Pantrigo, J.J.: Bayesian capsule networks for 3D human pose estimation from single 2D images. Neurocomputing **379**, 64–73 (2020). https://doi.org/10.1016/j.neucom.2019.09.101

17. Sabour, S., Frosst, N., Hinton, G.E.: Dynamic routing between capsules. In: Advances in Neural Information Processing Systems, vol. 30, pp. 3856–3866 (2017)

18. Shahroudy, A., Liu, J., Ng, T., Wang, G.: NTU RGB+D: a large scale dataset for 3D human activity analysis. In: IEEE Conference on Computer Vision and Pattern Recognition (CVPR), pp. 1010–1019 (2016). https://doi.org/10.1109/CVPR.2016.115

19. Si, C., Chen, W., Wang, W., Wang, L., Tan, T.: An attention enhanced graph convolutional LSTM network for skeleton-based action recognition. In: 2019 IEEE/CVF Conference on Computer Vision and Pattern Recognition (CVPR) (2019). https://doi.org/10.1109/CVPR.2019.00132

20. Song, S., Lan, C., Xing, J., Zeng, W., Liu, J.: An end-to-end spatio-temporal attention model for human action recognition from skeleton data. In: Proceedings of the 31st AAAI Conference on Artificial Intelligence, pp. 4263–4270 (2017)

21. Wang, H., Schmid, C.: Action recognition with improved trajectories. In: IEEE International Conference on Computer Vision, pp. 3551–3558 (2013). https://doi.org/10.1109/ICCV.2013.441

22. Wang, H., Wang, L.: Modeling temporal dynamics and spatial configurations of actions using two-stream recurrent neural networks. In: 2017 IEEE Conference on Computer Vision and Pattern Recognition (CVPR) (2017). https://doi.org/10.1109/CVPR.2017.387

23. Wang, P., Li, W., Li, C., Hou, Y.: Action recognition based on joint trajectory maps with convolutional neural networks. Knowl.-Based Syst. **158**, 43–53 (2018). https://doi.org/10.1016/j.knosys.2018.05.029

24. Yan, S., Xiong, Y., Lin, D.: Spatial temporal graph convolutional networks for skeleton-based action recognition. In: Proceedings of the 32nd AAAI Conference on Artificial Intelligence, pp. 7444–7452 (2018)

25. Yang, X., Tian, Y.: Super normal vector for activity recognition using depth sequences. In: IEEE Conference on Computer Vision and Pattern Recognition, pp. 804–811 (2014). https://doi.org/10.1109/CVPR.2014.108

26. Yang, Z., Li, Y., Yang, J., Luo, J.: Action recognition with spatio-temporal visual attention on skeleton image sequences. IEEE Trans. Circ. Syst. Video Technol. **29**(8), 2405–2415 (2019). https://doi.org/10.1109/TCSVT.2018.2864148

Towards Fairness in Classification: Comparison of Methods to Decrease Bias

Maitane Martinez-Eguiluz, Oier Irazabal-Urrutia,
and Olatz Arbelaitz-Gallego[✉] [iD]

Department of Computer Architecture and Technology, University of the Basque
Country (UPV/EHU), Manuel Lardizabal 1, 20018 Donostia, Spain
{mmartinez149,oirazabal003}@ikasle.ehu.eus, olatz.arbelaitz@ehu.eus
http://www.aldapa.eus

Abstract. It is said that with great power comes great responsibility.
Nowadays, we rely on machine learning systems to make decisions. Unfortunately these systems suffer from algorithmic biases; they often produce
results that are systemically prejudiced due to erroneous assumptions
in the machine learning process. Consequently these systems can contribute to increase biases in society and this is something we should
avoid undoubtedly. The importance of the topic and the effect it has in
the society has made it become an important research topic during the
last years giving rise to different solutions. In this work, we selected three
state-of-the-art techniques, decoupled classifiers, fairness constraints and
adversarial learning, that claim to reduce bias in machine learning algorithms and compared their performance over different databases and
fairness evaluation metrics. The obtained results show that there is no
system performing the best in all aspects and databases but gives some
hints to select the best option according to the objective.

Keywords: Machine learning · Algorithmic bias · Fairness · Evaluation

1 Introduction

Artificial Intelligence (AI) is having an increasing impact on our lives. Not only
do AI systems predict the weather or perform spam filtering [12], but also they
are able to evaluate the risk of recidivism in individuals [4] or decide whether
a person is worth lending credits [5]. These systems are backed up by machine
learning algorithms trained over large databases where biased databases entail
biased systems, as well-trained models will reflect those biases [13]. Without
proper identification and reduction of such correlations, models will inadver-
tently magnify stereotypes [15].

Fortunately, solutions are already being proposed in different classification
tasks ranging from creating new "neutral" databases [3] or placing an adversary
to the classifier that penalises the predictability of gender/race based on the
outcome of the classifier [13]. Experts in the Natural Language Processing (NLP)
field have also shown a deep concern because word embeddings have produced
relationships like "man is to programmer what woman is to homemaker" [2].

E. Alba et al. (Eds.): CAEPIA 2021, LNAI 12882, pp. 86–95, 2021.
https://doi.org/10.1007/978-3-030-85713-4_9

In addition, a debate resides in the community of fairness in classification on whether sensitive data such as gender, race, or religion should be used alongside other data at the training and classification stages. Moreover, the legality and ethics of using those attributes vary depending on country, jurisdiction, etc. [5]. This sense of "fairness through unawareness" is ineffective due to redundancy and correlation between attributes, enabling the classifier predict sensitive attributes through other pieces of information [8].

In this context, we considered important to evaluate the impact of different state-of-the-art debiasing techniques to reduce gender bias in classification tasks. We selected three techniques that rely on different foundations from one another and analysed how they can improve fairness to different classifiers. Some of these techniques, will not only incorporate the sensitive attribute to the classification data, but they will treat them as special values, crucial for the correct performance of the models.

The paper proceeds summarising the background in Sect. 2 and describing the methods selected for comparison and the metrics used to compare them in Sects. 3 and 4. Then the experiments carried out are described in Sect. 5 to continue with the description of the results in Sect. 6 and finish with conclusions and further work in Sect. 7.

2 Background

An increasing concern about fairness (or lack thereof) on multiple fields has risen [12] due to a higher academic interest in machine learning [10], which led to an emergence of multiple distinct approaches for sorting out the consequent issues.

Buolamwini and Gebru [3] worry about the disparity in accuracy of classifiers with respect to gender and skin colour and point out how urgently attention is needed on this matter if companies want to rely on fair systems. They blame the underrepresentation of minorities in databases and introduce a collection balanced both in gender and skin colour. Dwork et al. [5] sustain that machine learning systems face a trade off between fairness and accuracy. They present the notion of Decoupled Classifiers, training separate classifiers for each group, and extend their work by using transfer learning to address underrepresentation of minority groups. Slack et al. [10] propose two algorithms: (a) A model-agnostic algorithm that provides interpretable conditions for when a model is behaving fairly. (b) A meta-learning algorithm that intends to efficiently train models with few samples at hand while maintaining balanced fairness and accuracy.

Zafar et al. [12] introduce a mechanism to control the degree of fairness relatively precisely and apply the mechanism to two classifiers: logistic regression and support vector machines. The same authors also introduce a new notion of unfairness in another paper called *disparate mistreatment* [11], defined in terms of misclassification rates. They then provide measures of *disparate mistreatment* for decision boundary-based classifiers. Beutel et al. [1] use an adversarial training procedure to remove information about the sensitive attribute and observe the effects on fairness properties. They find out that a small database is enough for their models and that data itself guides a notion of fairness to the model. Zhang et al. [13], frequently citing and comparing [1], present a framework using adversarial learning for mitigating bias. Their objective is to maximise the ability of the predictor to correctly output the class while minimising the adversary's ability to predict the protected attribute.

Zhao et al. [15] focus on bias on visual recognition problems with supported captions sourced from web corpora. They (a) identify and quantify bias on those databases, (b) evaluate how models amplify that bias and (c) propose a calibration algorithm that introduces corpus-level constraints to classifiers for reducing bias. Garg et al. [6] show that word embeddings used in Natural Language Processing (NLP) convey 100 years of gender and ethnic stereotypes and demonstrate how dynamics of embeddings reflect the change of stereotipical attitudes towards women and ethnic minorities. Zhao et al. [14] perform a thorough analysis on the gender bias on ELMo embeddings (deep contextualized word representations [9]) and explore two methods for mitigating the disparity. Bolukbasi et al. [2] also present a similar concern over the discrimination of embeddings trained on Google News and provide a methodology for removing that bias. Nevertheless, a countering criticism of debiased embeddings has already emerged. Gonen and Goldberg [7] argue that although bias is reduced by definition, the actual effect is hidden instead of removed, making the debiasing superficial.

3   Selected Methods

In this work we analysed the behaviour of regular binary classifiers working with one sensitive attribute with binary values comparing and contrasting the performances of Decoupled Classifiers [5], Fairness Constrains [12] and Adversarial Learning [13].

3.1   Decoupled Classifiers

The core concept resides in training a separate classifier for each group and it can be applied on top of any type of machine learning model [5]. In addition it allows deducing how the relevance of each attribute varies from group to group. The decoupling procedure introduces fairness using a loss function that takes into account the outputs from both classifiers and penalises differences across the predictions in each group (see Eq. 1).

$$\frac{\lambda}{n} \sum_{i=1}^{n} |y_i - z_i| + \frac{1-\lambda}{n} \sum_{k=1}^{K} \left| \sum_{i:a_i=k} z_i - \frac{1}{K} \sum_i z_i \right|, \tag{1}$$

where z is the outcome of the model, y the true class, a the sensitive attribute and K the number of groups. The left term in the outermost sum computes the mean absolute error (MAE) and the right term calculates the difference in positives across groups, which can be summarised as adding accuracy and fairness, respectively. $\lambda \in [0,1]$ is used as an interpolating value for weighing the relevance of accuracy and fairness in the loss, which makes the relation between them explicit.

3.2   Fairness Constraints

Two different approaches for balancing accuracy and fairness were proposed: the first one aims to maximise accuracy under fairness constraints and the second aims to maximise fairness under accuracy constraints. The former and selected method enables a granular control over the strictness of fairness requisites and does not use the sensitive attribute for training the model. Zafar et al. [12] propose to measure unfairness as the covariance (Eq. 2) between the users' sensitive attribute a and the signed distance from the users' data to the decision boundary $w^T x$.

$$\frac{1}{n} \sum_{i=1}^{n} (a_i - \bar{a}) w^T x_i \tag{2}$$

The goal of this method is to find the parameters w that minimise cross entropy loss function under the following constraints:

$$
\begin{aligned}
&\min L(w) \\
&\text{s.t.} \ \frac{1}{n} \sum_{i=1}^{n} (a_i - \bar{a}) w^T x_i \leq c \\
&\quad \ \frac{1}{n} \sum_{i=1}^{n} (a_i - \bar{a}) w^T x_i \geq -c
\end{aligned}
\tag{3}
$$

where L is the loss function and $c \geq 0$ is the covariance threshold. Lowering c towards 0 will introduce stricter constraints, whilst potentially sacrificing loss.

3.3   Adversarial Learning

Based on the concept of Generative Adversarial Networks (GANs), Zhang et al. [13] adapted the model so that the generative model acts as a predictor by determining z given x and the adversary tries to guess a based on z and y. The objective is to minimise the ability to predict a based on z. Figure 1 illustrates the structure of the GAN.

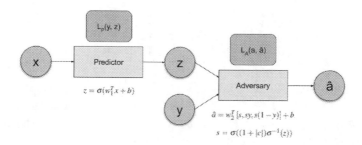

Fig. 1. Schema of the proposed adversarial learning system

The predictor will be a regular logistic regression of the form $z = \sigma(w_1^T x + b)$ and the adversary will calculate $\hat{a} = w_2^T [s, sy, s(1-y)] + b$, where $s = \sigma((1 + |c|)\sigma^{-1}(z))$, w_2 is a three weight vector and $\hat{a}$ denotes the prediction of the sensitive attribute a. 1 is added to $|c|$ to keep the adversary away from ignoring y by setting $c = 0$, which can be a tough local minimum to escape. We chose MSE (Mean Square Error) as loss function for both models. Parameter w_1 of the predictor is modified according to the losses of the predictor and adversary (L_p and L_a). w_1 (represented as w for conciseness) is modified according to the following expression:

$$\nabla_w L_p - proj_{\nabla_w L_a} \nabla_w L_p - \alpha \nabla_w L_a \qquad (4)$$

For example, SGD (Stochastic Gradient Descent) would update the parameters under the learning rate lr the following way:

$$w' = w - lr(\nabla_w L_p - proj_{\nabla_w L_a} \nabla_w L_p - \alpha \nabla_w L_a) \qquad (5)$$

Ignoring the central term in Eq. 4, we can see that the weights for the predictor need to be adjusted according to the gradients of both loss functions. The loss regarding the adversary is allegedly scaled by α to avoid getting stuck on local minima. The authors propose to dynamically set α for the Adult database. However, our experiments showed a value of 0.1 to work overall well.

4 Fairness Metrics

Since an inherent trade-off between accuracy and fairness is reported [10], we also selected other metrics.

Demographic parity, also known as the lack of disparate impact [10], is the ratio between positives in the minority and majority group (Eq. 6). A value closer to 1 indicates that the proportion of positives in both groups is similar, achieving demographic parity when the ratio equals 1. Reaching demographic parity is desirable in situations where changes are needed to give more opportunities to minorities.

$$\frac{P(z = 1 | a = 0)}{P(z = 1 | a = 1)} \qquad (6)$$

Equal opportunity is met when the true positive rates (TPR) are equal across the sensitive groups. This metric only requires non-discrimination in the positive group [8], often allowing for a higher accuracy [10]. It can be written as:

$$\frac{P(z = 1 | a = 0, y = 1)}{P(z = 1 | a = 1, y = 1)} \qquad (7)$$

Bias score evaluates the correlation between a sensitive attribute and another non-sensitive attribute by computing Eq. 8 where $c(z = i, a = j)$ counts the number of appearances of $z = i$ and $a = j$ altogether [15]. Thus, the proportion of each group in the positively classified examples is observed. A value closer to 0.5 indicates less bias.

$$\frac{c(z = 1, a = 0)}{c(z = 1, a = 0) + c(z = 1, a = 1)} \tag{8}$$

Reaching the optimal value can be of great use when the equality in the number of positives between groups is required instead of the equality in the proportion. For example, in 50/50 campaigns that demand parity in the number of men and women.

5   Experimental Setup

We gathered different databases and transformed them in order to follow a common standard and implemented the fairness metrics and the techniques chosen to mitigate bias. Finally, we tested the techniques and evaluated the performances over the transformed databases using a 10-fold cross-validation strategy.

5.1   Databases

5 databases were used for experiments, two of them used in the referenced papers (Adult ([4,12,13]) and COMPAS ([4,10,11]), other two, Credit and Hepatitis, publicly available at https://openml.org and a private database from our environment, Infor. Adult is used to predict whether an individual's income is greater than \$50,000 per year based on census data. The goal in COMPAS database is predicting the risk of recidivism of a jail inmate (we discarded some attributes of the original database due to their high number of missing values). Credit database is used to predict whether a requester is worth lending a credit. Hepatitis database (3 attributes discarded due to missing values) is used to predict whether a patient diagnosed with hepatitis will survive. Finally the aim of Infor database is to predict whether kids around 10 to 12 years depict a computer programmer as a woman.

All databases were processed so that in the case of the sensitive attribute, the minority group was assigned with the value $a = 0$ and the majority held $a = 1$. Regarding the class, the value that corresponds to the positive outcome was set to $y = 1$ and negative to $y = 0$. Continuous values were normalised in the range $[0, 1]$, discrete attributes with less than 10 unique values were one-hot encoded and, on the contrary, in discrete attributes with 10 or more unique values we replaced the most common with 1 and the rest with 0, in order to avoid excessive dimensionality. Their characteristics can be found in Table 1.

5.2   Classifier Implementation

The whole project was coded in Python, mostly using scikit-learn library. In the case of decoupled classifiers, our experiments compared the results of decoupling on top of logistic regression (LR) (optimal parameters found using the *lbfgs* algorithm proposed by default in scikit-learn), multilayer perceptron (MLP) (2 hidden layers with 30 neurons, maximum iterations for convergence 10,000 and by default values for the rest of parameters) and support vector machine (SVM) (using the *Radial Basis Function* kernel (RBF)) in order to observe the impact of decoupling in different classifiers. For Fairness Constraints we used the implementation provided by the authors. For each database, we ran two tests: one without the fairness constraints and the other with maximum constraints by setting the covariance threshold $c = 0$. Finally, the adversarial model was developed using the pytorch library. The most delicate part of the process was implementing Eq. 4, as no method in the library would make such calculation.

Table 1. Characteristics of the databases used for experiments

Database	Feat.	Protected	Examples					Bias Score	Dem. Parity
			$y = 0$		$y = 1$		Total		
			$a = 0$	$a = 1$	$a = 0$	$a = 1$			
Adult	14	sex	9592	15128	1179	6662	32561	0.15	0.36
COMPAS	12	race	3326	4009	2175	1528	11038	0.59	1.43
Credit	20	gender	191	109	499	201	1000	0.71	1.12
Hepatitis	16	sex	0	32	16	107	155	0.13	1.30
Infor	20	sex	214	31	243	378	866	0.39	0.58

5.3   Performance Measuring

To asses fairness, the performance of an algorithm cannot be measured with a single metric. In this work, for each of the implemented options, we calculated the next five metrics: accuracy, joint loss (calculated using Eq. 1), demographic parity, equal opportunity and bias score. Demographic parity and the bias score were also calculated as baseline for the databases (see Table 1).

6   Results

The results of the experiments are summarised in Table 2. The best values for each of the metrics and databases appear marked in bold.

Overall, decoupling results in an increase in both accuracy and fairness as the majority of accuracies (Adult-LR and Hepatitis-MLP are the exceptions) grow while equal opportunity tends to converge towards 1, MLP being the best performing model among the three. However, demographic parity seems to improve as often as it worsens. On the other hand, fairness constraints almost consistently improves fairness metrics while slightly sacrificing accuracy. Finally, the adversarial model scores the worst accuracies although sometimes achieving the best fairness scores. In addition the comparison of the obtained demographic parity and bias score values to the ones calculated in the original databases shows that the methods tend to improve them generally. Remember that underrepresentation can impact on bias scores and make it fall in contradiction with other scores if the database presents a large disproportion of men and women (or whichever values the sensitive attribute may hold), as stated in Sect. 4.

Table 2. Summary of the results obtained for the experiments.

	Decoupled classifiers						Fairness constraints		Adversarial
	LR		MLP		SVM				
	Coup	Decoup	Coup	Decoup	Coup	Decoup	Unconstr	Constr	
Adult									
Accuracy	0.850	0.849	0.845	**0.855**	0.840	0.840	0.851	0.852	0.815
Joint loss	0.149	0.150	0.154	0.149	0.156	0.155	**0.148**	**0.148**	0.159
Dem. parity	0.285	0.286	0.344	0.339	0.263	0.269	0.299	0.304	**0.438**
Equal opp	0.789	0.787	0.872	**1.073**	0.732	0.788	0.826	0.835	1.082
Bias Score	0.123	0.124	0.145	0.143	0.115	0.117	0.129	0.130	**0.178**
COMPAS									
Accuracy	0.757	0.757	0.756	**0.759**	0.749	0.750	0.757	0.753	0.678
Joint loss	0.198	0.196	0.199	0.199	0.196	0.197	0.198	**0.189**	0.242
Dem. parity	2.379	2.205	2.289	2.357	2.005	2.199	2.375	**1.222**	1.429
Equal opp	1.483	1.432	1.488	1.571	1.304	1.384	1.477	0.962	**0.997**
Bias Score	0.703	0.687	0.695	0.701	0.666	0.686	0.702	**0.548**	0.587
Credit									
Accuracy	0.754	0.768	0.706	**0.843**	0.755	0.793	0.760	0.753	0.702
Joint loss	0.269	0.261	0.298	**0.191**	0.275	0.246	0.266	0.259	0.317
Dem. parity	1.146	1.186	1.145	1.087	1.165	1.177	0.868	**0.998**	0.991
Equal opp	1.052	1.097	1.033	1.153	1.085	1.107	0.934	1.030	**0.996**
Bias Score	0.718	0.725	0.718	0.708	0.722	0.724	0.281	0.310	**0.688**
Hepatitis									
Accuracy	0.839	0.845	0.806	0.800	0.852	0.852	**0.858**	0.826	0.394
Joint loss	0.279	0.273	0.302	0.308	0.276	0.273	**0.263**	0.295	0.518
Dem. parity	1.153	1.230	1.164	1.219	1.114	1.198	1.230	**1.048**	0.808
Equal opp	1.024	1.092	1.056	1.126	**0.993**	1.070	1.081	0.946	0.787
Bias Score	0.117	0.124	0.118	0.123	0.114	0.121	**0.124**	0.108	0.085
Infor									
Accuracy	0.722	0.739	0.714	**0.898**	0.730	0.767	0.721	0.709	0.717
Joint loss	0.247	0.202	0.256	**0.118**	0.224	0.177	0.252	0.232	0.227
Dem. parity	0.602	0.845	0.565	0.563	0.735	0.880	0.573	**0.999**	1.005
Equal opp	0.634	0.895	0.624	0.944	0.774	0.975	0.605	0.994	**1.003**
Bias Score	0.402	0.485	0.387	0.386	0.451	**0.496**	0.390	0.527	0.529

7   Conclusions

In this paper, we incorporated state-of-the-art bias reducing techniques to different supervised classifiers. Their impact was evaluated using several metrics that measure fairness in classification tasks in five databases with different characteristics to evaluate how well the various models adapt to different circumstances. Having said that, we consider that from a fairness point of view the constrained classifier is the most appropriate method closely followed by the decoupled classifiers.

The biggest negative aspect of decoupled classifiers is the inconsistency with demographic parity. The difference with respect to their coupled respectives does not seem to have any clear tendency if we compare results from different databases. For instance in Credit, some models improve the metric while others do not. If we were to choose one decoupled classifier, it would be the decoupled multilayer perceptron (MLP) as it scores the best accuracy amongst all classifiers in all experiments except for Hepatitis. On the contrary, the constrained logistic regression seems to always improve fairness at a small cost of accuracy with respect to its unconstrained variant. Moreover, the results are competing with the ones of decoupled classifiers and are sometimes significantly better as in the case of demographic parity in many databases. Adversarial models fall into the third place because they showed to be rather inconsistent in their performance. For example, the adversarial model gets almost perfect fairness scores with the Credit database but it has the worst scores in Hepatitis. We believe this is a hyperparameter issue, as the authors of the technique propose a custom hyperparameter tuning for their experiment over Adult database. In fact, our results on that database are relatively acceptable.

All in all, we believe that fairness constraints are the most appropriate technique for mitigating binary bias, where gender takes part, due to its adaptability to several databases where the shape of data is not uniform or balanced or where the training set is limited in size. For example: the Hepatitis database has only 155 samples.

Although some concluding remarks could be done, this work opens a wide field to explore. One of the main assumptions we made was binarising both; the class and the sensitive attribute. However, key information might be lost by grouping different values together. For example, how should we group men, women and non-binary people? On the other hand, there are many more proposals of new techniques that could be analysed and probably some are being developed at this moment. Also, techniques may be fused together to form hybrid models that could improve our goal.

Acknowledgements. This work was funded by the Basque Government (ADIAN, IT-980-16; PRE-2013-1-887, BOPV/2013/128/3067); and by the Ministry of Economy and Competitiveness of the Spanish Government and the ERDF (PhysComp, TIN2017-85409-P).

References

1. Beutel, A., Chen, J., Zhao, Z., Chi, E.H.: Data decisions and theoretical implications when adversarially learning fair representations (2017)
2. Bolukbasi, T., Chang, K.W., Zou, J.Y., Saligrama, V., Kalai, A.T.: Man is to computer programmer as woman is to homemaker? debiasing word embeddings. In: Lee, D.D., Sugiyama, M., Luxburg, U.V., Guyon, I., Garnett, R. (eds.) Advances in Neural Information Processing Systems 29, pp. 4349–4357. Curran Associates, Inc., Barcelona (2016), http://papers.nips.cc/paper/6228-man-is-to-computer-programmer-as-woman-is-to-homemaker-debiasing-word-embeddings.pdf

3. Buolamwini, J., Gebru, T.: Gender shades: Intersectional accuracy disparities in commercial gender classification. In: Friedler, S.A., Wilson, C. (eds.) Proceedings of the 1st Conference on Fairness, Accountability and Transparency. Proceedings of Machine Learning Research, 23–24 February 2018, vol. 81, pp. 77–91. PMLR, New York (2018), http://proceedings.mlr.press/v81/buolamwini18a.html

4. Celis, L.E., Huang, L., Keswani, V., Vishnoi, N.K.: Classification with fairness constraints: a meta-algorithm with provable guarantees. In: Proceedings of the Conference on Fairness, Accountability, and Transparency (FAT 2019), pp. 319–328. Association for Computing Machinery, New York (2019). https://doi.org/10.1145/3287560.3287586

5. Dwork, C., Immorlica, N., Kalai, A.T., Leiserson, M.: Decoupled classifiers for fair and efficient machine learning (2017)

6. Garg, N., Schiebinger, L., Jurafsky, D., Zou, J.: Word embeddings quantify 100 years of gender and ethnic stereotypes. Proc. Natl Acad. Sci. 115(16), E3635–E3644 (2018). https://doi.org/10.1073/pnas.1720347115, https://www.pnas.org/content/115/16/E3635

7. Gonen, H., Goldberg, Y.: Lipstick on a pig: debiasing methods cover up systematic gender biases in word embeddings but do not remove them (2019)

8. Hardt, M., Price, E., Price, E., Srebro, N.: Equality of opportunity in supervised learning. In: Lee, D.D., Sugiyama, M., Luxburg, U.V., Guyon, I., Garnett, R. (eds.) Advances in Neural Information Processing Systems 29, pp. 3315–3323. Curran Associates, Inc. (2016), http://papers.nips.cc/paper/6374-equality-of-opportunity-in-supervised-learning.pdf

9. Peters, M.E., Neumann, M., Iyyer, M., Gardner, M., Clark, C., Lee, K., Zettlemoyer, L.: Deep contextualized word representations (2018)

10. Slack, D., Friedler, S.A., Givental, E.: Fairness warnings and fair-MAMAl: learning fairly with minimal data. In: Proceedings of the 2020 Conference on Fairness, Accountability, and Transparency (FAT 2020), pp. 200–209. Association for Computing Machinery, New York (2020). https://doi.org/10.1145/3351095.3372839

11. Zafar, M.B., Valera, I., Gomez Rodriguez, M., Gummadi, K.P.: Fairness beyond disparate treatment & disparate impact: Learning classification without disparate mistreatment. In: Proceedings of the 26th International Conference on World Wide Web (WWW 2017) . pp. 1171–1180. International World Wide Web Conferences Steering Committee, Republic and Canton of Geneva, CHE (2017). https://doi.org/10.1145/3038912.3052660

12. Zafar, M.B., Valera, I., Rodriguez, M.G., Gummadi, K.P.: Fairness constraints: mechanisms for fair classification (2015)

13. Zhang, B.H., Lemoine, B., Mitchell, M.: Mitigating unwanted biases with adversarial learning. In: Proceedings of the 2018 AAAI/ACM Conference on AI, Ethics, and Society (AIES 2018). pp. 335–340. Association for Computing Machinery, New York (2018). https://doi.org/10.1145/3278721.3278779

14. Zhao, J., Wang, T., Yatskar, M., Cotterell, R., Ordonez, V., Chang, K.W.: Gender bias in contextualized word embeddings (2019)

15. Zhao, J., Wang, T., Yatskar, M., Ordonez, V., Chang, K.W.: Men also like shopping: Reducing gender bias amplification using corpus-level constraints (2017)

Hypothesis Scoring and Model Refinement Strategies for FM-Based RANSAC

Alberto Ortiz$^{(\boxtimes)}$ [ID], Esaú Ortiz, Juan José Miñana[ID], and Óscar Valero[ID]

Department of Mathematics and Computer Science, University of the Balearic Islands, and IDISBA (Institut d'Investigacio Sanitaria de les Illes Balears), Palma de Mallorca, Spain
{alberto.ortiz,esau.ortiz,jj.minana,o.valero}@uib.es

Abstract. Robust model estimation is a recurring problem in application areas such as robotics and computer vision. Taking inspiration from a notion of distance that arises in a natural way in fuzzy logic, this paper modifies the well-known robust estimator RANSAC making use of a Fuzzy Metric (FM) within the estimator main loop to encode the compatibility of each sample to the current model/hypothesis. Further, once a number of hypotheses have been explored, this FM-based RANSAC makes use of the same fuzzy metric to refine the winning model. The incorporation of this fuzzy metric permits us to express the distance between two points as a kind of degree of nearness measured with respect to a parameter, which is very appropriate in the presence of the vagueness or imprecision inherent to noisy data. By way of illustration of the performance of the approach, we report on the estimation accuracy achieved by FM-based RANSAC and other RANSAC variants for a benchmark comprising a large number of noisy datasets with varying proportion of outliers and different levels of noise. As it will be shown, FM-based RANSAC outperforms the classical counterparts considered.

Keywords: Model estimation · RANSAC · Fuzzy metric · 2D straight line estimation

1 Introduction

Solving model estimation problems is a fundamental component of numerous applications in robotics, specially when addressing perception tasks. Nowadays, facing this kind of problem requires to cope with new challenges due to an

This work is partially supported by projects PGC2018-095709-B-C21 (MCIU/AEI/ FEDER, UE), EU-H2020 BUGWRIGHT2 (GA 871260) and ROBINS (GA 779776), and PROCOE/4/2017 (Govern Balear, 50% P.O. FEDER 2014–2020 Illes Balears). This publication reflects only the authors views and the European Union is not liable for any use that may be made of the information contained therein.

© Springer Nature Switzerland AG 2021
E. Alba et al. (Eds.): CAEPIA 2021, LNAI 12882, pp. 96–105, 2021.
https://doi.org/10.1007/978-3-030-85713-4_10

increased use of potentially poor, low-cost sensors, and the ever growing deployment of robotic devices which may operate in potentially unknown environments. In general terms, the underlying algorithms need to be capable of being robust against, in particular, strong uncertainty levels. In this regard, a *robust estimator* is able to correctly find the original model that supposedly the input data fits to, even when the data is noisy and contains outliers, i.e. data items which are not consistent with the original model due to an arbitrary bias affecting them (For the interested reader, [7] details the concepts, techniques and technical issues surrounding robust estimation).

The Random Sample Consensus algorithm (RANSAC) [4] is one of these robust estimation techniques. Given a dataset comprising both inliers and outliers, the most distinctive feature of RANSAC is the use of random sampling and a voting scheme to find the optimal set of model parameters. RANSAC is widely used nowadays, so much that it has become common in fields such as robotics and computer vision.

Fuzzy methodologies (together with other soft computing paradigms, such as probabilistic methods, machine learning, evolutionary computing and swarm intelligence) have been used since their birth to deal with imprecise data, targeting on the design of systems that are able to cope with uncertainty one way or another and even degrade gracefully if needed [8]. As already mentioned, robotics, and in general perception, is one of the areas where this capability achieves more relevance, particularly when autonomy is a distinctive feature.

In this work, we propose a variant of RANSAC which avoids discriminating between inliers and outliers by means of the use of a Fuzzy Metric (FM) in the sense of I. Kramosil and J. Michalek [10] that provides a degree of compatibility for each data sample with regard to the current model. The aforesaid fuzzy metric is besides used in a final model refinement step that is incorporated after the main hypothesis selection loop.

In the following, Sect. 2 overviews RANSAC, Sect. 3 introduces a fuzzy metric for RANSAC, Sect. 4 describes our approach based on the previous fuzzy metric, while Sect. 5 reports on a number of experiments to illustrate the performance achieved, and Sect. 6 concludes the paper.

2   Overview of RANSAC and Some Variants

Regarding model estimation, a common measure of estimation robustness is the breakdown point (BDP), defined as a percentage threshold on the outlier rate beyond which the technique under consideration is no longer robust to outliers. RANSAC is one of those robust estimators with BDP higher than fifty percent. Fifty percent is the limit of the Least Median of Squares (LMedS) [18], another robust estimator that has also enjoyed high popularity as a high BDP technique. Least Trimmed Squares (LTS) and Minimum Probability of Randomness (MINPRAN) are other high-BDP algorithms [Olu16], although less popular than RANSAC and LMedS. The BDP for others, such as the M-estimators family [HR11], is below 50%. Applications in statistics typically require less than fifty percent BDP, since outliers in this context are anomalies or exceptions in the data. However, the case is often different in robotics and computer vision applications, where outliers are defined with respect to the best among competing models, each describing well a fraction of the input data.

By randomly generating hypotheses on the model parameters, RANSAC tries to achieve a maximum consensus in the input dataset in order to deduce the inliers. Once the inliers are discriminated, they are used to estimate the parameters of the underlying model by regression. In more detail, instead of using every sample in the dataset to perform the estimation as in traditional regression techniques, RANSAC tests in turn many random sets of samples. Since picking an extra point decreases exponentially the probability of selecting an outlier-free sample [3], RANSAC takes the Minimum Sample Set size (MSS) to determine a unique candidate model, thus increasing its chances of finding an all-inlier sample set. This model is assigned a score based on the cardinality of its consensus set. Finally, RANSAC returns the hypothesis that has achieved the highest consensus, and the corresponding model is refined through a last minimization step that only involves the inliers found.

Searching for an all-inlier sample, RANSAC typically runs for N iterations:

$$N = \frac{\log{(1 - \rho)}}{\log{(1 - (1 - \omega)^s)}} \tag{1}$$

where ρ is the desired probability of success, i.e. at least one of the considered random sets is outlier-free, s is the size of the MSS for the problem at hand and ω is the ratio of outliers (see [4] for the details on Eq. (1)).

There have been a number of efforts aiming at enhancing the standard RANSAC algorithm, e.g. MSAC, MLESAC, MAPSAC, PROSAC, R-RANSAC, LO-RANSAC and U-RANSAC [2], since it, while robust, has its drawbacks regarding accuracy, efficiency, stability and response time [16,17]. Among these variants, there is a very reduced set adopting fuzzy methodologies [11,20]. In both cases, the authors address a homography fitting problem, which, in [11], is solved by discriminating data samples into the good, bad and vague fuzzy sets using a fuzzy classifier, while [20] defines a triangle-type membership function for the set of inliers and combines this with a Monte Carlo method for sample selection. It must be pointed out that the two aforementioned variants of RANSAC differ significantly from the one described in this paper.

3   On Fuzzy Metrics and RANSAC

In [10], a notion of fuzzy metric was introduced by adapting to the fuzzy approach the concept of statistical metric due to Menger. From now on, we assume that the reader is familiar with the basic notions of fuzzy sets and t-norms (we refer the reader to [9] for a deep treatment on them).

Nowadays, by a fuzzy metric space, in the sense of Kramosil and Michalek (see [12]), we are referring to a triple $(X, M, *)$ where X is a non-empty set, $*$ is a continuous t-norm and M is a fuzzy set on $X \times X \times]0, \infty[$ satisfying, for each $x, y, z \in X$ and $\theta, \mu \in]0, \infty[$, the axioms below:

(KM1) $M(x, y, \theta) = 1$ for each $\theta \in]0, \infty[$ if and only if $x = y$.
(KM2) $M(x, y, \theta) = M(y, x, \theta)$.
(KM3) $M(x, z, \theta + \mu) \geq M(x, y, \theta) * M(y, z, \mu)$.
(KM4) The assignment $M_{x,y} :]0, \infty[\rightarrow [0, 1]$ is a left-continuous function, where $M_{x,y}(\theta) = M(x, y, \theta)$ for each $\theta \in]0, \infty[$.

On account of the previous concept, the value $M(x, y, \theta)$ can be interpreted as a degree of nearness between two points $x, y \in X$ with respect to a parameter $\theta \in]0, \infty[$. The larger the value of $M(x, y, \theta)$, the closer the points x and y are, with respect to θ. Observe that, for two distinct points $x, y \in X$, the degree of nearness can be 1 for some $\theta_0 \in]0, \infty[$, but such a degree can only be 1 for all $\theta \in]0, 1[$ whenever x and y are the same point.

This notion of fuzzy metric has been studied extensively from a mathematical point of view in the literature. Besides, it is worth mentioning that such a kind of measurement has been shown to be useful, for instance, in image filtering and in problems related to perceptual colour difference. For a thorough treatment, we refer the reader to [1,6,13–15] and references therein.

A celebrated example of fuzzy metric is the so-called standard fuzzy metric [5], which is induced from a classical metric. Let us recall that, given a metric space (X, d), the triple (X, M_d, min) constitutes the standard fuzzy metric space, where min denotes the minimum t-norm and M_d is the fuzzy set defined on $X \times X \times]0, \infty[$ given by

$$M_d(x, y, \theta) = \frac{\theta}{\theta + d(x, y)}, \text{ for each } x, y \in X, \theta \in]0, \infty[.$$

Note that for the standard fuzzy metric, the degree of nearness between two points $x, y \in X$ only can be 1, for some $\theta_0 \in]0, \infty[$, whenever x and y are the same point. Moreover, the degree of nearness between two points can never be 0.

With the aim of proposing a fuzzy metric that can be a useful tool for RANSAC, and that is to encode the compatibility of each sample to the current model/hypothesis, we introduce, in Theorem 1, a general technique to generate fuzzy metrics from classical metrics. To this end, let us denote by $\mathbb{N}$ the set of positive integer numbers and let us recall that the family of Yager t-norms $(*_Y^\lambda)_{\lambda \in [0, \infty]}$ is given as follows [9]:

$$x *_Y^\lambda y = \begin{cases} x *_D y, & \text{if } \lambda = 0; \\ \min\{x, y\}, & \text{if } \lambda = \infty; \\ \max\left\{1 - \left((1 - x)^\lambda + (1 - y)^\lambda\right)^{\frac{1}{\lambda}}, 0\right\}, & \text{otherwise.} \end{cases}$$

Theorem 1. *Let (X, d) be a metric space and let $n \in \mathbb{N}$. Then $(X, M_d^n, *_Y^{\frac{1}{n}})$ is a fuzzy metric space, where $*_Y^{\frac{1}{n}}$ denotes the Yager t-norm for $\lambda = \frac{1}{n}$ and M_d^n is defined by*

$$M_d^n(x, y, \theta) = \begin{cases} 1 - \frac{d^n(x,y)}{\theta^n}, & \text{if } x, y \in X, \theta \in]0, \infty[\text{ such that } d(x, y) \leq \theta; \\ 0, & \text{otherwise.} \end{cases} \tag{2}$$

Proof. Next we show that axioms **(KM1)**-**(KM4)** are satisfied, for each $x, y, z \in X$ and $\theta, \mu \in]0, \infty[$.

(KM1) Let $x, y \in X$ and suppose that $M_d(x, y, \theta) = 1$ for all $\theta \in]0, \infty[$. We have that $d(x, y) \leq \theta$ and $\frac{d^n(x,y)}{\theta^n} = 0$ for all $\theta \in]0, \infty[$. It follows that $d(x, y) = 0$. The fact that d is a metric on X gives that $x = y$. Contrarily, assume that $x = y$. Since d is a metric on X, we obtain that $d(x, y) = 0$, whence $d(x, y) \leq \theta$ for all $\theta \in]0, \infty[$. Moreover, $M_d^n(x, y, \theta) = 1 - \frac{0}{\theta^n} = 1$ for all $\theta \in]0, \infty[$.

(KM2) It is obvious due to the symmetry of d, i.e. $d(x, y) = d(y, x)$ for all $x, y \in X$.

(KM3) Let $x, y, z \in X$ and $\theta, \mu \in]0, \infty[$. We are going to prove that

$$M_d^n(x, z, \theta + \mu) \geq M(x, y, \theta) *_Y^{\frac{1}{n}} M(y, z, \mu).$$

To this end, observe that $d(x, z) \leq d(x, y) + d(y, z)$ for all $x, y \in X$.
We distinguish two possible cases:

Case 1. Suppose that $d(x, z) \leq \theta + \mu$. Observe that $M_d^n(x, y) \leq 1 - \frac{d^n(x,y)}{\theta^n} \leq 1 - \frac{d^n(x,y)}{(\theta+\mu)^n}$ and $M_d^n(y, z) \leq 1 - \frac{d^n(y,z)}{\mu^n} \leq 1 - \frac{d^n(x,y)}{(\theta+\mu)^n}$. Moreover, we have that $M_d^n(x, z, \theta + \mu) = 1 - \frac{d^n(x,z)}{(\theta+\mu)^n}$. Therefore,

$$M_d^n(x, z, \theta + \mu) \geq 1 - \frac{(d(x,y) + d(y,z))^n}{(\theta + \mu)^n} \geq$$

$$1 - \left(\left(1 - \left(1 - \frac{d^n(x,y)}{(\theta + \mu)^n} \right) \right)^{\frac{1}{n}} + \left(1 - \left(1 - \frac{d^n(y,z)}{(\theta + \mu)^n} \right) \right)^{\frac{1}{n}} \right)^n$$

$$= \left(1 - \frac{d^n(x,y)}{(\theta + \mu)^n} \right) *_Y^{\frac{1}{n}} \left(1 - \frac{d^n(y,z)}{(\theta + \mu)^n} \right) \geq M_d^n(x, y, \theta) *_Y^{\frac{1}{n}} M_d(y, z, \mu).$$

Case 2. Suppose that $d(x, z) > \theta + \mu$. In such a case, observe that $M_d(x, z, \theta + \mu) = 0$ Moreover, either $d(x, y) > \theta$ or $d(y, z) > \mu$. Indeed, if $d(x, y) \leq \theta$ and $d(y, z) \leq \mu$, then $d(x, z) \leq d(x, y) + d(y, z) \leq \theta + \mu < d(x, z)$, which is a contradiction. Therefore, either $M_d^n(x, y) = 0$ or $M_d(y, z) = 0$. Thus $0 = M_d^n(x, y, \theta) *_Y^{\frac{1}{n}} M_d(y, z, \mu)$. So $M_d(x, z, \theta + \mu) = M_d^n(x, y, \theta) *_Y^{\frac{1}{n}} M_d(y, z, \mu)$.

(KM4) Let $x, y \in X$. Then, the assignment $(M_d^n)_{x,y} :]0, \infty[\to [0, 1]$ given by $(M_d^n)_{x,y}(\theta) = M_d^n(x, y, \theta)$, for each $\theta \in]0, \infty[$, is defined as follows

$$(M_d^n)_{x,y}(\theta) = \begin{cases} 0, & \text{if } \theta < d(x, y) \\ 1 - \frac{d^n(x,y)}{\theta^n}, & \text{if } \theta \geq d(x, y) \end{cases},$$

which, obviously, is (left-)continuous on $]0, \infty[$.

We conclude that $(X, M_d^n, *_Y^{\frac{1}{n}})$ is a fuzzy metric space, as claimed. $\qquad\square$

It must be stressed that one can find particular cases of metric spaces in which the degree of nearness between two points provided by the fuzzy metric in Eq. (2) can be 0. This is a relevant fact, as mentioned before, because the standard fuzzy metric is not able to achieve it.

4   FM-Based RANSAC

As already described, RANSAC adopts a *hypothesize-and-verify* approach to fit a model to data contaminated by random noise and outliers: i.e. for every hypothesis/model considered, data samples are classified into inliers and outliers by comparing the fitting error with a threshold τ_I related to data noise, and that model accumulating the largest number of inliers is the one finally chosen as solution of the estimation problem. This simple approach has been systematically used for robust estimation of model parameters in the presence of arbitrary noise, although, along the years, alternative implementations have been proposed to counteract the misbehaviours and shortcomings that have been detected.

In this work, we focus on three facets of RANSAC: (1) *samples classification* into inliers and outliers, which we avoid to prevent the estimator from explicitly, and prematurely, deciding which samples are relevant; (2) *model scoring*, for which we replace the pure cardinality of the inlier set of plain RANSAC by an expression involving the individual fitting errors, similarly to what MSAC and MLESAC do [19]; and (3) *model refinement* once the main hypothesis-checking loop has finished, for which we adopt an iterative re-weighting scheme that makes use of all the available data samples without any distinction between inliers and outliers, contrarily to plain RANSAC, and other variants, that adopt least squares regression for the set of inliers (notice that the distinction between inliers and outliers depends on the current model under consideration, and thus changes with every model).

Algorithm 1 describes formally the RANSAC variant that is proposed in this work. The details regarding points (1)–(3) above can be found next:

1. **Samples classification.** As already mentioned, no distinction is made between inliers and outliers, but we make use of the fuzzy metric introduced in Theorem 1 to obtain a compatibility value $\phi \in [0, 1]$ between each sample x_i and the current model $M_{\widehat{\Theta}_k}$, given the fitting error $\epsilon(x_i; M_{\widehat{\Theta}_k})$. Although the compatibility value is obtained by means of the aforesaid metric and, thus, it depends on the set of parameters (d, Φ) with $\Phi = (n, \theta)$, in the following we will denote it by $\phi(\epsilon; \Phi)$ in order to make clear that such a value refers to the fitting error ϵ.

2. **Model scoring.** The individual compatibility values $\phi(\epsilon; \Phi)$ are aggregated by simple summation to obtain the model score (step 6 in Algorithm 1) and hence the *so-far-the-best-model* is given by the maximum score found up to the current iteration (steps 7–9 of Algorithm 1).

3. **Model refinement.** Once a sufficient number of hypotheses/models have been considered, we re-estimate the winning model using iterative weighted least squares, where the compatibility values $\phi(\epsilon; \Phi)$, calculated for the fitting

---

Algorithm 1. FM-based RANSAC

Input: D - dataset comprising samples $\{x_i\}$
      $\phi(\epsilon\,;\,\Phi)$ - FM compatibility value for fitting error ϵ and parameters Φ
      $k_{\max}$ - maximum number of iterations of the main loop, as given by Eq. (1)
      $t_{\max}$ - maximum number of iterations of the refinement stage
Output: $M_{\widehat{\Theta}}$ - estimated model, whose parameters are compactly represented by $\widehat{\Theta}$

1: $k := 0,\ \varphi_{\max} := -\infty$
2: **for** $k := 1$ **to** $k_{\max}$ **do**   ▷ find maximum consensus model $M_{\widehat{\Theta}}$
3:     select randomly a minimal sample set S_k of size s from D
4:     estimate model $M_{\widehat{\Theta}_k}$ from S_k
5:     calculate fitting errors $\epsilon(x_i; M_{\widehat{\Theta}_k}), \forall x_i \in D$
6:     find model score $\varphi_k := \sum_{x_i \in D} \phi(\,\epsilon(x_i; M_{\widehat{\Theta}_k})\,;\,\Phi\,)$
7:     **if** $\varphi_k > \varphi_{\max}$ **then**
8:         $\varphi_{\max} := \varphi_k,\ M_{\widehat{\Theta}}^0 := M_{\widehat{\Theta}_k}$
9:     **end if**
10: **end for**
11: $t := 0$
12: **repeat**   ▷ refine model $M_{\widehat{\Theta}}$
13:     calculate fitting errors $\epsilon(x_i; M_{\widehat{\Theta}}^t), \forall x_i \in D$
14:     estimate model $M_{\widehat{\Theta}}^{t+1}$ using weights $\phi(\epsilon(x_i; M_{\widehat{\Theta}}^t)\,;\,\Phi)$
15:     $t := t + 1$
16: **until** convergence or $t \geq t_{\max}$
17: **return** $M_{\widehat{\Theta}}^t$

---

errors resulting from the current model, are used as weights for the new, refined model (steps 12–16 of Algorithm 1). The loop iterates until changes in Θ are negligible (or after a maximum number of iterations).

5   Experimental Results

In this section, we report on the performance of FM-based RANSAC for a number of experiments that include a comparison with plain RANSAC and MSAC (their computational requirements are similar to ours). For illustration purposes, all experiments involve the estimation of 2D lines described by $\Theta = (a, b, c)$, corresponding to a straight line in general form $ax + by + c = 0$.

5.1   Experimental Setup

For testing purposes, we generate synthetic datasets with points stemming from 2D lines in different orientations and positions. Each dataset contains a total of 300 points which comprise both inliers and outliers, the latter in a proportion equal to ω. Given a random point p over a line $\Theta = (a, b, c)$, i.e. $ap_x + bp_y + c = 0$, whose normal vector is $\boldsymbol{n}$, an inlier p_I of the dataset is generated by shifting p along $\boldsymbol{n}$ using a 0-mean Gaussian distribution with standard deviation σ, i.e.

Table 1. Estimation accuracy and number of iterations of the refinement stage for (a) different outlier ratios ω, (b) different noise magnitudes σ and (c) different settings for $\tau_I, \theta = \kappa \cdot \sigma$. Whenever they are kept constant, $\sigma = 1$, $\omega = 0.4$ and $\kappa = 3$. Lighter background means higher performance.

(a)

ω	RANSAC	MSAC	ours $n=1$	ours $n=2$		ω	ours $n=1$	ours $n=2$
			$\mu[\varepsilon]$ (°)				$\mu[t]$	
0.60	4.43	3.14	1.51	1.55		0.60	11.83	10.81
0.50	3.03	2.33	1.02	1.07		0.50	9.63	8.43
0.40	2.13	1.81	0.86	0.88		0.40	8.55	7.23
0.20	1.58	1.53	0.67	0.66		0.20	7.64	6.12

(b)

σ	RANSAC	MSAC	ours $n=1$	ours $n=2$		σ	ours $n=1$	ours $n=2$
2.00	6.76	6.87	3.76	3.78		2.00	21.02	17.68
1.00	2.13	1.81	0.86	0.88		1.00	8.55	7.23
0.50	1.32	0.89	0.39	0.44		0.50	5.65	5.04
0.25	1.05	0.62	0.23	0.29		0.25	4.60	4.31

(c)

κ	RANSAC	MSAC	ours $n=1$	ours $n=2$		κ	ours $n=1$	ours $n=2$
4.00	2.85	2.09	1.01	1.10		4.00	7.75	6.88
3.00	2.13	1.81	0.86	0.88		3.00	8.55	7.23
2.50	2.03	1.88	0.82	0.81		2.50	9.56	7.91
2.00	2.18	2.18	0.85	0.82		2.00	12.22	10.04
1.00	3.60	3.58	1.82	1.82		1.00	33.16	27.79

$p_I = p + \mathcal{N}(0, \sigma) \cdot n$. Outliers p_O are uniformly generated within a rectangular area containing the straight line, ensuring that they lie out of a $\pm 3\sigma$ stripe along the line. For every combination (σ, ω), we generate a total of 500 datasets.

Regarding hypothesis generation within the main loop, in all experiments, the size of the MSS is always $s = 2$ points. Besides, the number of iterations $k_{\max}$ is calculated according to Eq. (1), with $\rho = 99\%$. The parameters of $\phi(\epsilon; \Phi)$, $\Phi = (\theta, n)$, are set as follows: $\theta = \kappa \cdot \sigma$, as well as τ_I for RANSAC/MSAC, considering different values for κ; $n = 1$ or 2, as indicated for each experiment. Finally, to compare properly RANSAC, MSAC and the FM-based RANSAC, we make use of the same sequence of MSS's to avoid the effect of randomness.

5.2   Results and Discussion

In the following, to measure the estimation accuracy, we make use of the average $\mu[\varepsilon]$ of the angle ε between the true and the estimated normal vector; we as well report on the average number of iterations spent during model refinement $\mu[t]$.

On the one hand, Table 1 shows performance results for several outlier ratios ω and Gaussian noise magnitudes σ. In sight of these results, it is worth noting that: (1) the estimation accuracy of the FM-based RANSAC is above that of plain RANSAC and MSAC in all cases; (2) the most substantial differences are found for higher values of ω and σ; (3) the value of θ in ϕ does not seem to be critical, since very similar errors result for $\kappa = 2$–4; (4) estimation accuracy does not differ significantly between $n = 1$ and $n = 2$; (5) as for the number of iterations of the refinement stage t, it tends to be lower for $n = 2$ with regard to

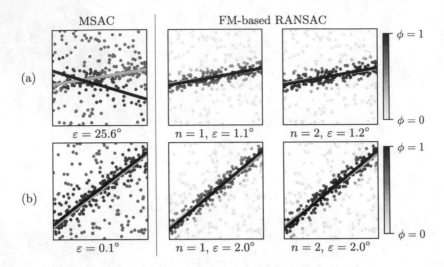

Fig. 1. (a) Best and (b) worst estimations found in 500 datasets for FM-based RANSAC in comparison with MSAC. The true models M_{Θ^*} are (a) $0.15x - 0.99y + 0.00 = 0$ and (b) $0.60x - 0.80y + 0.00 = 0$. The noise parameters in both cases are $(\sigma, \omega) = (1, 0.4)$ and $\kappa = 3$. The colour code is as follows: true/estimated model as gray/black lines, MSAC: inliers/outliers as blue/red dots, FM-based RANSAC: $\phi(\epsilon(x_i; M_{\hat{\Theta}}); \Phi)$ coded in gray scale. (Color figure online)

$n = 1$, and the difference becomes larger when the magnitude of noise is higher, i.e. $\sigma = 2$; (6) a correct setting of κ also reduces t.

On the other hand, Fig. 1 reports on the best- and the worst-case estimations for the FM-based RANSAC in comparison with MSAC for 500 datasets; that is to say, the best case is the case for which FM-based RANSAC outperforms MSAC the most, and the worst case is the case in which MSAC outperforms FM-based RANSAC the most. As can be observed, in both cases, data samples are correctly scored by the FM-based RANSAC, and the estimated and true models are almost identical even for the worst case.

6   Conclusions

In this paper, we have introduced a new Fuzzy Metric (FM) and proposed a variant of RANSAC which avoids discriminating between inliers and outliers by means of the use of such an FM, which provides a compatibility value for each data sample with respect to the current model. These compatibility values are aggregated next to score the model against other hypotheses generated inside the main RANSAC loop. The output model is refined at the latest stage by means of an iterated re-weighting least-squares scheme making use of the same FM. Experimental results show good performance for the FM-based RANSAC against other implementations of RANSAC, actually outperforming its classical counterparts.

References

1. Camarena, J., Gregori, V., Morillas, S., Sapena, A.: Fast detection and removal of impulsive noise using peer groups and fuzzy metrics. J. Vis. Commun. Image Represent. **19**(1), 20–29 (2008)
2. Choi, S., Kim, T., Yu, W.: Performance evaluation of RANSAC family. In: Proceedings of British Machine Vision Conference, pp. 42.1–42.11 (2009)
3. Chum, O., Matas, J., Kittler, J.: Locally optimized RANSAC. In: Michaelis, B., Krell, G. (eds.) DAGM 2003. LNCS, vol. 2781, pp. 236–243. Springer, Heidelberg (2003). https://doi.org/10.1007/978-3-540-45243-0_31
4. Fischler, M.A., Bolles, R.C.: Random sample consensus. Commun. ACM **24**(6), 381–395 (1981)
5. George, A., Veeramani, P.: On some results in fuzzy metric spaces. Fuzzy Sets Syst. **64**(3), 395–399 (1994)
6. Gregori, V., Miñana, J., Morillas, S.: Some questions in fuzzy metric spaces. Fuzzy Sets Syst. **204**, 71–85 (2012)
7. Huber, P.J., Ronchetti, E.M.: Robust Statistics. Wiley, Hoboken (2011)
8. Kacprzyk, J., Pedrycz, W. (eds.): Springer Handbook of Computational Intelligence. Springer, Heidelberg (2015). https://doi.org/10.1007/978-3-662-43505-2
9. Klement, E., Mesiar, R., Pap, E.: Triangular Norms. Springer (2000). https://doi.org/10.1007/978-94-015-9540-7
10. Kramosil, I., Michalek, J.: Fuzzy metrics and statistical metric spaces. Kybernetika **11**(5), 334–336 (1975)
11. Lee, J., Kim, G.: Robust estimation of camera homography using fuzzy RANSAC. In: Gervasi, O., Gavrilova, M.L. (eds.) ICCSA 2007. LNCS, vol. 4705, pp. 992–1002. Springer, Heidelberg (2007). https://doi.org/10.1007/978-3-540-74472-6_81
12. Miñana, J., Valero, O.: A duality relationship between fuzzy metrics and metrics. Int. J. Gen Syst . **47**(6), 593–612 (2018)
13. Morillas, S., Gregori, V., Peris-Fajarnés, G.: New adaptive vector filter using fuzzy metrics. J. Electron. Imaging **16**(3), 1–15 (2007). 033007
14. Morillas, S., Gregori, V., Peris-Fajarnés, G., Latorre, P.: Isolating impulsive noise color images by peer group techniques. Comput. Vis. Image Underst. **110**(1), 102–116 (2008)
15. Morillas, S., Gregori, V., Peris-Fajarnés, G., Sapena, A.: Local self-adaptive fuzzy filter for impulsive noise removal in color image. Signal Process. **8**(2), 390–398 (2008)
16. Oluknami, P.O.: On the sample consensus robust estimate paradigm: comprehensive survey and novel algorithms with applications. M.Sc. Thesis, University of KwaZulu-Natal, Durban, South Africa (2016)
17. Raguram, R., Chum, O., Pollefeys, M., Matas, J., Frahm, J.M.: USAC: a universal framework for random sample consensus. IEEE Trans. Pattern Anal. Mach. Intell. **35**(8), 2022–2038 (2013)
18. Rousseeuw, P.J.: Least median of squares regression. J. Am. Stat. Assoc. **79**(388), 871–880 (1984)
19. Torr, P., Zisserman, A.: MLESAC: a new robust estimator with application to estimating image geometry. Comput. Vis. Image Underst. **78**(1), 138–156 (2000)
20. Watanabe, T., Kamai, T., Ishimaru, T.: Robust estimation of camera homography by fuzzy RANSAC algorithm with reinforcement learning. J. Adv. Comput. Intell. Intell. Inform. **19**(6), 833–842 (2015)

Evaluation of the Transformer Architecture for Univariate Time Series Forecasting

Pedro Lara-Benítez[(✉)], Luis Gallego-Ledesma, Manuel Carranza-García, and José M. Luna-Romera

Division of Computer Science, University of Sevilla, 41012 Seville, Spain
plbenitez@us.es

Abstract. The attention-based Transformer architecture is earning increasing popularity for many machine learning tasks. In this study, we aim to explore the suitability of Transformers for time series forecasting, which is a crucial problem in different domains. We perform an extensive experimental study of the Transformer with different architecture and hyper-parameter configurations over 12 datasets with more than 50,000 time series. The forecasting accuracy and computational efficiency of Transformers are compared with state-of-the-art deep learning networks such as LSTM and CNN. The obtained results demonstrate that Transformers can outperform traditional recurrent or convolutional models due to their capacity to capture long-term dependencies, obtaining the most accurate forecasts in five out of twelve datasets. However, Transformers are generally more difficult to parametrize and show higher variability of results. In terms of efficiency, Transformer models proved to be less competitive in inference time and similar to the LSTM in training time.

Keywords: Time series · Forecasting · Attention · Transformers · Deep learning

1 Introduction

Time series forecasting (TSF) is an important problem in machine learning with many practical applications in different domains such as energy demand [7], finance [19], or retail industries [5]. In recent years, deep learning (DL) models have become the most popular approach for TSF [20]. Architectures such as recurrent or convolutional networks have been specifically designed to deal with time series data, outperforming traditional statistical methods. DL models can automatically learn complex patterns without any prior assumptions on the data, achieving superior forecasting performance and being more scalable.

Long Short-Term Memory (LSTM) and convolutional (CNN) networks are among the most widely used architectures for TSF over the past years. More recently, Transformer models are gaining attention as a powerful alternative for

© Springer Nature Switzerland AG 2021
E. Alba et al. (Eds.): CAEPIA 2021, LNAI 12882, pp. 106–115, 2021.
https://doi.org/10.1007/978-3-030-85713-4_11

time series processing. Unlike recurrent models, this architecture does not deal with the data in sequential order. Transformers can access any part of the history of the sequence using self-attention mechanisms, which makes them a potentially better solution to model long-term dependencies in the data.

This work presents an extension of the study conducted in [8], which provides the most extensive review of traditional deep learning techniques for TSF. In this study, we evaluate the performance of Transformer models under the same conditions and compare it with the best performing architectures that were LSTM and CNN. The experimental study uses 12 datasets with more than 50,000 time series from different fields to evaluate the forecasting precision and computational efficiency of the models. More than 200 architecture configurations of Transformer models are tested on each dataset, and the suitability of different hyperparameter choices is analyzed in-depth.

In summary, the main contributions of the study are the following:

- An extensive experimental study on Transformers models for univariate TSF.
- A comparative analysis with traditional state-of-the-art DL models
- A thorough evaluation of different architecture and hyperparameter configurations of attention-based models for TSF.

The rest of the paper is organized as follows. Section 2 presents related studies. Section 3 describes the methodology and the materials used. Section 4 reports the experimental results. Section 5 presents the conclusions and future work.

2 Related Work

Deep learning architectures have become the most effective alternative for forecasting across related time series, since they allow building accurate global models that can learn shared features and dynamics. The study presented in [8] reviews the advantages and limitations of several DL models that have been proposed for TSF such as Long Short-Term Memory Networks (LSTM), Gated Recurrent Units (GRU), Echo State Networks (ESN), or Temporal Convolutional Networks (TCN). This study concludes that LSTM and CNNs provide the most robust performance across all the studied databases.

Very recently, attention-based models have also been applied to TSF with success. Some works have aimed to improve recurrent DL techniques using attention. For instance, in [3], an attention mechanism is used to enhance the selection of relevant timesteps in the past history for an encoder-decoder architecture using LSTMs. However, the Transformer architecture, which is purely based on self-attention mechanisms is recently earning more popularity. Transformers were first presented for machine translation in [21], showing since then an outstanding capacity to generalize to other tasks such as computer vision or sequence modeling. A self-attention model for capturing information across several dimensions (time, location, and measurements) was proposed in [14] for forecasting over geo-tagged time series. Later, an enhanced version of Transformer was presented in [10], which introduced causal convolution in the self-attention module in order to make the model more sensitive to the local context. Furthermore, they also provide some modifications to reduce the memory cost of Transformers, making it more feasible to deal with long time series. A novel Temporal Fusion Transformer was proposed in [12], combining recurrent and attention layers to learn temporal dependencies at different scales over several real-world datasets. A deep Transformer model for influenza-like illness forecasting is presented in [23], which outperforms LSTM and Seq2Seq models. The self-attention of Transformers showed better forecasting performance than the linear attention used in Seq2Seq architectures.

3   Materials and Methods

This section describes the Transformer architecture for time series forecasting and the experimental setup. For reproducibility purposes, the complete implementation of the experiments is published at [9].

3.1   Attention-Based Deep Neural Network

The Transformer is a deep learning architecture based on attention mechanisms. The Scaled Dot-Product Attention algorithm, introduced in [21], aimed to give the models the capacity to focus on the most relevant elements of long sequences. This is achieved by computing a weighted sum of the values (V), where the weights are computed applying the softmax function to the dot products of the queries (Q) with the keys (K), scaled by the square root of the dimension of the keys (d_k).

$$Attention(Q, K, V) = softmax(\frac{QK^T}{\sqrt{d_k}})V \tag{1}$$

A variant of this algorithm, called Multi-Head attention, is used in the Transformer. This version applies h learnable linear projections to the queries, keys, and values before applying attention individually over each projection. Then, the results of each attention are concatenated before the last linear projection.

The original Transformer consisted of an encoder and a decoder. However, in this study, we consider a decoder-only architecture introduced in recent works as a more problem-agnostic model [10]. As can be seen in Fig. 1, the Transformer consists of several stacked decoder blocks that pass the encoding from the previous decoder as the input to the following blocks.

Each decoder block is composed of a first masked self-attention layer followed by a multi-head attention layer and a feed-forward block. Furthermore, all the sub-layers use a residual connection followed by dropout and batch normalization layers, to improve the capacity of generalization of the network [13]. In addition, to model the sequential information of the time series, a positional encoded vector, generated with sine and cosine functions, is added to the input sequences.

The network is fed with a time series of fixed size ($forecast\_horizon$) and the target output is the same sequence right shifted. In order to prevent the

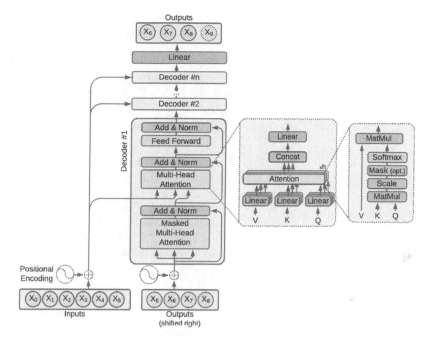

Fig. 1. Transformer architecture. In this example, the *past history* and *forecasting horizon* arc 6 and 4 respectively.

model from paying attention to values in the future, a mask is used before the softmax function. The mask sets all upper triangular elements to $-\infty$ so that future information has no importance in the attention layer. Hence, the network will learn to predict the next value of the input sequence based only on the previous values. Afterwards, the multi-head attention is performed over the previous *past_history* elements of the sequence.

For multi-step-ahead forecasting problems, the inference is carried out by calling the model iteratively *forecast_horizon* times. Hence, the last prediction is included in the input to compute the next value. As this method propagates the error along the prediction sequence, to help model convergence during training, the teacher forcing scheme [22] is used, including the actual value at each new prediction.

3.2   Experimental Study

In this subsection, we present the design of the experimental study carried out to evaluate the Transformer architecture. The results obtained from the different architecture configurations over 12 datasets are analyzed and compared statistically with the state-of-the-art deep learning models.

Table 1. Description of datasets. Columns N, FH, M and m refer to number of time series, forecast horizon, maximum length and minimum length respectively.

#	Datasets	N	FH	M	m	Description	Ref.
1	CIF2016o12	57	12	108	48	Financial and artificially generated	[24]
2	CIF2016o6	15	6	69	22		
3	ExchangeRate	8	6	7588	7588	Exchange rates of 8 countries	[6]
4	M3	1428	18	126	48	Monthly time series of different domains	[15]
5	M4	48000	18	2794	42		[16]
6	NN5	111	56	735	735	Daily ATMs cash withdrawals	[17]
7	SolarEnergy	137	6	52560	52560	Solar power production records	[18]
8	Tourism	336	24	309	67	Tourism data from Australia, Hong Kong, and New Zealand	[1]
9	Traffic	862	24	17544	17544	Occupancy rates of California Department of Transportation	[2]
10	Traffic-metr-la	207	12	34272	34272	Traffic speed of the highways of Los Angeles and the Bay area	[11]
11	Traffic-perms-bay	325	12	52116	52116		
12	WikiWebTraffic	997	59	550	550	Web traffic of Wikipedia pages	[4]

Table 2. Parameter grid search.

(a) Model architecture parameters.						(b) Training parameters.	
Transformer		LSTM		CNN		Past history	1.25, 2, 3
d_{model} 16, 128, 256		Units	32, 64, 128	Filters	16, 32, 64	Batch size	32, 64
Layers 2, 3, 4		Layers	1, 2, 4	Layers	1, 2, 4	Epochs	5
h 4, 8		Return Seq	True, False	Pool size	0, 2	Optimizer	Adam
						Learning rate	Same as [21]
						Normalization	minmax, zscore

3.2.1   Datasets

For the experimental study, we have used the same 12 publicly available datasets selected in [8], each of them with multiple related time series. These datasets, described in Table 1, present a wide diversity of characteristics in terms of length, domains, complexity, and seasonality.

3.2.2   Model Parametrization

This study aims to evaluate the performance of the Transformer model for TSF problems, in terms of both accuracy and efficiency. To this end, we have conducted an exhaustive grid search for both the architecture and training hyperparameters. As a result, a total of 216 Transformer models with different configurations have been trained and evaluated over each dataset. Furthermore, we compare the Transformer with the LSTM and CNN networks, as they achieved the best results in the previous study [8].

Table 2 presents the parameter search carried out for each architecture. For the Transformer, the dimension of the model (d_{model}), the number of stacked decoders (*layers*), and the number of linear projections in the multi-head attention (h) are fine-tuned. The possible values have been chosen based on what is commonly used in the literature, while also ensuring a fair comparison between architectures. Therefore, the same training hyper-parameters as in [8] are used, except for the learning rate, which is varied along the training process as indicated in the original study [21].

3.2.3   Evaluation Procedure

For evaluating the models, the last part of each individual time series (forecast horizon) is used as the test set, while the rest is used as training data. The same preprocessing steps as in [8] are applied, using the Multi-Input Multi-Output (MIMO) strategy to transform the time series into training instances that can feed the DL models.

This study analyses the best results obtained with each type of network, as well as the distribution of results of the different parameter configurations. The efficiency of the models is compared in terms of both training and inference time. The weighted absolute percentage error (WAPE) and the mean absolute error (MAE) metrics are used to measure the predictive performance:

$$WAPE = \frac{\frac{1}{n}\sum_{i=1}^{n}|y_i - o_i|}{\frac{1}{n}\sum_{i=1}^{n} y_i} \times 100\% \quad (2) \qquad\qquad MAE = \frac{1}{n}\sum_{i=1}^{n}|y_i - o_i|, \quad (3)$$

With the obtained results, a statistical analysis is carried out. Hommel's post-hoc analysis is conducted to find if there are significant differences between the performance of the models. Furthermore, we perform a paired Wilcoxon signed-rank test in order to study the statistical differences among the architecture configurations of each type of model.

4   Results and Discussion

This section presents the experimental results, which have been carried out using a computer with an NVIDIA RTX 2080 Ti 12GB GPU and an Intel i7-8700 CPU. An appendix with the full report of the results can be found at [9].

4.1   Forecasting Accuracy

Table 3 reports the best WAPE and MAE results obtained by the Transformer, LSTM, and CNN networks for each time series dataset. Overall, the three architectures achieved similar results. Specifically, the LSTM lead the ranking 5 out of 12 datasets for both metrics, the Transformer achieves the top results 4 times, while the CNN wins only in 3 datasets for each metrics. It is important to mention that Transformers obtain the most accurate predictions in popular forecasting competitions such as M3 or M4, which are also the two largest datasets. On average, the LSTM obtains the first position in the ranking, closely followed by the Transformer. In fact, Hommel's post-hoc analysis carried out determines that there are no significant differences between the Transformer and the LSTM, while they are both significantly better than the CNN.

Table 3. Best WAPE and MAE results obtained with each type of architecture for all datasets.

Datasets		WAPE			MAE		
		Transformer	LSTM	CNN	Transformer	LSTM	CNN
1	CIF2016o12	**11.207**	12.475	12.479	12,564.18	**11,732.31**	12,762.73
2	CIF2016o6	16.157	**15.352**	17.143	**2,182,435.2**	3,636,929.7	2,833,131.5
3	ExchangeRate	0.303	**0.300**	0.335	0.0021	**0.0019**	0.0020
4	M3	**12.490**	15.282	15.612	**659.18**	700.25	709.44
5	M4	**13.587**	14.281	14.256	**588.38**	597.54	593.71
6	NN5	18.637	**18.589**	18.852	3.570	**3.538**	3.572
7	SolarEnergy	13.550	12.452	**11.717**	2.246	2.066	**1.977**
8	Tourism	18.68	19.081	**18.497**	2,202.11	2,280.09	**1,969.58**
9	Traffic	33.541	**31.960**	34.406	0.0121	**0.0114**	0.0124
10	Traffic-metr-la	3.418	3.359	**3.337**	2.029	2.009	**1.991**
11	Traffic-perms-bay	1.333	**1.314**	1.433	0.885	**0.870**	0.946
12	WikiWebTraffic	**46.110**	46.477	46.914	**11.796**	12.063	12.106
	Mean ranking	1.833	**1.750**	2.416	1.916	**1.833**	2.250

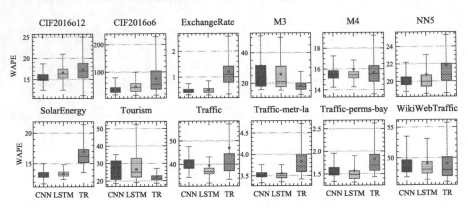

Fig. 2. Distribution of WAPE results obtained by each model architecture for each dataset.

Table 4. Architecture configuration analisys.

(a) Training hyper-parameters.				(b) Model architecture.	
	LSTM	CNN	**TR**		**TR**
Batch size	32**	64**	=	Layers	2**, 3*
Past History factor	1.25**	1.25**	1.25**	d_{model}	16**, 128*
Normalization Method	minmax**	zscore**	=	h	4*

Figure 2 presents the distributions of WAPE obtained by each model for each dataset. In general, we can observe that the Transformer is more sensitive to the model parametrization than the other architectures, as it presents a wider distribution. In order to analyze the results obtained with the different architecture parameters and training hyper-parameters, we use the Wilcoxon statistical test. The results of this test are reported in Table 4, where ** indicates that it is the best value with a significant statistical difference compared to the rest ($p < 0.05$), the * indicates that there is a certain tendency suggesting that it is better to choose that parameter ($p < 0.2$), and = means there are no significant differences between choosing any of the possible parameters.

4.2   Computation Time

We have also evaluated the different architectures in terms of computational efficiency. Figure 3 reports the distribution of training and inference time measured for each architecture. It is worth noting that the Transformer differs significantly from the other models in terms of inference time. This is due to the particularity of the Transformer architecture, which iterates generating single-step predictions for multi-step-ahead forecasting problems. Therefore, while CNN and LSTM compute a multiple steps prediction with a single call, the transformer will have to be called several times, specifically *forecasting_horizon* times. This behaviour is illustrated in Fig. 4, where we can see how the inference time is directly proportional to the prediction horizon. More precisely, on average, the transformer generates a single prediction in 3.2 milliseconds. However, as it has to be called for each prediction horizon, the inference time increases to almost 200 when the horizon reaches 59 time steps.

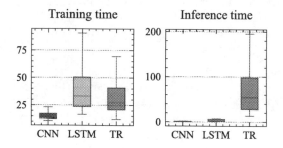 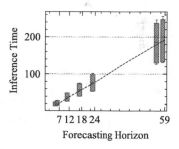

Fig. 3. Distribution of training and inference time by instance measured in milliseconds.

Fig. 4. Inference time of the transformer versus forecasting horizon.

In terms of training time, the Transformer is faster than the LSTM but not as fast as the CNN. The results show that in terms of the speed/accuracy trade-off, the CNN is the best one in terms of computation efficiency but with lower accuracy while, LSTM and Transformer behave similarly, achieving good forecasting accuracy but having a significantly slower training process compared to the CNN.

5   Conclusions

In this paper, we evaluated the performance of the Transformer architecture for time series forecasting in terms of accuracy and computational efficiency. An extensive experimental study over 12 datasets and different architecture configurations was carried out. The results are compared with long-short term memory (LSTM) and convolutional (CNN) networks, which are considered the state of the art in the field. The conclusion obtained from the analysis of the results of these experiments are summarized below:

- The Transformer architecture achieves state-of-the-art forecasting accuracy, obtaining similar results to the LSTM and outperforming CNNs.
- Transformers provide a better accuracy/speed trade-off than LSTM in training time. However, the Transformer training process is significantly slower compared to the CNN.
- The inference time of the Transformer architecture is severely influenced by the single-step prediction scheme used, which makes it slower than the other architectures.
- Finding the best architecture configuration for Transformers is a complex task as it presents a wider WAPE distribution than the other models.

In summary, the conclusions obtained from analyzing the results establish the Transformer architecture at the level of the state-of-the-art deep learning techniques for univariate time series forecasting. In future studies, alternative architecture variations such as convolutional attention or sparse attention should be considered. Another future study should work on non-auto-regressive models to reduce the inference time of the Transformers. Furthermore, we aim to study the use of multi-dimensional Transformers for dealing with spatio-temporal grid data.

Funding. This research has been funded by FEDER/Ministerio de Ciencia, Innovación y Universidades – Agencia Estatal de Investigación/Proyecto TIN2017-88209-C2 and by the Andalusian Regional Government under the projects: BIDASGRI: Big Data technologies for Smart Grids (US-1263341), Adaptive hybrid models to predict solar and wind renewable energy production (P18-RT-2778). We are grateful to NVIDIA for their GPU Grant Program that has provided us high-quality GPU devices for carrying out the study.

References

1. Athanasopoulos, G., Hyndman, R.J., Song, H., Wu, D.C.: Tourism forecasting part two (2010). www.kaggle.com/c/tourism2
2. Dua, D., Graff, C.: UCI machine learning repository (2017). http://archive.ics.uci.edu/ml
3. Fan, C., et al.: Multi-horizon time series forecasting with temporal attention learning. In: Proceedings of the 25th ACM SIGKDD International Conference on Knowledge Discovery & Data Mining, KDD 2019, pp. 2527–2535 (2019). https://doi.org/10.1145/3292500.3330662

4. Google: Web traffic time series forecasting competition (2017). www.kaggle.com/c/web-traffic-time-series-forecasting
5. Karmy, J., Maldonado, S.: Hierarchical time series forecasting via support vector regression in the European travel retail industry. Expert Syst. Appl. **137**, 59–73 (2019). https://doi.org/10.1016/j.eswa.2019.06.060
6. Lai, G., Chang, W.C., Yang, Y., Liu, H.: Modeling long- and short-term temporal patterns with deep neural networks. arXiv:1703.07015 (2017)
7. Lara-Benítez, P., Carranza-García, M., Luna-Romera, J.M., Riquelme, J.C.: Temporal convolutional networks applied to energy-related time series forecasting. Appl. Sci. **10**(7), 2322 (2020)
8. Lara-Benítez, P., Carranza-García, M., Riquelme, J.C.: An experimental review on deep learning architectures for time series forecasting. Int. J. Neural Syst. **31**(03), 2130001 (2021). https://doi.org/10.1142/S0129065721300011. pMID: 33588711
9. Lara-Benítez, P., Gallego-Ledesma, L., Carranza-García, M.: Time Series Forecasting - Deep Learning (2021). https://github.com/pedrolarben/TimeSeriesForecasting-DeepLearning
10. Li, S., et al.: Enhancing the locality and breaking the memory bottleneck of transformer on time series forecasting. arXiv:1907.00235 (2020)
11. Li, Y., Yu, R., Shahabi, C., Liu, Y.: Diffusion convolutional recurrent neural network: Data-driven traffic forecasting. arXiv:1707.01926 (2017)
12. Lim, B., Arik, S.O., Loeff, N., Pfister, T.: Temporal fusion transformers for interpretable multi-horizon time series forecasting. arXiv:1912.09363 (2020)
13. Luo, P., Wang, X., Shao, W., Peng, Z.: Towards understanding regularization in batch normalization. arXiv preprint arXiv:1809.00846 (2018)
14. Ma, J., Shou, Z., Zareian, A., Mansour, H., Vetro, A., Chang, S.F.: CDSA: cross-dimensional self-attention for multivariate, geo-tagged time series imputation. arXiv:1905.09904 (2019)
15. Makridakis, S., Hibon, M.: The M3-competition: results, conclusions and implications. Int. J. Forecast. **16**(4), 451–476 (2000). https://doi.org/10.1016/S0169-2070(00)00057-1
16. Makridakis, S., Spiliotis, E., Assimakopoulos, V.: The M4 competition: 100,000 time series and 61 forecasting methods. Int. J. Forecast. **36**(1), 54–74 (2020). https://doi.org/10.1016/j.ijforecast.2019.04.014
17. NNGC: NN5 time series forecasting competition for neural networks (2008). http://www.neural-forecasting-competition.com/NN5
18. NREL: Solar power data for integration studies (2007). www.nrel.gov/grid/solar-power-data.html
19. Sezer, O., Gudelek, M., Ozbayoglu, A.: Financial time series forecasting with deep learning: a systematic literature review: 2005–2019. Appl. Soft Comput. J. **90** (2020). https://doi.org/10.1016/j.asoc.2020.106181
20. Torres, J., Hadjout, D., Sebaa, A., Martínez-Álvarez, F., Troncoso, A.: Deep learning for time series forecasting: a survey. Big Data **9**(1), 3–21 (2021). https://doi.org/10.1089/big.2020.0159
21. Vaswani, A., et al.: Attention is all you need (2017)
22. Williams, R.J., Zipser, D.: A learning algorithm for continually running fully recurrent neural networks. Neural Comput. **1**(2), 270–280 (1989). https://doi.org/10.1162/neco.1989.1.2.270
23. Wu, N., Green, B., Ben, X., O'Banion, S.: Deep transformer models for time series forecasting: the influenza prevalence case. arXiv:2001.08317 (2020)
24. Štěpnička, M., Burda, M.: Computational Intelligence in Forecasting (CIF) (2016). https://irafm.osu.cz/cif

Optimization and Search

Automatic Generation of Interrelated Organisms on Virtual Environments

Santiago Pacheco$^{(\boxtimes)}$ ⓘ, Nicolas Ottonello, and Sergio Nesmachnow ⓘ

Universidad de la República, Montevideo, Uruguay
{santiago.pacheco,nicolas.ottonello,sergion}@fing.edu.uy

Abstract. This article presents a novel method for generating multiple species of organisms on virtual environments, with interrelated behaviors. The proposed system (AGIO) strives to keep a balance between the exploration of diverse species, the evolution of interesting and connected behaviors, and the control of the user over the generated organisms. Experimental results of a C++ implementation proves that AGIO is capable of generating different species and basic animal conducts, while keeping behaviors of the organisms interrelated. Multiple relations between different species were observed on the generated organisms. Furthermore, the performance of the organisms was comparable to that of a human player.

Keywords: Neuroevolution · A-Life · Video games

1 Introduction

Many articles in the field of artificial life (A-Life) have focused on how artificial systems can mimic behaviors found on natural living systems [9]. However, few proposals have focused on the applicability of those methods into industry sectors that deal with interactive simulations, such as the video game industry, where there are design restrictions imposed on the system.

Background agents with simple behaviors (e.g., animals), are commonly used to improve player experience on video games. These agents demand considerable work to be designed, modeled, and programmed. Specific techniques are needed to handle the animals behavior or graphical representation [7]. A-Life models are able to generate many organisms with rich behaviors [12], but they do not usually provide a way to control the resulting organisms, making their use into video games impractical. A system that combines an A-Life model with a control mechanism would be useful to reduce the work required to create background agents.

This article proposes *Automatic Generation of Interrelated Organisms* (AGIO), a framework for generating diverse organisms with interrelated behaviors using Evolutionary Algorithms (EAs) and Artificial neural networks (ANNs) along with a morphology model that allows the user to restrict and control the generated organisms. The main contributions include: i) a system that can generate tens of different species with interrelated behaviors, while providing the

E. Alba et al. (Eds.): CAEPIA 2021, LNAI 12882, pp. 119–128, 2021.
https://doi.org/10.1007/978-3-030-85713-4_12

user with control over the generated organisms, ii) a user controllable morphology model, and iii) the decoupling of the organisms generation from the in-world representation.

2   Related Works

Animal generation within the A-Life has been based on the framework by Sims [12]. Creatures were defined as a hierarchy of rigid joints with ANNs used to control the forces applied on each joint, and for communication. The system was able to generate organisms with different morphological structures and behaviors, capable of different tasks such as swimming, running, jumping, and following a light source.

The ERO framework [8] extended Sims's work by using historical markers for a less destructive recombination. ERO proved to be a powerful tool for A-Life research [4,11], but it does not allow controlling the morphology or behavior of the organisms. Furthermore, ERO is tightly coupled to scenarios with a specific morphology semantic and physics motor, thus limiting its applicability on general interactive simulations, like video games, where a system design is provided beforehand.

Deep reinforcement learning has been applied for agent control in video games, even outperforming humans in complex games [2,14]. While useful, these models require a significantly larger computation power than the available on current consumer hardware. Moreover, they are commonly used from the point of view of the player, which is not compatible with background agents [3].

AGIO provides a new framework for organism generation that offers more control on both morphology and behaviour of organisms, thus making it more suitable to be used on interactive simulations with predetermined restrictions.

3   Automatic Generation of Interrelated Organisms

This section describes the proposed method for organism and behavior generation.

3.1   Overall Description

AGIO was conceived to provide control over the generated organisms by applying a restrictive morphology model. The user is responsible of defining the actions the organisms can perform, the information (*sensors*) they have, and how those actions and sensors can combine.

Unlike ERO and other related algorithms, AGIO decouples the logical representation of the organisms from the in-world representation. Organisms are abstractly defined as a set of components and parameters, with the in-world representation left to the user. The action policy for the organisms is stochastic, to encourage exploration [6]. The probabilities of each action are computed from the sensors values by a single ANN on each organism.

The NEAT neuroevolutionary framework [13] is used to generate the topology and train the ANNs, defined as an arbitrary weighted directed graph with input, output and internal nodes. NEAT includes a speciation model that preserves innovation on new ANNs and the use of historical markers to preserve semantic during recombination. Each species on AGIO has an associated NEAT population which evolves the networks for the organisms of that species. NEAT was chosen as optimizer for the proposed model mainly due to four reasons: i) it has proved to be useful on this context [4,5,8], ii) it does not require handcrafting ANN architectures, iii) it can generate recurrent ANNs, and iv) it finds small networks, leading to low memory consumption and decision time.

3.2 Representation: Morphology and Parameters

In AGIO, a species is a set of representations of solutions that share a morphology and interact in the evolutionary process. Organisms are represented by a morphology, a set of numerical values (*parameters*) and an ANN. Parameters are either required (they exist on all organisms), or optional.

Actions and sensors of organisms are aggregated into components, which are joined into different groups. Groups have a minimum and maximum number of components to pick when creating the organisms. The morphology is defined as a set of components, determining the actions and sensors each organism has. In turn, organism parameters are continuous numeric values over a user-defined range, evolved alongside the behavior. Parameters allow to model arbitrary features of the organisms, such as movement speed or skin hue. They are incorporated into a NEAT genome, so that behavior and parameter evolution remains coupled.

Figure 1 presents an example representation, including its ANN, for a possible jumping herbivore organism with a parameter defining the jump distance.

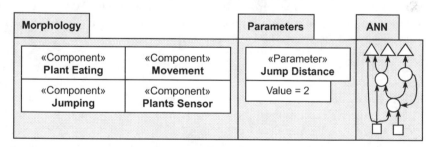

Fig. 1. Example organism representation. On the ANN squares are sensors (inputs), circles are hidden nodes and triangles actions (outputs)

3.3 Evolutionary Operators

Initialization. The number of species evolved is defined by the population size and the minimum number of organisms per species. The initialization operator generates morphologies by randomly selecting components from groups. Each morphology corresponds to one different species. A NEAT population (population members are named *individuals*, to differentiate them from AGIO organisms) is created for each species, using the standard NEAT initialization. Optional parameters are included with 0.5 probability according to a uniform distribution. Both required and optional parameters are initialized with a random value drawn from a uniform distribution on the corresponding range. Then, AGIO organisms of each species are created by pairing a morphology with a random NEAT individual, which contains the ANN of the organism and the parameters values.

Selection. The selection operator applied is Stochastic Universal Sampling, which provides an appropriate selection pressure to guide the search.

Recombination. The recombination operator is a variant of the semantic-driven operator applied in NEAT, extended to handle organism parameters. A standard arithmetic crossover is applied (i.e., the offspring value is the average of the values from both parents) for all parameters of the second parent that are also present in the first. Crossover is only performed within each AGIO species.

Mutation. A traditional mutation operator based on modifying existing connections or adding a new structure to the underlying ANN is applied. The mutation operator in NEAT was extended to consider parameters. Two mutations were implemented, applied equiprobably: i) *destructive mutation*, which randomly sets a parameter value according to a uniform distribution in the parameter range, assigning the individual a new historical marker; and ii) *Gaussian mutation*, which adds to the parameter a random value drawn from a Gaussian distribution $N(0, \sigma)$ multiplied by the length of the parameter range. The sum is restricted to the corresponding parameter range. Gaussian mutation does not modify markers.

Evolution Model, Replacement, and Stopping Criterion. A traditional generational evolution model is applied: after the fitness evaluation process, all NEAT populations advance to their next generation; new NEAT individuals are generated, which replace the ones from the previous generation. AGIO organisms are assigned randomly selected NEAT individuals and the iterative evolutionary process continues for a fixed number of generations.

3.4   Fitness Evaluation

Organisms are evaluated on batches randomly selected from the AGIO population. The size of the batches is equal to the simulation size, that is, the number of organisms in the simulation, which is separated from the population size. This separation is needed because the simulation size can affect the expected behavior (i.e., the competition between organisms) but the population size is a parameter to be adjusted for the evolutionary search and as such should not affect the expected behavior. A user defined simulation function is executed multiple times for each batch. The returned fitness value is the average of the fitness values obtained on each simulation.

3.5   Species Exploration

Evolving all possible species simultaneously is not feasible, since there is an arbitrary number of possible species as components and groups are user defined.

Therefore, a fixed number of species is evolved at the same time, replacing as needed.

Species to be replaced are selected considering their evolutionary progress (p_t), defined by Eq. 1, where t is the number of generations since the creation of the species, $\hat{f}_t$ is the average fitness of the k top individuals of the species, and s_t is a double smoothed average fitness defined by Eq. 2, in order to reduce the influence of random variations caused by differences in the evaluation from one generation to the next ($\lambda \in [0,1]$ is the smoothing factor).

$$p_0 = 0;\ p_t = (1 - \alpha_t) \cdot p_{t-1} + \alpha_t\, \frac{s_t - s_{t-1}}{s_{t-1}} \tag{1}$$

$$s_0 = \hat{f}_0;\ s_t = (1 - \alpha_t) \cdot s_{t-1} + \alpha_t \cdot \hat{f}_t,\ \text{where}\ \alpha_t = \frac{\lambda \cdot t + 1}{t + 1} \tag{2}$$

Replacement occurs when the species progress is below a threshold (β) for a certain number of consecutive generations. When replaced, the top k individuals of the species for the current generation, and the best individual since $t = 0$, are stored into a registry [10]. Then, the initialization operator is applied, trying to create a new species. If a new species is created, new AGIO organisms are generated for that species. Otherwise the current species is considered as if it where new (species reset) for the following process. Then, a new NEAT population is created, but instead of starting from a default ANN, the registry is queried for entries corresponding to the new species, and the ANNs of the best individuals are used as initialization if found. After creating the new NEAT population, the AGIO organisms are reassigned random NEAT individuals.

3.6   Output

The output consists on the registry entries for all found species, where each entry contains a set of fit organisms, as described on Sect. 3.5. Only the ANN and parameters values are stored for each organism, as the morphology (set of selected components) is implicitly defined by the species it belongs to. During evolution the ANN are defined by the reference NEAT implementation, but to improve performance and encapsulate the algorithm ANNs for the final organisms are converted to a directed graph stored on a linear array, where each node has an array of incoming and outgoing connections which index the linear node array, alongside storing the connection weight. The activation function is an exponential sigmoid as in NEAT. Activation values are propagated from incoming to outgoing connections, starting with the input (sensor) nodes, until all the outputs have received at least one incoming value. This optimized implementation is functionally equivalent to the internal NEAT representation, so that the evolved weights can be used directly.

4   Experimental Evaluation

This section describes the experiments performed to evaluate AGIO.

4.1   Methodology and Experiments

Overall Description. Three experiments were performed, evaluating the capabilities of AGIO to generate basic animal behaviors, keep species interrelated, and compare to a human player.

Two test systems were considered over a cyclic discrete 2D environment and a set of components groups. The simulations performed 300 steps. On each step, each organism decided an action to perform. Fifty independent executions of each simulation were executed on a C++ implementation with multi-threaded population evaluation running on a Razer Blade 15 (2019). Source code of the implementation and the complete results of the experimental analysis is available on the project website [1].

Basic Animal Behavior. Two species (prey-predator) were evolved in a square of 55 × 55 cells. One species mimics herbivores, having an action to eat plants (uniformly distributed in the environment, with a 0.01 probability of occurrence in each cell). The other species mimics carnivores, with an action to eat herbivores. 20 organisms were simulated (10 of each species). Two sensors report the distance to the nearest plant or herbivore on each axis. The eat action is only valid if the $\mathcal{L}_1$ norm distance to the nearest plant is 1 or less for herbivores, or 2 or less for carnivores, otherwise it is considered a failed action and ignored.

On each simulation, the fitness of all individuals started at 0 and increased by 1 for each successful eat action. Two relevant metrics were studied for both species: the number of times the organisms fed and the proportion of successful feeding actions with respect to the attempted feeding actions.

Species Interrelations. The capability of AGIO to generate interrelations between species was evaluated on a complex scenario with 50 organisms of up to 24 species (herbivores, carnivores, and omnivores). Optional components, such as detecting competitors or jumping (according to a range parameter) were also included.

The fitness function was computed as the accumulated value of the *health* of organisms. Health started at a fixed positive value; reduced with failed feeding actions, and increased with successful ones. When health reached 0, the organism was considered dead, unable to perform actions and assigned a low fitness value. A dead organism was not retired from the simulation until it was eaten by another.

The experiment consisted on obtaining a baseline fitness for each species and comparing it to the fitness when another species was not present on the simulation. If those species are related, then the fitness values should vary. First 100 simulations were executed, recording the fitness values of each species. Then for each species 100 simulations were performed removing that species from the simulation. The species (namely, A and B) were analysed in a pairwise fashion. The baseline fitness values of A where compared to the fitness values of A when B was not on the simulation using a two sample Kolmogorov–Smirnov test. A was said to be related with B if the test p-value was 0.05 or less.

Simulations used an environment of 50 × 32 cells of three types: *ground* (with no special effect); *water*, which reduce the health of organisms with the walker component, but not those with a walker/swimmer component; and *wall* cells, which block the movement of the organisms, but can be jumped by organisms with a jump component. Five scenarios were considered in the environment, varying the number and location of water and wall cells.

Comparison with a Human Player. Since the organisms generated by AGIO are expected to interact with players in the context of video games, an experiment was developed where a person interacted by controlling one of the organisms from a randomly selected omnivore species evolved on the complex system.

Two tests were carried out, changing the amount of information provided to the player. On the first test, only the numerical values of the sensors were shown and the player was asked to decide an action to execute by typing the index. The second test built on the first, adding a short explanatory text for the displayed information. The current fitness and ranking inside the species individuals was shown on both to provide the player with a guideline of his performance.

4.2 Parameters Setting

Parameters setting experiments were performed to adjust AGIO parameters, while default values were used for NEAT parameters [13]. A sensitivity analysis detected the parameters that most impacted the number of species and mean fitness: the minimum number of organisms per species (me), the smoothing parameter λ, and the progress threshold β. These three parameters and two relevant parameters of the evolutionary search, the population size as a factor of the simulation size (pop_mul) and the generations count ($\#gen$), were adjusted by testing all possible combinations of three candidate values per parameter. Two evaluation metrics were considered: the number of species found and the (normalized) fitness. The best results were obtained using the configuration $me = 50$, $\lambda = 0.025$, $\beta = 0.001$, $pop\_mul = 30$, $\#gen = 400$.

4.3 Results

Basic Animal Behavior. Figure 2 presents the number of successful feeding actions for each species using AGIO (black) and the proportion of successful feeding actions (red). Vertical dashed blue lines mark the species reset due to stagnancy.

Carnivores showed a steep improvement on successful feeding actions and proportion during the first 100 generations, and then became stagnant which caused several resets on subsequent generations. Herbivores showed a steep improvement on successful feeding actions, reaching a mean of 12 on the first 30 generations, with no significant progress on the following generations. While species reset on the carnivores provided no improvement, the herbivores reset on generation 224 was followed by a quick and significant improvement on the successful actions proportion.

Regarding the computational efficiency, the execution of the experiment took 729 s. Overall, this experiment validated the capability of AGIO to generate organisms with basic animal behavior and showed that the reset mechanism can aid by efficiently finding new and better behaviors.

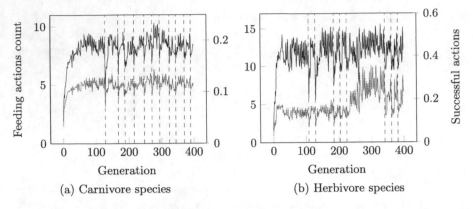

(a) Carnivore species   (b) Herbivore species

Fig. 2. Feeding actions for organisms of each species (—— count, ----- proportion) (Color figure online)

Species Interrelations. Table 1 reports species considered to be related and the mean fitness difference (Δ_f) expressed as a percentage of the baseline. Experiment execution took 2986 s.

Table 1. Relations between species and mean fitness difference.

Species 1		Species 2		Δ_f	Species 1		Species 2		Δ_f
Id	Type	Id	Type		Id	Type	Id	Type	
16	Carnivore	0	Herbivore	−11.99%	18	Omnivore	10	Herbivore	−11.48%
16	Carnivore	2	Omnivore	−12.69%	7	Herbivore	11	Carnivore	−4.47%
0	Herbivore	6	Carnivore	10.18%	18	Omnivore	13	Herbivore	−7.80%
16	Carnivore	6	Carnivore	−11.83%	0	Herbivore	14	Carnivore	10.71%
15	Carnivore	7	Herbivore	−6.91%	16	Carnivore	15	Carnivore	−13.87%
2	Omnivore	8	Omnivore	5.18%	2	Omnivore	16	Carnivore	6.66%
13	Herbivore	9	Omnivore	−5.50%	15	Carnivore	16	Carnivore	−2.75%
1	Omnivore	10	Herbivore	−4.27%	7	Herbivore	17	Carnivore	5.29%
12	Omnivore	10	Herbivore	1.56%	13	Herbivore	17	Carnivore	−6.80%
16	Carnivore	10	Herbivore	−10.89%	16	Carnivore	19	Carnivore	−9.87%

Multiple relations were observed, including long chains of relations ($16 \rightarrow 15 \rightarrow 7 \rightarrow 17$), transitive relations ($16 \rightarrow 0 \rightarrow 6, 16 \rightarrow 6$) and symmetric relations ($15 \rightarrow 16, 16 \rightarrow 15$). Herbivores presenting relations to other herbivores or being negatively impacted by the absence of carnivores and omnivores shows that relations other than direct prey-predator dependencies were formed too.

This experiment demonstrated that AGIO is able to generate species having interrelated behaviors and can present complex graphs of relations.

Human Comparison. Figure 3 presents the fitness of the organism controlled by the player and three randomly selected organisms of the same species controlled by AGIO. Graphs (a) and (b) correspond to different species meaning the fitness values are not comparable.

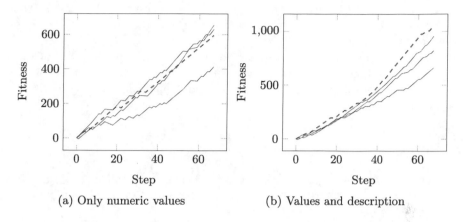

(a) Only numeric values   (b) Values and description

Fig. 3. Random AGIO organisms (——) vs. player controlled organism (- - -)

The first experiment consisted in only giving the player the numeric values of the sensors. Under this condition, the player showed worse performance than the AGIO organisms, as shown on Fig. 3a. The best organism generated by AGIO reached a fitness of 656, compared to 595 of the best organism by the player. Adding the descriptions notably improved the player performance (Fig. 3b), allowing him to quickly surpass all AGIO organisms. In that case, the human player obtained a 10% advantage over the best of the selected organisms at the end of the simulation.

The results of the experiment that compared the proposed method with a human player showed that the behavior of the individuals generated by AGIO compares favorably to what a human player can achieve when presented with similar conditions.

5   Conclusions and Future Work

This article presented AGIO, a new method for multiple agent generation on interactive simulations. The proposed method builds upon previous ideas from evolutionary approaches for A-Life by defining a general algorithm that provides user control over the generated organisms. Furthermore, AGIO does not depend on the in-world representation and is able to develop relations between the organisms. These features differentiates AGIO from previous evolutionary methods in the related literature.

Experimental results showed AGIO to be capable of generating tens of diverse species with basic animal behavior and a complex graph of relations between them. The behavior of the generated organisms proved to be comparable to the one achieved by a human player, an important accomplishment considering that player interaction is a critical component for interactive simulations, like the ones needed in video games.

The performance of the system proved to be adequate for its use on real time simulations executing on consumer hardware such as the one employed for the experimental evaluation.

The main lines for future work include extending the proposed framework for considering continuous action spaces, exploring alternative neuroevolution algorithms to improve the generated ANNs, and dynamically tuning algorithmic parameters per species.

References

1. CeCal HPC group home site. http://www.fing.edu.uy/inco/grupos/cecal/hpc/agio
2. Badia, A.P., et al.: Agent57: Outperforming the Atari human benchmark (2020). arXiv:2003.13350
3. Bourg, D.M., Seemann, G.: AI for Game Developers. O'Reilly Media Inc., Sebastopol (2004)
4. Echegaray, S., Luo, W.: Simulation of animal behavior using neural networks. In: 2006 IEEE Region 5 Conference, pp. 99–102 (2006)
5. Jallov, D., Risi, S., Togelius, J.: EvoCommander: a novel game based on evolving and switching between artificial brains. IEEE Trans. Comput. Intell. AI Games 9(2), 181–191 (2017)
6. Kaelbling, L.P., Littman, M.L., Moore, A.W.: Reinforcement learning: a survey. J. Artif. Intell. Res. 4(1), 237–285 (1996)
7. Konieczny, A., Pelletier, J.: Grounding wildlife in the mountains of far cry 4. In: Game Developers Conference (2015)
8. Krčah, P.: Evolutionary development of robotic organisms. Master's thesis. Charles University, Praga, Czech Republic (2007)
9. Langton, C.: Artificial Life. Addison-Wesley, Boston (1988)
10. Lehman, J., Stanley, K.: Abandoning objectives: evolution through the search for novelty alone. Evol. Comput. 19(2), 189–223 (2011)
11. Lehman, J., Stanley, K.: Evolving a diversity of virtual creatures through novelty search and local competition. In: Proceedings of the 13th Annual Conference on Genetic and Evolutionary Computation, pp. 211–218 (2011)
12. Sims, K.: Evolving virtual creatures. In: Proceedings of the 21st Annual Conference on Computer Graphics and Interactive Techniques, pp. 15–22 (1994)
13. Stanley, K., Miikkulainen, R.: Evolving neural networks through augmenting topologies. Evol. Comput. 10(2), 99–127 (2002)
14. Vinyals, O., et al.: Grandmaster level in StarCraft II using multi-agent reinforcement learning. Nature 575(7782), 350–354 (2019)

Asynchronous Vector Iteration
in Multi-objective Markov Decision Processes

Ekaterina Sedova, Lawrence Mandow, and José-Luis Pérez-de-la-Cruz[✉]

Univ. de Málaga, Andalucía Tech, Dpt. Lenguajes y Ciencias Comp., Málaga, Spain
ekaterina.sedova@tum.de, {lawrence,perez}@lcc.uma.es

Abstract. This paper presents new algorithms to solve Multi-Objective Markov Decision Processes (MOMDPs). Namely, we present Multi-objective Dynamic Programming variants of Value Iteration such that the values for every state are updated in some heuristic order. The performance of these algorithms is evaluated applying them to benchmark problems with two and three objectives.

1 Introduction

Multi-objective Markov decision processes (MOMDPs) are Markov decision processes in which rewards given to the agent are not scalar values, but numerical vectors. In recent years there has been a growing interest in considering theory and applications of multi-objective Markov decision processes and multi-objective Reinforcement Learning, e.g. see [6], and [3]. In this paper we define and study several algorithms for finding solutions to MOMDP problems with finite and discrete state and action spaces. These algorithms are multi-objective variants of the Dynamic Programming *vector iteration* procedure, differing in the order in which state vectors are updated.

The paper is structured as follows: in Sect. 2 necessary concepts about MOMDPs, Dynamic Programming and (single-objective) Value Iteration are summary presented. Then we describe the new algorithms (Sect. 3) and present and discuss the results obtained in a set of experiments (Sect. 4). Finally some conclusions are drawn.

2 Antecedents

A MOMDP is defined by a tuple $(\mathcal{S}, \mathcal{A}, p, \boldsymbol{r}, \gamma)$, where: $\mathcal{S}$ is a finite set of states; $\mathcal{A}(s)$ is the finite set of actions available at $s \in \mathcal{S}$; p is a probability distribution such that $p(s, a, s')$ is the probability of reaching state s' immediately after taking action a in state s; $\boldsymbol{r}$ is a function such that $\boldsymbol{r}(s, a, s') \in \mathbb{R}^q$ is the reward obtained after taking action a in state s and immediately transitioning to state s'; and $\gamma \in (0, 1]$ denotes the current value of future rewards. We consider MOMDPs with a set of goal states $S_{goal} \subset \mathcal{S}$. Goal states have no actions available. We will also consider MOMDPs with an initial state s_{init}. The agent is assumed to begin the interaction starting from this state.

Supported by: Plan Propio de Investigación de la Universidad de Málaga - Campus de Excelencia Internacional Andalucía Tech. L. Mandow is supported by project Rhea P18-FR-1081 funded by Junta de Andalucía (co-financed by FEDER funds), Spain.

E. Alba et al. (Eds.): CAEPIA 2021, LNAI 12882, pp. 129–138, 2021.
https://doi.org/10.1007/978-3-030-85713-4_13

A MOMDP can model the interaction of an agent with an environment at discrete time steps. The goal is to maximize the expected accumulated (additive) discounted reward (EADR) over time. A policy π determines the action to take in state s at time step i. Let random variables S_t, R_t denote the state, and the vector reward received at time step t. The vector value $\boldsymbol{v}_\pi$ is the EADR starting at state s and applying policy π,

$$\boldsymbol{v}_\pi(s) = \mathbb{E}\Big[\sum_{k=0}^{\infty} \gamma^k R_{t+k+1} \mid S_t = s\Big] \tag{1}$$

Vector values define a partial order *dominance* relation. Given two vectors $\boldsymbol{u} = (u_1, \dots u_q), \boldsymbol{v} = (v_1, \dots v_q)$, we define the following relations: (a) Dominates or equals, $\boldsymbol{u} \succeq \boldsymbol{v}$ iff for all i, $u_i \geq v_i$; (b) Dominates, $\boldsymbol{u} \succ \boldsymbol{v}$ iff $\boldsymbol{u} \succeq \boldsymbol{v}$ and $\boldsymbol{u} \neq \boldsymbol{v}$; Given a set of vectors $X \subset \mathbb{R}^q$, we define the subset of nondominated, or Pareto-optimal, vectors as $\mathrm{ND}(X) = \{\boldsymbol{u} \in X \mid \nexists \boldsymbol{v} \in X, \boldsymbol{v} \succ \boldsymbol{u}\}$. The solution to a MOMDP is given by the $\mathbb{V}(s)$ sets of all states, which denote the values of all nondominated policies.

The solution of a scalar MDP can be computed by Dynamic Programming methods like Value Iteration (VI). The core of VI is the so called *Bellman update*, i.e., the computation of a new value $V_t(s)$ for a state s from the old values of neighbor states,

$$V_t(s) = max_{a \in A}[\sum_{s'} P(s'|a, s)[R(s'|a, s) + \gamma V_{t-1}(s')]]. \tag{2}$$

The *residual* $Res(s)$ is defined as $|V_t(s) - V_{t-1}(s)|$. In basic VI, updates are carried out synchronously, i.e., considering all states in some arbitrary order and updating all of them with the values of the prior iteration. This has some potential inefficiencies, and several asynchronous variants have been proposed [5] and compared experimentally [2]. In these variants: (i) subscript t refers to steps of execution, not complete updates; and (ii) some non arbitrary order of updating is defined, in the hope of achieving better efficiency. For instance, in *Forwards VI* a depth-first search of the state space is performed beginning from the start state s_{init}. On the contrary, in *Backwards VI* the state space is updated beginning from the goal states. Finally, in *Improved Prioritized Sweeping VI* state updates are ordered according to the ratio of their *residuals* to the new values.

Considering again MOMDP, VI was adapted by White to the multi-objective setting [8] and proved to converge. The main modification is due to the fact that for each state s', $\mathbb{V}(s')$ is a set of vector values, so the update for $\mathbb{V}(s')$ is now a set arising from all suitable combinations of vectors of $\mathbb{V}(s_1'), \dots, \mathbb{V}(s_n')$ where $s_1', \dots, s_n'$ are the states reachable by a certain action a. More concretely, let us denote by $T(a)$ the Cartesian product $\mathbb{V}(s_1') \times \dots \times \mathbb{V}(s_n')$. Let $\sigma = (\sigma_1, \dots, \sigma_n) \in T(s)$ be a tuple of vector values. We will denote the updated value by $\text{WBB}(s, \mathbb{V})$ where s is the updated state, and $\mathbb{V}$ is the set of vectors giving the values $\mathbb{V}(s')$ of the neighboring states. Then

$$\text{WBB}(s, \mathbb{V}) = ND[\cup_{a \in A} \cup_{\sigma \in T(a)} \sum_i P(s_i|a, s)[R(s_i|a, s) + \gamma \sigma_i)]]. \tag{3}$$

Additionally, since the algorithm approximates the solution, a convergence check is needed to avoid infinite computations. This could be just the number of steps done, or perhaps some function of the residuals. Algorithm 1 is the basic VI for MOMDPs.

Algorithm 1. Synchronous Multi-Objective Vector Iteration Algorithm

---

Output $\mathbb{V}$, the set of non-dominated vector values of every state
1: Initialize $\mathbb{V}$ (mandatory $\mathbb{V}(s) = \{\mathbf{0}\}\ \forall s \in S_{goal}$)
2: converged = **False**
3: **while not** converged **do**
4:     $\mathbb{V}_{old} \leftarrow \mathbb{V}$
5:     **for** $\forall\ s \in S \setminus S_{goal}$ **do**
6:         $\mathbb{V}(s) = \text{WBB}(s, \mathbb{V}_{old})$
7:     **end for**
8:     converged = $checkConvergence()$
9: **end while**

---

3 Algorithms

In this section we will present the three algorithms defined in this research. These algorithms are the result of adapting the idea of asynchronous updating to the basic VI (Algorithm 1).

The first algorithm is *Forwards Multi-Objective Vector Iteration Algorithm* or FWVI (Algorithm 2). After initialization, the main loop (lines 5 9) is executed while the convergence condition is not satisfied. In each execution of the loop the agent starts at the initial state s_{init} and throws a depth-first forwards search (procedure DFS) in the graph (line 7). DFS first updates the *visited* value of the state passed as argument (line 11) and then makes further calls to DFS with all possible successor states such that their *visited* value is smaller that the current iteration count (lines 12–15), i.e. each reachable state is visited by DFS only once at each iteration. When finally DFS reaches a goal state, nothing needs to be done and recursively returns to its callers. Otherwise, after all successors of state s have been parsed the update rule given by procedure WBB is executed for s (line 17) before returning. Notice that WBB has the current updated values $\mathbb{V}$ as argument.

Given a pair of states s, s', if there exists an action a such that $P(s'|a, s) > 0$, then FWVI considers that s' is a successor of s and s' is taken into account in line 12. Notice that in the single objective version of Forwards VI the successors taken into account are just those connected by the action determined by a greedy policy. However, that restriction makes little sense in the multi-objective case, where there are many nondominated values and hence many possible "greedy" policies. We also assume goal nodes have no successors.

The second algorithm is *Backwards Multi-Objective Vector Iteration Algorithm* or BWVI (Algorithm 3). After initialization, the main loop (lines 5–21) is executed while the convergence condition is not satisfied. In each execution of the loop, the set of states to be updated is stored in a list *Queue* initially containing all goal states (line 7). While *Queue* is not empty, BWVI extracts a state s from it (line 9) and appends all the predecessors of s not yet considered in the present execution of the loop at the end of the *Queue* (lines 13–18). We have considered two variants of BWVI, depending of the criterion followed in the extraction (FIFO or LIFO). Unless s is a goal state, its value is updated (line 11), and the procedure is repeated on the new content of *Queue*.

Algorithm 2. Forwards Multi-Objective Vector Iteration Algorithm

---

Output $\mathbb{V}$, the set of non-dominated vector values of every state

1: $iter \leftarrow 0$
2: $visited[s] \leftarrow 0 \; \forall s \in S$
3: Initialize $\mathbb{V}$ (mandatory $\mathbb{V}(s) \leftarrow \{\mathbf{0}\} \; \forall s \in S_{goal}$)
4: converged = **False**
5: **while not** converged **do**
6:      $iter \leftarrow iter + 1$
7:      DFS($s_{init}, iter$)
8:      converged = $checkConvergence()$
9: **end while**
10: **procedure** DFS($s, iter$)
11:      $visited[s] \leftarrow iter$
12:      **for** $s_{succ} \in S_{succ}(s)$ **do**
13:          **if** $visited[s_{succ}] < iter$ **then** DFS($s_{succ}, iter$)
14:          **end if**
15:      **end for**
16:      **if** $s \notin S_{goal}$ **then**
17:          $\mathbb{V}(s) \leftarrow$ WBB($s, \mathbb{V}$)
18:      **end if**
19: **end procedure**

Given a pair of states s, s', if there exists an action a such that $P(s|a, s') > 0$, then BWVI considers that s' is a predecessor of s and s' is appended to *Queue*. In order to get the set of predecessors (and even that of goal states), a certain amount to preprocessing is needed; we assume that it can be easily done. Such is the case of the MOMDPs considered in Sect. 4. Notice again that in the single objective version of Backwards VI the predecessors taken into account are just those connected by the action determined by a certain policy.

The definition of the predicate *converged* is not explicit in the code of Algorithms 2 and 3. The condition implemented in our experiments (see Sect. 4) is that the value $\mathbb{V}(s_{init})$ has not been modified in the last C executions of the main loop. Notice that due to the limited precision of the computations, it is not enough to check that $\mathbb{V}(s_{init})$ has not changed in the last execution. A value of $C = 3$ has been selected for our experiments.

The third and last algorithm is *Improved Prioritized Sweeping-Based Multi-Objective Vector Iteration Algorithm* or IPS (Algorithm 4). Like in BWVI, states are updated backwards along the state space, starting at goal states. On the other hand, IPS uses a priority queue to decide which state gets updated next. In the single-objective version of this algorithm the priority of each state is the quotient between the state value difference of the last two adjacent iterations and the current state value. However, things are a little more complex for IPS.

First at all, a suitable definition must be provided for the *residual*, i.e., for a scalar representing the change done by the last update to the value $\mathbb{V}(s)$ of a state (remember that $\mathbb{V}(s)$ is now a set of vectors). The residual will be given by a function $Res(\mathbb{V}, \mathbb{W})$

Algorithm 3. Backwards Multi-Objective Vector Iteration Algorithm

---

Output $\mathbb{V}$, the set of non-dominated vector values of every state

1: $iter \leftarrow 0$;
2: $visited[s] \leftarrow 0 \; \forall s \in S$
3: Initialize $\mathbb{V}$ (mandatory $\mathbb{V}(s) \leftarrow \{\mathbf{0}\} \; \forall s \in S_{goal}$)
4: converged = **False**
5: **while not** converged **do**
6:      $iter \leftarrow iter + 1$
7:      Queue $\leftarrow S_{goal}$
8:      **while** Queue is not empty **do**
9:          $s \leftarrow$ Queue.popNext()   ▷ first element if FIFO, last if LIFO
10:          **if** $s \notin S_{goal}$ **then**
11:              $\mathbb{V}(s) \leftarrow \text{WBB}(s, \mathbb{V})$
12:          **end if**
13:          **for** $s_{pred} \in S_{pred}$ **do**
14:              **if** $visited[s_{pred}] < iter$ **then**
15:                  Queue.append(s_{pred})
16:                  $visited[s_{pred}] \leftarrow iter$
17:              **end if**
18:          **end for**
19:      **end while**
20:      converged $\leftarrow checkConvergence()$
21: **end while**

---

that takes into account all values in two sets $\mathbb{V}, \mathbb{W}$ and all components of the vectors (objectives). We define the residual as,

$$Res(\mathbb{V}, \mathbb{W}) = \begin{cases} \infty, & \text{if size}(\mathbb{V}) \neq \text{size}(\mathbb{W}) \\ \max_{V \in \mathbb{V}, W \in \mathbb{W}} \|V - W\|_\infty & \text{otherwise} \end{cases} \quad (4)$$

where $\|X\|_\infty$ is the value of the *maximum norm* of X, given by $\max_i |X_i|$. Additionally, IPS uses the updated value $updtd$ to define the priority of every state, that is given by the ratio residual/updated value. The most direct option is to define $updtd$ as V_j where j is the index for which $\|V - W\|$ reaches the maximum, where V and W are given by $\text{argmax}_{V \in \mathbb{V}, W \in \mathbb{W}} \|V - W\|_\infty$. To simplify notation, we will assume that $Res(\mathbb{V}, \mathbb{W})$ returns $updtd$ as a second value.

After initialization, the main loop (lines 5–31) is executed while the priority queue is not empty. When all priorities are 0, IPS will remove all states from the queue and finally halt. That could imply nontermination; however, we use a limited precision implementation of the algorithm as described in [4], so finally all residuals and priorities will be 0.

In the main loop the first state s is extracted from the queue (line 6), which is ordered in decreasing order of priority. If s is nongoal and its the residual value is zero (line 7), then nothing is done; otherwise, IPS selects all predecessors s_{pred} of s and updates the values $\mathbb{V}(s_{pred})$ of each of them (line 10), keeping a copy of old values, residual and priority. The new residual and priority of s_{pred} are then calculated (lines 12–18),

Algorithm 4. Improved Prioritized Sweeping-Based Vector Iteration Algorithm

---

Output $\mathbb{V}$, the set of non-dominated vector values of every state

1: Initialize $\mathbb{V}$ (mandatory $\mathbb{V}(s) \leftarrow \{\mathbf{0}\} \; \forall s \in S_{goal}$)
2: $priority[s] \leftarrow 0 \; \forall s \in S$
3: $residual[s] \leftarrow 0 \; \forall s \in S$
4: Queue $\leftarrow S_{goal}$
5: **while** Queue is not empty **do**
6:      $s \leftarrow$ Queue.$pop(0)$ ▷ pop the first element
7:      **if** $residual[s] > 0$ **or** $s \in S_{goal}$ **then**
8:          **for** $s_{pred} \in S_{pred}$ **do**
9:              $\mathbb{V}_{old} \leftarrow \mathbb{V}(s_{pred})$
10:             $\mathbb{V}(s_{pred}) \leftarrow$ WBB$(s_{pred}, \mathbb{V})$
11:             oldPrio, oldResidual $\leftarrow priority[s_{pred}], \leftarrow residual[s_{pred}]$
12:             $res, v \leftarrow Res(\mathbb{V}(s_{pred}), \mathbb{V}_{old})$
13:             $residual[s_{pred}] \leftarrow res$
14:             **if** $v \neq 0$ **then**
15:                 $priority[s_{pred}] \leftarrow |res/v|$
16:             **else**
17:                 $priority[s_{pred}] \leftarrow 0$
18:             **end if**
19:             **if** oldPrio $< priority[s_{pred}]$ **and** $s_{pred} \in$ Queue **then**
20:                 remove all s_{pred} instances from Queue
21:             **else if** oldPrio $> priority[s_{pred}]$ **and** $s_{pred} \in$ Queue **then**
22:                 $priority[s_{pred}] \leftarrow$ oldPrio
23:                 $residual[s_{pred}] \leftarrow$ oldResidual
24:                 continue
25:             **else if** oldPrio $= priority[s_{pred}]$ **and** $s_{pred} \in$ Queue **then**
26:                 continue
27:             **end if**
28:             insert s_{pred} into Queue keeping Queue in decreasing order of priority
29:         **end for**
30:     **end if**
31: **end while**

---

and finally s_{pred} is inserted in the priority queue according to the value calculated (line 28). However, some care must be taken for this operation, because there can be other occurrences of s_{pred} in the queue; so some checks must be done (lines 19–27).

4   Experimental Results and Discussion

This section describes the evaluation of the algorithms introduced in Sect. 3 over different environments: several variants of the biobjective Deep Sea Treasure environment [7], and the three objective Resource Gathering environment [1].

All our variants of the Deep Sea Treasure environment define their state spaces using the grid depicted in Fig. 1(left), but differ in the sets of available actions. A submarine (the agent) has its initial state at the top left corner. Its goal is to find treasures that lie on the bottom of the sea which are also the absorbing states. The rewards of the treasures can be seen in the picture while the black squares denote the sea ground which is inaccessible to the agent.

There are two objectives the agent takes into account. First, the time criterion: for every movement inside the grid the agent is rewarded with a value of -1. The second objective is the treasure reward: the agent receives it when it transitions to one of the absorbing states, for all other transitions the value is 0. The goal is to maximize both rewards.

We consider several versions of this environment. The first one is DST-Right-Down (DSTRD). It is an environment with deterministic dynamics and the action space consisting of only two actions: right and down. This feature makes DSTRD non-cyclic. Another variant is the deterministic cyclic DST. Its action space includes moves to the right, down, left and up. Finally, we take DSTRD with stochastic dynamics into consideration. Being in state $s \in S$ and taking action $a \in A$, the agent has an 80% chance of moving in the intended direction, and with a 20% probability it moves in another (randomly chosen) allowed direction. In case only one action is possible in state s, it moves in the only available direction in 100% of the cases. In all versions $\gamma = 1$.

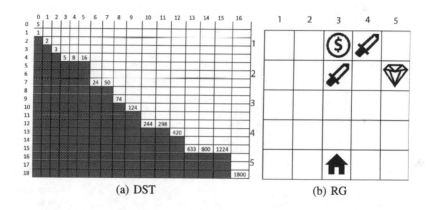

(a) DST   (b) RG

Fig. 1. Environments for the experiments

To compare the performance metrics for these environment settings, we consider various DST configurations. By configuration we imply a state space defined only over a subset of the grid's columns. For example, configuration 6 means that we only consider the first 6 columns of the DST grid while configuration 17 means we consider the whole grid (see Fig. 1(left)).

The Resource Gathering (RG) environment [1] is probabilistic and has three objectives. An agent moves in a grid depicted in Fig. 1(right). The agent starts in its home location (cell (3, 5)) and can collect one item for each of two kinds of resources: gold (cell (3, 1)), and gems (cell (5, 2)). There are also two enemy states in cells (4, 1) and (3, 2). If the agent steps into one of them, there is a 10% chance it gets attacked and returns home losing all resources it has gathered in previous steps. The agent receives its three rewards (gold, gem, attack) as soon as it returns back to the home location which is also considered as the final state.

The action space consists of 4 actions: up, down, left, right. The objective space has three dimensions. The first one represents the enemy attack: along this dimension the agent gets the value of −1 if it gets attacked, otherwise the value stays zero. The second objective is the reward for gathering gold. Its value is 1 for the transition to the final state if the gold has been successfully gathered in the past, and zero in all other cases. The third objective is the reward for gathering gems, and is updated by the same rules as the gold objective. We set $\gamma = 0.9$ for this environment.

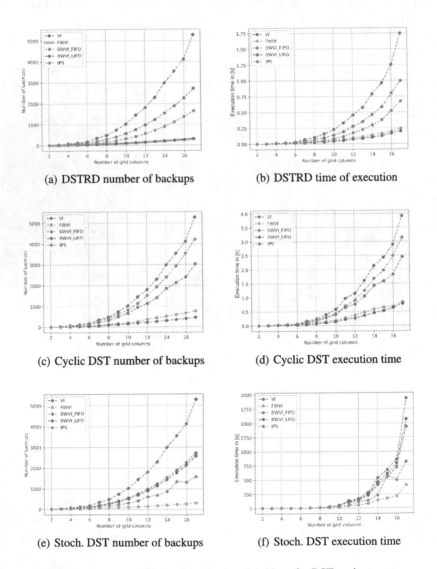

(a) DSTRD number of backups

(b) DSTRD time of execution

(c) Cyclic DST number of backups

(d) Cyclic DST execution time

(e) Stoch. DST number of backups

(f) Stoch. DST execution time

Fig. 2. Performance of the multi-objective algorithms for DST environments

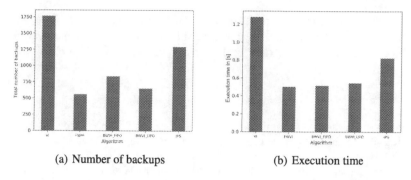

(a) Number of backups   (b) Execution time

Fig. 3. Performance of the multi-objective algorithms for the RG environment

Algorithms were implemented in Python. Experiments were carried out on a general-use personal computer with Intel Core i5-CPU, at 1.3-GHz, 3 MB cache, 2 cores and 4 threads.

Figure 2 shows the results of the algorithms when applied to the different variants of the DST environment. The horizontal axis displays the size (or configuration) of the problem, i.e. the number of columns in the environment. The vertical axis displays performance metrics, given by total number of state backups (left) and total time in seconds (right) until convergence. Precision (see [4]) was set to 0.1.

As expected, all algorithms and environments show exponential growth both in time and number of backups with the size of the problem. The worst performance is always that of the synchronous multi-objective algorithm (VI). For DSTRD, the best performance is by far that of BWVI-LIFO, being that of FWIV approximately the same. BWVI-FIFO is not so good, and it is outperformed by IPS. For cyclic DST, execution time is greater. The best performance is again that of BWVI-LIFO, being that of FWIV approximately the same. But now BWVI-FIFO outperforms IPS. Finally, for stochastic DSTRD, execution time is two orders of magnitude greater. FWVI is the best algorithm, and both versions of BWVI show little improvement over synchronous VI.

Figure 3 shows the results of the algorithms when applied to the RG environment. Precision (see [4]) was set to $1e - 6$. Total number of state backups and total time until convergence are shown for the different algorithms. Best performance is shown by FWVI with little difference over BWVI.

Globally, these results are consistent with those found by [2] for the scalar case. In their experiments IPS also showed worse performance in complex cases when compared to forwards and backwards VI.

5   Conclusions and Future Work

We have presented some new variants of Value Iteration algorithms for multi-objective MDPs. In these variants states are updated asynchronously following a certain order (forwards, backwards, or according to a priority heuristics). In the standard grid environments used as benchmarks, all variants present some improvement over basic Value Iteration. However, there are great differences among them. In our experiments the best results in "difficult" environments (stochastic DST and 3-objective RG) are given by forwards exploration, which also performs well in simpler environments. Future work includes more extensive evaluations of the algorithms over different problems.

References

1. Barrett, L., Narayanan, S.: Learning all optimal policies with multiple criteria. In: Proceedings of the 25th International Conference on Machine Learning, pp. 41–47 (2008)
2. Dai, P., Hansen, E.A.: Prioritizing Bellman backups without a priority queue. In: Proceedings of the Seventeenth International Conference on International Conference on Automated Planning and Scheduling, pp. 113–119. AAAI Press (2007)
3. Drugan, M., Wiering, M., Vamplew, P., Chetty, M.: Special issue on multi-objective reinforcement learning. Neurocomputing **263**, 1–2 (2017)
4. Mandow, L., Pérez de la Cruz, J.L., Pozas, N.: Multi-objective dynamic programming with limited precision. arXiv:2009.08198 (2020)
5. Mausam, A.K.: Planning with Markov decision processes. An AI perspective. In: Synthesis Lectures on Artificial Intelligence and Machine Learning. Morgan & Claypool (2012)
6. Roijers, D.M., Whiteson, S.: Multi-objective decision making. In: Synthesis Lectures on Artificial Intelligence and Machine Learning. Morgan & Claypool (2017)
7. Vamplew, P., Dazeley, R., Berry, A., Issabekov, R., Dekker, E.: Empirical evaluation methods for multiobjective reinforcement learning algorithms. Mach. Learn. **84**, 51–80 (2011)
8. White, D.J.: Multi-objective infinite-horizon discounted Markov decision processes. J. Math. Anal. Appl. **89**, 639–647 (1982)

Influence of the Alternative Objective Functions in the Optimization of the Cyclic Cutwidth Minimization Problem

Sergio Cavero$^{(\boxtimes)}$, Eduardo G. Pardo, and Abraham Duarte

Universidad Rey Juan Carlos, Madrid, Spain
{sergio.cavero,eduardo.pardo,abraham.duarte}@urjc.es

Abstract. The quality of the solutions to a combinatorial optimization problem is usually measured using a mathematical function, named objective function. This function is also used to guide heuristic procedures through the solution space, helping to detect promising search directions (i.e., it helps to compare the quality of different solutions). However, this task becomes very hard when many solutions are evaluated with the same value by the objective function. This fact commonly occurs in either max-min/min-max optimization problems. In those situations, a key strategy relies on the introduction of an alternative objective function. This function helps to determine which solution is more promising when the compared ones achieve the same value of the original objective function. In this paper we study the Cyclic Cutwidth Minimization Problem (CCMP), which is an example of a min-max optimization problem. Particularly, we analyze the influence in the search of using alternative objective functions within local search procedures. Also, we propose two alternative objective functions for the CCMP and compare its performance against a previously introduced one. Finally, we explored the combination of more than one alternative function.

Keywords: Cyclic cutwidth · Graph layout problem · Combinatorial optimization · Flat landscape

1 Introduction

In this work, we analyze the influence in the search of using multiple objective functions for a min-max optimization problem, the Cyclic Cutwidth Minimization Problem (CCMP). The CCMP has been widely used to model and formulate a variety of real-world applications. Particularly, the applications of the CCMP can be found in circuit design, migration of telecommunication networks, or graph drawing, among others [5,15].

This research has been supported by the Ministerio de Ciencia, Innovación y Universidades (Grant Refs. PGC2018-095322-B-C22 and FPU19/04098) and by C. Madrid and European Regional Development Fund (Grant Ref. P2018/TCS-4566).

E. Alba et al. (Eds.): CAEPIA 2021, LNAI 12882, pp. 139–149, 2021.
https://doi.org/10.1007/978-3-030-85713-4_14

The CCMP belongs to a family of optimization problems, usually denoted as Graph Layout Problems (GLP), where the objective consists of defining an embedding of a graph (known as the input graph) into another graph (known as the host graph). Given an input graph $\mathcal{G} = (V_\mathcal{G}, E_\mathcal{G})$ and a host graph $\mathcal{H} = (V_\mathcal{H}, E_\mathcal{H})$, where $V_\mathcal{G}$ and $V_\mathcal{H}$ represent the set of vertices of the input and host graphs, and $E_\mathcal{G}$ and $E_\mathcal{H}$ represent the set of edges of the input and host graphs respectively, we formally define an embedding with two functions: the first one, φ, assigns each vertex of the input graph to a vertex of the host graph, $\varphi : V_\mathcal{G} \rightarrow V_\mathcal{H}$; the second one assigns each edge of the input graph to a path of the host graph, $\psi : E_\mathcal{G} \rightarrow P_\mathcal{H}$, being $P_\mathcal{H}$ the set of all feasible paths of $\mathcal{H}$. Let us remember that a path in a connected graph between two vertices, u and v, denoted as $p(u, v)$, is defined as a sequence of edges which join them.

The most studied problems within the GLP family are those in which the host graph has a regular structure, such as paths, cycles, or trees [6, 18]. The CCMP is a particular Graph Layout Problem where the host graph is restricted to be a cycle. Therefore, in this case, $\mathcal{H}$ is a 2-regular, Eulerian, Hamiltonian, and unit-distance graph which satisfies that $|V_\mathcal{H}| = |E_\mathcal{H}| = |V_\mathcal{G}|$. Given an embedding φ and an edge $(u, v) \in E_\mathcal{G}$, the function ψ assigns the edge (u, v) to a path of $\mathcal{H}$ with an ending in $\varphi(u)$ and another ending in $\varphi(v)$. Notice, that when the host graph is a cycle, there are only two possible paths (avoiding loops) between each pair of vertices. Furthermore, in this specific problem, ψ assigns the shortest path to $(u, v) \in E_\mathcal{G}$. More formally:

$$\psi((u, v)) = \underset{p(\varphi(u),\varphi(v))\in P_\mathcal{H}}{\arg\min} \quad \{|p(\varphi(u), \varphi(v))|\} \, \forall \, (u, v) \in E_\mathcal{G}. \tag{1}$$

However, since ψ can be derived from φ, to ease the notation we use only φ in the rest of the document to denote an embedding.

Let us illustrate these concepts with an example. In Fig. 1a we depict an example of an input graph $\mathcal{G}$ with $|V_\mathcal{G}| = 5$ and $|E_\mathcal{G}| = 5$, and with vertices labeled alphabetically (A,B,C,D,E). In Fig. 1b we show a possible embedding of $\mathcal{G}$ in a host-cycle graph $\mathcal{H}$, such that $|V_\mathcal{H}| = |V_\mathcal{G}| = 5$. The host graph is depicted in dashed black lines, and its vertices have been labeled with numbers from 1 to 5. In this example, the specific function φ' is defined as follows: $\varphi'(A) = 1$, $\varphi'(B) = 2$, $\varphi'(C) = 3$, $\varphi'(D) = 4$, and $\varphi'(F) = 5$. Finally, in Fig. 1c we represent the two possible paths between a pair of vertices 1 and 3, which are currently hosting the vertices A and C. In particular, $p_1 = \{(1, 2), (2, 3)\}$ and $p_2 = \{(3, 4), (4, 5), (5, 1)\}$. According to Eq. 1, the path p_1 is assigned to the edge (A,C) since it achieves to have the minimum cardinality.

With the previous definitions at hand, we next introduce the CCMP. Let us start by defining the "cut" of an edge of the host graph, $(w, z) \in E_\mathcal{H}$, for a particular embedding φ as the number of edges of the input graph which have associated a path which contains the edge (w, z). More formally:

$$\mathrm{cut}((w, z), \varphi) = |\{(u, v) \in E_\mathcal{G} : (w, z) \in \psi((u, v))\}|. \tag{2}$$

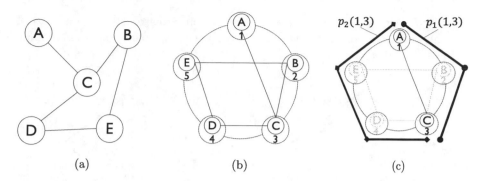

Fig. 1. (a) Input graph $\mathcal{G}$. (b) A possible embedding, φ' of $\mathcal{G}$. (c) The two possible paths (p_1 and p_2) between 1 and 3.

Given an input graph G and a particular embedding φ, the objective function of the CCMP (denoted as ccw) is calculated as follows:

$$ccw(\mathcal{G}, \varphi) = \max_{(w,z) \in E_{\mathcal{H}}} \{\mathrm{cut}((w, z), \varphi)\}. \tag{3}$$

The purpose of the CCMP (defined in Eq. 4) is to find an embedding $\varphi^\star$ among all possible embedding, Φ, that minimizes the Eq. 3:

$$\varphi^\star \leftarrow \arg\min_{\varphi \in \Phi} \{ccw(G, \varphi)\}. \tag{4}$$

Let us illustrate the evaluation of a solution with an example. In Fig. 2 we depict the evaluation of two possible embeddings φ' and φ'', of the input graph presented in Fig. 1a. We have represented in bold lines outside the cycle, the paths in the host graph associated with each of the edges of the input graph. Then, the "cut" of each edge of the host graph is calculated as the number of paths that contain that edge (see Eq. 2). For example, in Fig. 2a, the edge $(1,2)$ is contained in the paths $p(\varphi(B), \varphi(E))$ and $p(\varphi(A), \varphi(C))$. Therefore, $\mathrm{cut}((1,2), \varphi') = 2$. Similarly, $\mathrm{cut}((2,3), \varphi') = 2$ and so on. Finally, the cyclic cutwidth, ccw, of the embedding φ' of graph $\mathcal{G}$ in a cycle is $ccw(\mathcal{G}, \varphi') = \max\{2, 2, 1, 1, 1\} = 2$. Similarly, the ccw, of the embedding φ'' of graph $\mathcal{G}$ in a cycle is $ccw(\mathcal{G}, \varphi'') = \max\{1, 2, 1, 1, 1\} = 2$.

The CCMP was introduced as a variant of the Cutwidth Minimization Problem (CMP) since both share the same objective function. Therefore, both problems share some properties. However, the host graph for the CMP is a path graph [5]. The CMP belongs to the $\mathcal{NP}$-hard class [10], but it has been exactly solved for some types of graphs with regular structure [11,23,28]. Moreover, it has been tackled from a heuristic perspective for general graphs [5,7,17,19,24]. The relationship between the CCMP and the CMP was formalized in [14] in terms of lower and upper bounds.

In the case of the CCMP, it has been widely studied for regular-structured input graphs, from both exact and asymptotic perspectives [1–4,9,13,14,20,25–27]. On the other hand, the CCMP has been tackled using heuristic approaches, a Memetic Algorithm [12], and a Multistart Tabu Search [4]. The last one is currently the best proposal in the literature, being able to find the best solutions for most of the studied instances.

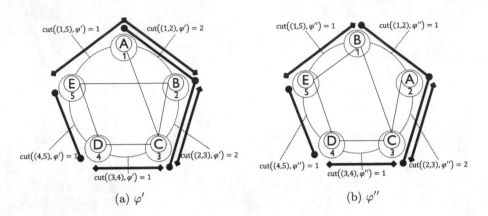

(a) φ'

(b) φ''

Fig. 2. Evaluation of two possible embedding of $\mathcal{G}$ in $\mathcal{H}$.

In this paper we study the impact of the use of alternative objective functions in local search procedures, when dealing with flat landscapes associated with the CCMP. Particularly, we propose two alternative objective functions for the CCMP and compare its performance against a previously introduced one.

The rest of the paper is organized as follows. In Sect. 2, we introduce the three alternative functions studied for the CCMP. Then, in Sect. 3, we describe the algorithmic strategy used to evaluate the alternative functions. Next, in Sect. 4, we compare and analyze the methods. Finally, in Sect. 5, we provide the overall conclusions as well as relevant directions for future research.

2   Alternative Evaluation Functions for the CCMP

The CCMP is a min-max optimization problem, where the objective function consists of minimizing a maximum value. These kinds of problems usually present flat landscapes or fitness landscapes [7,19,21], which means that many solutions are qualified with the same value of the objective function, although they are structurally different. In this context, the search presents additional challenges for search procedures, since determining the search direction is harder. This is because many times, when comparing two solutions, it is not possible to distinguish which one is more promising. This is the case of local search procedures, which usually determine the search direction based on the changes produced in the objective function during the search.

Some studies which handle problems with flat landscapes have proposed the use of alternative objective functions as a strategy to differentiate solutions qualified equally to the original objective function. In this context, the choice of an objective function should be done considering, first, the computational cost required to calculate it; second, the capacity to locate promising solutions that guide the heuristic procedure; and finally, the consistency, a solution should always be evaluated in the same way [21]. This strategy has also been used in the context of the CCMP [4] by proposing an alternative objective function for the problem. In this research, we describe this function and compare its performance with two new alternative objective functions proposed here for the CCMP.

Next, we describe each of the aforementioned functions. Let f_k be the number of edges of the host graph which have an associated "cut" equal to k. In mathematically terms:

$$f_k = |\{(w, z) \in E_{\mathcal{H}} : \text{cut}((w, z), \varphi) = k\}|. \tag{5}$$

In order to simplify the notation, we also refer to k_{max} as the value of the original objective function for a particular solution (i.e., $k_{max} = ccw(\mathcal{G}, \varphi)$).

The first alternative function studied, denoted as ccw_1, was introduced in [4] for the CCMP. However, some variations of this objective function can be found for other related problems such as the CMP [19] or the Cyclic Bandwidth Sum Problem (CBS) [21]. The rationale behind ccw_1 is to penalize those solutions with many edges with a "cut" value close to k_{max}. Considering that n is the number of vertices of the input graph ($n = |V_{\mathcal{H}}|$) this function is calculated as follows:

$$ccw_1(\mathcal{G}, \varphi) = \sum_{k=1}^{k_{max}} n^k \cdot f_k. \tag{6}$$

The second alternative objective function, denoted as ccw_2, is proposed for the first time in this paper in the context of the CCMP. However, it has been also related to other optimization problems, such as the CBS [21] or the Minimum Linear Arrangement [16]. The rationale of this function is to favor those embeddings with a sum of the "cut" associated with each edge of the host graph, as small as possible. This function is calculated as follows:

$$ccw_2(\mathcal{G}, \varphi) = \sum_{k=1}^{k_{max}} k \cdot f_k. \tag{7}$$

Finally, the third objective function is also proposed here for the first time in the context of the CCMP. It is inspired by the ideas proposed for the CBS problem [21,22]. The rationale behind this function is to penalize the occurrence of edges with a small "cut" value associated. This function is calculated as follows:

$$ccw_3(\mathcal{G}, \varphi) = \sum_{k=1}^{k_{max}} n^{k_{max}-k+1} \cdot f_k. \tag{8}$$

Notice that, when comparing two solutions to any of the previous functions, we consider that the one which minimizes the particular alternative function is more promising. Despite the fact that the previous functions are not equivalent to minimize the CCMP, they are useful as a tie-break criterion.

The cost of the three objective functions previously introduced, in terms of computational complexity is $\mathcal{O}(n)$, since all of them include a sum from 1 to k_{max}, which, in the worst case, could have a value of $\lfloor n/2 \rfloor$.

Let us illustrate the use of the alternative objective functions with an example. As the reader might have noticed, the two solutions depicted in Fig. 2 are equal in terms of the original objective function value (i.e., $ccw(\mathcal{G}, \varphi') = ccw(\mathcal{G}, \varphi'') = 2$). However, we can find differences between them when evaluating the solutions with the alternative objective functions previously introduced (i.e., $ccw_1(\mathcal{G}, \varphi') = 65$, while $ccw_1(\mathcal{G}, \varphi'') = 45$; $ccw_2(\mathcal{G}, \varphi') = 7$, while $ccw_2(\mathcal{G}, \varphi'') = 6$; and $ccw_3(\mathcal{G}, \varphi') = 85$, while $ccw_3(\mathcal{G}, \varphi'') = 105$).

3   Algorithmic Evaluation Strategy

To analyze the performance of the different alternative objective functions presented in Sect. 2, we propose the use of a random constructive procedure combined with a local search procedure based on the insert move. A local search is a heuristic procedure that follows an intensification strategy that aims to find a local optimal solution in a particular neighborhood. The insert move is a classic operator in GLP problems [4,17], and it consists of unassigning a vertex of the input graph and then assigning it to another vertex of the host graph. We formally denote $\mathcal{N}(\varphi)$ as the neighborhood associated to the insert move, i.e., the set of embeddings that can be reached from φ, by applying the insert operator. In mathematical terms:

$$\mathcal{N}(\varphi) = \{Insert(\varphi, u, w) : \forall u \in V_{\mathcal{G}}, \forall w \in V_{\mathcal{H}}, w \neq \varphi(u)\}. \tag{9}$$

Therefore, for an input graph with n vertices, the size of the neighborhood is $n \cdot (n-1)$. Notice that we propose the use of a best improvement strategy. This strategy consists of taking into account all possible movements of a solution, before choosing the best one. The rationale of using this procedure to test the alternative objective functions is to let the functions the chance of comparing as many solutions as possible during the search.

Algorithm 1 summarizes the steps followed by our local search procedure. Given G, an input graph, and φ, an initial solution generated by the random constructive procedure, all possible solutions of $\mathcal{N}(\varphi^\star)$ are visited (steps 6–13), where $\varphi^\star$ is the best solution found so far (which is initially equal to φ). If a solution of $\mathcal{N}(\varphi^\star)$ is better than the current one (step 9), it becomes the best new solution found (steps 9–12). If there is no solution that improves the current one, the procedure ends (step 4), and the best solution is returned (step 17).

To determine which solution is better after a move, we use the procedure isBetter described in Algorithm 2. Particularly, it compares two solutions considering the original objective function ccw and, if a tie is found, the tie is broken using one of the alternative objective functions defined in Sect. 2 ($i \in \{1, 2, 3\}$).

Algorithm 1. Local search procedure.

```
1: Procedure LocalSearch (G, φ)
2:   improve ← True
3:   φ* ← φ
4:   while improve do
5:     improve ← False
6:     for all u ∈ V_G do
7:       for all w ∈ V_H do
8:         φ' ← Insert(φ*, u, w)
9:         if isBetter(φ', φ) then
10:          φ ← φ'
11:          improve ← True
12:        end if
13:      end for
14:    end for
15:    φ* ← φ
16:  end while
17:  return φ*
```

Algorithm 2. Procedure to compare two solutions.

```
1: Procedure isBetter (φ', φ)
2:   if ccw(φ') < ccw(φ) then
3:     return True
4:   else if (ccw(φ') == ccw(φ)) and (ccw_i(φ') < ccw_i(φ)) then
5:     return True
6:   else
7:     return False
8:   end if
```

---

4   Experimental Results

In this section, we evaluate the performance of the three alternative objective functions for the CCMP introduced in Sect. 2 and also, the combination of each of them. The experimentation has been carried out over 19 instances obtained from the Harwell-Boeing collection [8]. These instances represent problems from scientific and engineering disciplines. The algorithms have been coded in Java, and all experiments have been executed on an Intel(R) Core(TM) i7-1065G7 CPU at 1.30 GHz with a Windows 10 operating system.

In all the experiments we run each algorithm 50 times for any of the 19 instances considered and we collect the best values found per instance. Particularly, we report the average of the best solutions found (Avg.), the deviation to the best solution found in the experiment (Dev. (%)), the CPU time in seconds (CPUt(s)), and the number of best solutions found in the experiment (# Best).

In Table 1 we compare the performance of using the original objective function ccw in isolation in the Local Search procedure (LS), and its combination with an alternative objective function for tie-breaking purposes: ccw_1 (LS$_1$),

Table 1. Influence of the alternative objective function in the local search.

	C	C+LS	C+LS$_1$	C+LS$_2$	C+LS$_3$
Avg.	62.21	52.68	20.79	21.05	20.58
Dev. (%)	322.25	254.56	3.85	8.85	3.82
CPUt(s)	0.01	52.35	138.98	122.59	81.55
# Best	0	0	12	9	12

ccw_2 (LS$_2$), and ccw_3 (LS$_3$). Notice that, all local search procedures start from the same initial solution generated by a random constructive procedure (C).

As expected, C+LS is able to improve considerably the solutions generated by C, although it quickly reaches a local optimum due to the flat landscape of the problem. When the main objective function is supported by any of the three alternative objective functions (whatever the alternative objective function is) the Avg. is considerably reduced. Moreover, C+LS is not able to achieve any of the best solutions found, which are distributed among C+LS$_1$, C+LS$_2$ and C+LS$_3$. Despite the small differences among the methods C+LS$_3$ seems to be the best one, since it achieves the smallest deviation and the largest number of best solutions in a shorter amount of time. To complement this experiment, we have used Wilcoxon's signed rank test to compare the differences between the objective function values of the best solutions found for each pair of procedures. When comparing C+LS with either C+LS$_1$, C+LS$_2$ or C+LS$_3$ the p-value obtained is 0.00014 (the three comparisons obtained the same p-value), which indicates significant differences between procedures. Therefore, we can conclude that the use of an alternative function produces significant better results than using only the original objective function for the CCMP. However, we did not find significant differences among the results obtained with any of them. As an additional experiment, since the constructive procedure is a very fast method, we let it run for up to 150 s, verifying that the obtained results (with an average deviation of 264.76% and 0 best solutions found) are far from the values obtained by the rest of the methods.

Despite the fact that the three proposed alternative objective functions obtained very good results, the tested methods performed differently when observing the results obtained for each instance separately. In the next experiment, we study whether the combination of more than one alternative objective function allows us to find a better and robust procedure. Particularly, since we used a multi-start procedure to compare the methods, we now propose to change the alternative objective function used in each iteration. For instance, we have combined C+LS$_1$ and C+LS$_2$ in the procedure C+LS$_{12}$ by executing alternatively C+LS$_1$ and C+LS$_2$, until 50 executions are reached. Similarly, C+LS$_{13}$ combines C+LS$_1$ with C+LS$_3$. C+LS$_{23}$ combines C+LS$_2$ and C + LS$_3$. Finally, all procedures are combined in C+LS$_{123}$ by executing alternatively C+LS$_1$, C+LS$_2$ and C+LS$_3$ until 50 executions are reached. The results obtained are reported in Table 2. At a first glance, the combination of the procedures allowed

Table 2. Combination of the proposed procedures.

	C+LS$_1$	C+LS$_2$	C+LS$_3$	C+LS$_{12}$	C+LS$_{13}$	C+LS$_{23}$	C+LS$_{123}$
Avg.	20.79	21.05	20.58	20.84	20.42	20.58	20.42
Dev. (%)	3.85	8.85	3.82	4.99	0.86	3.83	0.59
CPUt(s)	138.98	122.59	81.55	130.78	110.27	102.07	115.03
# Best	12	9	12	10	14	12	15

us find higher quality solutions. Particularly, we observed that C+LS$_{123}$ is able to decrease the Avg. and Dev. (%), while it found the largest number of best solutions. However, the statistical tests performed indicate that the differences found are not significant for the instances tested.

5   Conclusions

In this paper we have studied the effect of flat landscapes that usually arises in min-max/max-min optimization problems in search procedures. Particularly, we have focused on the study of the Cyclic Cutwidth Minimization Problem, consisting of embedding an input graph into a host-cycle graph while minimizing the maximum cut in the host graph. To handle with this problem, we introduced the use of an alternative objective function. Particularly, we compiled a previous function used in the context of the problem and proposed two new functions.

The experiments carried out demonstrated that the use of an alternative objective function with tie-breaking purposes, in combination with the original one, showed a better performance for the CCMP, since the method avoids getting stuck in flat landscapes. We have also revealed an insight about the advantage obtained when more than one alternative objective function is combined within the same procedure, since the methods follow different search directions. Future work should be focused on a deeper analysis of this strategy.

References

1. Abbott, H.: Hamiltonian circuits and paths on the n-cube. Can. Math. Bull. **9**(5), 557–562 (1966)
2. Aschenbrenner, R.: A proof for the cyclic cutwidth of q5. Cal State University, San Bernardino, REU Project (2001)
3. Castillo, C.: A proof for the cyclic cutwidth of q6. Cal State University, San Bernardino, REU Project (2003)
4. Cavero, S., Pardo, E.G., Laguna, M., Duarte, A.: Multistart search for the cyclic cutwidth minimization problem. Comput. Oper. Res. **126**, 105–116 (2021)
5. Cohoon, J., Sahni, S.: Heuristics for the backplane ordering. J. VLSI Comput. Syst. **2**(1–2), 37–60 (1987)
6. Díaz, J., Petit, J., Serna, M.: A survey of graph layout problems. ACM Comput. Surv. (CSUR) **34**(3), 313–356 (2002)

7. Duarte, A., Pantrigo, J.J., Pardo, E.G., Sánchez-Oro, J.: Parallel variable neighbourhood search strategies for the cutwidth minimization problem. IMA J. Manag. Math. **27**(1), 55–73 (2016)
8. Duff, I.S., Grimes, R.G., Lewis, J.G.: Users' guide for the harwell-boeing sparse matrix collection (release i) (1992)
9. Erbele, J., Chavez, J., Trapp, R.: The cyclic cutwidth of qn. California State University, San Bernardino USA, Manuscript (2003)
10. Gavril, F.: Some np-complete problems on graphs. Technical Report, Computer Science Department, Technion (2011)
11. Harper, L.H.: Optimal numberings and isoperimetric problems on graphs. J. Comb. Theory **1**(3), 385–393 (1966)
12. Jain, P., Srivastava, K., Saran, G.: Minimizing cyclic cutwidth of graphs using a memetic algorithm. J. Heuristics **22**(6), 815–848 (2016)
13. James, B.: The cyclical cutwidth of the three-dimensional and four dimensional cubes. Cal State University, San Bernardino McNair Scholar's Program Summer Research Journal (1996)
14. Johnson, M.: The linear and cyclic cutwidth of the complete bipartite graph. Cal State University, San Bernardino, REU Project (2003)
15. Makedon, F., Sudborough, I.: On minimizing width in linear layouts. Discrete Appl. Math. **23**(3), 243–265 (1989)
16. Martí, R., Pantrigo, J.J., Duarte, A., Pardo, E.G.: Branch and bound for the cutwidth minimization problem. Comput. Oper. Res. **40**(1), 137–149 (2013)
17. Pantrigo, J.J., Martí, R., Duarte, A., Pardo, E.G.: Scatter search for the cutwidth minimization problem. Ann. Oper. Res. **199**(1), 285–304 (2012)
18. Pardo, E.G., Martí, R., Duarte, A.: Linear layout problems. In: Martí, R., Panos, P., Resende, M.G. (eds.) Handbook of Heuristics, pp. 1–25. Springer, Cham (2016). https://doi.org/10.1007/978-3-319-07153-4_45-1
19. Pardo, E.G., Mladenović, N., Pantrigo, J.J., Duarte, A.: Variable formulation search for the cutwidth minimization problem. Appl. Soft Comput. **13**(5), 2242–2252 (2013)
20. Rios, F.R.: Complete graphs as a first step toward finding the cyclic cutwidth of the n-cube. Cal State University. San Bernardino McNair Scholar's Program Summer Research Journal (1996)
21. Rodriguez-Tello, E., Lardeux, F., Duarte, A., Narvaez-Teran, V.: Alternative evaluation functions for the cyclic bandwidth sum problem. Eur. J. Oper. Res. **273**(3), 904–919 (2019)
22. Rodriguez-Tello, E., Narvaez-Teran, V., Lardeux, F.: Dynamic multi-armed bandit algorithm for the cyclic bandwidth sum problem. IEEE Access **7**, 40258–40270 (2019)
23. Rolim, J., Sýkora, O., Vrt'o, I.: Optimal cutwidths and bisection widths of 2- and 3-dimensional meshes. In: Nagl, M. (ed.) WG 1995. LNCS, vol. 1017, pp. 252–264. Springer, Heidelberg (1995). https://doi.org/10.1007/3-540-60618-1_80
24. Santos, V.G.M., de Carvalho, M.A.M.: Tailored heuristics in adaptive large neighborhood search applied to the cutwidth minimization problem. Eur. J. Oper. Res. **289**(3), 1056–1066 (2021)
25. Schröder, H., Sýykoa, O., Vrt'o, I.: Cyclic cutwidth of the mesh. In: Pavelka, J., Tel, G., Bartošek, M. (eds.) SOFSEM 1999. LNCS, vol. 1725, pp. 449–458. Springer, Heidelberg (1999). https://doi.org/10.1007/3-540-47849-3_33

26. Schröder, H., Sỳkora, O., Vrt'o, I.: Cyclic cutwidths of the two-dimensional ordinary and cylindrical meshes. Discrete Appl. Math. **143**(1-3), 123–129 (2004)
27. Sciortino, V., Chavez, J., Trapp, R.: The cyclic cutwidth of a $p_2 \times p_2 \times p_n$ mesh. Cal State University, San Bernardino, REU Project (2002)
28. Thilikos, D.M., Serna, M., Bodlaender, H.L.: Cutwidth II: algorithms for partial w-trees of bounded degree. J. Algorithms **56**(1), 25–49 (2005)

A Similarity Measure of Gaussian Process Predictive Distributions

Lucia Asencio Martín and Eduardo C. Garrido-Merchán[✉]

Universidad Autónoma de Madrid, Madrid, Spain
lucia.asencio@estudiante.uam.es, eduardo.garrido@uam.es

Abstract. Some scenarios require the computation of a predictive distribution of a new value evaluated on an objective function conditioned on previous observations. We are interested on using a model that makes valid assumptions on the objective function whose values we are trying to predict. Some of these assumptions may be smoothness or stationarity. Gaussian process (GPs) are probabilistic models that can be interpreted as flexible distributions over functions. They encode the assumptions through covariance functions, making hypotheses about new data through a predictive distribution by being fitted to old observations. We can face the case where several GPs are used to model different objective functions. GPs are non-parametric models whose complexity is cubic on the number of observations. A measure that represents how similar is one GP predictive distribution with respect to another would be useful to stop using one GP when they are modelling functions of the same input space. We are really inferring that two objective functions are correlated, so one GP is enough to model both of them by performing a transformation of the prediction of the other function in case of inverse correlation. We show empirical evidence in a set of synthetic and benchmark experiments that GPs predictive distributions can be compared and that one of them is enough to predict two correlated functions in the same input space. This similarity metric could be extremely useful used to discard objectives in Bayesian many-objective optimization.

1 Introduction

Regression problems involve the prediction of the value y associated with the evaluation of a point $\mathbf{x} \in \mathbb{R}^d$ in an objective function or unknown ground truth $f(\mathbf{x})$, where d is the number of dimensions of $\mathbf{x}$ [1,14]. Let $\mathcal{X}$ be a subset of $\mathbb{R}^d$ called the input space. Supervised learning finds the values of the machine learning (ML) algorithm hyper-parameters $\boldsymbol{\theta}$ that make the algorithm calculate an accurate prediction of $f(\mathbf{x})$ via fitting the algorithm with a dataset $\mathcal{D} = \{(\mathbf{x}_i, y_i) | i = 1, ..., n\}$, where $\mathbf{x}_i$ are points labelled with values y_i. ML algorithms then perform predictions $y^\star$ of new points $\mathbf{x}^\star$. If the ML algorithm does not compute an uncertainty $\sigma(\mathbf{x})$ of its predictions y, the user of the regression will not know the degree of certainty of the predictions done by the ML algorithm. This is the case of Deep neural networks, that do not provide uncertainty. Gaussian processes (GPs) [12] and Bayesian neural networks compute

© Springer Nature Switzerland AG 2021
E. Alba et al. (Eds.): CAEPIA 2021, LNAI 12882, pp. 150–159, 2021.
https://doi.org/10.1007/978-3-030-85713-4_15

uncertainties of its predictions. A GP model is equivalent to a fully connected deep neural network with infinite number of hidden units in each layer [11]. GPs have successfully been used for regression problems where the uncertainty $\sigma(\mathbf{x})$ of the predictions y is important [15].

GPs have also been used as probabilistic surrogate models in Bayesian optimization (BO) [16]. BO deals with the optimization of black-box functions. A black-box is a function whose analytical expression is unknown. Hence, its gradients are not accessible. It is very expensive to evaluate and the function evaluations are potentially noisy. The estimation of the generalization error of ML algorithms is considered to be a black-box function. We find other applications in structure learning of probabilistic graphical models [2] or even subjective tasks as suggesting better recipes [4]. When not only one but several black-boxes are optimized, we deal with the Multi-objective BO scenario [9]. If these objectives need to be optimized under the presence of constraints, we deal with the constrained multi-objective scenario [5]. BO suggest one point per evaluation, but it also can suggest several points in the constrained multi-objective scenario [6]. Typically, these problems involve the optimization of less than 4 objectives. Many objective optimization has dealt with the optimization of more than 4 objectives [3]. This scenario has not been targeted by BO. An approach to solve this scenario is to get rid of objectives that can be explained through the other objectives. In BO, these objectives are modelled by GPs. If we had a similarity measure of the predictive distribution computed by a GP over an input space $\mathcal{X}$, we could use it to propose an approach for the many objective BO scenario. This is precisely the motivation for this paper: proposing a specialist GP predictive distribution similarity metric to be used in the many objective BO scenario.

The purpose of our measure is to detect a GP that is so similar to another GP that we can stop fitting it in many objective BO. Hence, we cannot just apply the KL divergence, as it is just a similarity measure of probability distributions. Let $\boldsymbol{\theta}$ represent the set of parameters of a distribution $\mathcal{P}$. The KL divergence between two probability density functions $p(\boldsymbol{\theta})$ and $q(\boldsymbol{\theta})$ over continuous variables is given by the following expression:

$$\mathrm{KL}(p(\boldsymbol{\theta})\|q(\boldsymbol{\theta})) = \int_{-\infty}^{\infty} p(\boldsymbol{\theta}) \log(\frac{p(\boldsymbol{\theta})}{q(\boldsymbol{\theta})}) d\boldsymbol{\theta} \,. \tag{1}$$

As we can see, KL is not focused on things like the importance of the point and its neighbourhood that maximizes the objective function $f(\mathbf{x})$ but in all the probability distribution support. Our measure differs from KL divergence in the fact that we focus on particular characteristics of the GP predictive distribution that are relevant for discarding a GP in a hypothetical many objective BO scenario.

In this work, we focus on comparing GP predictive distributions, as it is the arguably most widely used model in BO [16]. Nevertheless, our measure could also be applied to the predictive distributions of Bayesian neural networks or Random forests, widening its applicability.

The paper is organized as follows. First, we briefly review the fundamental concepts of GPs. These concepts will be useful to better understand the purpose of our proposed measure. Then, we include a section describing our proposed similarity measure. We add empirical evidence of the practical use of this measure in an experiments section. Lastly, we illustrate conclusions about this work and further lines of research.

2   Gaussian Processes

A Gaussian Process (GP) is a collection of random variables (of potentially infinite size), any finite number of which have (consistent) joint Gaussian distributions [15]. We can also think of GPs as defining a distribution over functions where inference takes place directly in the space of functions [15]. A GP can be used for regression of a function $f(\mathbf{x})$.

Let $\mathbf{X} = (\mathbf{x}_1, ... \mathbf{x}_N)^T$ be the training matrix and $\mathbf{y} = (y_1, ..., y_N)^T$ be a vector of labels to predict. We define as a dataset $\mathcal{D} = \{(\mathbf{x}_i, y_i) | i = 1, ..., n\}$ the set of labeled instances. A GP is fully characterized by a zero mean and a covariance function $k(\mathbf{x}, \mathbf{x}')$, that is, $f(\mathbf{x}) \sim \mathcal{GP}(\mathbf{0}, k(\mathbf{x}, \mathbf{x}'))$.

Given a set of observed data $\mathcal{D} = \{(\mathbf{x}_i, y_i) | i = 1, ..., n\}$, where $y_i = f(\mathbf{x}_i) + \epsilon_i$ with ϵ_i some additive Gaussian noise, a GP builds a predictive distribution for the potential values of $f(\mathbf{x})$ at a new input point $\mathbf{x}^\star$. This distribution is Gaussian. The GP mean, $\mu(\boldsymbol{x})$, is usually set to 0. Namely, $p(f(\mathbf{x}^\star) | \mathbf{y}) = \mathcal{N}(f(\mathbf{x}^\star) | \mu(\mathbf{x}^\star), v(\mathbf{x}^\star))$, where the mean $\mu(\mathbf{x}^\star)$ and variance $v(\mathbf{x}^\star)$ are respectively given by:

$$\mu(\mathbf{x}^\star) = \mathbf{k}_\star^T (\mathbf{K} + \sigma^2 \mathbf{I})^{-1} \mathbf{y}, \tag{2}$$

$$v(\mathbf{x}^\star) = k(\mathbf{x}_\star, \mathbf{x}_\star) - \mathbf{k}_\star^T (\mathbf{K} + \sigma^2 \mathbf{I})^{-1} \mathbf{k}_\star, \tag{3}$$

where $\mathbf{y} = (y_1, ..., y_N)^T$ is a vector with the observations collected so far; σ^2 is the variance of the additive Gaussian noise ϵ_i; $\mathbf{k}_\star = \mathbf{k}(\mathbf{x}_\star)$ is a N-dimensional vector with the prior covariances between the test point $f(\mathbf{x}^\star)$ and each of the training points $f(\mathbf{x}_i)$; and $\mathbf{K}$ is a $N \times N$ matrix with the prior covariances among each $f(\mathbf{x}_i)$, for $i = 1, ..., N$. Each element $\mathbf{K}_{ij} = k(\mathbf{x}_i, \mathbf{x}_j)$ of the matrix $\mathbf{K}$ is given by the covariance function between each of the training points $\mathbf{x}_i$ and $\mathbf{x}_j$ where $i, j = 1, ..., N$ and N is the total number of training points. The particular characteristics assumed for $f(\mathbf{x})$ (e.g., level of smoothness, additive noise, etc.) are specified by the covariance function $k(\mathbf{x}, \mathbf{x}')$ of the GP. A popular example of covariance function is the squared exponential, given by:

$$k(\mathbf{x}, \mathbf{x}') = \sigma_f^2 \exp\left(-\frac{r^2}{2\ell^2}\right) + \sigma_n^2 \delta_{pq}, \tag{4}$$

where r is the Euclidean distance between $\mathbf{x}$ and $\mathbf{x}'$, ℓ is a hyper-parameter known as length-scale that controls the smoothness of the functions generated from the GP, σ_f^2 is the amplitude parameter or signal variance that controls the range of variability of the GP samples and $\sigma_n^2 \delta_{pq}$ is the noise variance that applies when the covariance function is computed to the same point $k(\mathbf{x}, \mathbf{x})$. Those are hyper-parameters of the GP. Let $\boldsymbol{\theta}$ be the set of all those hyper-parameters. We can find point estimates for the hyper-parameters $\boldsymbol{\theta}$ of the GP via optimizing the log marginal likelihood. The marginal likelihood is given by the following expression:

$$\log p(\mathbf{y}|\mathcal{X}, \boldsymbol{\theta}) = -\frac{1}{2}\mathbf{y}^T(\mathbf{K} + \sigma_n^2 I)^{-1}\mathbf{y} - \frac{1}{2}\log|\mathbf{K} + \sigma_n^2 I| - \frac{n}{2}\log 2\pi. \quad (5)$$

The previous analytical expression can be optimized to obtain a point estimate $\boldsymbol{\theta}^\star$ for the hyper-parameters $\boldsymbol{\theta}$. We can optimize it through a local optimizer such as L-BFGS-B [19] and via the analytical expression of the marginal likelihood gradient $\nabla_{\boldsymbol{\theta}} \log(\mathbf{y}|\mathbf{X}, \boldsymbol{\theta}) = (\partial \log(\mathbf{y}|\mathbf{X}, \boldsymbol{\theta}/\partial\theta_1, ..., \partial \log(\mathbf{y}|\mathbf{X}, \boldsymbol{\theta})/\partial\theta_M)^T$ whose partial derivatives are given by:

$$\frac{\partial}{\partial\theta_j}\log(\mathbf{y}|\mathbf{X}, \boldsymbol{\theta}) = \frac{1}{2}\mathbf{y}^T\mathbf{K}^{-1}\frac{\partial\mathbf{K}}{\partial\theta_j}\mathbf{K}^{-1}\mathbf{y} - \frac{1}{2}\mathrm{tr}(\mathbf{K}^{-1}\frac{\partial\mathbf{K}}{\partial\theta_j})$$

$$= \frac{1}{2}\mathrm{tr}((\boldsymbol{\alpha}\boldsymbol{\alpha}^T - \mathbf{K}^{-1})\frac{\partial\mathbf{K}}{\partial\theta_j}), \quad (6)$$

where $\boldsymbol{\alpha} = \boldsymbol{K}^{-1}\mathbf{y}$ and M is the number of hyper-parameters.

3   The Similarity Measure

Let $f(\mathbf{x})$, $g(\mathbf{x})$ be two GPs. Let us work under the assumption that their covariance functions $k(\mathbf{x}, \mathbf{x})$ have similar analytical expressions (e.g., both are squared exponential functions). Given a set $\mathbf{X}_\star$ of input points, we can compute $\mu_f(\mathbf{X}_\star)$ and $\mu_g(\mathbf{X}_\star)$, the predicted mean vectors for each process, as well as $v_f(\mathbf{X}_\star(\mathbf{X}_\star)$ and $v_g(\mathbf{X}_\star)$, their covariance matrices.

We now define a notion of distance between these two processes, firstly presenting its mathematical expression:

$$\begin{aligned} d(f(\mathbf{x}), g(\mathbf{x})) = &\varepsilon_1 d_1\left(T(\mu_f(\mathbf{X}_\star)), \mu_g(\mathbf{X}_\star), \delta\right) \\ &+ \varepsilon_2 d_2\left(v_f(\mathbf{X}_\star), v_g(\mathbf{X}_\star)\right) + \\ &(1 - \varepsilon_1 - \varepsilon_2)\left(1 - \rho\left(\mu_f(\mathbf{X}_\star), \mu_g(\mathbf{X}_\star)\right)\right). \end{aligned} \quad (7)$$

As it can be seen, the measure is given following a weighted sum model (WSM [18]). The WSM contains three components to which we will refer as

$$\begin{aligned} s_1 &= \varepsilon_1 d_1\left(T(\mu_f(\mathbf{X}_\star)), \mu_g(\mathbf{X}_\star)\delta\right), \\ s_2 &= \varepsilon_2 d_2\left(v_f(\mathbf{X}_\star), v_g(\mathbf{X}_\star)\right), \\ s_3 &= (1 - \varepsilon_1 - \varepsilon_2)\left(1 - \rho\left(\mu_f(\mathbf{X}_\star), \mu_g(\mathbf{X}_\star)\right)\right). \end{aligned} \quad (8)$$

The objective of s_1 and s_3 is to describe the distance between both mean vectors, while s_2 aims to reflect the distance between the covariance matrices. We will now analyze each of these components and their respective parameters.

The first one, s_1, is given in terms of a tolerance δ, a transformation function T and a distance function d_1 between the mean vectors.

The election of T describes when two mean vectors $\mu_f(\mathbf{X}_\star) \neq \mu_g(\mathbf{X}_\star)$ should be considered equal. For example, since we will be optimizing these vectors, if $\mu_f(\mathbf{X}_\star) = 2\mu_g(\mathbf{X}_\star)$, their critical points will be the exact same and we might want to consider them as a single vector. Although T can be chosen by the user depending on their needs, the proposed implementation provides a function $T(\mu_f(\mathbf{X}_\star)) = a\mu_f(\mathbf{X}_\star) + b\mathbf{1}$, where $a > 0$ and b are scalars chosen with the least squares method to give the best fit of $\mu_f(\mathbf{X}_\star)$ onto $\mu_g(\mathbf{X}_\star)$. This transformation reflects the fact that two vectors that are proportional and whose difference is constant behave in the same way in terms of optimization.

With function $d_1(\cdot)$, the user is able to choose in which way they want to measure the distance between $T(\mu_f(\mathbf{X}_\star))$ and $\mu_g(\mathbf{X}_\star)$. Several options are given to the user in our implementation, each of them being convenient depending on the nature of the problem modeled by the GP. Some of these options are to define d_1 as the number (or percentage) of points where $T(\mu_f(\mathbf{X}_\star)) \neq \mu_g(\mathbf{X}_\star)$, or as a p-norm ($d_1 = \|\mu_g(\mathbf{X}_\star) - T(\mu_f(\mathbf{X}_\star))\|_p$) which includes euclidean norm, infinity norm, etc.

Lastly, with δ the user is allowed to change the desired level of tolerance given to d_1, i.e. the distance is calculated only among the vectors' elements where the chosen d_1 is greater than δ in its element-wise operations. For example, if we chose a 1-norm as d_1, s_1 would be computed as $\sum_{|\mu_g - T(\mu_f)| > \delta} |\mu_g(\mathbf{X}_\star) - T(\mu_f(\mathbf{X}_\star))|$.

The other weighted sum term used to compare the two mean vectors is s_3. It is the only fixed term in the sum, and it represents the Pearson correlation coefficient between the GP means.

This coefficient is defined as

$$\rho(\mu_f(\mathbf{X}_\star), \mu_g(\mathbf{X}_\star)) = \frac{\mathbb{E}[(\mu_f(\mathbf{X}_\star) - \overline{\mu_f(\mathbf{X}_\star)})(\mu_g(\mathbf{X}_\star) - \overline{\mu_y(\mathbf{X}_\star)})]}{\sigma_{\mu_f}\sigma_{\mu_g}}, \qquad (9)$$

where $\overline{\mu(\cdot)}$ denotes the mean value of a vector μ and σ_μ is its standard deviation.

The reason we were first interested in this operator is because of its interpretation. The coefficient $\rho(\mu_f(\mathbf{X}_\star), \mu_g(\mathbf{X}_\star))$ ranges from -1 to 1. If it equals 1, there is a (positive) linear equation describing $\mu_g(\mathbf{X}_\star)$ in terms of $\mu_f(\mathbf{X}_\star)$; if it equals -1, this linear equation has a negative slope and, when it is 0, no linear correlation between $\mu_f(\mathbf{X}_\star)$ and $\mu_g(\mathbf{X}_\star)$ exists.

Moreover, following Eq. (9), ρ increases whenever $\mu_f(\mathbf{X}_\star)$ and $\mu_g(\mathbf{X}_\star)$ both increase or decrease. It decreases when their growth behaviour is different. This is very valuable for our problem, since we need to identify whether two vectors are increasing and decreasing in a similar fashion, i.e., their maximums and minimums lie around the same positions.

We found this to be the most accurate way of detecting similar processes, since it detects that sample vectors of functions like x^6 and x^2, which would a priori seem very different using any conventional vector distance (one grows much faster than the other) behave essentially the same: they both decrease from $-\infty$ to 0, have a minimum in 0 and increase towards ∞.

Lastly, the addend s_2 is intended to measure the distance between both predictive variances, and therefore any matrix norm could be used for this purpose.

We have not found the matrices distance to be significant when it comes to deciding whether two GPs should be optimized analogously, although this might be because of working under the assumption that $f(\mathbf{X}_\star)$ and $g(\mathbf{X}_\star)$ have similar covariance functions. In case the user wants to make use of the matrices similarity, note that entrywise matrix norms should be preferred over the ones induced by vector norms because of their lower computational cost [8].

As future work, these matrices could be used to measure the uncertainty of the distance between two GPs, since they represent the uncertainty of the GPs' predictions.

4   Experiments

For all the experiments, we have set the parameter $\delta = 0$ and, since we didn't found the covariance matrices distance to be significant under our hypothesis, we used $\varepsilon_1 = 0.25$ and $\varepsilon_2 = 0$ (therefore ρ's weight is 0.75). For the transformation T, the previously explained linear transformation using the least squares method was used. We have chosen d_1 to be the average relative distance between the points in the two mean vectors, i.e., the mean of the vector given by $|T(\mu_f(\mathbf{X}_\star)) - \mu_g(\mathbf{X}_\star)|$ divided by the subtraction of the greatest element found in the two vectors minus the smallest.

For the following examples, various GPs were fitted taking sample vectors from benchmark functions. We will now discuss some of the results obtained by applying our measure to find the distance between them.

We will start with some uni-dimensional toy functions. We have chosen to compare three GPs from which we know that two of them are very similar and that the third one behaves differently from the other two. A plot of their mean vectors can be seen in Fig. 1. The first one models a Michalewicz function (defines as $f_1(x) = -\sin x \left(\sin \frac{x^2}{\pi}\right)^{2m}$) with parameter $m = 50$, the second one a Michalewicz function with $m = 100$ and the third one models a parabola x^2. The correlation between the predicted means of the two Michalwicz GPs is 0.97, and the average relative distance between them is 0.02. In total, the distance calculated by our measure is 0.02 over 1, i.e., these GPs are very similar according to our function. On the other hand, when comparing the Michalewicz GP that has $m = 100$ with the parabola, we obtain a correlation of 0.12, which reflects how different their growth behaviour is, and an average relative distance of 0.27. In total a distance of 0.72 over 1.

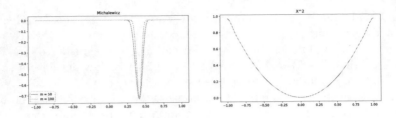

Fig. 1. Toy functions for one dimension

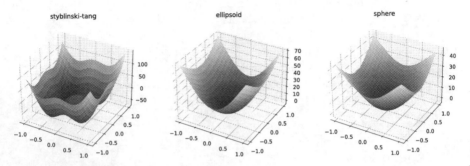

Fig. 2. Bowl-shaped functions

We now compare three 2D bowl-shaped processes: one of them modelling a Styblinski-Tang function, another one an ellipsoid and the third one a sphere.

The Syblinski-Tang function is given by $f_2(\mathbf{x}) = \frac{1}{2} \sum_{i=1}^{2} \left(x_i^4 - 16x_i^2 + 5x_i \right)$, the ellipsoid is $f_3(\mathbf{x}) = \sum_{i=1}^{2} \sum_{j=1}^{i} x_j^2$ and the sphere function is $f_4(\mathbf{x}) = x_1^2 + x_2^2$ Since the three are bowl shaped, they are somewhat similar, but from Fig. 2 we can tell that Styblinski-Tang is slightly different from the others. Indeed, when we compare the sphere and the ellipsoid processes we obtain a 0.94 correlation between their predicted mean vectors, and 0.06 is their average relative distance. Overall, the distance is 0.05 which means these two functions are very similar. In contrast, when we compare the ellipsoid with the Styblinski-Tang process, we obtain a correlation of 0.74: a value which is close to 1, reflecting the fact that both shapes are similar in a way, but not as close as in the previous comparison because the Styblinski-Tang bowl is different from the ellipsoid. The average relative distance is 0.13 (again a value which is greater than before) and the total distance of 0.22 over 1, which shows that these processes are similar, but not as much as the previous ones.

We will now compare two processes modelling two functions that we know are not similar, illustrated in Fig. 3. The first one is a Griewank function $f_5(\mathbf{x}) = \frac{1}{4000} \left(x_1^2 + x_2^2 \right) - \cos(x_1) \cos\left(\frac{x_2}{\sqrt{2}} \right) + 1$, and the second one a levy function $f_6(\mathbf{x}) = \sin^2(\pi w_1) + (w_1 - 1)^2 \left(1 + 10 \sin^2(\pi w_1 + 1) \right) + (w_2 - 1)^2 \left(1 + \sin^2(2\pi w_2) \right)$ where $w_i = 1 + (x_i - 1)\frac{1}{4}$.

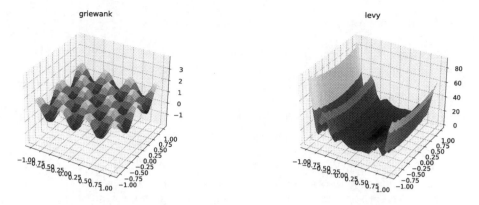

Fig. 3. Griewank and Levy functions

Because of how different their shapes are, the correlation between the predicted mean is 0.04, almost no correlation at all. Their average relative distance is 0.16, and the distance between the processes is 0.75 over 1.

Finally, we will be comparing some Ackley functions. Recall that an ackley function depending on parameters a, b and c is given by

$$f_7(\mathbf{x}) = -a \exp\left(-b\sqrt{\frac{1}{d}\sum_{i=1}^{2} x_i^2}\right) - \exp\left(-\frac{1}{2}\sum_{i=1}^{2} \cos(cx_i)\right) + a + e$$

We first compare two processes with fixed $a = 20$ and $b = 0.2$. The parameter c equals π for one process and 6π for the other, which results in unsimilar predicted means plots as can be seen in Fig. 4. The correlation between them is 0.31, and the average relative distance 0.15, giving an overall distance of 0.55 over 1. Lastly, we compare two Ackley processes which, despite having different a values, have a very similar shape (Fig. 4). We chose $b = 0.2, c = 2\pi$ and $a = 70$ for one process and $a = 100$ for the other. Their correlation is very close to 1, 0.98, and their average relative distance is 0.01. A total distance of 0.01, which means these processes are indeed very similar in their shape.

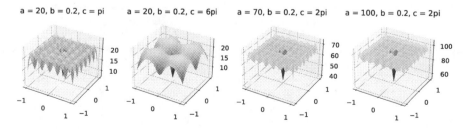

Fig. 4. Ackley functions

5   Conclusions

In this paper, we have proposed a similarity metric for GP predictive distributions in order to be used in a many objective BO scenario [10]. Thanks to this metric, we are able to measure how similar are the predictions given by two GP predictive distributions. We have illustrated the results of this measure in a set of synthetic and benchmark functions. This measure will be used in multi-objective BO, that could be parallel or constrained, when there are more than 3 objectives.

The metric can also incorporate the uncertainty of the GP prediction mean. The intuition is that the areas whose uncertainty on the prediction is low need to add more weight that unexplored areas. Suppose that two GP predictive distributions differ in their predictions in an unexplored area. It is fair to assume that they may be more similar than if they differ on an explored area. We intend to incorporate this property to the GP similarity measure in future work. Another possible use of this metric is its application for the cognitive architectures of brain inspired autonomous robots [7]. In this architecture, every objective can model a particular emotion, that conditions the policy of the robot. The robot wants to simultaneously optimize conflicting emotions like happiness, social contacts or being full of energy. As human beings are only phenomenally conscious of a small set of emotions in every moment, we can imitate that behavior by discarding redundant emotions through this metric and making the global workspace only aware of the most relevant emotions [13,17].

Acknowledgments. Authors gratefully acknowledge the use of the facilities of Centro de Computacion Cientifica (CCC) at Universidad Autónoma de Madrid. The authors also acknowledge financial support from Spanish Plan Nacional I+D+i, grants TIN2016-76406-P and from PID2019-106827GB-I00 /AEI /10.13039/501100011033.

References

1. Bishop, C.M.: Pattern Recognition and Machine Learning. Springer, New York (2006)
2. Córdoba, I., Garrido-Merchán, E.C., Hernández-Lobato, D., Bielza, C., Larranaga, P.: Bayesian optimization of the PC algorithm for learning Gaussian Bayesian networks. In: Herrera, F., et al. (eds.) Conference of the Spanish Association for Artificial Intelligence, pp. 44–54. Springer, Cham (2018). https://doi.org/10.1007/978-3-030-00374-6
3. Fleming, P.J., Purshouse, R.C., Lygoe, R.J.: Many-objective optimization: an engineering design perspective. In: Coello Coello, C.A., Hernández Aguirre, A., Zitzler, E. (eds.) EMO 2005. LNCS, vol. 3410, pp. 14–32. Springer, Heidelberg (2005). https://doi.org/10.1007/978-3-540-31880-4_2
4. Garrido-Merchán, E.C., Albarca-Molina, A.: Suggesting cooking recipes through simulation and Bayesian optimization. In: Yin, H., Camacho, D., Novais, P., Tallón-Ballesteros, A.J. (eds.) IDEAL 2018. LNCS, vol. 11314, pp. 277–284. Springer, Cham (2018). https://doi.org/10.1007/978-3-030-03493-1_30

5. Garrido-Merchán, E.C., Hernández-Lobato, D.: Predictive entropy search for multi-objective Bayesian optimization with constraints. Neurocomputing **361**, 50–68 (2019)
6. Garrido-Merchán, E.C., Hernández-Lobato, D.: Parallel predictive entropy search for multi-objective Bayesian optimization with constraints. arXiv preprint arXiv:2004.00601 (2020)
7. Garrido-Merchán, E.C., Molina, M., Mendoza, F.M.: An artificial consciousness model and its relations with philosophy of mind. arXiv preprint arXiv:2011.14475 (2020)
8. Hendrickx, J.M., Olshevsky, A.: Matrix P-norms are NP-hard to approximate if p $\neq$ 1,2,∞ (2009)
9. Hernández-Lobato, D., Hernandez-Lobato, J., Shah, A., Adams, R.: Predictive entropy search for multi-objective Bayesian optimization. In: International Conference on Machine Learning, pp. 1492–1501 (2016)
10. Ishibuchi, H., Tsukamoto, N., Nojima, Y.: Evolutionary many-objective optimization: a short review. In: 2008 IEEE Congress on Evolutionary Computation (IEEE World Congress on Computational Intelligence), pp. 2419–2426. IEEE (2008)
11. Lee, J., Bahri, Y., Novak, R., Schoenholz, S.S., Pennington, J., Sohl-Dickstein, J.: Deep neural networks as Gaussian processes (2018)
12. MacKay, D.J.C.: Introduction to Gaussian processes. NATO ASI Ser. F Comput. Syst. Sci. **168**, 133–166 (1998)
13. Merchán E.C.G., Molina, M.: A machine consciousness architecture based on deep learning and Gaussian processes. arXiv preprint arXiv:2002.00509 (2020)
14. Murphy, K.P.: Machine Learning: A Probabilistic Perspective. MIT Press, Cambridge (2012)
15. Rasmussen, C.E.: Gaussian processes in machine learning. In: Bousquet, O., von Luxburg, U., Rätsch, G. (eds.) ML -2003. LNCS (LNAI), vol. 3176, pp. 63–71. Springer, Heidelberg (2004). https://doi.org/10.1007/978-3-540-28650-9_4
16. Snoek, J., Larochelle, H., Adams, R.P.: Practical Bayesian optimization of machine learning algorithms. Adv. Neural Inf. Process. Syst. **25**, 2951–2959 (2012)
17. Soto, F.M.M.: Artificial conciousness: an approach to autonomous agents based in a global workspace model. Science **385**(6362), 486–492 (2017)
18. Triantaphyllou, E.: Multi-Criteria Decision Making Methods: A Comparative Study. Applied Optimization 44. Kluwer Academic Publishers, Dordrecht (2000)
19. Zhu, C., Byrd, R.H., Peihuang, L., Nocedal, J.: Algorithm 778: L-BFGS-B: Fortran subroutines for large-scale bound-constrained optimization. ACM Trans. Math. Softw. (TOMS) **23**(4), 550–560 (1997)

Towards Automatic Bayesian Optimization: A First Step Involving Acquisition Functions

Luis C. Jariego Pérez and Eduardo C. Garrido Merchán[✉]

Universidad Autónoma de Madrid, Madrid, Spain
luis.jariego@estudiante.uam.es, eduardo.garrido@uam.es

Abstract. Bayesian Optimization (BO) is the state of the art technique for the optimization of black boxes, i.e., functions where we do not have access to their analytical expression nor its gradients, are expensive to evaluate and its evaluation is noisy. A BO application is automatic hyperparameter tuning of machine learning algorithms. BO methodologies have hyperparameters that need to be configured such as the surrogate model or the acquisition function (AF). Bad decisions over the configuration of these hyperparameters implies obtaining bad results. Typically, these hyperparameters are tuned by making assumptions of the objective function that we want to evaluate but there are scenarios where we do not have any prior information. In this paper, we propose an attempt of automatic BO by exploring several heuristics that automatically tune the BO AF. We illustrate the effectiveness of these heurisitcs in a set of benchmark problems and a hyperparameter tuning problem.

1 Introduction

Optimization problems, which task assuming minimization is to retrieve the minimizer $\mathbf{x}^* = \arg\max f(\mathbf{x}) \mid f : \mathbb{R}^n \to \mathbb{R}, \quad \mathbf{x}^*, \mathbf{x} \in \mathcal{X} \in \mathbb{R}^n$, are often solved easily when we have access to the gradient of the function that we want to optimize. Nevertheless, there exist a plethora of scenarios where we do not have access to these gradients. Typically, metaheuristics [12] like genetic algorithms [5] are used in this setting. Genetic algorithms and metaheuristics in general are useful when the evaluation of the function is cheap whether the cheap definiton refers to computational time or other resources such as the budget of the optimization process. This is not always the case. For example, we may consider an scenario when the function to optimize requires to configure a robot [3] or training a deep neural network [9]. We can not afford in these scenarios a high number of evaluations. Ideally, we would like to consider a method that suggest as an approximation $\hat{\mathbf{x}}^* \approx \mathbf{x}^*$ of the optimum of the problem in the least number of evaluations as possible. An approximated solution to the true minimizer of the problem would be one with low absolute regret at the end of the optimization process $r = |f(\hat{\mathbf{x}}) - f(\mathbf{x})|$, i.e. a local optima, not necessarily close, w.r.t. some distance metric in $\mathbb{R}^n$, in the input space to the minimizer.

© Springer Nature Switzerland AG 2021
E. Alba et al. (Eds.): CAEPIA 2021, LNAI 12882, pp. 160–169, 2021.
https://doi.org/10.1007/978-3-030-85713-4_16

Moreover, we can even consider a more complicated scenario that the one described if the function that we want to optimize $f(\cdot)$ is modelled as a latent variable that we cannot observed as it has been contaminated by some random variable, for example, a gaussian random variable, hence observing $y = f(\cdot) + \mathcal{N}(0, \sigma)$ where σ is i.i.d. $\forall \mathbf{x} \in \mathcal{X}$. In other words, for any two similar points of the input space we observe a, without loss of generality, gaussian distribution $\mathcal{N}(0, \sigma)$. Functions whose analytical expression is unknown, the evaluations are costly and the observation is contaminated with noise are often referred to as black boxes. Non convex Black box optimization has been dealt with success by BO methodologies [2], being the current state of the art approach.

The most popular example of such an optimization is the task of automatic Machine Learning tuning of the hyperparameters or the hyperparameter problem of machine learning algorithms [20], such as the PC algorithm [4], but also all kinds of subjective tasks like Suggesting Cooking Recipes [7] or other applications belonging to robotics, renewable energies and more [19].

Automatic Hyperparameter Tuning of Machine Learning algorithms is a desirable process that BO can tackle, but the BO procedure also have hyperparameters that need to be fixed a priori. As we are going to see in more detail in the next section, BO needs to fit a probabilistic surrogate model M, such as a Gaussian Process (GP) [18], in every iteration to the observations. This GP or other model have a set of hyperparameters θ associated with it. An Acquisition Function (AF) $\alpha(\cdot) : \mathbb{R}^n \rightarrow \mathbb{R}^n$ is then built in every iteration from the GP, or other model, that tries to represent an optimal tradeoff between the uncertainty given by the probabilistic model in every point of the input space and its prediction. The AF is a free hyperparameter of BO and it could be a bad choice depending on the problem. There are an infinite number of AFs $\alpha \in \mathcal{A}$, being $\mathcal{A}$ the functional space of possible AFs. There is no single AF that is the best for every problem. A bad choice on these and other hyperparameters of BO lead to bad results in the optimization process. Hence, we ideally need a process that performs automatic BO without the need of also hyperparametrize the BO algorithm. This work tries to attempt this problem and starts dealing with the automatic decision of which AF should we use by performing different heuristics. We hypothesize that an automatic BO algorithm will deliver better results than having to manually tune the hyperparameters of BO in problems where we do not have prior information about them.

This paper is organized as follows, in Sect. 2 we introduce the fundamental theory of BO and GP. Then, in Sect. 3, we exhibit our proposed approaches for BO. We introduce a set of benchmark experiments and a real experiment to show the utility of our approach in an experiments section. Finally, a conclusions and further work section summarizes the paper.

2   BO Issues for Automatic Optimization

The BO algorithm is executed in an iterative fashion, where it uses a probabilistic surrogate model $M(\theta)$ as a prior over functions $p(F)$ which functional space $\mathcal{F}$

contains all the hypotheses about the objective function $f(\cdot)$ that we want to get the maximum of $\mathbf{x}^* = \arg\max f(\mathbf{x})$. This model M, hyperparametrized by a set θ, is typically a GP [18], but other models such as Bayesian Neural Networks [21] and Random Forests [15] are also used. In order for BO to work, we need to assume that the function f can be sampled from it $p(F)$. Hence, depending on the problem, different models may be optimal and even some of them may led to bad result, being hence the model and its hyperparameters a hyperparameter of BO. For example, if we consider the popular GP for a problem, if the objective function is not stationary and we do not do any transformation of the input space to treat this property of the objective function, the GP does not serve as a prior for that function and independently of the other hyperparameters of the BO algorithm and of the number of evaluations, we are going to retrieve bad results.

Even by choosing the same probabilistic surrogate model M we need to define the correct hyperparameters $\theta \in \Theta$ for that model. In the typical case of a GP, a wrong choice of kernel can imply that the function that we want to optimize is no longer on the functional space that the GP defines. Even by optimizing the rest of the GP hyperparameters by a maximum likelihood procedure or taking an ensemble of different GPs with hyperparameters sampled from a hyperparmeter distribution, as they depend on the choice of kernel, that optimization procedure would be useless, leading again the BO algorithm to bad results.

BO uses the predictive distribution of the model in every point $\mathbf{x}$ of the input space $\mathcal{X}$ to build an AF $\alpha(M(\mathcal{X}|\theta))$. This AF represents the utility of evaluating every point $\mathbf{x} \in \mathcal{X}$ in order to retrieve the optimum of the objective function in the, in the standard BO algorithm, next step of the iteration, being a myopic optimization procedure. The literature contains different AFs that try to represent the optimal trade off between exploration of the space areas that have not been yet explored and the exploitation of previously good evaluated results. Some of these AFs are the following ones:

Probability of Improvement: $\mathrm{PI}(\mathbf{x}) = \Phi(\dfrac{f(\mathbf{x}_{best}) - \mu(\mathbf{x})}{\sigma(\mathbf{x})})$. This AF basically represents, for each point of the space, the probability of this point to be better if evaluated than the best observed value retrieved so far.

Expected Improvement: $\mathrm{EI}(\mathbf{x}) = \sigma(\mathbf{x})(\gamma(\mathbf{x})\Phi(\gamma(\mathbf{x})) + \phi(\gamma(\mathbf{x})))$. The previous function does not take into account, for every point and sample function of the probabilistic model, how much does the point improve the maximum value found. Expected improvement represents a theoretical improvement over the probability of improvement by considering this quantity.

Lower Confidence Bound: $\mathrm{LCB}(\mathbf{x}) = \mu(\mathbf{x}) - \kappa\sigma(\mathbf{x})$. This AF is representing a tradeoff between the prediction of the probabilistic model in each point of the space $\mu(\mathbf{x})$ and exploration over unknown areas given by the uncertainty of the model in each point of the space $\sigma(\mathbf{x})$. The κ parameter assigns a weight for each quantity.

But there are a lot more, in fact, we could generate an infinite number of possible AFs. As in the case of the probablistic surrogate model, the decision of the chosen AF conditions the optimization. For example, if the function is monotonic, we do not need a heavy exploratory based AF. On the other way, if the objective function is contaminated by a high level of noise, the exploitation criterion is practically useless. There is no single best AF for every scenario, as the no free lunch theorem states [14].

for $t = 1, 2, 3, \ldots, max\_steps$ **do**

    1: Find the next point to evaluate by optimizing the AF:

    $\mathbf{x}_t = \arg \max_{\mathbf{x}} \quad \alpha(\mathbf{x}|\mathcal{D}_{1:t-1})$.

    2: Evaluate the black-box objective $f(\cdot)$ at $\mathbf{x}_t$: $y_t = f(\mathbf{x}_t) + \epsilon_t$.

    3: Augment the observed data $\mathcal{D}_{1:t} = \mathcal{D}_{1:t-1} \bigcup \{\mathbf{x}_t, y_t\}$.

    4: Update the GP model using $\mathcal{D}_{1:t}$.

end

Result: Optimize the mean of the GP to find the solution.

Algorithm 1: BO of a black-box objective function.

BO have more hyperparameters, as for example the optimization algorithm of the AF, typically a grid search over the space of the AF and a local optimization procedure such as the L-BFGS algorithm [6]. The sampling procedure for the hyperparameter distribution of the probabilistic surrogate model, the number of samples and more. Varying the values of those hyperparameters condition the quality of the final recommendation. We have observed that despite the fact that BO is an excellent optimization procedure, it is not automatic and we need to choose wisefully the hyperparameters. This is possible if we have prior knowledge about the objective function, but this is not a scenario that always happens.

Hence, we ideally need a procedure to search for the best BO hyperparameters, concretely the model and the acquisition, as the function is being optimized. This work is a first step towards this goal. We explore different simple heuristics to determine if they affect to the optimization behaviour. We have only focused on the AFs, but the selection of a particular probabilistic surrogate model while the optimization is being performed is also an essential issue to deliver automatic BO.

The next section will illustrate the first possible methods that we can execute to perform a simple search of the possible AFs belonging to the set $\mathcal{A}$ of all possible AFs to build from a probabilistic surrogate model.

3   Heuristic Driven Bayesian Optimization

In this work, we begin to explore the possibilities of combining AFs in order to build criteria that satisfies the majority of the problems or that it adapts to the optimization process.

Formally, if we have a set $\mathcal{A}$ of AFs, we are going to build criteria that combines these AFs.

We hypothesize that different GP states of an underlying objective function need different AFs in order to discover which is the optimum of the underlying function. Which is in contrast to the typical BO algorithm that just uses the same AF for all the iterations.

We propose, given the same probabilistic surrogate model, using different AFs or linear combinations between AFs in the same BO algorithm. For every iteration, a different AF will be used, defining now for BO problems not an AF as in standard BO but an AF generator $\mathcal{G}$ that generates for every iteration $t = 1..N$ a different AF $\alpha_t(\cdot) \in \mathcal{A}$. These generators can use any possible AF as seeds for the generation of AFs in every iteration. We illustrate different approaches for an AF generator that are basically heuristics that search the best possible AF.

In practice, we have explored combinations of Standard AFs used in the BO literature. We formulate the hyperparameter tuning of AFs for BO as a search problem and start tackling it with heuristics to observe how the global behaviour of BO is conditioned.

We propose the following approaches over the AFs described in the previous section. As it has been described, we could use an extended set of AFs like including PES [13], MES [22] or any other. We also hypothesize that the behaviour of the heuristics will improve with the addition of more and more diverse AFs to the seed set of AFs that we consider. The heuristics that we propose are, in first place, the Random criteria, basically defined by placing un uniform distribution U over the functional set of AFs $\mathcal{A}$ and sampling from it in every iteration. For every iteration a different AF $\alpha(\cdot)_t$ is going to be executed. We hypothesize that the optimization process will be enriched by the random execution of different criteria, obtaining good results. In our case, as we only consider the EI, LCB and PI acquisitions, the criterion will be given by the following expression: $Rand(\mathbf{x}) = U(PI(\mathbf{x}), EI(\mathbf{x}), LCB(\mathbf{x}))$., but in the general case it would be: $Rand(\mathbf{x}) = U(\mathcal{A})$.

We could perform the same logic as in the Random case but performing a Sequential criterion. $Seq(\mathbf{x}, n_{iter}) = Cands(\mathbf{x})[n_{iter} mod(n_{cands})]$. We model here all the acquisitions in an ordered list and sample them sequentially, one acquisition for every iteration. We have proposed this two initial strategies in an analogy with respect to the grid search and random search, hypothesizing that they fully explore the set of seed AFs and enriching the optimizing process results.

If we assume that all the AFs can be valid in any time of the optimization process and retrieve different but interested results, then, a logical suggestion will be to consider a linear combination over all the considered AFs, that is the weighted AF criterion, defined by the following expression: $\alpha_w(\mathbf{x}|\mathcal{A}, \mathbf{w}) = \sum_{i=1}^{|\mathcal{A}|} w_i \alpha_i(\mathbf{x}) : \sum_{i=1}^{|\mathcal{A}|} w_i = 1$. In our particular case the weighted criterion function would be $\alpha_w(\mathbf{x}) = \kappa_{PI} PI(\mathbf{x}) + \kappa_{EI} EI(\mathbf{x}) + \kappa_{LCB} LCB(\mathbf{x})$.

Lastly, lots of metaheuristics and machine learning algorithms include mechanisms such as the mutation probability in genetic algorithms or dropout in deep neural networks that act as regularizers, enforcing exploration and preventing from overfitting, improving the results. We hypothesize that we can establish an analogy for the AF search so we introduce a noised criterion, that basically transforms the acquisition in a latent functional variable and contaminates it with i.i.d gaussian noise to enforce exploration: $f(\mathbf{x}) = g(\mathbf{x}) + acquisition\_noise \mathcal{N}(0, \mathbf{I})$.

All these approaches are heuristic but explore a space defined by the set $\mathcal{A}$. Our procedure combines AFs like this: The weighted AF criterion contains a weight for each AF to measure its the importance. This is a generalization of common BO but does not solve the automatic BO scenario. If, instead of being hardcoded by the user, these weights were adapted as the problem is being optimized or in function of the problem, the optimization would be automatic. As a first attempt towards automatic BO, we propose to use a Metaoptimization of the weights $\mathbf{w}$ using BO over the weight space $\mathcal{R}^{|\mathcal{A}|} \in [0,1]^{|\mathcal{A}|}$. We define a search space of $|\mathcal{A}|$ weights that are associated with their respective AFs. Then, we execute a standard BO procedure that gives us the weights that minimize the predicted error by the underlying BO algorithm. By performing this double loop, the weights are optimized and the underlying BO algorithm is automatic. Nevertheless, the upper BO algorithm still needs to be tuned but we can study several problems to adjust a reasonable prior over the weight space.

4   Experiments

We carry out several experiments to evaluate the performance of the described heuristics in the previous section. We also compare the approaches to a pure exploration method based on Random Search [1]. The set of seeds AFs and the proposed ones have been implemented in SkOpt [16]. In each experiment carried out in this section we report average results and the corresponding standard deviations. The results reported are averages over 100 repetitions of the corresponding experiment. Means and standard deviations are estimated using 200 bootstrap samples. The hyperparameters of the underlying GPs are maximized through maximum likelihood in the optimization process. The AF of each method is maximized through a grid search.

4.1   Benchmark Experiments

We test the proposed AFs and compare with GP-Hedge over a set of benchmark problems, namely, the Branin, 3-dimensional Hartmann and 3-dimensional Rastrigin functions. We plot the results in Figs. 1, 2 and 3.

   We can observe that, for the Branin function, the best method is the weighted AF optimized by the metaoptimization process. GP-Hedge method also delivers good results, tying at the end with the weighted AF. We hypothesize that the good behaviour of the ensemble AFs (weighted and hedge) is a consequence given by the fact that every seed adds some value in the problem. Separated, although, they do not provide good results.

   We observe a different behaviour in the Hartmann function, where only the pure exploitation AFs (EI and PI) report a good result. This happens due to the shape of Hartmann, where exploration is a bad strategy as with pure exploitation we can reach to the optimum. We can observe empirically that EI is better than PI as it considers the amount of improvement over the incumbent. Ensemble AFs, as they consider exploration or other criteria rather than EI and PI lose

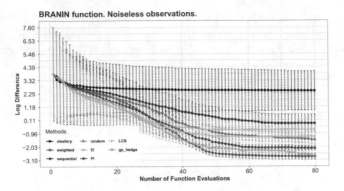

Fig. 1. Means and standard deviations of the log difference w.r.t the absolute regret of the maximizer of the different considered AFs in the Branin Function.

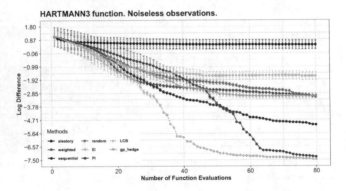

Fig. 2. Means and standard deviations of the log difference w.r.t the absolute regret of the maximizer of the different considered AFs in the Hartmann Function.

performance, but they are not as bad as LCB, which is not a good strategy here. This property of ensemble AFs guarantees that they are not as bad as the worst case in any scenario.

In the Rastrigin function, we can observe that the random methods do not perform well but the others tie, performing a better result. No AF seems to govern, maybe all locating just local optima of Rastrigin. The large standard deviations of the Rastrigin function may be explained for different reasons, first is the shape of the function with lots of local optima, each repetition may end in different points and hence the deviation is big. Other explanations are the optimization of the AF being done with a grid search. We need to perform a L-BGFS optimization of the maximum valued point retrieved by this search to discard the hypothesis that the large deviations are happening for local optima. Another important fact is to consider a hyperparameter distribution of the GPs to sample from it with an algorithm such as slice sampling instead of simply optimizing

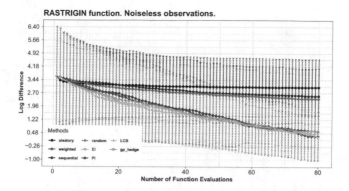

Fig. 3. Means and standard deviations of the log difference w.r.t the absolute regret of the maximizer of the different considered AFs in the Rastrigin Function.

the hyperparameters through maximum likelihood, incurring in overfitting of the model as BO performs a small number of evaluations.

4.2 Real Experiment

In this section we perform a hyperparameter tuning problem of the learning rate, minimum samples split and maximum tree depth of a Gradient Boosting Ensemble classifier on the Digits Dataset. We do not find the issues of the Rastrigin function in this problem as, typically, the shape of the estimation of the generalization error function for machine learning algorithms is smooth, so we expect that the retrieved results by BO in this case will not contain a high standard deviation and favour the weighted criterion. The results can be seen in Fig. 4.

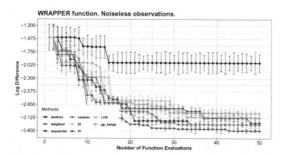

Fig. 4. Means and standard deviations of the log difference w.r.t a perfect classification error of the different considered AFs in the Hyperparameter Tuning of a Gradient Boosting Ensemble.

As we can see, the weighted criterion is the best one in this problem, that might contain some local optima and irregularities as the random search also work pretty well. Maybe due to certain combinations of parameters that generates good results. There is a lot more to do for automatic BO but the first necessary step towards that goal is to explore the set of all possible AF through, as in this case, generators of linear combinations of AFs that, in average, produce great results.

5   Conclusions and Further Work

The proposed approaches provide alternatives for Hyperparameter Tuning problems with respect to the standard AFs. There is still a lot of work to do for automatic BO, such as doing a similar approach as this one but with probabilistic graphical models and AF optimizers. In future work, we would like to build a dataset from a plethora of GP states and try to train a deep neural network that learns to predict which is the best AF to use or even the best point to consider given the dataset and the state of the current GP. We would like to test whether if the transformations made in the input space to deal with integer [8] and categorical-valued variables [10] change the behaviour of the given AF heuristics. The final purpose of this research is to employ automatic BO for the optimization of the hyperparameters of the machine learning architecture of the creative robots that exhibit human behaviour [11,17] to test machine consciousness hypotheses.

Acknowledgements. Authors gratefully acknowledge the use of the facilities of Centro de Computacion Cientifica (CCC) at Universidad Autónoma de Madrid. The authors also acknowledge financial support from Spanish Plan Nacional I+D+i, grants TIN2016-76406-P and from PID2019-106827GB-I00/AEI/10.13039/501100011033.

References

1. Bergstra, J., Bengio, Y.: Random search for hyper-parameter optimization. J. Mach. Learn. Res. **13**, 281–305 (2012)
2. Brochu, E., Cora, V.M., De Freitas, N.: A tutorial on Bayesian optimization of expensive cost functions, with application to active user modeling and hierarchical reinforcement learning. arXiv preprint arXiv:1012.2599 (2010)
3. Calandra, R., Gopalan, N., Seyfarth, A., Peters, J., Deisenroth, M.P.: Bayesian gait optimization for bipedal locomotion. In: Battiti, R., Brunato, M., Kotsireas, I., Pardalos, P.M., (eds.) Learning and Intelligent Optimization LION 12 2018. LNCS, vol. 11353, pp. 274–290. Springer, Cham (2019). https://doi.org/10.1007/978-3-030-05348-2
4. Córdoba, I., Garrido-Merchán, E.C., Hernández-Lobato, D., Bielza, C., Larranaga, P.: Bayesian optimization of the PC algorithm for learning Gaussian Bayesian networks. In: Herrera, F., et al. (eds.) Conference of the Spanish Association for Artificial Intelligence. LNCS, pp. 44–54. Springer, Cham (2018). https://doi.org/10.1007/978-3-030-00374-6

5. Davis, L.: Handbook of Genetic Algorithms
6. Gao, G., Reynolds, A.C., et al.: An improved implementation of the LBFGS algorithm for automatic history matching. In: SPE Annual Technical Conference and Exhibition. Society of Petroleum Engineers (2004)
7. Garrido-Merchán, E.C., Albarca-Molina, A.: Suggesting cooking recipes through simulation and Bayesian optimization. In: Yin, H., Camacho, D., Novais, P., Tallón-Ballesteros, A.J. (eds.) IDEAL 2018. LNCS, vol. 11314, pp. 277–284. Springer, Cham (2018). https://doi.org/10.1007/978-3-030-03493-1_30
8. Garrido-Merchán, E.C., Hernández-Lobato, D.: Dealing with integer-valued variables in Bayesian optimization with Gaussian processes. arXiv preprint arXiv:1706.03673 (2017)
9. Garrido-Merchán, E.C., Hernández-Lobato, D.: Predictive entropy search for multi-objective Bayesian optimization with constraints. Neurocomputing **361**, 50–68 (2019)
10. Garrido-Merchán, E.C., Hernández-Lobato, D.: Dealing with categorical and integer-valued variables in Bayesian optimization with Gaussian processes. Neurocomputing **380**, 20–35 (2020)
11. Garrido-Merchán, E.C., Molina, M., Mendoza, F.M.: An artificial consciousness model and its relations with philosophy of mind. arXiv preprint arXiv:2011.14475 (2020)
12. Glover, F.W., Kochenberger, G.A.: Handbook of Metaheuristics, vol. 57. Springer, Boston (2006). https://doi.org/10.1007/978-1-4419-1665-5
13. Hernández-Lobato, J.M., Hoffman, M.W., Ghahramani, Z.: Predictive entropy search for efficient global optimization of black-box functions. In: Advances in Neural Information Processing Systems, pp. 918–926 (2014)
14. Ho, Y.-C., Pepyne, D.L.: Simple explanation of the no-free-lunch theorem and its implications. J. Optim. Theory Appl. **115**(3), 549–570 (2002)
15. Kotthoff, L., Thornton, C., Hoos, H.H., Hutter, F., Leyton-Brown, K.: Auto-WEKA 2.0: automatic model selection and hyperparameter optimization in WEKA. J. Mach. Learn. Res. **18**(1), 826–830 (2017)
16. Markov, S.: Skopt documentation
17. Merchán, E.C.G., Molina, M.: A machine consciousness architecture based on deep learning and Gaussian processes. arXiv preprint arXiv:2002.00509 (2020)
18. Rasmussen, C.E.: Gaussian processes in machine learning. In: Bousquet, O., von Luxburg, U., Rätsch, G. (eds.) ML 2003. LNCS (LNAI), vol. 3176, pp. 63–71. Springer, Heidelberg (2004). https://doi.org/10.1007/978-3-540-28650-9_4
19. Shahriari, B., Swersky, K., Wang, Z., Adams, R.P., De Freitas, N.: Taking the human out of the loop: a review of Bayesian optimization. Proc. IEEE **104**(1), 148–175 (2015)
20. Snoek, J., Larochelle, H., Adams, R.P.: Practical Bayesian optimization of machine learning algorithms. In: Advances in Neural Information Processing Systems, pp. 2951–2959 (2012)
21. Springenberg, J.T., Klein, A., Falkner, S., Hutter, F.: Bayesian optimization with robust Bayesian neural networks. In: Advances in Neural Information Processing Systems, pp. 4134–4142 (2016)
22. Wang, Z., Jegelka, S.: Max-value entropy search for efficient Bayesian optimization. In: Proceedings of the 34th International Conference on Machine Learning, vol. 70, pp. 3627–3635. JMLR.org (2017)

Solving the Permutation Heijunka Flow Shop Scheduling Problem with Non-unit Demands for Jobs

Joaquín Bautista-Valhondo[✉] [iD]

IOC ETSEIB, Universitat Politècnica de Catalunya, Avenue Diagonal 647, 08028 Barcelona, Spain
joaquin.bautista@upc.edu

Abstract. In this paper a problem of job sequences in a workshop is presented, taking into account non-unit demands for these and whose objective is to obtain manufacturing sequences satisfying the Quota property with a minimum total completion time for all the jobs (C_{max}). Two procedures are proposed to solve the problem: Mixed Integer Linear Programming and a Metaheuristic based on Multi-start and Local Search. The two proposed procedures are tested using instance set Nissan-9Eng.I, in both cases giving rise to highly satisfactory performance both in quality of solutions obtained and in the CPU times required.

Keywords: Flow Shop Scheduling Problem · Overall demand · Heijunka · Mixed Integer Linear Programming · Multi-start · Local search

1 Preliminaries

The *Flow Shop Scheduling Problem* (FSP) is a sequencing problem that has received considerable attention from professionals and researchers in recent decades due in part to the wide range of production environments it can model [1].

A recent version of FSP is the $Fm/\beta/\gamma/d_i$ family of sequencing problems ([2, 3]), which is to establish an application between the elements of a set T of ordinals (T elements) corresponding to the positions in the production sequence:$\pi(T) = (\pi_1, \ldots, \pi_T)$, and the elements of a set J of jobs or products (D elements, with $D = T$).

The jobs or products in group J are classified into exclusive types or classes, J_i, satisfying the following properties: $J = \bigcup_{i \in I} J_i$ and $J_i \cap J_{i'} = \emptyset, \forall \{i, i'\} \in I$, where I is the set of job types ($i = 1, \ldots, n$).

In $Fm/\beta/\gamma/d_i$ problems, the β parameter can take the permutation (prmu) or blocking (block) values, while the γ parameter corresponds the efficiency metrics to optimize (C_{max}, C_{med}, etc.), vector d represents the demand plan for the considered job types, and d_i symbolizes the number of jobs of type $i \in I$ within J; $d_i = |J_i| \forall i \in I$, satisfying: $\sum_{\forall i} d_i = D = T$.

© Springer Nature Switzerland AG 2021
E. Alba et al. (Eds.): CAEPIA 2021, LNAI 12882, pp. 170–181, 2021.
https://doi.org/10.1007/978-3-030-85713-4_17

The units of J travel in order through a set K of m stations on an assembly line arranged in series and the production of a job of type $i \in I$ requires a heterogeneous processing time $p_{i,k}$ in workstation $k \in K$ ($k = 1, \ldots, m$).

The purpose of problems $Fm/\beta/\gamma/d_i$ is to obtain a sequence of replicated jobs or products (d_i), in a line with m machines, with the possibility of blocking or not, according to the β parameter, and with the objective of optimizing the efficiency metric represented by the γ parameter.

Therefore, using the notation proposed by Graham et al. [4], both the $Fm/prmu/\gamma$ problems ([5–7]) as the $Fm/block/\gamma$ problems ([8–10]) are particular cases of the family $Fm/\beta/\gamma/d_i$, when $d_i = 1$ for all $i \in I$.

On the other hand, completing all jobs in the shortest time possible (min C_{max}) is not the only desirable objective when establishing a product manufacturing sequence. In production environments that are governed by the Just-in-Time manufacturing ideals ([11]), the production sequences must have properties that are linked to the Heijunka concept [12], whose meaning is to achieve regularity of production. The incorporation of Heijunka in production sequence problems can be characterized by three methods:

a. Restrictions: Imposing minimum and maximum manufacturing levels on the job types or products ($i = 1, \ldots, n$) in each manufacturing cycle ($t = 1, \ldots, T$).
b. Objective function: Maximizing the constancy of the product manufacturing rates and/or the component consumption rates.
c. Mixed characterization: There is also the possibility of establishing a mixed characterization of Heijunka, which incorporates into the sequence models the two previous methods [13]: (a) restrictions and (b) an objective function.

In this work, the first characterization has been added to the genuine $Fm/prmu/C_{max}/d_i$ problem to achieve sequences with minimum makespan (C_{max}: time that elapses from the start of work to the end) and with some properties that propitiate the regularity of production through restrictions.

The remaining text has the following structure. Section 2 is dedicated to presenting the problem under study. Section 3 describes the algorithm that was designed. In Sect. 4, a case study with its data is shown, as well as the procedures used and their results. Finally, Sect. 5 offers some conclusions about this work.

2 Heijunka $Fm/prmu/C_{max}/d_i$

To incorporate Heijunka, we will indicate that the sequence $\pi(T) = (\pi_1, \ldots, \pi_T)$, which is composed of T units of jobs, has the property of preservation of the production mix if the set of restrictions (1) is satisfied. We also call this property *Quota property*:

$$\lambda_i t \leq X_{i,t} \leq \lambda_i t \Leftrightarrow |X_{i,t} - \lambda_i t| < 1 \forall i \forall t, \text{ and } X_{i,T} = d_i \forall i \tag{1}$$

where:

- I : set of product types, $i = 1, \ldots, |I|$
- T: set of manufacturing cycles in every demand plan, $t = 1, \ldots, |T|$; $T \equiv |T|$
- d_i : demand for units of type $i \in I$ in an arbitrary demand plan
- λ_i : proportion of units of type $i \in I$: $\lambda_i = d_i/T \ \forall i \in I$
- $X_{i,t}$: number of units of type $i \in I$ in the partial sequence $\pi(t) \subseteq \pi(T)$: Actual production associated with the partial sequence $\pi(t)$.

The *Quota property* (1) impose that the actual production $X_{i,t}$, for every product $i \in I$ and every manufacturing cycle $t \in T$, must be an integer as close as possible to its ideal production $\lambda_i t$. The ideal production $(\lambda_i t)$ is defined as the quota of manufacturing time given to a product $(i \in I)$ until the end of each production cycle $(t = 1, \ldots, |T|)$.

Under such conditions, we can present a model for the $Fm/prmu/C_{max}/d_i$ that accounts for two types of aspects:

A.1 Technical-productive in JIT manufacturing context: Quota property to enforce preservation of the production mix in the Heijunka manufacturing sequence $\pi(T)$.

A.21 Processing time efficiency: objective function to minimize the maskespan C_{max}.

Effectively, assuming the following data is known:

- The set of job types $(I : i = 1, \ldots, |I|)$ and the set of stations $(K : k = 1, \ldots, |K|)$.
- The processing times $p_{i,k}(i \in I \wedge k \in K)$ of the operations.
- The demand vectors $\vec{d} = (d_1, \ldots, d_{|I|})$ and production mix $\vec{\lambda} = (\lambda_1, \ldots, \lambda_{|I|})$.

The problem is finding a Quota sequence of T jobs $\pi(T) = (\pi_1, \ldots, \pi_T)$ with minimum makespan C_{max} that satisfies the demand plan represented by the vector $\vec{d}$. The formulation of the model is as follows:

$$\min Z = \sum_{t=1}^{T} \sum_{i=1}^{n} z_{i,t} \prec \min C_{max} = \max_{\forall k \forall t}\left[C_{k,t}\right] \equiv C_{m,T} \tag{2}$$

$$C_{k,t} = S_{k,t} + p_{\pi_t,k} \forall k \in K \forall t = 1, \ldots, T \tag{3}$$

$$S_{k,t} = max\left(C_{k,t-1}(\pi_{t-1}), C_{k-1,t}(\pi_t)\right) \forall k \in K \forall t = 1, \ldots, T \tag{4}$$

$$X_{i,t} = |\{\pi_\tau \in \pi(t) \subseteq \pi(T) : \pi_\tau = i \in I\}| \forall i \in I \forall t = 1, \ldots, T \tag{5}$$

$$\left|X_{i,t} - \lambda_i t\right| < 1 + d_i \times z_{i,t} \forall i \in I \forall t = 1, \ldots, T \tag{6}$$

$$X_{i,T} = d_i \forall i \in I \tag{7}$$

$$C_{k,0} = 0 \, \forall k \in K \tag{8}$$

$$C_{0,t} = 0 \, \forall t = 1, \ldots, T \tag{9}$$

$$z_{i,t} \in \{0, 1\} \forall i \in I \forall t = 1, \ldots, T \tag{10}$$

In the model, the function (2) is composed of two hierarchical objectives: the first is oriented to find a sequence $\pi(T)$ that satisfies the Quota property ($Z = 0$) and the second expresses the minimization of the time of completion of the last job or product π_T of the production sequence $\pi(T)$ in the last machine ($k = m$); that is: $C_{max} \equiv C_{m,T}$. The equality (3) determines the minimum time of completion of the t-th job π_t in machine $k \in K : C_{k,t}(\pi_t)$. The equality (4) determines the minimum star time $S_{k,t}$ of the t-th job π_t in $\pi(T)$ in machine $k \in K$. Formula (5) serves to count the number of jobs of type $i \in I$ in the partial sequence $\pi(t) \subseteq \pi(T)$. Conditions (6) are used to count the number of violations of the Quota property in the sequence $\pi(T)$ using the binary variables $z_{i,t}$. The equalities (7) impose the satisfaction of the demand plan ($d_i \forall i \in I$). Conditions (8) and (9) set the start of completion times. Finally, conditions (10) force the $z_{i,t}$ variables to be binary.

3   MS-LS: A metaheuristic for Heijunka $Fm/prmu/C_{max}/d_i$

Similar to [13] the proposed metaheuristic, MS-LS, consists of a first constructive phase, which provides an initial solution through a randomized greedy procedure, and a second phase, called the improvement phase, which uses local search procedures to reach the local optima in one or more specific neighborhoods.

After setting a prefixed number of iterations (construction plus improvement), the proposed metaheuristic obtains a manufacturing sequence $\pi(T) = (\pi_1, \ldots, \pi_T)$ that satisfies the Quota property and also serves the objective of minimizing the completion time of the last job in the last workstation: C_{max}.

3.1   Phase 1: Multi-start for the Construction of a *Quota* Sequence

Formally, a *Quota sequence* is any solution according to model MQS that follows.
MQS: Maxsat-*Quota-Sequence*Model

$$\min \mathcal{Z}_{sum} = \sum_{t=1}^{T}\sum_{i=1}^{n} z_{i,t} \Leftrightarrow \max \mathcal{Z}'_{sum} = \sum_{t=1}^{T}\sum_{i=1}^{n}(1 - z_{i,t}) \tag{11}$$

$$\sum_{i=1}^{n} x_{i,t} = 1 \; \forall t = 1, \ldots, T \tag{12}$$

$$\sum_{t=1}^{T} x_{i,t} = d_i \; \forall i \in I \tag{13}$$

$$X_{i,t} - \sum_{\tau=1}^{t} x_{i,\tau} = 0 \; \forall i \in I \; \forall t = 1, \ldots, T \tag{14}$$

$$x_{i,t} = \begin{Bmatrix} 1 \Leftrightarrow \hat{\pi}_t = i \\ 0 \Leftrightarrow \hat{\pi}_t \neq i \end{Bmatrix} \forall i \in I \; \forall t = 1, \ldots, T \tag{15}$$

$$z_{i,t} = \begin{Bmatrix} 1 \Leftrightarrow |X_{i,t} - \lambda_i t| \geq 1 \\ 0 \Leftrightarrow |X_{i,t} - \lambda_i t| < 1 \end{Bmatrix} \forall i \in I \; \forall t = 1, \ldots, T \tag{16}$$

Where $z_{i,t}$ ($\forall i \forall t$) is a binary variable equal to 1 if and only if $|X_{i,t} - \lambda_i t| \geq 1$, and $x_{i,t}$ ($\forall i \forall t$) is a binary variable that equals 1 if and only if a unit of type of product $i \in I$ occupies position t of the manufacturing sequence $\pi(T)$. Obviously, the goal is to obtain sequences with $\mathcal{Z}_{sum} = 0$.

Attending to (16), we can construct Quota sequences (or closed to them) minimizing the sum of absolute deviations $|X_{i,t} - \lambda_i t|$; this is:

$$\min G = \sum_{t=1}^{T}\sum_{i=1}^{n} |X_{i,t} - \lambda_i t| \tag{17}$$

Taking into account (17), we construct a sequence of jobs $\pi(T) = (\pi_1, \ldots, \pi_T)$, which assign progressively at each stage $t(t = 1, \ldots, T)$ a job from the $CL(t)$ list of candidates that can be drawn to occupy the position t of the manufacturing sequence. So, when stage t is reached, it is added to the sequence consolidated in the previous stage, $\pi(t-1)$, a job $i \in CL(t)$ (see Algorithm A1).

For a job type $i \in I$ to enter the list $CL(t)$ of stage t, it must meet the following two conditions (line 7 from A1):

(a)   The job type does not have its demand fulfilled: $n_i = X_{i,t-1} < d_i$.
(b)   The job type must not violate the *Upper Quota Property*: $n_i + 1 \leq \lambda_i t$.

Once the $CL(t)$ list is built, we order the candidate jobs $i \in CL(t)$ according to the following priority index:

$$g_i^{(t)} = |n_i + 1 - \lambda_i t| + \sum_{\forall j \in I: j \neq i} |n_j - \lambda_j t| \forall i \in CL(t) \tag{18}$$

With the help of the $g_i^{(t)}$ index, the jobs from the list $CL(t)$ are ordered increasing order and the $\overline{CL}(t)$ is constructed (line 13 from A1).

A1: Algorithm 1 for the constructive phase of the sequence of jobs: $\pi(T)$

1:   *// Initialization*
2:   **input** $\Lambda, I, K, D, (d_i, p_{i,k}) \forall i \in I \forall k \in K$
3:   **initialize** $T = D, t = 0, \pi(t) = \{\emptyset\}, (n_i = 0, \lambda_i = d_i/D) \forall i \in I$
4:   *// Create the candidate set*
5:   **while** $(t \leq T)$ **do**
6:      set $t = t + 1$
7:      set $CL(t) = \{i \in I: (n_i < d_i) \wedge (n_i + 1 \leq \lceil \lambda_i t \rceil)\}$
8:   *// Evaluate alternative*
9:      **for all** $(i \in CL(t))$ **do**
10:       set $g_i^{(t)} = |n_i + 1 - \lambda_i t| + \sum_{\forall j \in I: j \neq i} |n_j - \lambda_j t|$
11:      **end for**
12:   *// Sort alternatives*
13:      **sort** $CL(t)$: set $\overline{CL}(t)$ as the ordered list from $CL(t)$ according the $g_i^{(t)}$ values.
14:   *// Select alternative*
15:      set $pos_\Lambda = -int(-\Lambda \cdot |\overline{CL}(t)| \cdot RND) \equiv -int(-|\overline{RCL}(t, \Lambda)| \cdot RND)$
16:      set $i_\Lambda = i \in \overline{CL}(t): pos_i = pos_\Lambda$
17:   *// Update*
18:      set $n_{i_\Lambda} \leftarrow n_{i_\Lambda} + 1$
19:      set $\pi(t) = \pi(t - 1) \cup \{i_\Lambda\}$
20:   **end while**
21:   *// End Algorithm 1*

After this ordering, the list $\overline{CL}(t)$ is reduced through a mechanism that is a function of the admission factor Λ (percentage of candidate jobs), with this operation, the restricted list $\overline{RCL}(t, \Lambda)$ is obtained (line 15 in A1), which coincides with $\overline{CL}(t)$ when $\Lambda = 100\% = 1$, while if $\Lambda = 1/|I|$, the best candidate job from such lists is selected at each stage t.

Algorithm A1 does not always provide a sequence $\pi(T)$ that satisfies the *Lower Quota Property*: $\lambda_i t \leq X_{i,t}, \forall i \forall t$; So, after running it, Algorithm 2 starts up.

A2: Algorithm 2 for the constructive phase of the Quota sequence of jobs: $\hat{\pi}(T)$

1:   // *Initialization*
2:   **input** $I, K, D, \pi(T) = (\pi_1, \dots, \pi_T), (d_i, p_{i,k})\ \forall i \in I\ \forall k \in K$
3:   **initialize** $T = D, t = 0, quota = false,\ \lambda_i = d_i/D\ \forall i \in I$
4:   // *Quota Property*
5:   **while** $(t \leq T)$ **do**
6:     set $t = t + 1$
7:     **for all** $(i \in I)$ **do**
8:       set $X_{i,t} = |\{\pi_\tau \in \pi(t) = (\pi_1, \dots, \pi_t) \subseteq \pi(T): \pi_\tau = i \in I\}|$
9:       **if** $\lfloor \lambda_i t \rfloor \leq X_{i,t} \leq \lceil \lambda_i t \rceil$ **then**
10:        set $quota = true$
11:      **else**
12:        set $quota = false$
13:        **exit while**
14:      **end if**
15:    **end for**
16:    set $\hat{\pi}(t) = \pi(t)$
17: **end while**
18: **if** $quota = false$ **then**
19:    **solve MAXSAT**: set $\hat{\pi}(T) \leftarrow maxsat(\pi(T), \lfloor \lambda_i t \rfloor \leq X_{i,t} \leq \lceil \lambda_i t \rceil)$
20: **end if**
21: // *End Algorithm 2*

The MAXSAT procedure (Line 19 from A2) is an exchange procedure that solves the problem of maximum satisfaction of restrictions MQS: $\left[|X_{i,t} - \lambda_i t| < 1, \forall i \forall t \right]$, which provides as a solution a sequence $\hat{\pi}(T)$ that does satisfy the *Quota* property in all of the manufacturing cycles.

3.2 Phase 2: Improvement of the *Quota* Sequence Through Local Search

The improvement phase start with a *Quota* sequence $\hat{\pi}(T)$ in which four descent algorithms are run consecutively and repetitively in 4 neighborhoods (2 exchange and 2 insertion) until none of them improves the best solution that is achieved during the iteration. From two *Quota* sequences, the one that offers the least total completion time (C_{max}) is selected. The descent algorithms are based on the exchange and insertion of jobs, and they are oriented to the exploration of sequence cycles in both increasing and decreasing order. The four descent algorithms are:

(i) *Forward exchange*: for all t position of the current sequence, $\hat{\pi}(T)$, it is determined the job type that is in that position and it is searched the next closest locus, $t' > t$, that is occupied by the same type (i.e. $\hat{\pi}_t = \hat{\pi}_{t'}$); if no such locus exists, then its value is set by making $.t' = T + 1$ Just after, the tentative exchange between $\hat{\pi}_t$ and the jobs located in the range $[t + 1, t' - 1]$ of the sequence is made. The first exchange that reduces the total completion time C_{max} is consolidated as long as the resulting sequence satisfies the Quota property. While there is improvement this algorithm is repeated.

(ii) *Backward exchange:* this procedure is similar to the previous one, but in this case the search is performed for $t = T$ to 1 step -1. Obviously, if the previous closest locus, $t'(t' < t)$, with the same job type $(\hat{\pi}_t = \hat{\pi}_{t'})$ does not exist, it is considered $t' = 0$. This action is repeated while there is improvement.

(iii) *Forward insertion:* for all t position of the current sequence, $\hat{\pi}(T)$, the job type in the t position is detected and it is searched the next closest locus $t'(t' > t)$ that is occupied by the same type $(\hat{\pi}_t = \hat{\pi}_{t'})$; if these locus does not exist, it is considered $t' = T + 1$. Following, the $\hat{\pi}_t$ job is inserted in the range of sequence positions $[t + 1, t' - 1]$. Then, the first insertion that leads to reduce C_{max} is done as long as the resulting sequence satisfies the Quota property. This procedure is repeated while there is improvement.

(iv) *Backward insertion:* this insertion procedure is similar to (iii) with respect to the neighbourhood, and analogous in the search for types of jobs to (ii). Also, this action is repeated while there is improvement.

4 Case Study: Nissan BCN Engine Plant

The computational experience proposed here is focused on comparing the MS-LS (proposed metaheuristic) and MILP (Mixed Integer Linear Programming) procedures in terms of the quality of the solutions and the CPU times. As in [2] and [3], the analysis is related to a case study of the Nissan plant in Barcelona: an assembly line of nine types of engines grouped into three families (SUVs, Vans and Trucks).

The production line under study employs 42 operators work in shifts of 8 h. The significant data of this case are the following: 21 workstations $|K| = 21$, 9 job types $|I| = 9$, processing times $p_{i,k}(\forall i \in I, \forall k \in K)$ with values between 89s and 185s, 23 engine demand plans $|E| = 23$ (corresponding to the Nissan-9Eng.I instances) and daily demand of 270 jobs for all demand plans: $T \equiv D_\varepsilon = 270 jobs(\forall \varepsilon \in E)$.

The compiled codes of the procedures that we have selected in this work are MILP and MS-LS.

Table 1 shows the best results with respect to C_{max} and CPU Time from MILP and MS-LS, and for the 23 datasets of the problem $\varepsilon \in E$. In the Table 1, the column headings represent the following characteristics:

$\varepsilon \in E$. Identification number of the instances for Plan#1 to Plan#23

C_{max}. Best makespan value obtained for procedure MILP or MS-LS

LB. C_{max} lower limit for the Heijunka $Fm/block/C_{max}/d_i$ problem obtained for MILP

Gap. Relative gap between C_{max} and LB.

The relative gap values between C_{max} are calculated using (19).

$$Gap(\varepsilon) = (C_{max}(\varepsilon) - LB(\varepsilon))/LB(\varepsilon) \forall \varepsilon \in E \qquad (19)$$

The characteristics of the two procedures are:

- MILP: Heijunka $Fm/prmu/C_{max}/d_i$ Model: (i) Objective function for minimizing the C_{max} value of the Quota production sequence; (ii) implementation for IBM ILOG CPLEX solver (Optimization Studio v.12.2, win-x86-64); (iii) maximum CPU time of 900 s allowed for solving each instance (23 instances). The average CPU time used by each demand plan to find the best solution is equal to 213.82 s.
- MS-LS: Is a Multi-start algorithm with Local search focused on minimizing the total completion time C_{max} in Quota manufacturing sequences. The maximum number of iterations for each demand plan from Nissan-9Eng.I instances is equal to 10 with 5 candidate admission factors $\Lambda = (1/|I|, 0.25, 0.5, 0, 75, 1)$, which generates in the constructive phase 1150 solutions and 7060 improved solutions (improvement phase) in 115 executions. MS-LS uses on average a CPU time equal to 56.55 s to find the best solution for each demand plan.

An analysis of Table 1 reveals the following:

- Procedure MILP obtains and ensures optimal solutions in 19 of the 23 instances with 270 jobs (23 instances Nissan-9Eng.I) when the Heijunka $Fm/prmu/C_{max}/d_i$ problem is solved.
- Procedure MS-LS obtains optimal solutions in 10 of the 23 instances with 270 jobs when the Heijunka $Fm/prmu/C_{max}/d_i$ problem is solved.
- The average value of the relative gap between C_{max} and LB achieved by MILP is 0.001% in a range of values between 0.000% and 0.012%.
- The average value of the relative gap between C_{max} and LB achieved by MS-LS is 0.005% in a range of values between 0.000% and 0.018%.
- The average CPU times used by MILP are approximately 213.82 s for each instance of 270 jobs in a range of values between 6.51 and 900.38 s, when a maximum CPU time equal to 900 s is imposed on CPLEX to solve each instance.
- The average CPU time used by MS-LS is equal to 56.55 s within a range of values between 3.91 and 251.38 s, when 10 iterations are performed with the algorithm.
- Considering that the cost of production loss is 137.14 euros per production minute [14] and that the current production time available to manufacture 270 engines is equal to 50770 s, transforming the original assembly line into a Heijunka Permutation Flow Shop would save an average of 1161.12 euros a day.

Table 1. Results for Nissan-9Eng.I instances using procedures MILP and MS-LS. *CPU* columns show the CPU time (in seconds) spent solving each instance.

$\varepsilon \in E$	MILP				MS-LS		
	LB	C_{max}	Gap	CPU	C_{max}	Gap	CPU
1	50100	50100	0.000%	150.98	50104	0.008%	5.50
2	50180	50180	0.000%	391.35	50188	0.016%	46.70
3	50303	50303	0.000%	46.08	50303	0.000%	15.34
4	50170	50170	0.000%	55.08	50170	0.000%	251.38
5	50385	50385	0.000%	25.81	50394	0.018%	123.41
6	50202	50202	0.000%	11.76	50204	0.004%	3.91
7	50397	50397	0.000%	32.38	50397	0.000%	196.16
8	50126	50128	0.004%	900.30	50131	0.010%	23.57
9	50378	50378	0.000%	11.06	50378	0.000%	5.82
10	50625	50625	0.000%	7.16	50625	0.000%	12.64
11	50084	50085	0.002%	900.31	50088	0.008%	30.16
12	50196	50196	0.000%	55.65	50196	0.000%	211.54
13	50129	50135	0.012%	900.27	50136	0.014%	12.69
14	50223	50223	0.000%	233.21	50224	0.002%	123.73
15	50242	50242	0.000%	16.58	50243	0.002%	13.13
16	50123	50126	0.006%	900.38	50131	0.016%	12.41
17	50273	50273	0.000%	75.83	50275	0.004%	4.29
18	50273	50273	0.000%	41.66	50275	0.004%	8.95
19	50481	50481	0.000%	6.51	50481	0.000%	23.91
20	50100	50100	0.000%	111.85	50100	0.000%	52.20
21	50307	50307	0.000%	10.12	50307	0.000%	5.99
22	50545	50545	0.000%	7.58	50545	0.000%	83.46
23	50157	50157	0.000%	25.85	50158	0.002%	33.69
Av	50260.80	50261.35	0.001%	213.82	50263.17	0.005%	56.55
Max	50625	50625	0.012%	900.38	50625	0.018%	251.38
Min	50084	50085	0.000%	6.51	50088	0.000%	3.91

5 Conclusions

In this work, a manufacturing sequence model is presented which incorporates the Heijunka concept into the $Fm/prmu/C_{max}/d_i$ problem.

Two methods have been used to solve the problem. The first of them is based on Mixed Integer Linear Programming and the CPLEX solver (a commercial Software from IBM) has been used solving all 23 instances from the Nissan-9Eng.I set. The second method, with which the same instances have been solved, is MS-LS algorithm in whose constructive phase initial solutions are generated satisfying the Quota property, while in the second phase the solutions are improved using 4 neighborhood (exchange, insertion) and attending to the criterion of minimum total completion time (C_{max}).

Both procedures have been highly competitive with the problem, since they have been able to optimally solve a high percentage of the instances using reasonable CPU times. Specifically, procedure MILP (CPLEX) obtains and ensures optimal solutions in 19 of the 23 instances with 270 using an average CPU time equal to 213.82 s for each instance with an average value of the relative gap between C_{max} and the lower bound equal to 0.001%. For its part, MS-LS has been able to obtain 10 optimum within 23 instances using an average CPU time equal to 56.55 s for each instance with an average *Gap* equal to 0.005%. Therefore, it can concluded that both procedures are valid to solve the Heijunka $Fm/prmu/C_{max}/d_i$ problem.

In view of the results, it can be concluded that there has been a technical tie in the quality of the solutions offered by MILP and MS-LS. However, MS-LS has been shown 3.78 times faster than MILP (IBM CPLEX solver) in the proposed experiment, while MILP has also served to calculate lower bounds for the purpose of comparing the two procedures.

Acknowledgments. This work has been funded by the Ministry of Economy and Competitiveness of the Government of Spain through project OPTHEUS (ref. PGC2018-095080-B-I00), including European Regional Development Funds (ERDF).

References

1. Pinedo, M.L.: Scheduling -Theory, Algorithms, and Systems. 5th edn. Springer, Cham (2016). https://doi.org/10.1007/978-3-319-26580-3
2. Bautista, J., Alfaro, R.: Transformación de una línea de montaje de modelos mixtos en un taller de flujo regular: Caso de estudio en la factoría Nissan de Barcelona. Dirección y Organización **69**, 99–110 (2019)
3. Bautista, J., Alfaro, R.: Mixed integer linear programming models for Flow Shop Scheduling with a Demand Plan of Job Types. CEJOR **28**, 5–23 (2020)
4. Graham, R.L., Lawler, E.L., Lenstra, J.K., Rinnooy Kan, A.H.G.: Optimization and approximation in deterministic sequencing and scheduling: a survey. Ann. Discrete Math. **5**, 287–326 (1979)
5. Taillard, E.: Some efficient heuristic methods for the flow shop sequencing problem. Eur. J. Oper. Res. **47**, 65–74 (1990)
6. Reeves, C.R.: A genetic algorithm for flowshop sequencing. Comput. Oper. Res. **22**, 5–13 (1995)
7. Aggoune, R.: Minimizing the makespan for the flow shop scheduling problem with availability constraints. Eur. J. Oper. Res. **153**, 534–543 (2004)
8. Ronconi, D.P.: A note on constructive heuristics for the flowshop problem with blocking. Int. J. Prod. Econ. **87**, 39–48 (2004)
9. Bautista, J., Cano, A., Companys, R., Ribas, I.: Solving the Fm|block|Cmax problem using Bounded Dynamic Programming. Eng. Appl. Artif. Intell. **25**, 1235–1245 (2012)
10. Ozolins, A.: Improved bounded dynamic programming algorithm for solving the blocking flow shop problem. CEJOR **27**, 15–38 (2019)

11. Monden, Y.: Toyota Production System: An Integrated Approach to Just-In-Time, 4th edn. Productivity Press, New York (2011)
12. Matzka, J., Di Mascolo, M., Furmans, K.: Buffer sizing of a Heijunka Kanban system. J. Intell. Manuf. **23**, 40–60 (2012)
13. Bautista, J., Alfaro, R.: A GRASP algorithm for *Quota* sequences with minimum work overload and forced interruption of operations in a mixed product assembly line. Progress Artif. Intell. **7**, 197–211 (2018)
14. Bautista, J., Alfaro, R.: An expert system to minimize operational costs in mixed-model sequencing problems with activity factor. Expert Syst. Appl. **104**, 185–201 (2018)

Real-World Applications

Nearest Neighbors-Based Forecasting for Electricity Demand Time Series in Streaming

L. Melgar-García[1]($^{(\boxtimes)}$), D. Gutiérrez-Avilés[2], C. Rubio-Escudero[2], and A. Troncoso[1]

[1] Data Science and Big Data Lab, Pablo de Olavide University, 41013 Seville, Spain
{lmelgar,atrolor}@upo.es
[2] Department of Computer Science, University of Seville, Seville, Spain
{dgutierrez3,crubioescudero}@us.es

Abstract. This paper presents a new forecasting algorithm for time series in streaming named StreamWNN. The methodology has two well-differentiated stages: the algorithm searches for the nearest neighbors to generate an initial prediction model in the batch phase. Then, an online phase is carried out when the time series arrives in streaming. In particular, the nearest neighbor of the streaming data from the training set is computed and the nearest neighbors, previously computed in the batch phase, of this nearest neighbor are used to obtain the predictions. Results using the electricity consumption time series are reported, showing a remarkable performance of the proposed algorithm in terms of forecasting errors when compared to a nearest neighbors-based benchmark algorithm. The running times for the predictions are also remarkable.

Keywords: Forecasting · Nearest neighbors · Streaming time series · Electricity demand

1 Introduction

The explosive increase of global data, based on technology improvements, has led to the gathering of information as an automatic and relatively inexpensive task [16], taking us to the big data era. Data science offers a solution to gain knowledge from these enormous amounts of data, by means of adapting the existing models to the big data paradigm. This adaptation is a challenge for the research community.

There are several fields in which the application of the new big data analysis techniques represent a great improvement in problem solving, such as the energy consumption forecasting [17,25]. Governments and private companies are focusing on this topic as the improvement in the prediction levels will have both economic and environmental positive consequences [22]. In this sense, some classifiers have already been successfully applied to electricity consumption forecast

© Springer Nature Switzerland AG 2021
E. Alba et al. (Eds.): CAEPIA 2021, LNAI 12882, pp. 185–195, 2021.
https://doi.org/10.1007/978-3-030-85713-4_18

[24], such as the weighted k-nearest neighbors classifier (WKNN). The WKNN [4] is a generalization of the k-nearest neighbors method (KNN) [2] that assigns weights to the neighbors based on their distance from the element to predict.

The direct application of these methods to the big data domain is not feasible due to the computational needs, in terms of time and memory. Several proposals have adapted nearest neighbor proposals to the big data paradigm using the Apache Spark distributed computation framework [16,21,22].

Data streams are generated in many practical applications as temporally ordered, fast changing and massive flows of data [13]. Mining these data streams is concerned with extracting knowledge structures represented in models and patterns in non-stopping streams of information [6], and the research on this area has gained a high attraction. In this proposal, we go a step further and propose a general purpose forecasting algorithm based on nearest neighbors for big volumes of streams of data, to create a method capable to be integrated in real-world systems in which data are constantly generated as streams, such as the demand prediction in the electricity market.

In this work, we propose the StreamWNN algorithm for streaming time series forecasting based on nearest neighbors. This algorithm consists of two phases: a batch phase to generate an initial model, and an online phase for forecasting in real time by using the model previously created in the batch phase. The proposal has been applied to a dataset of 497,832 samples of electrical energy consumption in Spain.

The rest of the paper is structured as follows. Section 2 describes a review of the state of the art approaches related to data streaming and forecasting analysis int the electricity market. Section 3 presents the methodology applied for time series forecasting in streaming. The experimental setup along with the results obtained using electricity demand time series can be found in Sect. 4. Finally, in Sect. 5, the final considerations extracted from this work are presented.

2   Related Works

A wide range of approaches for data streaming analysis is currently emerging. The primary trend of this research field is the development of machine learning methodologies to the streaming environments. From this perspective, the authors in [26] presented an online version of the support vector machine model to predict air pollutant levels from the monitored air pollutant in Hong Kong. An online version of the linear discriminant analysis algorithm for dimension reduction was presented in [14]. On the other hand, it has carried out research efforts to develop frameworks for adaptation of standard machine learning methods to streaming [10]. Another streaming framework is SAMOA presented in [1], where the authors developed an API to apply machine learning algorithms to streams of data in a big data context. Different algorithms to analyze data streams from the Internet of Things (IoT) networks are also currently being developed. In [5], the authors presented a streaming linear regression method to forecast streams data generated by IoT networks. Finally, several surveys have been published about the streaming analysis. In this sense, the authors in [20] analyzed the difference between the real-time processing and the stream processing of big data, and by contrast, a survey of the open-source technologies that support big data in a real-time/near real-time environments was introduced in [15].

Concerning researches focused on forecasting for the electricity demand time series data, in addition to the nearest neighbors for a big data environment proposed in [22] and the new big data-based multivariate and multi-output forecasting approach in [21], other approaches have been published. In [7], the authors applied decision gradient boosted trees and random forest ensemble methods to the electricity demand problem. Also, deep learning techniques have been applied to predict energy power consumption in big data environments [23]. A Temporal Convolutional Network has been used in [11] for demand energy forecasting. A complete review of deep learning architectures for time series forecasting was published in [12]. On the other hand, several streaming techniques have been applied to this problem. In [3], the authors presented an incremental pattern characterization algorithm to mine data streams from smart meters of RMIT University for the purpose of applying it to electricity consumption analysis and forecasting. The authors in [8] proposed a complete data streaming analysis system combining an online clustering model and neural-networks to predict in real-time the electricity load demand from sensor networks.

Besides the forecasting, other problems related to energy have been addressed. The authors in [19] presented a methodology to extract electric energy consumption patterns in big data time series based on the application of the distributed version of the k-means algorithm. In [9] the authors presented a big data system to classify fraudulent behaviors of the leading electricity company in Spain. Regarding the streaming environment, an incremental ensemble learning method is developed for the on-line classification of the electricity pricing in Australia in [18]. Furthermore, in [27], the authors presented the DStreamEPK algorithm, a new streaming clustering method applied to electric power data.

3   Methodology

This Section presents the proposed algorithm, named StreamWNN, for streaming time series forecasting based on nearest neighbors.

The time series forecasting problem consists in predicting the next h values from the historical past values. The StreamWNN forecasting algorithm has of two phases: a batch phase to generate an initial model, and an online phase for forecasting in real time by using the model created in the batch phase.

A time series X_t is defined as a set of ordered chronologically values $\{x_1, ..., x_t\}$ and can be always transformed into N instances formed by features and class as follows:

$$X_t = \{(x^1, y^1), ..., (x^N, y^N)\} \quad x^i \in \mathbb{R}^w \quad y^i \in \mathbb{R}^h \tag{1}$$

where x^i are the features of the $i-th$ instance, representing the past w values to the class y^i formed by the next h values. For the batch phase, the time series X_t

from Eq. (1) is divided into training set and test set. Then, the prediction method based on nearest neighbors searches for the k closest neighbors to a window composed of the past w values to the h values to be predicted. Afterwards, a weight is calculated for each neighbor depending on its distance to the past values window. Thus, the initial model M consists of the pairs of the features of the instances from the test set and a list of the classes corresponding to the neighbors of theses features from the training set. That is:

$$M = <x^i, <y(n_1(x^i)), ..., y(n_K(x^i))>> \tag{2}$$

where K is the number of neighbors, x^i are the w features of the $i - th$ instance of the test set, $n_j(x^i)$ is the $j - th$ neighbor of the x^i and $y(n_j(x^i))$ is the class corresponding to the $j - th$ neighbor.

When a time series is received in streaming, a temporal data stream ds_t can be a chunk of the time series of length w, that is, $ds_t = <x_t, x_{t+1}, ..., x_{t+w-1}>$. For the online phase, once the ds_t data stream is received, the nearest neighbor of the ds_t from test set is obtaining by this equation:

$$x^* = arg \min_{x^i \in Test} d(x^i, ds_t) \tag{3}$$

Then, the prediction is obtained using the K neighbors of x^* and weights already computed in the M model from Eq. (2). In particular, the prediction is made by applying a weighted average of the h samples following those k closest neighbors. Thus, the StreamWNN algorithm predicts by means of the following equation:

$$\widehat{y}(ds_t) = \frac{1}{\sum_{j=1}^{K} w_j^*} \sum_{j=1}^{K} w_j^* y(n_j(x^*)) \tag{4}$$

where $n_j(x^*)$ is the $j - th$ neighbor of x^*, $y(n_j(x^*))$ is the class corresponding to the $j - th$ neighbor, and w_j^* is the weight associated to the $j - th$ neighbor. This weight depends on the distance, with a greater weight to the closest neighbors and a smaller weight to the farthest neighbors according to a distance d. In this work, the Euclidean distance has been chosen, and the weights are defined by:

$$w_j^* = \frac{1}{d^2(x^*, n_j(x^*))} \tag{5}$$

Consequently, it is possible to obtain forecasts in real time as the prediction consists of making an average with neighbors and weights previously computed in the batch phase using the historical data.

4   Experimental Results

This section specifies the dataset used in the experimentation and reports the results obtained after the application of the proposed streaming algorithm. In particular, Sect. 4.1 describes the dataset and the experiments carried out, specifying in each case the parameters of the algorithm. Finally, in Sect. 4.2 the results of the experimentation are shown and discussed.

4.1   Dataset and Experimental Setup

The experimentation uses a dataset of 497,832 samples of electrical energy consumption in Spain. Each sample has 12 attributes related to electricity. For this work, only two attributes are used: the energy demand in megawatt (MW) and the date and time of the measured value.

In particular, the dataset contains 1 sample for every 10 min during 9 years and 6 months, starting the 1 January 1st 2007 and finishing June 21st 2016. The whole dataset is chronologically divided into 3 sets of data: training, test and streaming sets. The training and test sets are approximately a 70% of the dataset: the training set contains data from January 1st 2007 to August 23rd 2011 and the test set contains data from August 24th 2011 to August 19th 2013. The algorithm predicts almost 3 years, i.e., the streaming set is from August 20th 2013 to June 21st 2016.

In this study, the experiments are carried out with the same parameters and prediction horizons established in [22]. Each of the four experiments has a different horizon: 4, 8, 12 and 24 hours. As the dataset contains 1 sample each 10 min, the prediction horizons are 24, 48, 72 and 144 samples, respectively. The goal is to analyze the behaviour of the algorithm for different prediction horizons considering the optimal parameters of [22].

The parameters for each experiment are listed below, where h is the prediction horizon, w corresponds to the number of past values used for predicting the next h values and K is the number of nearest neighbors of the training set to consider when creating the M model, as defined in Sect. 3:

- For the prediction horizon $h = 24$, optimal parameters are $w = 144$ and $K = 4$.
- For the prediction horizon $h = 48$, optimal parameters are $w = 288$ and $K = 2$.
- For the prediction horizon $h = 72$, optimal parameters are $w = 576$ and $K = 4$.
- For the prediction horizon $h = 144$, optimal parameters are $w = 864$ and $K = 4$.

4.2   Results

The four experiments are run on a cluster located at the Data Science and Big Data Laboratory in Pablo de Olavide University. The cluster is formed by 4 nodes: 3 slaves and 1 master. The whole cluster has 4 Processors Intel(R) Core(TM) i7-5820K CPU with 48 cores, 120 GB of RAM memory. It uses Ubuntu 16.04.1 LTS, Apache Spark 2.3.4, HDFS on Hadoop 2.7.7 and Apache Kafka 2.11.

The metrics used to evaluate the performance of the algorithm are the mean absolute percentage error (MAPE), expressed as a percentage, and the mean absolute error (MAE), expressed in MW [24]. Table 1 presents the above-mentioned metrics of error when forecasting the streaming set of data for the different prediction horizons. Moreover, the maximum, minimum and standard deviation (st. dev.) of the MAPE for the streaming set are depicted. It can be noticed that both MAPE and MAE increase with higher values of the prediction horizon. Considering that in this work the offline summary model is not updated, the standard deviation and values of MAPE and MAE lead to think that the offline summary model represents in an accurate way the streaming data.

Table 1. Metrics of errors for different prediction horizons

h	w	k	Maximum MAPE	Minimum MAPE	St. dev. MAPE	MAPE	MAE
24	144	4	33.0031	0.2464	2.0745	2.4288	670.1298
48	288	2	31.2719	0.4101	2.0842	2.7617	766.8640
72	576	4	34.3861	0.6002	2.8199	3.3535	933.9924
144	864	4	29.3277	0.6548	3.6136	3.8465	1072.8357

Figures 1 and 2 show the worst forecasts (the maximum MAPE) and the best ones (the minimum MAPE) for each prediction horizon, respectively. They both show the real and forecasted electricity demand values in the vertical axis and the hours of the day in the horizontal axis. Each sub-figure includes the day (in format day/month/year) and the horizon of the maximum or minimum MAPE. All worst days correspond to public holidays in Spain: in summer for the prediction horizons 24 and 48 and, in winter for the prediction horizons 72 and 144. For prediction horizons 24, 48 and 72, it can be observed abrupt changes at the last time sample of the horizon as the following forecasted values correspond to the next prediction horizon on the same day. On the other hand,

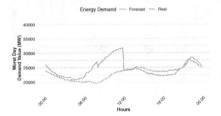

(a) h=24. Horizon: from 08:00AM to 11:50AM. Day: 16/08/2015

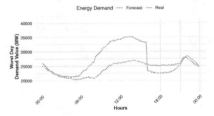

(b) h=48. Horizon: from 08:00AM to 15:50PM. Day: 16/08/2014

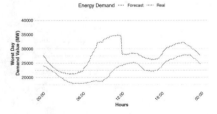

(c) h=72. Horizon: from 00:00AM to 11:50AM. Day: 25/12/2013

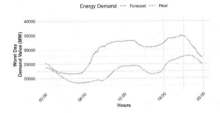

(d) h=144. Horizon: The whole day. Day: 25/12/2014

Fig. 1. Days with the worst forecasts for each h horizon

Fig. 2 shows that, in these days, the data used in the offline phase represents well the online data because even without any update of the summary offline model, the forecasted values are quite accurate.

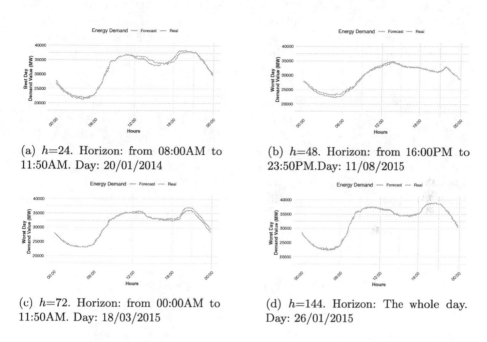

(a) h=24. Horizon: from 08:00AM to 11:50AM. Day: 20/01/2014

(b) h=48. Horizon: from 16:00PM to 23:50PM.Day: 11/08/2015

(c) h=72. Horizon: from 00:00AM to 11:50AM. Day: 18/03/2015

(d) h=144. Horizon: The whole day. Day: 26/01/2015

Fig. 2. Days with the best forecasts for each h horizon

Table 2 shows the MAE obtained when applying the algorithm recently published in [22] and the proposed StreamWNN algorithm using the same set of data and the same parameters for comparison purposes. It can be observed that the error of the proposed algorithm is higher just for $h = 24$. However, the MAEs of the StreamWNN are quite smaller than the ones in [22] for all the other prediction horizons.

Table 2. The MAE (in MW) for the StreamWNN and the algorithm in [22].

h	[22]	StreamWNN
24	524.14	670.13
48	920.87	766.86
72	1313.40	933.99
144	1514.92	1072.84

Figure 3 represents the mean values for each hour, both of the forecasted and of the real energy demand values of the $h = 24$ prediction horizon setup. The representation of the other three forecast horizons is very similar. It confirms that the forecast results have behave very similar to the ones of the real data.

Besides the good performance, a streaming algorithm has to provide timely results during the online phase. Even if the offline phase of the streaming algorithm is not limited in execution time, the offline phase of the proposed algorithm is fast considering the huge amount of data, both in training and test sets. The offline phase of the proposed algorithm for $h = 24$ takes 222.09 s, 167.16 s for $h = 48$, 153.47 s for $h = 72$ and 122.50 s for $h = 144$.

The online execution time for all four prediction horizons is presented in Fig. 4. This figure shows for every 200 iterations of the algorithm, the time in seconds from the beginning of the online phase. The number of iterations for each experiment is different as w and h changes. In addition, as smaller these values are, less time is taken to compute the iterations (as in the offline phase). It can be observed that the algorithm increases linearly the execution time as more iterations have been previously made, which is very important in streaming algorithms. Considering these results, a forecast of h values is made in an average of 1.4 s for $h = 24$, 1.6 s for $h = 48$, 1.9 s for $h = 72$ and 2.3 s for $h = 144$. These results are presented in Table 3.

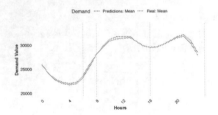 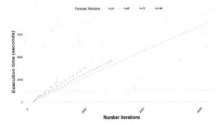

Fig. 3. Hourly average of the actual and forecasted energy demand

Fig. 4. Execution time of the online phase versus number of iterations

Table 3. Computation times (in seconds) for different prediction horizons

h	Offline phase time	Online prediction time of h values
24	222.09	1.4
48	167.16	1.6
72	153.47	1.9
144	122.50	2.3

5 Conclusions

The StreamWNN algorithm for time series forecasting in the streaming environment has been proposed. The StreamWNN consists of two stages: an offline or batch phase and an online phase. The first stage creates a summary prediction model with the K nearest neighbors for each window of w samples and their next h samples of the training set. Afterwards, in the second stage, the time series of the streaming set are processed satisfying the streaming requirements. When streams arrive, the model predicts the h next values with a weighted average using the selected K nearest neighbor from the batch prediction model. The algorithm has been applied to an electricity demand time series dataset containing records over nine years. The performance of the algorithm has been evaluated with the MAPE and MAE error metrics for each prediction horizon. A good performance has been shown when comparing these errors with a benchmark algorithm, that used the same dataset and parameters.

The future works will be focused on some characteristics of the algorithm such as updating the summary batch model considering the knowledge of the previous time series streams, detecting novelties and outliers in the streams or studying the process to select the optimal values of the parameters.

Acknowledgements. The authors would like to thank the Spanish Ministry of Science, Innovation and Universities for the support under project TIN2017-88209-C2.

References

1. Bifet, A., Morales, G.F.: Big data stream learning with SAMOA. In: Proceedings of the IEEE International Conference on Data Mining Workshop (ICDM), pp. 1199–1202 (2015)
2. Cover, T., Hart, P.: Nearest neighbor pattern classification. IEEE Trans. Inf. Theory **13**(1), 21–27 (1967)
3. De Silva, D., Yu, X., Alahakoon, D., Holmes, G.: Incremental pattern characterization learning and forecasting for electricity consumption using smart meters. In: Proceedings of the IEEE International Symposium on Industrial Electronics, pp. 807–812 (2011)
4. Dudani, S.A.: The distance-weighted k-nearest-neighbor rule. IEEE Trans. Syst. Man Cybern. **6**(4), 325–327 (1976)
5. Fernández, A.M., Gutiérrez-Avilés, D., Troncoso, A., Martínez-Álvarez, F.: Real-time big data analytics in smart cities from LoRa-based IoT networks. In: Martínez Álvarez, F., Troncoso Lora, A., Sáez Muñoz, J.A., Quintián, H., Corchado, E. (eds.) SOCO 2019. AISC, vol. 950, pp. 91–100. Springer, Cham (2020). https://doi.org/10.1007/978-3-030-20055-8_9
6. Gaber, M.M., Zaslavsky, A., Krishnaswamy, S.: Mining data streams: a review. ACM SIGMOD Rec. **34**(2), 18–26 (2005)
7. Galicia, A., Talavera-Llames, R., Troncoso, A., Koprinska, I., Martínez-Álvarez, F.: Multi-step forecasting for big data time series based on ensemble learning. Knowl. Based Syst. **163**, 830–841 (2019)
8. Gama, J., Rodrigues, P.P.: Stream-based electricity load forecast. In: Kok, J.N., Koronacki, J., Lopez de Mantaras, R., Matwin, S., Mladenič, D., Skowron, A. (eds.) PKDD 2007. LNCS (LNAI), vol. 4702, pp. 446–453. Springer, Heidelberg (2007). https://doi.org/10.1007/978-3-540-74976-9_45

9. Gutiérrez-Avilés, D., et al.: SmartFD: a real big data application for electrical fraud detection. In: de Cos Juez, F., et al. (eds.) HAIS 2018. LNCS, vol. 10870, pp. 120–130. Springer, Cham (2018). https://doi.org/10.1007/978-3-319-92639-1_11

10. He, H., Chen, S., Li, K., Xu, X.: Incremental learning from stream data. IEEE Trans. Neural Networks **22**(12), 1901–1914 (2011)

11. Lara-Benítez, P., Carranza-García, M., Luna-Romera, J.M., Riquelme, J.C.: Temporal convolutional networks applied to energy-related time series forecasting. Appl. Sci. **10**(7), 2322 (2020)

12. Lara-Benítez, P., Carranza-García, M., Riquelme, J.C.: An experimental review on deep learning architectures for time series forecasting. Int. J. Neural Syst. **31**(03), 2130001 (2021)

13. Li, Y., Li, D., Wang, S., Zhai, Y.: Incremental entropy-based clustering on categorical data streams with concept drift. Knowl. Based Syst. **59**, 33–47 (2014)

14. Liu, L.P., Jiang, Y., Zhou, Z.H.: Least square incremental linear discriminant analysis. In: Proceedings of the IEEE International Conference on Data Mining, pp. 298–306 (2009)

15. Liu, X., Iftikhar, N., Xie, X.: Survey of real-time processing systems for big data. In: Proceedings of the International Database Engineering and Applications Symposium, pp. 356–361 (2014)

16. Maillo, J., Ramírez, S., Triguero, I., Herrera, F.: kNN-IS: an iterative spark-based design of the k-nearest neighbors classifier for big data. Knowl. Based Syst. **117**, 3–15 (2017)

17. Martínez-Álvarez, F., Troncoso, A., Riquelme, J.C., Aguilar-Ruiz, J.S.: Energy time series forecasting based on pattern sequence similarity. IEEE Trans. Knowl. Data Eng. **23**(8), 1230–1243 (2010)

18. Ng, W.W.Y., Zhang, J., Lai, C.S., Pedrycz, W., Lai, L.L., Wang, X.: Cost-sensitive weighting and imbalance-reversed bagging for streaming imbalanced and concept drifting in electricity pricing classification. IEEE Trans. Ind. Inform. **15**(3), 1588–1597 (2019)

19. Pérez-Chacón, R., Luna-Romera, J.M., Troncoso, A., Martínez-Álvarez, F., Riquelme, J.C.: Big data analytics for discovering electricity consumption patterns in smart cities. Energies **11**(3), 683 (2018)

20. Shahrivari, S.: Beyond batch processing: towards real-time and streaming big data. Computers **3**(4), 117–129 (2014)

21. Talavera-Llames, R., Pérez-Chacón, R., Troncoso, A., Martínez-Álvarez, F.: MV-kWNN: a novel multivariate and multi-output weighted nearest neighbours algorithm for big data time series forecasting. Neurocomputing **353**, 56–73 (2019)

22. Talavera-Llames, R., Pérez-Chacón, R., Troncoso, A., Martínez-Álvarez, F.: Big data time series forecasting based on nearest neighbours distributed computing with spark. Knowl. Based Syst. **161**, 12–25 (2018)

23. Torres, J.F., Galicia, A., Troncoso, A., Martínez-Álvarez, F.: A scalable approach based on deep learning for big data time series forecasting. Integr. Comput. Aided Eng. **25**(4), 335–348 (2018)

24. Troncoso, A., Riquelme-Santos, J.M., Gómez-Expósito, A., Martínez-Ramos, J.L., Riquelme-Santos, J.C.: Electricity market price forecasting based on weighted nearest neighbors techniques. IEEE Trans. Power Syst. **22**(3), 1294–1301 (2007)

25. Troncoso, A., Riquelme, J.C., Aguilar-Ruiz, J.S., Riquelme-Santos, J.M.: Evolutionary techniques applied to the optimal short-term scheduling of the electrical energy production. Eur. J. Oper. Res. **185**(3), 1114–1127 (2008)

26. Wang, W., Men, C., Lu, W.: Online prediction model based on support vector machine. Neurocomputing **71**(4–6), 550–558 (2008)
27. Zhang, X., Qian, Z., Shen, S., Shi, J., Wang, S.: Streaming massive electric power data analysis based on spark streaming. In: Li, G., Yang, J., Gama, J., Natwichai, J., Tong, Y. (eds.) DASFAA 2019. LNCS, vol. 11448, pp. 200–212. Springer, Cham (2019). https://doi.org/10.1007/978-3-030-18590-9_14

Towards Combining Object Detection and Text Classification Models for Form Entity Recognition

María Villota, Gonzalo Santamaría, César Domínguez[✉], Jónathan Heras, Eloy Mata, and Vico Pascual

Department of Mathematics and Computer Science, Universidad de La Rioja, Logroño, Spain
{maria.villota,gonzalo.santamaria,cesar.dominguez,jonathan.heras, eloy.mata,vico.pascual}@unirioja.es

Abstract. Due to the increasing volume of forms that are generated in a daily basis, the automatic extraction of the information included in these template-based documents is greatly demanded. However, this is not a straightforward task due to the great diversity of templates with different location of form entities, and the quality of the scanned documents. In this work, we have made a first step towards form entity recognition by combining computer vision and natural language processing techniques. First, we have applied state-of-the-art deep object detection and semantic segmentation models for localising the position of form entities based only on visual features. Afterwards, we have studied different transfer learning approaches (fine-tuning and feature extraction) for classifying the text content of the localised form entities. The studied models require low computational and image resources, making them a feasible alternative to state-of-the-art models even if their performance is slightly worse.

Keywords: Form understanding · Object detection · Semantic segmentation · Text classification

1 Introduction

Forms are a widespread type of document used in lots of fields including administration, medicine, finance, or insurance [5]. Forms are used as an appropriate way to collect and communicate data following a structured format; and, nowadays, there is an enormous demand in digitising forms, and interpreting the data included in them [28]. Forms are either provided under a born digital format (such as PDF, HTML, or documents included in web applications), or included in a scanned image that comes from a form written or printed on a paper [5]. In this work, we have focused on the task of form understanding from scanned documents.

This work was partially supported by Ministerio de Ciencia e Innovación and FEDER Funds [RTC-2017-6640-7], Ministerio de Economía y Competitividad [MTM2017-88804-P], and Ministerio de Ciencia e Innovación [PID2020-115225RB-I00].

E. Alba et al. (Eds.): CAEPIA 2021, LNAI 12882, pp. 196–205, 2021.
https://doi.org/10.1007/978-3-030-85713-4_19

Form understanding can be defined as the process of automatically extracting information from a form [12], and it is usually approached by analysing both textual contents and organisational structures [28]. Form understanding on scanned documents remains a challenging task due to the diversity of templates, structures, layouts, and formats that can greatly vary from one form to another; and, also due to the different quality of the scanned document images [30]. In this context, there is a feature that is shared by all forms: they contain a collection of interlinked entities built as key-value (or label-value) pairs [28], together with other entities such as headers or images. Therefore, form understanding can be seen as a two-step process. In a first step, the spatial layout and written information is analysed to localise the position of form entities and to identify them as questions, answers, or other entities present in the form; this step is known as *form entity recognition*. Subsequently, the extracted entities are interlinked to understand their relationships in a task called *form entity linking* [12].

In this work, we have made a first step towards tackling form entity recognition by combining computer vision and natural language processing techniques; the main differences of our approach with other existing methods are detailed in Sect. 2. Our approach has been tested in the FUNSD dataset [12], described in Sect. 3, and we can highlight the following contributions of this work.

- First, we have conducted a study of several state-of-the-art deep detection and semantic segmentation models for localising the position of form entities based only on visual features, see Sect. 4. The best model achieved a F1-score of 0.71.
- Additionally, we have explored two different transfer learning approaches (fine-tuning and feature extraction) for classifying the text in form entities, see Sect. 5, achieving a F1-score of 0.81.
- Finally, we have publicly released all the code and models developed in this work https://github.com/mavillot/FUNSD-Information-Extraction.

2   Related Work

Form understanding is a task that, up to now, has received little attention in the literature [12]. The scarcity of works in this area is mainly based on the absence of datasets of forms due to the sensitive information included in these documents. Therefore, a recent and important milestone in this area was the publication of the FUNSD dataset [12] in 2019, which was the first publicly available dataset that was developed with form understanding purposes. This was a fully annotated dataset of image forms from noisy and old scanned documents. Moreover, baselines and metrics for the tasks of form entity recognition and form entity linking were provided. In particular, different text localisation models at the word level (including Tesseract, EAST, Google Vision, and Faster R-CNN) were combined with a multi-layer perceptron for form entity recognition obtaining a F1-score of 0.57. For the task of form entity linking a binary classifier constructed using again a multi-layer perceptron achieved a F1-score of 0.04.

Since its publication, the FUNSD dataset has been used as a benchmark by several works. LayoutLM [30] proposed a pre-training method of text and layout for document image understanding task. The method joins text, position, 2-D position and image embeddings. Text and position embeddings are inspired by the BERT language model [6] trying to input textual information. 2-D position embeddings denote the relative position of tokens in the document, and image embeddings try to capture appearance features such as font directions, types and colours. The LayoutLM method was pre-trained on a great number of unlabelled documents in different domains. More concretely, the IIT-CDIP Test Collection [14], which contains more than 6 million scanned documents, was used. Then, the model was fine-tuned using the embeddings on different contexts. In particular, the model was applied to form entity recognition on the FUNSD dataset achieving the best performance (F1-score of 0.79) when using text, layout, and image information at the same time on a pre-trained model on 11M document pages. Recently, an improved version of this method, named LayoutLMv2, was presented in [31]. Among other characteristics, the new method integrates the document text, layout and image information in the pre-trained phase. When this improved model was applied to form entity recognition on the FUNSD dataset, a F1-score of 0.84 was obtained. A different approach was used in [9], where the authors created a model called BROS that also used 2-D positional embeddings following 1-D BERT embeddings. This work includes a novel area-masking pre-training strategy designed for text blocks on 2-D space, and defines a graph-based decoder to capture the semantic relation between text blocks. Following LayoutLM, this method was also pre-trained in the IIT-CDIP Test Collection, and it obtained a F1-score of 0.81 when it was applied to form entity recognition on the FUNSD dataset.

Finally, a multimodal method to extract key-values pairs and build the hierarchy structure in documents for form entity linking in the FUNSD dataset was proposed in [28]. The form structure was considered as a tree-like hierarchy of text fragments, and the parent-child relation corresponds to key-value pairs in forms. In particular, given the hierarchical structure in the form, the superior counterpart for each text fragment was predicted. This work obtained a mAP of 0.72. The problem of entity linking was also addressed by BROS [9] by including a graph-based decoder. When the BROS model was applied to the task of entity linking in the FUNSD dataset, a F1-score of 0.67 was obtained.

The main drawback of both the LayoutML and BROS models is that they require a pre-training step on 11M images of old documents. Hence, in order to work properly with modern documents, a similar pre-training step will be required; however, as far as we are aware, such a dataset of modern documents does not currently exists. In our work, we have designed an approach for form entity recognition that does not require the pre-training step; namely, we first localise the position of the form entities based only on visual features; and, subsequently, we apply semantic labelling to the localised objects using text classification models. Currently, we have used the annotations provided by the FUNSD dataset, described in the following section, to construct both a localisation model and a text classifier. The next step, that remains as further work will be the connection of both models by using OCR over the form entities localised by the visual model.

3   FUNSD Dataset

The FUNSD Dataset [12] is a freely available dataset for form understanding in noisy scanned documents. This dataset contains 199 fully annotated images of forms that vary widely with respect to their structure and appearance. The dataset is available at https://guillaumejaume.github.io/FUNSD/. The forms come from different fields, e.g., marketing, advertising, and scientific reports. The documents were sampled from the form type document of the RVL-CDIP dataset [8] which is composed of real grey scale images from the 1980s and 1990s. The documents have a quality with various types of noise added by successive scanning and printing procedures, and a low resolution (around 100 dpi).

The annotations of each image is encoded in a JSON file. Each form is represented as a list of semantic entities that are interlinked. A semantic entity is described by a unique identifier, a label (chosen from four categories: question, answer, header, or other), a bounding box with the position of the entity, a list of words, and a list of links with the relationships among entities. For our work, the information about the links has not be considered. The 199 annotated forms contain more that 30,000 word-level annotations and around 10,000 entities. The dataset is split into 149 images in the training set and 50 in the testing set. The dataset statistics and class distribution of the semantic entities, as described in [12], are included in Table 1.

Table 1. FUNSD class distribution of the semantic entities

	Header	Question	Answer	Other	Total
Training	441	3,266	2,802	902	7,411
Testing	122	1,077	821	312	2,332

4   Vision Models for Detecting Form Entities

Form entity recognition in images can be framed either as an object detection or a semantic segmentation task. Algorithms for object detection determine the position, by means of a bounding box, and category of multiple objects in an image; whereas, semantic segmentation models provide a classification for each pixel of a given image. Currently, the most successful methods for both tasks are based on deep learning methods [16]. In this section, we present a study of several deep learning algorithms, both for object detection and semantic segmentation, applied to recognise the semantic entities of the FUNSD dataset.

For our experiments with object detection algorithms, we have trained 6 object detection models using 3 deep learning libraries: IceVision [25], that provides the Faster R-CNN [18] and EfficientDet [22] models; DarkNet [1], that supports the versions 3 and 4 of YOLO (the difference between these models is the backbone architecture and state of the art features employed for training the version 4 of YOLO) [26]; and Keras [3], that allows us to train FCOS [23] and FSAF [32] models. In order to train these models, we applied transfer learning by loading in them the corresponding backbone trained on the ImageNet classification challenge, and then fine-tuned the model for our task using a GPU Nvidia RTX 2080 Ti, and using the by-default hyper-parameters for these models. The trained models were evaluated using precision, recall, F1-score, and mAP in the testing set of the FUNSD dataset by considering only the localisation of text regions (localisation), and also by taking into account the class of those regions (detection), see Table 2. In both tasks, the best model was built using the version 4 of YOLO with a F1-score of 0.8 in the localisation task, and a 0.71 in the detection task.

Table 2. Results for the object detection and semantic segmentation models. The localisation columns corresponds with the results for the localisation of form regions; whereas, the detection columns also take into account the classification of those regions. A "-" indicates that such a metric was not provided in the original paper. The best results are highlighted in bold face.

	Localisation				Detection			
	Precision	Recall	F1-score	mAP	Precision	Recall	F1-score	mAP
Faster R-CNN	0.73	0.63	0.68	13.05	0.16	0.14	0.15	12.5
FCOS	0.76	0.40	0.53	9.60	0.57	0.30	0.40	19.93
FSAF	0.64	0.36	0.46	7.31	0.49	0.27	0.35	19.49
EfficientDet	0.76	0.06	0.11	2.27	0.09	0.01	0.01	4.83
YOLOv3	**0.81**	0.79	**0.8**	62.5	0.7	0.7	0.7	55.14
YOLOv4	0.8	0.81	**0.8**	**63.05**	0.7	0.72	0.71	**60.19**
DeepLab	0.76	0.55	0.64	11.27	0.36	0.42	0.39	17.99
HRNet	0.75	0.53	0.62	11.19	0.43	0.48	0.45	20.44
U-Net	0.74	0.54	0.63	11.10	0.27	0.43	0.33	13.57
FUNSD model [12]	0.70	**0.84**	0.76	-	-	-	0.57	-
BROS [9]	-	-	-	-	0.80	0.81	0.81	-
LayoutLM [30]	-	-	-	-	0.76	0.81	0.79	-
LayoutLMv2 [31]	-	-	-	-	**0.83**	**0.85**	**0.84**	-

In addition to the object detection models, we have trained three semantic segmentation algorithms: DeepLab [2] (with a Resnet 50 backbone), HRNet-Seg [27] (with an HRNet W30 backbone), and U-Net [19] (with a Resnet 34 backbone). All the architectures were trained with the libraries PyTorch [17] and FastAI [10] and using a GPU Nvidia RTX 2080 Ti, and using the by-default hyper-parameters for these models. In order to conduct the training process, we first transformed the bounding boxes of the form entities provided by the FUNSD dataset to masks. Analogously, the masks produced by the trained semantic segmentation models where transformed to bounding boxes (in order to compare them with the detection models) by taking the minimum enclosing bounding box of each segmented region. The F1-score of the segmentation models when classes are taken into account, see Table 2, ranges from 0.33 in the U-Net model to 0.45 in the HRNet model; and the F1-score when we only pay attention to the blocks ranges from 0.62 in the HRNet model to 0.64 in the DeepLab model. These results are similar to those obtained by the Faster R-CNN (the third best detection model), but far from those achieved by the YOLO algorithms.

We can notice that the performance of our models is far from that obtained with models such as LayoutLM [30,31] or BROS [9] which combine text, layout and visual features, see Table 2. As we have previously mentioned, the drawback of those models is that they require a pre-training step with 11M images, whereas our models are only trained with the FUNSD data. As we have mentioned in Scct. 2, this might be an issue when working with modern documents, since LayoutLM and BROS will require a new pretraining step with such kind of document. The models presented in this section do not suffer from such drawback, but are based only on the inspection of visual features; hence, we are not taking into account the textual information of forms. As shown in [9,30,31], such knowledge is relevant when trying to recognise different form entities, and it is explored in the following section.

5 Text Classification of Form Entities

Text classification is a natural language processing task that consists in categorising a text into a set of predefined classes. Nowadays, this task is mainly tackled using deep learning models [6], and, namely, by training transformer-based architectures [24]. As for the computer vision models, it is not feasible to train this kind of model from scratch, but transfer learning must be applied. In this section, we present two transfer learning approaches for text classification of the form entities of the FUNSD dataset.

In the first set of experiments, we have fine-tuned several transformer-based language models; namely, Albert [13], BERT [6], DistilBert [20], Roberta [15], and ULMFit [11]. For fine-tuning the models, we replaced the head of each language model (that is, the last layer of the model), with a new head adapted to the number of classes of the FUNSD dataset. Then, we trained the models for 5 epochs. All the networks used in our experiments were implemented in Pytorch [17], and have been trained thanks to the functionality of the libraries Hugging Face [29], Fastai [10] and Blur [7] using the GPUs provided by the Google Colab environment [4], and using the by-default hyper-parameters for these models. These models were evaluated using the weighted version of the accuracy, precision, recall, and F1-score in the testing set of the FUNSD dataset (see Table 3), and the best results (a weighted F1-score of 0.81) were achieved with the BERT architecture.

Table 3. Results for the text classification models. The first 5 rows provide the results for deep learning models fine-tuned on the FUNSD dataset; whereas the next 7 rows are classical machine learning models trained on the output of the last layer of a BERT model. The last three rows come from the state-of-the-art models. A "-" indicates that such a metric was not provided in the original paper. The best results are highlighted in bold face.

	Accuracy	Precision	Recall	F1-score
Albert	0.78	0.78	0.78	0.78
BERT	**0.82**	0.81	0.82	0.81
DistilBert	0.72	0.71	0.72	0.71
Roberta	0.71	0.69	0.71	0.69
ULMFit	0.75	0.76	0.75	0.76
KNN	0.80	0.81	0.80	0.81
Decision tree	0.79	0.79	0.79	0.79
SVM	0.80	0.80	0.80	0.80
Naive Bayes	0.79	0.79	0.79	0.79
Random forest	0.79	0.80	0.79	0.79
Neural network	0.81	0.81	0.81	0.81
Logistic regression	0.81	0.81	0.81	0.81
BROS [9]	-	0.80	0.81	0.81
LayoutLM [30]	-	0.76	0.81	0.79
LayoutLMv2 [31]	-	**0.83**	**0.85**	**0.84**

We have also tested a different transfer-learning approach for classifying the text of the FUNSD dataset. In particular, instead of replacing the last layer of the aforementioned text classification models, we used the last layer of the BERT model as feature extractor; and, subsequently, used such features to train 7 classical machine learning algorithms (namely, KNN, decision tree, SVM, naive Bayes, random forest, neural network, and logistic regression). The results obtained by these models, summarised in Table 3, show that all of them performed equally well (the 7 models reached a weighted F1-score close to 0.80). Moreover, three of the models achieved the same weighted F1-score of the best fine-tuned model with the advantage of not requiring a GPU for training.

It is worth noting that the text models presented in this section obtain results close to those obtained by models like LayoutLM or BROS, but without requiring the pre-training step. However, we are making two strong assumptions about the text extraction that were not made by the LayoutLM and BROS models.

First, we assume that the position of the text blocks is properly determined; this is an assumption that is almost solved with the computer vision methods presented in the previous section. Moreover, we assume that the text contained in those blocks is read properly. In spite of the existence of OCR methods for automatically reading text from documents [21], it was shown in [12] that those methods fail when working with the FUNSD dataset. Hence, further research is needed in those directions to successfully apply our approach.

6 Conclusions and Further Work

This work is a first step towards form entity recognition based on the combination of computer vision and natural language processing techniques. We have tested several deep object detection and semantic segmentation models to identify form entities by just using visual features. The YOLO v4 detection model has shown to be competitive, with a F1-score of 0.71, when compared with more complex approaches presented in the literature. In addition, we have explored the application of two transfer learning techniques for classifying the text of form entities. In such a study, we reached the conclusion that fine-tuning the BERT model produces the best result with a F1-score of 0.81. The studied models do not require a pre-training step, making them a feasible alternative to state-of-the-art models even if their performance is slightly worse.

Up to now, we have tackled the problem of form understanding from two different perspectives by using, independently, computer vision and natural language processing techniques. In the future, we plan to combine these two approaches to bring to the table the benefits of each of them. One of the main challenges will be a correct reading of the text included in the documents, since OCR techniques do not perform properly in the FUNSD dataset [12]. Moreover, we are interested in applying our models to more recent documents since the FUNSD dataset is formed by old documents. The main challenges here are the privacy concerns raised when using form documents, and the issues related to the annotation of these documents, a time-consuming task that is instrumental to train and evaluate any deep learning model.

References

1. Alexey, A.B.: YOLO darknet (2018). https://github.com/AlexeyAB/darknet
2. Chen, L.-C., Zhu, Y., Papandreou, G., Schroff, F., Adam, H.: Encoder-decoder with Atrous separable convolution for semantic image segmentation. In: Ferrari, V., Hebert, M., Sminchisescu, C., Weiss, Y. (eds.) ECCV 2018. LNCS, vol. 11211, pp. 833–851. Springer, Cham (2018). https://doi.org/10.1007/978-3-030-01234-2_49
3. Chollet, F., et al.: Keras (2015). https://github.com/fchollet/keras
4. Colaboratory team: Google colaboratory (2017). https://colab.research.google.com
5. Coüasnon, B., Lemaitre, A.: Recognition of tables and forms. In: Doermann, D., Tombre, K. (eds.) Handbook of Document Image Processing and Recognition, pp. 647–677. Springer, London (2014). https://doi.org/10.1007/978-0-85729-859-1_20

6. Devlin, J., et al.: BERT: pre-training of deep bidirectional transformers for language understanding. In: Proceedings of the 2019 Conference of the North American Chapter of the Association for Computational Linguistics: Human Language Technologies, Volume 1 (Long and Short Papers), pp. 4171–4186. Association for Computational Linguistics (2019). https://doi.org/10.18653/v1/N19-1423

7. Gilliam, W.: Blur: a library that integrates hugging face transformers with version 2 of the fastai framework (2021). https://github.com/ohmeow/blurr

8. Harley, A.W., Ufkes, A., Derpanis, K.G.: Evaluation of deep convolutional nets for document image classification and retrieval. In: Proceedings of the 13th International Conference on Document Analysis and Recognition (ICDAR 2015), pp. 991–995 (2015). https://doi.org/10.1109/ICDAR.2015.7333910

9. Hong, T., et al.: A pre-trained language model for understanding texts in document (2021). https://openreview.net/forum?id=punMXQEsPr0

10. Howard, J., Gugger, S.: FastAI: a layered API for deep learning. Information 11, 108 (2020). https://doi.org/10.3390/info11020108

11. Howard, J., Ruder, S.: Universal language model fine-tuning for text classification. In: Proceedings of the 56th Annual Meeting of the Association for Computational Linguistics (Volume 1: Long Papers), pp. 328–339. Association for Computational Linguistics (2018). https://doi.org/10.18653/v1/P18-1031

12. Jaume, G., Ekenel, H.K., Thiran, J.P.: FUNSD: a dataset for form understanding in noisy scanned documents. In: Proceedings of the 2019 International Conference on Document Analysis and Recognition Workshops (ICDARW), vol. 2, pp. 1–6. IEEE (2019). https://doi.org/10.1109/ICDARW.2019.10029

13. Lan, Z., et al.: Albert: A lite BERT for self-supervised learning of language representations. In: International Conference on Learning Representations (2020)

14. Lewis, D., Agam, G., Argamon, S., Frieder, O., Grossman, D., Heard, J.: Building a test collection for complex document information processing. In: Proceedings of the 29th Annual International ACM SIGIR Conference on Research and Development in Information Retrieval (SIGIR 2006), pp. 665–666. Association for Computing Machinery, New York, NY, USA (2006). https://doi.org/10.1145/1148170.1148307

15. Liu, Y., et al.: Roberta: a robustly optimized BERT pretraining approach. CoRR abs/1907.11692 (2019). http://arxiv.org/abs/1907.11692

16. Liu, Z., et al.: Swin transformer: hierarchical vision transformer using shifted windows. CoRR abs/2103.14030 (2021). http://arxiv.org/abs/2103.14030

17. Paszke, A., et al.: Pytorch: an imperative style, high-performance deep learning library. In: Advances in Neural Information Processing Systems, vol. 32, pp. 8024–8035. Curran Associates, Inc. (2019)

18. Ren, S., He, K., Girshick, R., Sun, J.: Faster R-CNN: towards real-time object detection with region proposal networks. Adv. Neural Inf. Process. Syst. 28, 91–99 (2015)

19. Ronneberger, O., Fischer, P., Brox, T.: U-Net: convolutional networks for biomedical image segmentation. In: Navab, N., Hornegger, J., Wells, W.M., Frangi, A.F. (eds.) MICCAI 2015. LNCS, vol. 9351, pp. 234–241. Springer, Cham (2015). https://doi.org/10.1007/978-3-319-24574-4_28

20. Sanh, V., et al.: DistilBERT, a distilled version of BERT: smaller, faster, cheaper and lighter. CoRR abs/1910.01108 (2019). http://arxiv.org/abs/1910.01108

21. Smith, R.: An overview of the tesseract OCR engine. In: Proceedings of the International Conference on Document Analysis and Recognition (ICDAR), vol. 2, pp. 629–633 (2007). https://doi.org/10.1109/ICDAR.2007.4376991

22. Tan, M., et al.: EfficientDet: scalable and efficient object detection. In: Proceedings of the 2020 IEEE/CVF Conference on Computer Vision and Pattern Recognition. IEEE (2020). https://doi.org/10.1109/CVPR42600.2020.01079
23. Tian, Z., Shen, C., Chen, H., et al.: FCOS: fully convolutional one-stage object detection. CoRR abs/1904.01355 (2019). http://arxiv.org/abs/1904.01355
24. Vaswani, A., et al.: Attention is all you need. In: Advances in Neural Information Processing Systems, vol. 30. Curran Associates, Inc. (2017)
25. Vazquez, L., et al.: IceVision: an agnostic object detection framework (2020). https://github.com/airctic/icevision
26. Wang, C.Y., Bochkovskiy, A., Liao, H.Y.M.: Scaled-yolov4: scaling cross stage partial network. CoRR (2021). http://arxiv.org/abs/2011.08036
27. Wang, J., Sun, K., Cheng, T., et al.: Deep high-resolution representation learning for visual recognition. IEEE Trans. Pattern Anal. Mach. Intell. (2020). https://doi.org/10.1109/tpami.2020.2983686
28. Wang, Z., Zhan, M., Liu, X., Liang, D.: DocStruct: a multimodal method to extract hierarchy structure in document for general form understanding. In: Proceedings of the Findings of the Association for Computational Linguistics (EMNLP 2020), pp. 898–908. Association for Computational Linguistics (2020). https://doi.org/10.18653/v1/2020.findings-emnlp.80
29. Wolf, T., et al.: Transformers: state-of-the-art natural language processing. In: Proceedings of the 2020 Conference on Empirical Methods in Natural Language Processing: System Demonstrations, pp. 38–45. Association for Computational Linguistics (2020). https://doi.org/10.18653/v1/2020.emnlp-demos.6
30. Xu, Y., Li, M., Cui, L., Huang, S., Wei, F., Zhou, M.: LayoutLM: pre-training of text and layout for document image understanding. In: Proceedings of the 26th ACM SIGKDD International Conference on Knowledge Discovery and Data Mining (KDD 2020), pp. 1192-1200. ACM (2020). https://doi.org/10.1145/3394486.3403172
31. Xu, Y., et al.: LayoutLMv2: multi-modal pre-training for visually-rich document understanding. CoRR abs/2012.14740 (2020). http://arxiv.org/abs/2012.14740
32. Zhu, C., He, Y., Savvides, M.: Feature selective anchor-free module for single-shot object detection. CoRR abs/1903.00621 (2019). http://arxiv.org/abs/1903.00621

A Collaborative Platform for the Detection of Non-inclusive Situations in Smart Cities

Alfonso González-Briones$^{(\boxtimes)}$ ⓘ, Iván García-Magariño ⓘ,
Jorge J. Gómez-Sanz ⓘ, Rubén Fuentes-Fernández ⓘ, and Juan Pavón ⓘ

Research Group on Agent-Based, Social and Interdisciplinary Applications
(GRASIA), Complutense University of Madrid, Madrid, Spain
alfonsogb@ucm.es
http://grasia.fdi.ucm.es

Abstract. The quality of daily life is a key factor in today's urban development. This is a complex aspect, as different groups of citizens understand it quite differently and have different needs. This is particularly important for people with disabilities. When thinking about solutions for smart cities, there are a few approaches for the identification of the problems or obstacles that their implementation poses for different groups of people. Addressing this issue requires tools that provide an interdisciplinary perspective, so the proposed smart solutions really promote the improvement of the quality and well-being of all citizens in cities. In this line, this paper presents a tool that facilitates collaboration among stakeholders through identifying and analysing the elements that prevent a smart city solution from being inclusive. The platform is based on visual novels that illustrate how the solution would work in real settings. Users comment on the novel, play with it to discover and evaluate the solution, and propose changes. Then, a natural language processing engine analyses their comments, and returns the identified non-inclusive situations, ideas for improvement or solutions, and the degree of affinity that each participant has with each of them. The tool has been validated in a mobility scenario. There, three groups of people with different needs used the tool to identify obstacles and non-inclusive situations. The results have been used to assess and improve the tool.

Keywords: Inclusive smart cities · Reduced mobility · Visual novels · Natural Language Processing · Collaborative design · Functional diversity

This work has been partially supported by the projects "Collaborative design for promoting wellness in inclusive smart cities (DColbici3)" (grant TIN2017-88327-R), funded by Spanish Ministry for Economy and Competitiveness under, and "Women, Disability and Inclusion (MILIEU)" (grant 952369) and "Reshaping Attention and Inclusion Strategies for Distinctively vulnerable people among the forcibly displaced (RAISD)" (grant 822688), of the Horizon 2020 research and innovation programme.

E. Alba et al. (Eds.): CAEPIA 2021, LNAI 12882, pp. 206–215, 2021.
https://doi.org/10.1007/978-3-030-85713-4_20

1   Introduction

Disability is gaining more visibility in our society; media awareness campaigns and the ageing of the population have both played a part in this progress. However, there is still much room for improvement in the development and evaluation of solutions that will make smart cities truly inclusive [8]. Each kind of disability has its particular set of characteristics, and in many cases there are known assistive measures for them. Some of these had already been integrated into urban development a few decades ago, such as the sound of traffic lights to allow people with visual impairment to know when they can cross the street, or enable people with mobility problems to go down the kerb when arriving at a zebra crossing. However, not all people with disabilities and situations have been considered equally, therefore, new solutions should be explored.

This progress is noticeable, but still not sufficient. Solution planning is usually done according to the criteria of urban planning staff, who are limited in number and more importantly, they generally do not suffer any type of disability and so they cannot provide an optimal solution from the perspective of a person with disability. One way to support urban planning decisions for the development of inclusive cities is by using simulation tools. Although existing ones are useful, they are mainly based on parametric models of disabilities, so there are multiple details they do not consider. This implies limitations regarding the correct understanding and interpretation of problems and situations, and it makes it difficult to evaluate solutions provided by citizens. To overcome these issues, more capabilities to gather, analyse and interpret the data provided by a platform are required, so it can detect specific instances of exclusion and provide ideas on how to counteract them as well as offer effective alternative solutions and decision-making. A key point here should be gathering feedback from citizens, to know whether the situation and proposed solutions are accepted and produce a positive feeling of inclusion.

This work presents an approach for the cooperative design of more inclusive cities. It considers that participants may have different levels of expertise and experience (i.e., from urban planners to citizens with disabilities), and all of them are needed to asses these complex solutions. The backbone of this approach is a platform called Dcolbici3. It models scenarios as visual novels that participants can play and comment on them to discover and evaluate the situations. The platform collects their opinions regarding those situations. Here, the example that has been focused on involves people with psychomotor disabilities or reduced mobility. The scenarios recreate their daily commuting in the city of Madrid to identify sites that impede their mobility. The platform analyses all the collected information using Natural Language Processing (NLP) techniques, so it is able to discover non-inclusive situations by interpreting users' comments. It uses sentiment analysis to identify the mood or subjective opinions.

The rest of the paper is structured as follows. Section 2 reviews state-of-the-art proposals in this area. Section 3 presents the platform and the visual novels it generates to facilitate the collaboration of citizens in the design of smart city solutions, with special emphasis on aspects of inclusion. Section 3.4 describes the evaluation process and the key results. Finally, Sect. 4 draws some conclusions and future work.

2   Related Work

Today's cities present obstacles to people with disabilities, which affects their quality of life. For instance, wheelchair users have to deal with roadworks, potholes and other obstacles that require them to make decisions and take action; people with hearing problems have to use their other senses, mainly vision, to avoid problems and compensate for the lack of sound; and people with visual impairment have to use hearing signals to detect and avoid obstacles in their daily lives. Tools are required to identify and solve these situations when designing smart cities through information gathering and analysis.

2.1   Detection of Non-inclusive Needs in Smart Cities

The first step when developing smart city solutions is to research and understand the needs of citizens. As previously indicated, each citizen may have different needs as a result of her/his condition. The detection and understanding of those needs have been widely studied in the last decades, especially with the rise and evolution of the Smart City concept [1,7]. Some of the first tools for the detection of non-inclusive situations were based on approaches that used technologies for the creation of 3D environments and on the use of multi-agent systems for the simulation of the behaviour of people with disabilities [9,12].

Tools are needed to understand the requirements for inclusiveness in smart cities; these tools must facilitate the direct participation of citizens. Once they are faced with a situation of potential non-inclusiveness, they could explain what problem they are facing, how they feel, how long it could take to resolve it, how and when the incident must be reported, what solutions or improvements they propose, or any other relevant information that could help solve the problem. This approach allows to collect information that people without certain problems or disabilities may not detect, and therefore not take into account. This offers an important evolutionary advantage with respect to the previously mentioned agent-based simulation systems. This interactive user process within the simulation provides quality information for the analysis, development and adoption of urban inclusion solutions [2,4,10].

Although citizen participation and simulations are being included in smart city studies with greater frequency, there is a lack of a widely accepted approach. The participation of citizens in the recreation of realistic smart city scenarios allows to obtain highly contextualised information. This reliable information is taken into account a posteriori for the improvement of the city's services. Simulation systems, experts or citizens alone cannot provide reliable and precise information, as they lack context. Thus, the contextualized experiences of the citizen must be the main element in providing information.

2.2 Analysis of the Information Collected from the Citizen Interaction

The participatory aspect is key for the collection of information and understanding of situations of non-inclusiveness, from the perspective of the affected. The information can be obtained from citizens with a specific type of disability and analysed to find out how a situation affects them. The required type of tool should have the ability to detect when there was a non-inclusive situation, whether the person was able to solve it or not in the specific circumstances, how much time was needed to overcome it, the feelings experienced by the person who faced this situation, and the reactions to the solutions proposed by the tool. The tool must also facilitate the extraction of ideas on ways of counteracting these problems and solutions to avoid exclusion if it occurred.

This type of tool must be able to admit a high degree of citizen participation, to enable anyone wishing to improve inclusiveness in their smart city to participate. Thus, the tool must have a pipeline for the stages of pre-processing multiple and diverse responses, analysis of information and presentation of the results. All this in an appropriate way to encourage new ideas and the identification of key inclusion aspects for each population group. NLP techniques support this kind of analysis as a mechanism for the automatic extraction of useful information from the multiple responses received in text format [6,11]. It is worth highlighting the use of opinion data mining techniques (better known as sentiment analysis).

In general, the answers of citizens on the collaborative platforms are not well-structured and are not adapted to the grammar of a given natural language, e.g., English or Spanish. In addition, the use of other language elements, such as idioms, proverbs, hyperboles or emojis, makes the extraction of meaning and its analysis complex. Such elements make it necessary to perform a pre-processing stage, at which the received information is cleaned and tokenised for subsequent analysis. Moreover, the platform must be able to classify the responses as options or sentiments. Option-type responses can be of various kinds, and they should be categorized into, for instance, "complaints," "suggestions," and "acknowledgments". When they are classified, the application of sentiment analysis can help understand the citizens' feeling in those responses. With this information, it is possible to make the final analysis and a graphic representation.

The analysis of the needs in this area evidences the potential contribution of this type of tool for the development of inclusive solutions in smart cities. Different techniques can be used to classify citizens into various categories within a population group, identify problems and classify citizens' responses and ideas for solving the detected problems. In this way, the aspect of data analysis is covered from a perspective that allows for an objective evaluation of the responses obtained on the collaborative platforms. This contributes to the achievement of the objective of eliminating or mitigating situations of non-inclusiveness, in search of an increase in the quality of daily life of all citizens.

3 DColbici3: Collaborative Platform for the Identification of Non-inclusive Situations in Smart Cities

The main objective of this work is to facilitate the participation of citizens in the detection of non-inclusive situations that affect the quality of life of certain groups in smart cities. To this end, a citizen-centred process of solution design is proposed. This is an interactive process where citizens recreate their daily lives in the form of visual novels. There, they can detect situations of non-inclusiveness and give feedback on them and how they think these could be solved or improved.

3.1 Design of Visual Novels as a Collaborative Platform

The development of a collaborative platform requires a robust mechanism for user interaction. In this case, it was important to make the choice of this mechanism considering that a large number of citizens will participate. In previous projects [2,5], we have realized that the use of text or graphic models (e.g., domain specific languages), makes operation difficult for most people. However, movies generated by simulations are much more accessible. In this line, we have explored the use of visual novels, where a user is the central element of the novel by participating in it, making decisions that condition the development of the novel, and providing answers. The implementation of visual novels in DColbici3 is facilitated by Monogatari (https://monogatari.io/), a JavaScript framework for the creation and distribution of visual novels. The platform allows for the interaction of the user, who can select options or answer questions. We also implemented geopositioning functions in visual novels among other aspects. This allows the platform to record whether users carry out the actions it requests them, in the place where they are requested to do so. The interaction that Monogatari enables meets the requirements set out in the review of the state-of-the-art. It is a framework that allows for the development of a collaborative platform and, among other functionalities, it can collect a variety of information from the novel created by the user: actions carried out, the user's opinion, and additional issues through geopositioning, e.g., avoiding obstacles.

On our platform, throughout the story, a series of options are offered to find out which one each citizen chooses. The subsequent analysis results in the discovery of the options preferred by different groups (e.g., people without disabilities or with motor or hearing disabilities) and in an understanding of why they are preferred. However, the bare choice of options is not enough to discuss collaboratively the improvement of inclusion in a smart city. For this reason, the platform shows text boxes to allow citizens to express their opinion regarding situations of exclusion in the novel. Additionally, the platform asks series of open-ended questions to collect opinions and ideas about a specific problem.

3.2 NLP for Collaborative Information Analysis

Most of the information gathered from the novel is from free answers. Figure 1 shows the pipeline of the analysis process of this information. The following sections detail each stage of the analysis process.

Fig. 1. Processing pipeline for the analysis of open responses.

Preprocessing: Cleaning Tokenisation. The analysis of the information contained in the comments, ideas, suggestions and feelings of the platform users is done using NLP techniques. They allow to extract the key information from the text, going through several stages.

The information provided by the user may contain irrelevant data, such as some emoticons, symbols, digits and even references to URLs or HTML tags, which must be discarded. A pre-processing stage cleans up the input data, eliminating the irrelevant data and words with no useful meaning. The platform removes the most common words in the language. Given that the Dcolbici3 collaborative platform has for now been developed for a Spanish-speaking public, the most common words are determiners, prepositions and conjunctions, such as "de," "la," "que," "el," "en," and "y". Then, the platform prepares the remaining input data (tokenises the responses) as arrays of strings containing tokens joined by spaces (n-grams), so that it can be further analysed.

Thanks to the transformation of words into tokens, the platform is able to know how many times or in which context certain words appear. This helps detect situations of non-inclusion and their possible solutions.

As noted before, the Dcolbici3 platform asks two types of questions. One is an "option" type, where the user chooses one of the several possible actions that can be taken. These choices change the development of the visual novel. The other one is a "sentiment" type of question, in which users share their feelings regarding the options they have chosen: if s/he has felt comfortable, if that option seems appropriate, or if other better solutions could be offered and why.

Sentiment Analysis. After the pre-processing of the raw responses collected by the platform, they can be studied using sentiment analysis models. Most of the tools and algorithms for carrying out these sentiment analyses are developed for their use with English-language texts. However, the DColbici3 platform offers the possibility to use the platform in Spanish. To overcome this issue and facilitate the initial development, the analysis system uses a Spanish-English translator, so that the analysis can be conducted satisfactorily. Here, the platform uses Googletrans, a Python library that implements the Google Translate API.

The sentiment analysis uses TextBlob (https://textblob.readthedocs.io/) in our platform. This is a Python library for processing text data. It provides an API that allows to perform common NLP tasks such as part-of-speech tagging, noun phrase extraction, or sentiment analysis, among others. TextBlob is used to obtain polarity and subjectivity metrics. The polarity is the feeling, whose value ranges from -1 to $+1$. Subjectivity is a measure of feeling that varies from objective to subjective, and the value goes from 0 to 1. It is preferable to observe the objective feeling than the subjective one, as it tends to provide both positive and negative comments despite the translation to English.

Categorization. As previously described, the visual novels on DColbici3 show three types of questions according to their possible responses: i) Questions to select an option (choice), ii) Questions to ask about the person's feeling on the choices made in the previous type of question (sentiment), and iii) open-ended questions where the user can propose solutions, improvements, or contributions to each case (proposals). The first type allows the platform to determine what kind of questions should be asked to the user further on. The second type is the one to which sentiment analysis is applied. The third type can be divided into three groups "Complaints," "Suggestions," and "Acknowledgements". Once that the text in the responses to "proposals" has been processed, the platform uses sklearn (NLP) (https://scikit-learn.org/) and SpaCy (https://spacy.io/) to categorize them into those groups. Word vectors are used to perform the analysis, as they achieve better classification results with less training data.

3.3   Experimental Set-Up

The case study that has been carried out to validate the DColbici3 platform has been specifically designed to detect non-inclusive situations for people with psychomotor disabilities, reduced mobility and people who, without any of these problems, could be affected in specific situations (e.g., carrying or pulling a shopping trolley). For this purpose, a common situation has been modelled, such as making a journey on foot in a city, here in Madrid (Spain) from the Moncloa Intermodal Transportation Hub to the Spain Square (*Plaza de España*). It is a straight way through the Princess Street (*calle de la Princesa*) of approximately 1.5 km with an average walking time of 19 min. What for most people is a normal walk, for people with some type of disability it may be an obstacle track.

To identify potential problems, DColbici3 reliably recreated this routine situation by developing a visual novel using the Monogatari framework. The visual novel includes elements and situations that usually occur in a city like Madrid. Some examples are the lack of elements that facilitate transport in some places (e.g., escalators at some metro stations), the presence of roadworks, or pavements that are partially or totally closed for pedestrians. These features are important in this context because they represent situations that people with special needs perceive as non-inclusive.

The validation of DColbici3 has been carried out by a group of 24 people. It included: i) 4 persons with disability (wheelchair), 10 persons with reduced mobility (children's carriage), and 10 persons with no mobility problem. The case study pursued the identification of obstacles and situations that are not inclusive for any of these groups.

(a) Decision-making in the visual novel.   (b) The user enters the answer.

Fig. 2. Interaction with the user during the development of the visual novel.

3.4   Results

During the visual novel, the platform asked a series of questions. Option-type questions made it possible to determine to which of these three groups the user belonged. Open-ended questions had also been asked to find out why some options are selected over others, and what feelings the users experience when making some of those choices. Figure 2 shows an interaction with the user by means of an open-ended question on a specific aspect.

First, the answers obtained through the platform were preprocessed. Then, the first step of the analysis process used the internal translator to translate the texts collected in Spanish, and then TextBlob to obtain the polarity of all the answers. In this case, the process was triggered manually by running the script, but it can be configured to run once every certain number of responses have been obtained. Figure 3 shows graphical representations of the results of the analysis conducted in the case study. The first image (a) shows the most repeated keywords in the case study: indicate ("indicar" in Spanish) with 9.5%, effort ("esforzar") with 7.1% and situation ("situación"), notify ("avisar"), signal ("señalar"), anticipation ("antelación"), request ("requerir"), report ("reportar") and incident ("incidencia") with 4.8%.

A quick glance at the keywords with the highest percentages gives a first insight into the problem detected in this case study (i.e., an "incident" occurs and is not "warned" or "signalled" "in advance"). Furthermore, looking at the other keywords with lower percentages gives a possible solution to the problem (i.e., the incident should be reported, creating an app would make it easier for the municipality). This possible solution is formed with the keywords: report ("reportar" in Spanish) and incidence ("incidencia") with 4.8%, should ("debería"), would facilitate ("facilitaría"), create ("crear"), app ("app"), and city council ("ayuntamiento") with 2.4%.

That result is very attractive for researchers from Social Sciences, as it allows them to create different case studies and evaluate possible situations of social exclusion, obtaining the problem perceived by a specific group of people and how to improve or solve this situation. Figures 3(b) and 4(a) respectively show the sentiment of each response received to a question (question 7) and of the options

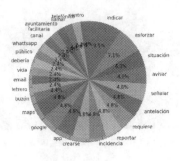
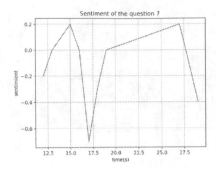

(a) Most repeated words (topics).　　(b) Sentiment of answer question 7.

Fig. 3. NLP analysis of the responses.

(question 5), and the time taken to respond, and Fig. 4(b) shows that the number of proposals for improvement was greater than the number of complaints.

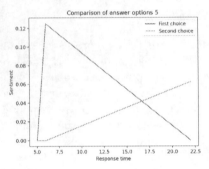
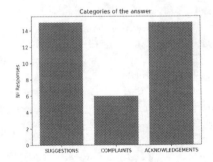

(a) Comparison of sentiments regarding options.　　(b) N° of responses for each type of question.

Fig. 4. Some graphs obtained from the analysis of the case study

4　Conclusions and Future Work

This study has presented a collaborative platform called Dcolbici3 designed to enable citizens to participate in the proposal and design of solutions for smart cities. In this case study, users watched the visual novel and commented on it to help detect problems, evaluate them and propose solutions for the inclusion of people with permanent or temporary mobility problems. The platform has analysed the users' feedback through different types of questions to detect and evaluate situations of non-inclusion in cities. This is possible thanks to the use of NLP-based analysis, which extracts the key information and the general feeling regarding a problem detected by people representing different social groups. It also compares users, groups of users, and the average behaviour regarding aspects like decisions made or the time required to play parts of the novel.

There are several issues to be addressed in future work. Firstly, there is ongoing work on the generation of the visual novel using Model-Driven Engineering (MDE), so that simulations can be developed more easily by people with no programming skills [3]. Secondly, the platform will incorporate additional analysis features for text. Third, this platform will be validated for other smart city development aspects than inclusion.

References

1. Camero, A., Alba, E.: Smart city and information technology: a review. Cities **93**, 84–94 (2019)
2. Cárdenas, M., Castillo, N.G., Gómez-Sanz, J., Pavón, J.: Participatory design with on-line focus groups and normative systems. In: Herrera, F., et al. (eds.) CAEPIA 2018. LNCS (LNAI), vol. 11160, pp. 66–75. Springer, Cham (2018). https://doi.org/10.1007/978-3-030-00374-6_7
3. Cárdenas, M., Sanz, J.G., Pavón, J.: Testing ambient assisted living solutions with simulations. In: Medina-Bulo, I., Merayo, M.G., Hierons, R. (eds.) ICTSS 2018. LNCS, vol. 11146, pp. 56–61. Springer, Cham (2018). https://doi.org/10.1007/978-3-319-99927-2_5
4. Cardullo, P., Kitchin, R.: Being a 'citizen' in the smart city: up and down the scaffold of smart citizen participation in Dublin, Ireland. GeoJournal **84**(1), 1–13 (2019)
5. Fuentes-Fernández, R., Gómez-Sanz, J.J.: Interpreting information in smart environments with social patterns. In: Slavkovik, M. (ed.) EUMAS 2018. LNCS (LNAI), vol. 11450, pp. 48–61. Springer, Cham (2019). https://doi.org/10.1007/978-3-030-14174-5_4
6. Indurkhya, N., Damerau, F.J.: Handbook of Natural Language Processing, vol. 2. CRC Press, Boca Raton (2010)
7. Kummitha, R.K.R., Crutzen, N.: Smart cities and the citizen-driven internet of things: a qualitative inquiry into an emerging smart city. Technol. Forecasting Soc. Change **140**, 44–53 (2019)
8. de Oliveira Neto, J.S., Kofuji, S.T.: Inclusive smart city: an exploratory study. In: Antona, M., Stephanidis, C. (eds.) UAHCI 2016. LNCS, vol. 9738, pp. 456–465. Springer, Cham (2016). https://doi.org/10.1007/978-3-319-40244-4_44
9. Pribyl, O., Svitek, M.: System-oriented approach to smart cities. In: 2015 Photonics North, pp. 1–8. IEEE (2015)
10. Simonofski, A., Asensio, E.S., De Smedt, J., Snoeck, M.: Citizen participation in smart cities: evaluation framework proposal. In: 2017 IEEE 19th Conference on Business Informatics (CBI). vol. 1, pp. 227–236. IEEE (2017)
11. Sun, S., Luo, C., Chen, J.: A review of natural language processing techniques for opinion mining systems. Inf. Fusion **36**, 10–25 (2017)
12. Zhao, Y., Pour, F.F., Golestan, S., Stroulia, E.: Bim Sim/3D: multi-agent human activity simulation in indoor spaces. In: 2019 IEEE/ACM 5th International Workshop on Software Engineering for Smart Cyber-Physical Systems (SEsCPS), pp. 18–24. IEEE (2019)

Electricity Consumption Time Series Forecasting Using Temporal Convolutional Networks

J. F. Torres[(✉)], M. J. Jiménez-Navarro, F. Martínez-Álvarez, and A. Troncoso

Data Science and Big Data Lab, Pablo de Olavide University, 41013 Seville, Spain
{jftormal,mjjimnav,fmaralv,atrolor}@upo.es

Abstract. Forecasting electricity demand is crucial for the management of smart grids to ensure a secure, reliable and sustainable supply. Recently, a variant of convolutional neural networks, called temporal convolutional networks, has emerged for data sequence, competing directly with deep recurrent neural networks in terms of execution time and memory requirements. In this work, we propose a deep temporal convolutional network to predict time series, namely, the electricity consumption with a 4-h forecast horizon. Results using nine and a half years of Spanish electricity load, with a 10-min sampling rate, are reported and discussed. In addition, the performance of the proposed model is compared with linear regression, decision trees, gradient boosted trees, random forests, deep feed forward neural networks that use different techniques to find the optimal hyper-parameters and a deep Long Short-Term Memory network. The proposed model reaches competitive results in terms of accuracy, with the smallest error verging on 1%.

Keywords: Deep learning · Temporal convolutional networks · Time series forecasting · Electricity consumption

1 Introduction

Getting to know the future has always been a big challenge. Since a huge amount electric energy cannot be stored, it is extremely important to generate as accurately as possible the electric energy necessary to cover the demand. Therefore, obtaining reliable predictions can make great social and economic impact, as well as generating knowledge that could be critical in decision-making. The research community is aware of this, so a large part of its studies has focused on the time series analysis and forecasting [16].

Forecasting methods used to predict future values in a time series are based on Box and Jenkins models [3], such as ARIMA, ARMA, ARCH or GARCH [28]. However, techniques based on machine learning and data mining are becoming increasingly important in time series forecasting nowadays. These techniques are widely used in various application fields such as energy [6], stock market [21], health [4], pollution [20], natural disasters [2], agriculture [27], or energy

© Springer Nature Switzerland AG 2021
E. Alba et al. (Eds.): CAEPIA 2021, LNAI 12882, pp. 216–225, 2021.
https://doi.org/10.1007/978-3-030-85713-4_21

resources [26], being some examples that can contribute to the fashioning of the future of humanity.

Within these techniques, deep learning models have had the greatest impact and growth in the last few years. This is due to the great progress that has been made in the area of hardware [15]. Once the hardware limitation has been solved, deep learning models have taken centre stage.

In this work, a deep Temporal Convolutional Network (TCN) is proposed to forecast energy demand for the next four hours. This TCN combines the power of convolutional networks to discover patterns with recurrent networks to deal with sequential data. Results using electricity demand from Spain for more of nine years measured with a 10-min frequency are reported. In addition, the performance of the proposed TCN is compared to various deep feed-forward neural networks, which differ in the way they obtain the optimal values of the hyper-parameters. The TCN shows a remarkable improvement in the prediction in terms of errors regarding other deep learning models.

The rest of the paper is structured as follows. Section 2 introduces the deep learning models recently published in the context of energy time series forecasting. The forecasting problem and the description of the TCN deep learning model can be found in Sect. 3. Section 4 discusses the most important results of short-term electricity consumption forecasting in the Spanish electricity market. Finally, the conclusions are presented in Sect. 5.

2   Related Work

It is well known that there are several architectures available in the literature, such as Deep Feed Forward, Recurrent, Convolutional or Adversarial networks, among others. The use of one architecture or another will depend on the characteristics of the problem to be solved. A comprehensive review of the different network architectures has been published in [8] while an experimental review on such architectures can be found in [12].

Deep learning models have been widely used for energy forecasting. Li et al. [13] used an enhanced deep learning model to manage the energy of an electric vehicle. In particular, the authors used the deep Q-learning model, obtaining a remarkable improvement in both energy loss and computational time. In [23], a real-time forecasting model combining Long Short-Term Memory (LSTM) and Convolutional Neural Network (CNN) architectures was presented. The model performance was evaluated using energy consumption data from a four-storey building in Bombay, India. In the same sense, the authors of [24] applied an LSTM-based model to analyse the energy consumption of buildings on the University of New York campuses.

One of the most promising architectures for time series forecasting due to its high efficiency is the TCN [1]. The authors in [19] introduced a TCN model to predict the electrical load and demonstrated that the model is able to efficiently detect the trend and multi-stationarity existing in the data. The authors presented in [11] a TCN network application for predicting energy time series.

In this paper, the authors forecast two time series comparing more than 1900 models. The results show that the TCN approach outperforms LSTM networks. Zhang et al. also applied a TCN network to predict the trend of water quality in [30]. Specifically, the authors proposed a multi-task network to predict multiple water quality variables. Li et al. performed a comparison of a TCN model with multilayer feed-forward neural networks, and also with recurrent networks, including state-of-the-art LSTM and Gated Recurrent Unit (GRU) recurrent networks in [14]. The authors demonstrated the effectiveness of the proposed model on two Australian datasets containing solar and meteorological data. TCNs were also applied in text analysis. A method that used a TCN as an encoder to infer the segmentation of written Chinese text was proposed in [9]. The authors compared the results with a Bi-LSTM network, obtaining better performance. In the same area of research, Shao et al. applied a TCN to predict messages in different social media in [22]. Traffic analysis has also been studied using TCN. The authors combined a ResNet and a TCN to predict traffic volume using a real-world dataset, showing the high efficiency of the model compared to other existing models [10]. Another area where TCNs are having a big impact is in the analysis of video and time-lapse images. Zhang et al. used a TCN to summarize generic videos in [29]. Another interesting work applying TCN to estimate density maps from different videos was published in [18]. Feng et al. used a TCN model to dynamically detect stress through facial photographs in [5].

However, although TCNs have been applied in many fields, to the authors' knowledge, very few published works on TCNs for predicting electricity consumption can be found in the literature.

3   Methodology

This section presents the proposed methodology to forecast time series in the electricity context using TCN.

Given a time series expressed as $[x_1, x_2, \ldots, x_t]$ the main goal of this work is to predict a finite set of future values, expressed as $[x_{t+1}, x_{t+2}, \ldots, x_{t+h}]$ based on a window of historical values. In this way, the problem can be formulated as:

$$[x_{t+1}, x_{t+2}, \ldots, x_{t+h}] = m(x_t, x_{t-1}, x_{t-2}, \ldots, x_{t-w}) \tag{1}$$

where the m function is the model to be found in the training phase, h means the number of values to be forecasted, also called prediction horizon, and w refers to the set of previous values used to make the prediction.

In this work, the model m is obtained by a deep TCN, with the aim of showing the efficiency of TCN in the prediction of electricity consumption time series. TCN is a variant of convolutional neural networks that has been targeted for sequence data analysis. Specifically, it is based on the propagation of convolutions through each time instant. These convolutions are not causal, i.e., there is no leakage of information from the future to the past, as in the case of recurrent networks. Figure 1 illustrates the architecture of a simple TCN network, where 1, 2 and 4 are the d dilation factors for the first, second and third layers, respectively. Another hyper-parameter depicted in the figure is the kernel size. This parameter indicates the spatial volume considered in the convolutional operations. The figure shows how these are set to 2, 2 and 1, respectively.

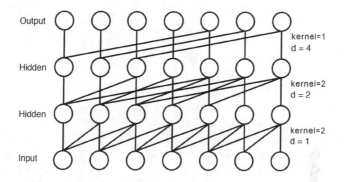

Fig. 1. Simple TCN architecture.

Dilated convolutions determine which values of a neuron in a previous layer will contribute to the next layer. In this way, the model is able to learn both local and temporal information. The dilated convolution can be expressed as a function, F_d, defined in Eq. (2) as follows:

$$F_d(x) = \sum_{i=0}^{K-1} f(i) \cdot x_{t-d \cdot i} \tag{2}$$

where d is the dilation factor parameter and f is a filter of size K.

In addition, TCNs have residual modules, which add the input data to the results obtained from the application of the dilated convolutions before providing the final activation of the layer. The equation that define a TCN model can be summarized as:

$$a_t^l = g(W_a^l F_d(a_t^{l-1}) + b_a^l + a_t^{l-1}) \tag{3}$$

where $F_d(\cdot)$ is the dilated convolution of d factor defined in Eq. (2), a_t^l is the value of the neuron of the l-th layer at time t, W_a^l and b_a^l are the weights and bias corresponding to the l-th layer, and g is the activation function.

4   Results

This section describes the results obtained by the TCN-based deep learning model when predicting the electricity demand for the next 24 values corresponding to 4 h ($h = 24$). First, Sect. 4.1 presents a description of the time series used. Then, Sect. 4.2 describes the experiments carried out and reports the forecasts and a comparison of the errors with other deep learning models.

All the experiments have been executed using TensorFlow 2.1.0 under Ubuntu 18.04 operating system. An Nvidia Titan V GPU has been used. This GPU has 12 GB of HBM2 memory, 5120 CUDA cores and 640 tensor cores, allowing a total of 3.8 TFLOPS of computational capacity in single precision.

4.1 Dataset Description

The dataset used in this study is a time series related to electricity consumption in Spain. The time series is composed of one variable over a period of 9 years and 6 months, specifically from January 2007 to June 2016. This series has a sampling frequency of 10 min, resulting into a dataset with a total of 497832 samples. The original dataset has been processed to convert the data into a supervised learning problem. For this purpose, an historical window size w was set. Due to previous analysis on the same dataset [25], it has been determined that the optimal value for w is 168. This means that a previous day and four hours will be used for the prediction of the next 4 h. The processing turns the series into a matrix composed of 20736 rows and 192 columns. To perform the learning model, the dataset has been split into 14515 instances for training (70%) and 6221 for test (30%).

4.2 Experimental Setting

Deep neural network-based models are highly sensitive to the values of different hyper-parameters. In this work it has been performed a trial-error optimization (TE) in order to obtain the optimal model. The final TCN model is composed of 3 layers. The first one is the input layer and is composed of 168 neurons, each of them corresponds to a time instant of the sample. A TCN layer is applied on the input layer by setting the following parameters: 64 filters, a kernel with size 144, the hyperbolic tangent as activation function and 1 stack. The dilations were set to {4, 8, 16, 24, 48}. Finally, a fully connected layer is applied. This layer consists of 24 neurons that will calculate the output of the network. Each of these neurons corresponds to the prediction at each time interval. The model has been trained over 300 epochs with a batch size of 256.

In order to assess the performance of the model, the well-known root mean squared error (RMSE), mean absolute error (MAE) and mean absolute percentage error (MAPE) measures have been selected. The formulas defining these errors are represented below:

$$RMSE = \sqrt{\frac{1}{n}\sum_{i=1}^{n}(p_i - a_i)^2} \tag{4}$$

$$MAE = \frac{1}{n}\sum_{i=1}^{n}|p_i - a_i| \tag{5}$$

$$MAPE = \frac{1}{n}\sum_{i=1}^{n}\frac{|p_i - a_i|}{a_i} \cdot 100 \tag{6}$$

where n, p_i and a_i mean the number of samples, predicted values and actual values at time instant i, respectively.

4.3   Analysis of Results

In this Section, the TCN is applied to obtain the forecasts from august 20, 2013 at 02:50 to june 21, 2016 at 23:40, resulting in a total of 49305 forecasted values.

In order to evaluate the performance of the proposed TCN model, the results are compared with other models published in the literature where the same data set was used. In [7], it can be found the application of linear regression (LR), decision trees (DT), gradient boosted trees (GBT) and random forests (RF). In addition, the TCN is compared with neural network models based on deep feed forward network (DFFN), with three different optimization approaches to obtain the optimal hyper-parameters. The first one, with an exhaustive grid search (GS), the second with a random search (RS), and the third with a random search applying a smoothing filter as a final training step. Finally, the TCN is also compared with a deep LSTM optimized using a RS. The values for RMSE, MAE and MAPE obtained by all these models are presented in Table 1.

It can be seen that the deep TCN model significantly outperforms all DFFN-based architectures, with a reported MAPE slightly greater than 1%, even if they have been trained with a hyper-parameter optimization strategy. The same applies to the other deep learning model, in which the improvement is even greater. Ensemble, trees and linear models also exhibit worse results in terms of the metrics selected. All the values can be found in Table 1.

Table 1. Errors obtained by the TCN and DFFN models.

Methods	Optimization	RMSE (MW)	MAE (MW)	MAPE (%)
LR	GS	2554.01	2014.58	7.34
DT	GS	1161.61	787.90	2.88
GBT	GS	1096.72	787.90	2.72
RF	GS	849.43	598.11	2.20
DFFN	GS	380.49	451.96	1.68
DFFN	RS	345.89	422.55	1.57
DFFN	RS+filter	251.14	369.19	1.36
LSTM	RS	545.90	398.77	1.45
TCN	TE	**180.43**	**310.01**	**1.13**

Figures 2 and 3 shows the best and worst predicted days of the entire test set, respectively. Both figures represent on their horizontal axis the 144 values corresponding to each of the measurements of a day in the 10-min interval. The best day corresponds to February 25, 2016, where the MAPE value was 5.87e–6, while the worst day corresponds to December 31, 2013 with a MAPE of 0.019. The worst predicted day coincides with a date marked on the calendar as New Year's Eve.

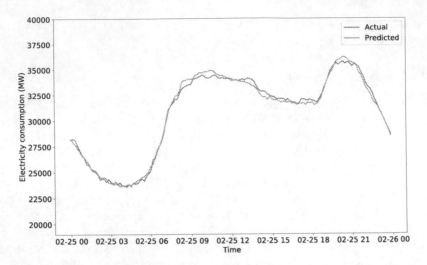

Fig. 2. Best daily prediction.

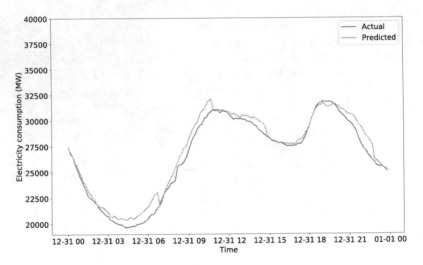

Fig. 3. Worst daily prediction.

The mean of the absolute errors for all months of the test set is depicted in Fig. 4. It can be seen that the worst predicted month is May 2016. This is due to the fact that 1 May is a day marked in the Spanish calendar as a public holiday, and therefore, the model obtained an error much higher than the mean.

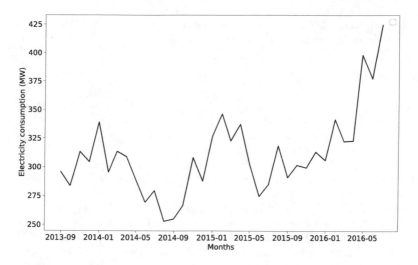

Fig. 4. Monthly average of the absolute errors for the test set.

In terms of computational cost, the TCN network competes directly with the LR, DT, GBT and RF models, being in the order of hours. However, the rest of the models based on deep learning require days of training.

5 Conclusions

In this work, we have proposed a deep learning model to forecast an energy-related time series. More precisely, a deep TCN model has been applied to obtain forecasts for the next 24 values using the electricity consumption time series in Spain during nine years and half with a measurement frequency of 10 min. The performance of the TCN has been evaluated comparing with other deep learning models in terms of MAE, MSE and MAPE. The results show that the model is highly competitive for time series forecasting, obtaining an error around 1%, resulting a relative improvement of 84.60%, 60.76%, 58.45%, 48.64%, 16.91%, 28.02%, 32.74% and 22.07% with regard to linear regression, decision trees, gradient boosted trees, random forests, the DFFN with random search and smoothing process, DFFN with random search only, DFFN with grid search and an deep LSTM, respectively.

Future work will be aimed at applying a hyper-parameter optimization strategy to study the scope for improvement of the TCN model and, more precisely, to adapt the use of the novel Coronavirus Optimization Algorithm [17] to be jointly used with TCN. In addition, an in-depth statistical analysis of all hyper-parameters will be carried out in order to determine the influence of each one. In the same way, tests will be carried out using other datasets to verify the effectiveness of the model.

Acknowledgments. The authors would like to thank the Spanish Ministry of Economy for the support under projects TIN2017-8888209C2-1-R.

References

1. Alla, S., Adari, S.K.: Beginning Anomaly Detection Using Python-Based Deep Learning. Apress (2019)
2. Asim, K.M., Martínez-Álvarez, F., Basit, A., Iqbal, T.: Earthquake magnitude prediction in Hindukush region using machine learning techniques. Nat. Hazards **85**, 471–486 (2017)
3. Box, G., Jenkins, G.: Time Series Analysis: Forecasting and Control. John Wiley and Sons, Hoboken (2008)
4. Bui, C., Pham, N., Vo, A., Tran, A., Nguyen, A., Le, T.: Time series forecasting for healthcare diagnosis and prognostics with the focus on cardiovascular diseases. In: Vo Van, T., Nguyen Le, T.A., Nguyen Duc, T. (eds.) BME 2017. IP, vol. 63, pp. 809–818. Springer, Singapore (2018). https://doi.org/10.1007/978-981-10-4361-1_138
5. Feng, S.: Dynamic facial stress recognition in temporal convolutional network. In: Proceedings of the Communications in Computer and Information Science, pp. 698–706 (2019)
6. Galicia, A., Talavera-Llames, R., Troncoso, A., Koprinska, I., Martínez-Álvarez, F.: Multi-step forecasting for big data time series based on ensemble learning. Knowl.-Based Syst. **163**, 830–841 (2019)
7. Galicia, A., Torres, J.F., Martínez-Álvarez, F., Troncoso, A.: A novel Spark-based multi-step forecasting algorithm for big data time series. Inf. Sci. **467**, 800–818 (2018)
8. Hadjout, D., Torres, J.F., Sebaa, A., Martínez-Álvarez, F., Troncoso, A.: deep learning for time series forecasting: a survey. Big Data **9**(1), 3–21 (2021)
9. Jiang, W., Wang, Y., Tang, Y.: A sequence-to-sequence transformer premised temporal convolutional network for chinese word segmentation. In: Proceedings of Parallel Architectures, Algorithms and Programming, pp. 541–552 (2020)
10. Kuang, L., Hua, C., Wu, J., et al.: Traffic volume prediction based on multi-sources GPS trajectory data by temporal convolutional network. Mobile Networks and Applications, pp. 1–13 (2020)
11. Lara-Benítez, P., Carranza-García, M., Luna-Romera, J.M., Riquelme, J.C.: Temporal convolutional networks applied to energy-related time series forecasting. Appl. Sci. **10**(7) (2020). https://doi.org/10.3390/app10072322
12. Lara-Benítez, P., Carranza-García, M., Riquelme, J.C.: An experimental review on deep learning architectures for time series forecasting. Int. J. Neural Syst. (3), 2130001 (2021)
13. Li, W., et al.: Deep reinforcement learning-based energy management of hybrid battery systems in electric vehicles. J. Energy Storage **36**, 102355 (2021)
14. Lin, Y., Koprinska, I., Rana, M.: Temporal convolutional neural networks for solar power forecasting. In: Proceedings of the International Joint Conference on Neural Networks, pp. 1–8 (2020)
15. Maji, P., Mullins, R.: On the reduction of computational complexity of deep convolutional neural networks. Entropy **20**(4), 305 (2018)
16. Martínez-Álvarez, F., Troncoso, A., Asencio-Cortés, G., Riquelme, J.C.: A survey on data mining techniques applied to electricity-related time series forecasting. Energies **8**(11), 13162–13193 (2015)

17. Martínez-Álvarez, F., et al.: Coronavirus optimization algorithm: a bioinspired metaheuristic based on the COVID-19 propagation model. Big Data **8**(4), 308–322 (2020)
18. Miao, Y., Han, J., Gao, Y., Zhang, B.: ST-CNN: spatial-temporal convolutional neural network for crowd counting in videos. Patt. Recogn. Lett. **125**, 113–118 (2019)
19. Mishra, K., Basu, S., Maulik, U.: DaNSe: a dilated causal convolutional network based model for load forecasting. In: Deka, B., Maji, P., Mitra, S., Bhattacharyya, D.K., Bora, P.K., Pal, S.K. (eds.) PReMI 2019. LNCS, vol. 11941, pp. 234–241. Springer, Cham (2019). https://doi.org/10.1007/978-3-030-34869-4_26
20. Navares, R., Aznarte, J.L.: Predicting air quality with deep learning LSTM: Towards comprehensive models. Ecol. Inform. **55**, 101019 (2020)
21. Roy, S.S., Mittal, D., Basu, A., Abraham, A.: Stock market forecasting using lasso linear regression model. In: Abraham, A., Krömer, P., Snasel, V. (eds.) Proceedings of the Afro-European Conference for Industrial Advancement, pp. 371–381 (2015)
22. Shao, J., Shen, H., Cao, Q., Cheng, X.: Temporal convolutional networks for popularity prediction of messages on social medias. In: Zhang, Q., Liao, X., Ren, Z. (eds.) CCIR 2019. LNCS, vol. 11772, pp. 135–147. Springer, Cham (2019). https://doi.org/10.1007/978-3-030-31624-2_11
23. Somu, N., Gauthama Raman M.R., Ramamritham, K.: A deep learning framework for building energy consumption forecast. Renew. Sustain. Energy Rev. **137**, 110591 (2021)
24. Sülo, I., Keskin, S.R., Dogan, G., Brown, T.: Energy efficient smart buildings: LSTM neural networks for time series prediction. In: Proceedings of the International Conference on Deep Learning and Machine Learning in Emerging Applications, pp. 18–22 (2019)
25. Torres, J.F., Galicia, A., Troncoso, A., Martínez-Álvarez, F.: A scalable approach based on deep learning for big data time series forecasting. Integr. Comput.-Aid. Eng. **25**, 335–348 (2018)
26. Torres, J.F., Troncoso, A., Koprinska, I., Wang, Z., Martínez-Álvarez, F.: Big data solar power forecasting based on deep learning and multiple data sources. Exp. Syst. **36**, e12394 (2019)
27. Vega-Márquez, B., Nepomuceno-Chamorro, I., Jurado-Campos, N., Rubio-Escudero, C.: Deep learning techniques to improve the performance of olive oil classification. Front, Chem. **7**, 929 (2020)
28. Witten, I.H., Frank, E.: Data Mining: Practical Machine Learning Tools and Techniques with Java Implementations. Morgan Kaufmann, San Francisco (1999)
29. Zhang, Y., Kampffmeyer, M., Liang, X., et al.: Dilated temporal relational adversarial network for generic video summarization. Multimedia Tools Appl. **78**(24), 35237–35261 (2019)
30. Zhang, Y., Thorburn, P.J., Fitch, P.: Multi-task temporal convolutional network for predicting water quality sensor data. In: Proceedings of Neural Information Processing Communications in Computer and Information Science, pp. 122–130 (2019)

Recognition of Teaching Activities from University Lecture Transcriptions

Daniel Diosdado[✉], Alberto Romero, and Eva Onaindia

VRAIN, Universitat Politècnica de València, Valencia, Spain
{dadiolo,alrofer}@inf.upv.es, onaindia@dsic.upv.es

Abstract. Research on language acquisition for academic purposes is not extensive. In this work, we propose to build a system for recognizing teaching activities from automatic transcriptions of classroom audio and video recordings centered on the professor's discourse. To this end, we identified the main teaching activities that cover the nature of the lecturer discourse when giving a course e.g. 'theoretical explanation', real-world practical example', interaction lecturer-student', 'course-related asides', etc. We labeled a dataset of lecture transcriptions from a repository with an approximate length of 50 h and we build a classifier by fine-tuning the XLM-RoBERTa model with a classification head on top of it. The results will show that our proposal is a promising step ahead towards recognition of discourse activities in academic contexts.

Keywords: Spoken academic lecture · Text classification · Transformer models

1 Introduction

This paper centers around recognition of human activity where low-level data come in the form of transcriptions of audio recordings and the objective is to identify the nature of the discourse. More specifically, we aim at recognizing teaching activities from automated lecture transcriptions of university classes.

Research on language acquisition for academic purposes is not extensive. The Language ENvironment Analysis (LENA) system is one of the few existing tools that records the language environment of small children by combining a wearable audio recorder with automated vocal analysis software [8,9]. Data collected from teachers wearing the LENA system while teaching regular mathematics lessons has been used to identify three common discourse activities: teacher lecturing, whole class discussion and student group work [13]. LENA provides timely feedback for teachers to improve their skills in classroom discourse management but it uses a proprietary voice identification and transcription system, and it is particularly limited to small children.

The project Decibel Analysis for Research in Teaching (DART) analyzes the volume and variance of STEM (Science Technology Engineering Mathematics) course audio recordings to predict how much time is spent on single voice (e.g.,

© Springer Nature Switzerland AG 2021
E. Alba et al. (Eds.): CAEPIA 2021, LNAI 12882, pp. 226–236, 2021.
https://doi.org/10.1007/978-3-030-85713-4_22

lecture), multiple voice (e.g., pair discussion), and no voice (e.g., clicker question thinking) activities [12]. DART aims at studying patterns of active learning by comparing lecture and non-lecture activity (multiple and no voice) in courses for STEM majors versus non-STEM majors.

Our work focuses on recognizing teaching activities in university classes, which typically are more of the type of lecture-based learning, and builds on automated transcriptions of the class recordings. LENA and DART provide a discourse activity classification based on speech processing from audio recordings. Our proposal however exploits language modeling, what allows us achieving a richer teaching activity classification based on the analysis of the nature of the discourse and not merely on the audio-recording data.

We used video and audio recordings of lectures registered at our university prior to 2020, where the voice of students is hardly audible, and so our proposal for the recognition of teaching activities focuses on analyzing the nature of the teacher discourse. That said, we present a system based on text classification to recognize the type of speech of a university lecturer out of automated transcriptions of class recordings. We identify a set of categories that characterize the spoken academic discourse and we design a classifier using a transformer-based language model, specifically a version of the BERT family transformer models [5]. We underscore our system aims for recognizing discourse activities across a variety of different university subjects, thus the focus is not on topic modeling but on analyzing the discourse of a speech communication where the communicative intent and modality of the lecturer matter. Our ultimate goal will eventually be to cross-check the classification results with the academic evaluation surveys of the lecturers and study correlations between teaching activities and student satisfaction.

The paper is organized as follows. Section 2 briefly summarizes the main characteristics of the spoken academic lecture. The following section presents the procedure for the data segmentation and labeling. Section 4 explains the construction of the classification model and Sect. 5 shows the experimental results. Finally, we present a discussion and conclusions in Sect. 6.

2   Spoken Academic Lecture

In linguistics, the term **genre** refers to types of spoken and written discourse recognized by a community; e.g. lectures, conversations, advertisements, novels, shopping lists, interviews and many more. Since our work is devoted to the speech used in university classes, our focus is on the **spoken academic discourse** genre, particularly on classroom genres, which are regarded as paramount for both students and faculty. Among the classroom genres, the seminar, tutorial, presentation and oral exams typically involve a high level of interaction between the presenter and the audience the activity is addressed to [6]. The **academic lecture**, however, is mostly considered an expository genre where interaction and communication between teachers and students are less frequent.

The academic lecture is becoming more and more relevant due to the increasing internationalization of higher education both from the point of view of students and lecturers [7]. Lectures have a highly informational focus, similarly to academic prose, and, at the same time, have interactive features as they are delivered under on-line production circumstances that resemble face-to-face conversations in the spoken mode [1,4]. Hence lectures are categorized by features that capture the informational purpose of the speech and by features displaying the spoken discourse. Some researchers examined the macro-structure of university lectures and the micro-features that contribute to this structure [15]:

- **Interaction**: important feature that indicates to which extent lecturers maintain contact with their audience so as to reduce the distance between themselves and their listeners as well as to ensure that what has been taught is in fact understood.
- **Theory or Content**: this is used to reflect the lecturer's purpose, which is to transmit theoretical information.
- **Examples of practical application**: in this phase speakers illustrate theoretical concepts through concrete examples familiar to students.

Besides the three aforementioned identifying features of a lecture, more recent research also point at the ability of lecturers to **express their attitudes**, to **relate personal experience** to the content of the lectures, to talk about **evaluation of materials**, and to use formal and informal languages, spoken and written (text in slideshows or other forms of text) [11].

3   Data Segmentation and Labeling

The data used in this work is a collection of automated transcriptions of class recordings of university subjects given in Spanish. We used an online transcription and translation platform for automated and assisted multilingual media subtitling that provides support for the transcription of video, audio and content of courses[1].

We selected a total of 27 audio recordings of lectures that covered scientific as well as technical matters, e.g. Statistics, Electronic Devices, Mathematics, Microprocessors, etc. All together, the selected recordings feature 3000 transcription minutes, half corresponding to male lecturers and the other half to female lecturers. Additionally, 6 out of the 27 selected videos were manually reviewed so the transcriptions of these lectures are much more reliable and accurate to the original discourse of the speaker. Table 1 shows an excerpt of the output file returned by the transcription platform. A viewer will see the text of section 23 on screen as a caption, then the text of section 24 and so on.

---

[1] MLLP transcriptions. https://ttp.mllp.upv.es/index.php?page=faq.

Table 1. Excerpt of a transcription.

Spanish	English
23	23
00:09:07,890 --> 00:09:11,020	00:09:07,890 --> 00:09:11,020
¿Vale? Como bien sabéis ya de	Okay? As you know from
teoria de circuitos no existen	circuit theory there aren't
24	24
00:09:11,020 --> 00:09:15,220	00:09:11,020 --> 00:09:15,220
resistencias de cualquier valor. ¿Vale?	resistors of any value. Okay?
Sino que los tenemos tabulados.	But we have them tabulated.
25	25
00:09:15,220 --> 00:09:18,560	00:09:15,220 --> 00:09:18,560
En el laboratorio tenemos resistencias	In the laboratory we have resistors
de la serie E doce y	of the E twelve series and

3.1   Academic Labels

We manually segmented the transcription files by identifying context switching in the text and deciding whether said context change was associated to a change in the teacher's discourse. Data segmentation was done along with data labeling; we previously decided on the academic labels to classify the discourse activities so that a context switching is detectable as a change of label. We reviewed each other's work to ensure consistency in the labeling process.

On the basis of the investigations on the academic lecture genre, we performed an exhaustive analysis of the audio & transcription files and put forward the hierarchy of academic labels shown in Fig. 1. The white nodes denote parts

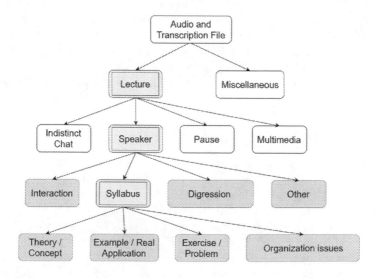

Fig. 1. Hierarchy of academic labels

of the audio file which do not have a readable transcription. The seven dark coloured leaf nodes are the academic activities we used to label the discourse segments. The meaning of each level is as follows:

Level 1: filtering out sounds from the audio file. The audio files of some recordings contain corrupted sections or unwanted sounds due to a sudden cutoff of the recording, background noise, errors in the recording or microphone feedback. We identify these damaged sections of the audio file as *Miscellaneous* and the rest is classified as audio that belongs to the *Lecture*.

Level 2: speaker identification. We distinguish the parts of the file in which the speaker (the lecturer) is talking from those in which they are not. The labels *Indistinct Chat*, *Pause* and *Multimedia* are used to mark sections of the audio file that contain an indistinguishable speaker.

Level 3: lecture-audience relationship. All the features at level 3 and 4 can be extracted from the transcription file since we end up with a file exclusively comprised of the discourse of the speaker after filtering the labels at level 1 and 2. The four labels at level 3 denote different ways for the lecturer to address the students. The key label *Syllabus* comprises the entire academic discourse around the specialized subject. *Interaction* denotes an exchange of communication between the lecturer and students; *Digression* is when a lecturer shifts to a more personal self and offers course-related asides; and *Other* refers to a speech unclassifiable under the other three labels which usually refers to the overall functioning of delivering the class and to non-course-related matters.

Level 4: content-based lecture structure. It includes the phases of a regular expository class around the syllabus of a subject, namely *Theory/Concept*, *Example/Real Application*, *Exercise/Problem* and *Organization issues*. Two remarks are worth mentioning: (a) the label *Exercise/Problem* accounts for a common practice in scientific/technical subjects but can be ignored in humanities and social science subjects; (b) *Organization issues*, which encompasses general course information like schedules, teaching practice or grading policy of interest for the carrying out of the syllabus, could also be classified as a subcategory of *Speaker* if we assume that students generally put much attention when the lecturer talks about organization matters.

We show now in Table 2 two examples of text segmentation and labeling in Spanish, and their English's translation.

4   Text Classification

For building our classifier for academic transcription segments, as we do not have much training data or the necessary hardware to train a NLP model from scratch, we employ transfer learning by using a pre-trained model and fine-tuning it to our task. To this end, we chose XLM-RoBERTa, a multi-lingual model that achieves a performance comparable to monolingual models in a variety of tasks such as named entity recognition, question answering, sentiment analysis, natural language inference, etc. The pre-trained XLM-RoBERTa model was downloaded from HuggingFace's Transformers repository [14]. We used *xlm-roberta-base* instead of the large version due to hardware restrictions.

Table 2. Examples of text segmentation and labeling

Spanish	English
¿Qué es lo que mide C M R R? Es la cantidad, lo que mide es la cantidad de ruido que un amplificador operacional es capaz de eliminar. ¿Vale? Al final normalmente las señales que queremos medir muchas de las señales que queremos de mi, medir son diferenciales.¿Vale? [Theory]	What does C M R R measure? It is the quantity, what it measures is the amount of noise that an operational amplifier is capable of removing. Okay? In the end, normally the signals that we want to measure, many of the signals that we want to me, to measure are differential. Okay? [Theory]
un ejemplo, la señal de electrocardiograma, encefalograma todas las señales biomédicas son diferenciales [Example]	an example, the electrocardiogram signal, encephalogram all biomedical signals are differential [Example]
¿De acuerdo? ¿Lo entendéis? ¿Sí o no? Sí. [Interaction]	Agreed? Do you understand it? Yes or no? Yes. [Interaction]
Vale, siguientes transparencias que os las dejaré, ahora lo escucháis un poquitín. A ver el video, el video, el video, vale, el vídeo. Si es que tengo una, unas, tengo unas preparadas, pero vale. [Organization]	Okay, next slides that I'll leave you, now you listen to it a little bit. Let's see the video, the video, the video, okay, the video. If I have one, some, I have some ready, but okay. [Organization]
¿Sí tengo una función de dos variables qué habéis deducido en cuanto a las derivadas? ¿A ver, quién me dice algo? ¿Quién me queda hacer un pequeño resumen, a ver, me hace alguien un pequeño resumen, a ver del vídeo? [Interaction]	If I have a function of two variables, what have you deduced regarding the derivatives? Let's see, who tells me something? Who is left for me to make a small summary, let's see, does someone make me a small summary, let's see of the video? [Interaction]

We set the maximum sequence length to 512 tokens, which is the maximum length supported by XLM-RoBERTa. The longer the sequence, the easier to classify a segment due to the larger amount of context information comprised in it. If the segment contains less than 512 tokens we apply padding, and for segments longer than 512 tokens we split them using a sliding window with a stride of $0.8 * \text{max\_seq\_length}$ (410 tokens).

We added a classification head on top of the pre-trained XLM-RoBERTa model. This classification head takes as input the segment representation contained in the embedding of the *classifier token* (a special token added at the beginning of the segment). The classification head consists of a dense layer of hidden size (768 units) with *tanh* activation function followed by a dense layer of seven units (one unit for each label/class associated to one academic activity) with *softmax* activation. The output of the classification head is a list containing the probability that the input segment belongs to each of the seven classes. We used the *Adam* algorithm with weight decay fix as optimizer and *categorical cross-entropy* as our loss function for fine-tuning.

The hyperparameters were tuned with the *Weights and Biases* framework [2] according to the model performance using Bayesian Optimization. The final values of the hyperparameters are: learning rate = 0.00005, 40 epochs, batch size of 8 segments (due to memory constraints), gradient accumulation steps of 32 (for a simulated batch size of 256 segments) and weight decay of 0.0007. We trained our model with a Nvidia Geforce RTX 3090.

Table 3. Distribution of our data by label. The number of tokens was obtained by using XLM-Roberta's tokenizer.

Label	Num segments	Total tokens	Avg. tokens	Max tokens
Theory/Concept	454	115885	255.25	3019
Exercise/Problem	537	77866	145.01	1481
Example/Real Appl.	347	63239	182.24	1845
Organization	260	37083	142.63	1989
Interaction	567	66326	116.98	3878
Digression	118	11857	100.48	647
Other	112	5416	48.36	297
Total	2395	377672	157.69	3878

Table 3 shows the composition of our dataset by class. For each class, we report the number of text segments, the total number of tokens, the average token length of the segments and the maximum length in tokens of a segment. As we can see in Table 3, our dataset is rather imbalanced, as some classes like Theory/Concept or Exercise/Problem are much more frequent than other classes like Digression or Other. This is reasonable and in line with the nature of the academic lecture, wherein the most part of the teacher's speech is devoted to the contents of the syllabus of the subject. As a result, the number of segments and the total number of tokens of the most populated classes is obviously higher.

We can draw some conclusions about the composition and structure of each class. The three academic labels *Theory/Concept*, *Exercise/Problem* and *Example/Real Application* make up 56% of the total number of segments, and 68% of the total number of tokens in the dataset. These classes also share a substantial part of their vocabulary with one another. The *Other* class is fairly regular as it is mostly composed of relatively short segments. This is indicated by the lowest value of the maximum number of tokens (297) in a segment and also by the lowest average number of tokens (48.36). In contrast, *Interaction* is highly irregular because it contains segments of variable length. *Interaction* is the class with the largest number of segments (567) and the longest segment (3878) while this class has about half the number of tokens of *Theory/Concept*, and its average number of tokens is closer to the less populated classes. We also observed that *Interaction* appears more frequently among segments of *Exercise/Problem*, either by the student asking for clarification or the teacher querying the students.

5   Experimental Results

We evaluated our model on the whole dataset using 10-fold cross-validation with stratify (each partition holds approximately one tenth of each class). We report the aggregated confusion matrix of the results in Fig. 2 and the values of precision, recall and F-score for each class in Table 4.

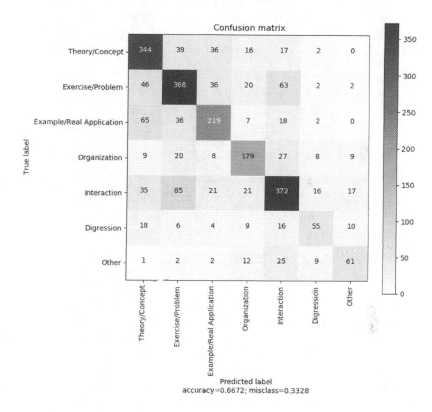

Fig. 2. Aggregated confusion matrix of 10-fold cross-validation

In the confusion matrix of Fig. 2, rows show the true label of the segments, i.e., the label we manually assigned to the segments, and columns represent the predicted class by our model. The values on the diagonal are the number of True Positives (TP); for each class, the values in the columns show the False Positives (FP) and the values in the rows show the number of False Negatives (FN).

Table 4 shows that the metrics of the class *Digression* fall behind the rest of the classes, followed by the class *Other*. *Digression* has the lowest recall among all classes, which is also confirmed by the high number of FN in Fig. 2 relative to the number of samples of this class. This reveals the difficulty of the model to correctly classify segments of *Digression*. We believe the reason for the poor performance of the model with classes *Digression* and *Other* is due to the low number of samples of these two classes in our dataset as well as the difficulty we experienced to correctly label the *Digression* samples.

It is also noticeable that the precision value of *Interaction* is higher than its recall value, and higher than the precision of the other classes. The fact that *Interaction* is the class with the largest proportion of samples correctly classified responds to the ability of the model to recognize the distinguishing characteristics of the discourse style in this class. In *Interaction* the teacher frequently uses the second person to address the students, for querying them or answering their questions. Interestingly, the model is able to identify the interaction teacher-student even not yet having transcriptions of the students' speech.

Table 4. Precision, Recall and F-Score by class.

Label	Precision	Recall	F-Score
Theory/Concept	0.664	0.758	0.708
Exercise/Problem	0.662	0.685	0.673
Example/Real Application	0.672	0.631	0.651
Organization	0.678	0.689	0.683
Interaction	0.692	0.656	0.673
Digression	0.585	0.466	0.519
Other	0.616	0.545	0.578

In Fig. 2, the majority of high values in the columns other than the diagonals are concentrated in three classes: *Theory/Concept*, *Example/Real Application* and *Exercise/Problem*. We can thus say our model has a certain bias towards this group of classes which otherwise seems reasonable since they are the most representative classes of the academic discourse of a lecturer and share a substantial part of their vocabulary. We also observe a significant amount of misclassifications between *Exercise/Problem* and *Interaction*. This happens because it is typically the case that students get more engaged during problem-solving than theory explanations.

The class *Theory/Concept* shows the highest recall but a lower precision value (low values in its row in Fig. 2 compared to the values in its column). This means the model is fairly successful in correctly classifying many of the segments labeled as *Theory/Concept*, but it also tends to classify as *Theory/Concept* segments that do not actually belong to this class. This reveals a slight bias towards this class which is probably due to *Theory/Concept* being the largest class in the dataset. The second highest F-score of the class *Organization* is likely explained by the particular vocabulary of this class, which easily distinguishes it from other classes, such as terms that denote dates, weekdays, grading system, explanations about laboratory activities, etc.

6   Conclusions and Future Work

Despite the low number of labeled samples for this type of NLP task, our model achieves a significant performance that confirms the adequacy of our labeling scheme for recognizing teaching activities from automated transcriptions. We observed that the three academic classes *Theory/Concept*, *Exercise/Problem* and *Example/Real Application* concentrate a large part of the errors because these classes make for more than half of the dataset and share a large part of their vocabulary. Misclassfications between *Interaction* and *Exercise/Problem* happen because many interactions student-lecturer take place during exercise solving in class. Additionally, the model achieves good results for the *Organization* class thanks to its distinctive and recognizable vocabulary (dates, grading, etc.).

A straightforward way to increase the performance of our model is by augmenting the size of the dataset [3, 10]. We plan to develop an automated segmentation process and use our classification model to help us augment the dataset. Additionally, we will consider using a Language Model to spellcheck the text and thus improve the quality of the transcriptions. Lastly, we intend to test XLM-RoBERTa-large and check if the superior performance of the large version over the base model [3] translates into a improvement in our classification model.

References

1. Biber, D.: Dimensions of Register Variation: A Cross-linguistic Comparison. Cambridge University Press, New York (1995)
2. Bicwald, L.: Experiment tracking with weights and biases (2020). https://www.wandb.com/. software available from wandb.com
3. Conneau, A., et al.: Unsupervised Cross-lingual Representation Learning at Scale (2020)
4. Csomay, E.: Academic lectures: an interface of an oral/literate continuum. NovELTy **7**(3), 30–48 (2000)
5. Devlin, J., Chang, M., Lee, K., Toutanova, K.: BERT: pre-training of deep bidirectional transformers for language understanding. CoRR abs/1810.04805 (2018). http://arxiv.org/abs/1810.04805
6. Fortanet-Gómez, I.: Honoris Causa speeches: an approach to structure. Discourse Stud. **7**(1), 31–51 (2005)
7. Fortanet-Gómez, I., Bellés-Fortuño, B.: Spoken academic discourse: an approach to research on lectures. Revista española de lingüística aplicada **1**(8), 161–178 (2005)
8. Ganek, H., Eriks-Brophy, A.: Language ENvironment analysis (LENA) system investigation of day long recordings in children: a literature review. J. Commun. Disord. **72**, 77–85 (2018)
9. LENA Research Foundation: The LENA research foundation (2014). http://www.lenafoundation.org/
10. Liu, Y., et al.: RoBERTa: A Robustly Optimized BERT Pretraining Approach (2019)
11. Malavska, V.: Genre of an academic lecture. Int. J. Lang. Lit. Cult. Educ. **3**(2), 56–84 (2016)

12. Owens, M.T., et al.: Classroom sound can be used to classify teaching practices in college science courses. Proc. Nat. Acad. Sci. **114**(12), 3085–3090 (2017). https://doi.org/10.1073/pnas.1618693114
13. Wang, Z., Pan, X., Miller, K.F., Cortina, K.S.: Automatic classification of activities in classroom discourse. Comput. Educ. **78**, 115–123 (2014)
14. Wolf, T., et al: Huggingface's transformers: state-of-the-art natural language processing. CoRR abs/1910.03771 (2019)
15. Young, L.: University Lectures - Macro-structure and Micro-features, pp. 159–176. Cambridge University Press, Cambridge Applied Linguistics (1995). https://doi.org/10.1017/CBO9781139524612.013

Train Route Planning as a Multi-agent Path Finding Problem

Mauricio Salerno$^{(\boxtimes)}$, Yolanda E-Martín, Raquel Fuentetaja, Alba Gragera, Alberto Pozanco, and Daniel Borrajo

Universidad Carlos III de Madrid, Madrid, Spain
{msalerno,agragera,apozanco}@pa.uc3m.es, {yescuder,rfuentet}@inf.uc3m.es, dborrajo@ia.uc3m.es

Abstract. The train routing and timetabling problem consists of setting routes and schedules of a set of vehicles given their initial timetables and a railway network. The number of vehicles, the complexity and limited capacity of the railway network, and the time constraints make this problem difficult to solve. In this paper, we model this problem as a Multi-Agent Pathfinding problem, and propose a Conflict-Based Search approach to solve it. In our approach, we consider the complex properties found in this scenario such as continuous time, agents that function as convoys of arbitrary length, arbitrary action duration, and railway networks to find a solution. We analyze and discuss our approach explaining the main difficulties and evaluate it on several scenarios.

Keywords: Train routing and timetabling · Multi-agent path finding · Heuristic search

1 Introduction

The Train Routing Problem (TRP) consists of routing a set of vehicles in railway network and assigning them tracks to arrive (depart) to (from) the station. The Train Timetabling Problem (TTP) consists of scheduling a set of vehicles without violating track capacities and satisfying some time constraints. Both problems can be studied separately, but they are directly related: scheduling a train not only depends on the railway network and departure and arrival times, but also on the route and all possible conflicts with other trains' routes. The combination of both problems is difficult to solve because of the number of trains, the complexity and limited capacity of the railway network, and the time constraints.

Both problems have been widely studied using different techniques such as Integer Linear Programming (ILP) [3], Mixed Integer Programming (MIP) [11,13], multi-objective linear programming [12], local search [4,7], heuristic search [6], or Constraint Satisfaction Problems (CSP) [14]. In this work, we study the Train Routing and Timetabling problems together as Multi-Agent Pathfinding (MAPF) problems [5]. A MAPF problem is the problem of finding paths for a set of agents such that every agent reaches its goal while avoiding collisions.

E. Alba et al. (Eds.): CAEPIA 2021, LNAI 12882, pp. 237–246, 2021.
https://doi.org/10.1007/978-3-030-85713-4_23

TRP has been already studied by previous works using a MAPF approach [2]. However, they relax the problem by making assumptions that hinder the use of such techniques in more realistic scenarios as: discrete time steps, unit-cost actions, vehicles losing dimensionality while stopped, and grid scenarios. Andreychuk et al. [1] study the MAPF problem under a more realistic setting, where agents have volume, there are arbitrary cost actions, and continuous time. The type of agents considered are 2D non rotating agents situated also in grids.

Our work is inspired by Atzmon et al. [2] and Andreychuk et al. [1], but we go one step forward by considering: (1) vehicles that keep their size throughout the whole process; (2) use the concept of *resources* to determine conflicts, which allows dealing with collision detection; and (3) more realistic railway networks.

The rest of the paper is organized as follows. First, we introduce a formal definition of the Train Routing and Timetabling Problem (TRTP) we address. Then, we define the algorithms we use to solve the problem. Finally, we present an empirical study in different scenarios, and the conclusions and future work.

2   Problem Definition

We define the Train Routing and Timetabling Problem (TRTP), as a tuple $(\mathcal{I}, \mathcal{R}, \mathcal{V}, \mathcal{T})$ where $\mathcal{I}$ represents the railway topology, defined by a set of segments S and a set of points P; $\mathcal{R}$ is a set of resources; $\mathcal{V}$ is a set of vehicles; and $\mathcal{T}$ is the initial route timetable for all vehicles. Every segment $s \in S$ has a starting point and an end point (s_s, s_e), where $s_s, s_e \in P$ and it is associated to one of two directions $d_s \in \{1, 2\}$, a length l_s, and a travel time t_s. Bidirectional segments are considered as different segments with opposite directions. Resources are the basis of the railway safety system. They are exclusive since they can only be occupied by a single vehicle at a time. Thus, each resource is defined by a set of segments $R \subseteq S$, such that $\forall i, j \; i \neq j \rightarrow R_i \cap R_j = \emptyset$. Each vehicle $v \in \mathcal{V}$ has a length l_v. We assume all vehicles can travel in both directions and have constant speed c. A route timetable for a vehicle v is a sequence of tuples $\langle p, d, [t_a, t_d], o \rangle$, where p is the position of the vehicle's head, d is the direction, $[t_a, t_d]$ is the time interval defining the arrival and departure times of the vehicle head to/from p, and o is the sequence of segments (from head to tail) that the vehicle occupies. p can be defined by either a point, an area, or a platform area.

An *area* is a subset of segments $A \subseteq S$. A *platform area* is a subset of platform segments in an area, $T \subseteq A$. Platforms are the only segments where passengers can board and alight.

The initial route timetable corresponds to the official train timetable, which is a partial definition of the vehicles' route. It must specify boarding/alighting times in platform areas, which will be considered as hard constraints. Thus, for each vehicle it could specify: (a) either an entry or internal point of the infrastructure along with the arrival time to it; (b) one or more areas where the vehicle has to stop, or platform areas where the vehicle has to board/alight passengers, along with the corresponding times; and (c) an exit point from the infrastructure to the external railway network.

A solution to a TRTP is a route timetable that completely defines all vehicles' paths along with the arrival and departure point times, such that there are no conflicts among vehicles and all arrivals and departures are performed on-time.

The following definitions refer to concepts which are relevant for finding a solution to the TRTP.

Definition 1 (Stop time). *Given the arrival/departure interval $[t_a^p, t_d^p]$ for a specific point p in the route of a vehicle v, the stop time of v at p is defined as $t_{stop}^p = t_d^p - t_a^p$. If $t_{stop} = 0$, p is a non-stopping point.*

Vehicles have an arbitrary length, which could be larger than the length of the segment where their head is situated. This implies that a vehicle might occupy several segments at the same time. Thus, the solver needs to keep track of the segments' occupation as the route is being computed. Also, the solution must ensure that the route is safe, meaning that there are no collisions with other vehicles. In order to achieve that, the route must comply with resource exclusivity, which implies keeping track of the blocked resources and their releasing times.

Definition 2 (Occupied segments). *Let $(p_0, \ldots, p_i)$ be the points in the current route of a vehicle v, which determines a sequence of segments $(s_0, \ldots, s_{i-1})$, where each segment connects two consecutive route points. Let us assume that v's head is situated at point p_i, which means that the vehicle is in segment s_{i-1}. Let s_{i-k} be the first segment from head to tail for which $\sum_{j=1}^{k} l_{s_{i-j}} > l_v$. Then, v occupies, from head to tail, the sequence of segments $o = (s_{i-1}, \ldots, s_{i-k})$.*

This definition is illustrated in Fig. 1 (left), where there is a vehicle whose head is at p_i, and the complete vehicle occupies the segments from s_{i-1} to s_{i-k}.

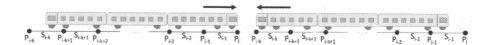

Fig. 1. Occupation and direction change scheme.

To ensure a solution that respects the railway safety system, we need to define the concept of *segment occupation time*, i.e., the time interval when a vehicle is occupying a segment. This interval starts when the vehicle's head arrives to the starting point of the segment and ends when the vehicle's tail leaves its end point. The upper bound of this interval is computed considering the head's departure time from the end point plus the time from head to tail. Formally:

Definition 3 (Segment occupation time). *Let $(p_0, \ldots, p_i)$ be the points in the current route of a vehicle v, and $o = (s_{i-1}, \ldots, s_{i-k})$ be the sequence of occupied segments. Then, the segment occupation time of s_{i-k} is defined by the time interval $[t_a^{p_{i-k}}, t_d^{p_{i-k+1}} + t_{head\text{-}tail}^v + t_{delay}^o]$, where $t_{head\text{-}tail}^v = l_v/c$ and $t_{delay}^o = t_{stop}^{p_i} + t_{stop}^{p_{i-1}} + \cdots + t_{stop}^{p_{i-k+2}}$.*

In this definition, the time from head to tail, $t^v_{head-tail}$, is computed considering the length of the vehicle and the constant speed c. The delay in leaving segment s_{i-k} is due to the (potential) stops of the vehicle's head in the points from p_{i-k+2} to p_i. As Fig. 1 (left) shows, these are the successive points where the vehicle can stop while its tail is still in segment s_{i-k}.

Resources are sets of exclusive segments. A resource is blocked when a vehicle enters in any of its segments [10]. When a resource is blocked, no other vehicles can use the resource until it is released. Note that a vehicle could block more than one resource at the same time. A resource is released when the vehicle's tail passes another resource plus a constant security time. Given the sequence o of occupied segments by a vehicle v, the list of blocked resources by v can be easily computed considering the segments in o and the resources they belong to. Given a resource $R = \{s_0, \ldots s_n\}$, it would be blocked by a vehicle v within the interval $[t_{block}, t_{release} + t_{safe}]$, where t_{block} is the arrival time of v's head to a segment in R; $t_{release}$ is the time when v's tail leaves the resource; and t_{safe} is an input constant. The segment occupation times are computed following Definition 3.

In this work we assume vehicles can change their direction at a given moment. To represent a direction change in the route schedule, we replace the vehicle's tail with its head and vice versa. We consider the time to move the new vehicle's head to the nearest point in the opposite direction (referred as *setting time*) plus a *maneuver time*, t_m. Let $(p_i, d, [t^{p_i}_a, t^{p_i}_d], (s_{i-1}, \ldots, s_{i-k}))$ be the last tuple in the route schedule for a vehicle before a direction change. Then, the next tuple in its schedule, after the direction change, will be $(p_{i-k}, \bar{d}, [t^{p_i}_d + t_m + t_{set}, t^{p_{i-k}}_d], o)$. p_{i-k} is the nearest point in the opposite direction, given that when the head was at p_i the vehicle was occupying the previous segments to s_{i-k}. The opposite direction is denoted as $\bar{d}$. The arrival time to this nearest point is the departure time from p_i, $t^{p_i}_d$, plus the setting and maneuver times. $t^{p_i}_d$ refers now to the tail departure since there was a direction change. The setting time is $t_{set} = (\sum^k_{j=1} l_{s_{i-j}} - l_v)/c$, where the numerator is the total length of the occupied segments minus the vehicle's length. This is the distance from the position of the vehicle's tail before the direction change to the point p_{i-k}, the nearest one in the opposite direction. The occupied segments o when the vehicle's head is at p_{i-k} are computed following Definition 2.

Figure 1 illustrates a direction change. The left figure shows the initial position of the vehicle before the direction change, where its head is located at point p_i (right direction). The right figure shows the final position of the vehicle after the direction change (left direction). The setting time is the time taken to move the vehicle's head from its actual position in segment s_{i-k} (left figure) to point p_{i-k}, which is the head position after the direction change (right figure).

3   Graph Representation of the Railway Network

In railway networks there are certain turns that vehicles cannot take due to physical properties of the track topology. Figure 2 (left) shows a small railway network where a train cannot turn from C to F if it reaches C from B (orange train). However, the turn is possible if the train comes from D (grey train). Considering these physical restrictions when the network is represented as a graph would mean to deal with additional constraints to avoid impossible turns.

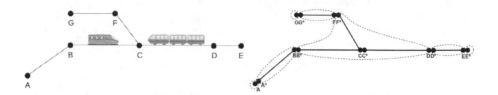

Fig. 2. Railway network with two vehicles (left) and corresponding DVG (right).

To overcome this issue, we represent the infrastructure as a Double Vertex Graph (DVG) [10], which consists of vertices (points) and edges (segments) that prevent impossible turns. We perform the search over this graph. The main idea of a DVG is that all vertices are duplicated, generating pairs (v, v°), where v and v° are joined vertices that represent the same point in the network. This association relies on a mapping function $\circ : V \mapsto V$ that for each vertex v returns its joined vertex $\circ(v)$ (or v°). This mapping function satisfies that $\circ(\circ(v)) = v$. During the search, reaching a vertex on the DVG implies to be moved automatically to its joined one, by applying the mapping function $\circ$. Therefore, the only allowed movements are those represented by the outgoing edges of the joined vertex. Outgoing edges do not include movements with impossible turns.

The infrastructure $\mathcal{I}$ is converted automatically into a DVG: each point v_i is converted into a double vertex (v_i, v_i°); each segment with direction d, defined by is starting and end points (v_s, v_e), generates the edge (v_s°, v_e); and each segment with direction $\bar{d}$, defined by points (v_s, v_e) generates the edge (v_s, v_e°). Figure 2 (right) shows the result of transforming the infrastructure in Fig. 2 (left) to a DVG. Thus, the infrastructure contains the segments: AB, BC, CD, DE, GF, FC (direction 1); BA, CB, DC, ED, FG, CF (direction 2).

A formal track topology, as defined by Montigel [10], includes both the DVG and the definition of resources, which guarantee safety in the railway system. Figure 2 (right) shows an example where resources represented with dashed lines. Considering the DVG, vertices connected by an edge belong to the same resource. Resource boundaries lie between joined vertices.

4   The TRTP as a MAPF Problem

In this section, we explain the approach followed to solve the TRTP problem as a MAPF problem. Specifically, we apply Conflict-Based Search (CBS) [15], where agents are trains and the search is performed over the formal track topology.

CBS consists of two search spaces: high-level and low-level. At the high level, the search is performed on a binary conflict tree (CT), which is created from the found conflicts. At the low level, the search seeks a path for a single agent consistent with the imposed restrictions. The main idea behind this type of search is to allow each agent to find its own path at the low level while checking that those paths are conflict-free at the high level.

In this work, each node $n \in$ CT is a state that consists of: (1) a set of constraints (initially empty); (2) a potential solution to the TRTP, $\mathcal{T}_n$, consisting of complete route timetable for each vehicle; and (3) the total cost of the solution. To ensure the safety of the system, constraints are defined over resources; only one vehicle can be located at the same time in the same resource.

Definition 4 (Conflict). *A conflict appears when there is an overlap of the time intervals of two agents occupying the same resource. A conflict over a resource $R \in \mathcal{R}$ is defined as a tuple $\langle v_1, v_2, [t_1, t_2], [t_3, t_4] \rangle$, where $v_1, v_2 \in \mathcal{V}$ are the vehicles involved in the conflict, and $[t_1, t_2], [t_3, t_4]$ are the respective resource occupation time intervals with $[t_1, t_2] \cap [t_3, t_4] \neq \emptyset$.*

During the high-level search, we select the next node $n \in$ CT with least cost. If n does not have any conflict, n is a solution and we return the conflict-free route timetable for each agent on n. Otherwise, the search continues expanding n. A conflict in n is arbitrarily chosen and we constrain each agent's search according to the occupation time interval of the other agent involved in the conflict. We define two constraints for each selected conflict, represented as $c_1 = (v_1, R, [t_3, t_4])$ and $c_2 = (v_2, R, [t_1, t_2])$. The former represents that the agent v_1 must not be in R during the time interval $[t_3, t_4]$, preventing it from occupying R while v_2 is inside (c_2 is similar, but in the opposite direction). Then, we generate two new successors n_1 and n_2 in the CT, with the same set of constraints as n, plus the new one generated to each vehicle. Hence, n_1 will restrict the solution of v_1 with c_1 while n_2 will do it to v_2 with c_2. A low-level search is performed for each node to find a new solution consistent with the new constraints.

The low-level search seeks a complete route timetable for a vehicle consistent with its initial timetable $\mathcal{T}_0$, and its constraints. We conduct a modified A*, using as heuristic the minimum travel time without considering changes of direction. A state is represented as $\langle p, d, t_a, T \rangle$, where p is the vehicle's position, d is the direction the vehicle is facing, t_a is the arrival time to p, and T is the vehicle's timetable (partial route used to determine the vehicle's current occupation). Applicable actions are moving actions from one point to another. Stops happen at the arrival vertex and the mapping function $\circ$ is applied on departure. Direction changes can be applied at any moment (but have lower priority).

Sub-goals of a vehicle can be either points or areas. If a sub-goal g is a point, the search can be easily guided using a heuristic function that estimates the cost of reaching that point from the current point. However, when g is an area this is not enough because each area has a set of n predefined platform segments. Any path that leads the vehicle to one of these segments within the specified time interval could be a valid solution. Then, for that case, we first perform a platform selection step by generating as many search nodes as platforms are in the area. All of these nodes have the same state, but differ in the goal point.

The search is performed as follows. For each node n, $g(n)$ is the t_a to the current point, defined in its state. We keep two open lists during the search. The first one stores nodes n that do not require a direction change to reach the goal. These are expanded according to their $f(n) = g(n) + h(n)$ value. The second one stores nodes that require at least a direction change. They are sorted according to $g(n)$, but only expanded when the first list is empty. This guarantees that direction changes are only performed when necessary. Applying a move action from point p to point p' implies: computing the departure time t_d from the current point p; generating a successor whose partial route includes p along with its time interval; and computing the arrival time, t'_a of the next current point p'. We do not consider stops unless this option violates a constraint. Thus, we set t_d equal to t_a whenever possible. The arrival time at p' is computed as the departure time from p plus the travel time $t_{pp'}$ of the current traveling segment, $t'_a = t_d + t_{pp'}$. If the node being expanded is a goal node, the departure time is set to ∞: this indicates that the vehicle will remain parked in the current segment(s). Then, the solution is returned. A stop is a t_d such that $t_a < t_d$. We only consider them when they are needed to avoid violating any constraint.

Definition 5 (Constraint Violation). *Given a state* $s = \langle p, d, t_a, T \rangle$ *and a successor state* $s' = \langle p', d', t'_a, T' \rangle$, *generated by applying a move action from* p *to* p' *to the current vehicle* v, *a constraint* $c = (v, R, [t_i, t_j])$ *for* v *is violated if the segment* (p, p') *belongs to* R *and either: (a)* $t_i < t_d < t_j$, *or (b)* $t_d < t_i$ *and* $t'_a > t_i$, *or (c)* $t'_a < t_i$, *the successor* s'' *of* s' *involves a movement through a segment which still belongs to* R, *and this movement generates a violation of* c.

In (a), the violation can only be solved in two ways: (1) making $t_d < t_i$, or (2) making $t_d > t_j$. Assuming that the vehicle does not stop at p (i.e. $t_d = t_a$ and $t'_a = t_a + t_{pp'}$), there is no chance to make $t_d < t_i$ since t_d is the earliest departure time. Therefore, we choose to solve the constraint violation making $t_d > t_j$ by setting $t_d = t_j + t_{safe}$, where t_{safe} is the constant security time defined for the network. Then, $t'_a = t_d + t_{pp'}$. It implies making a stop at p to delay entering the resource until the upper bound of the forbidden interval is reached. In (b), the solution is similar since an earlier departure from p would be needed to achieve $t'_a < t_i$. This is not possible because t_d is the earliest departure time (if the vehicle does not stop at p). In (c), the constraint violation cannot be checked at the expansion time of the current node (state s). At this point, it is a potential violation since we do not know neither the departure time in s' nor the arrival time in s'' until s' is expanded. In such scenario, we must create two child nodes to guarantee completeness. One is the current successor ($t_d = t_a$), which does not violate the constraint at the moment. The other node is created by making a stop at p, to delay its departure time to the upper bound of the forbidden interval. This is done by following (a) or (b). When the departure time in s' or the arrival time in s'' violates the constraint, the path is discarded.

This conflict resolution approach is also valid in those cases where a direction change is applicable (a direction change action generates an additional successor). In all cases, when selecting the departure time, the occupied segments, and their occupation times are computed following Definitions 2 and 3.

The final route timetable generated is optimal with respect to the travel time while complying with the imposed constraints. Considering the way constraints are created, the solution might not be optimal. Constraints are added using the vehicle's occupation time in the resource, not the minimum occupation time possible for that resource. So a solution that complies with the constraints might be more costly than one with different constraints.

5   Evaluation

We tested 3 networks, following experts' guidelines, of increasing size: 110, 148, and 312 segments, with 40, 55, and 115 resources respectively. We ran experiments with an increasing number of agents k, ranging from 2 to 10. The maximum number of agents seems to be low, but the networks are relatively small. Hence, we are testing the very complex scenarios due to a high percentage of the network occupied by agents. This parameter, denoted as %O, is computed as the number of initially occupied resources divided by the total number of resources in the network. We randomly assigned a different length to each agent from 5 to 25. For all networks, the average segment length is 20, so agents might occupy two segments in some cases. Each agent has associated a platform as goal.

We tested with three types of deadlines. To compute them, for each network, we ran 1000 problems with one agent having a random initial position and destination. The base deadline, b_d, is set to the maximum time needed for the agent to reach its destination among all runs. b_d is considered as a hard deadline in practice, since it is very unlikely the algorithm finds a solution for all agents that takes less time than b_d. The higher the number of agents in the network, the higher the number of conflicts, which causes delays over all vehicles. The other two deadlines are: $d = b_d \times 2$ (medium deadline); and $d = b_d \times 4$ (soft deadline).

We generated 100 random problems and ran them for each type of deadline and number of agents. We gave 60 s to the algorithm to solve each instance and report: (1) if the problem was solved within the time bound, S; (2) the sum of costs of all the agents' plans, SOC; (3) the makespan, MK, which is the time step at which the last agent reaches its destination; and (4) the time T in milliseconds needed to solve the problem.

Table 1 shows the results[1]. For the small network, we only report results up to 6 agents since with a higher number of agents none of the problems were solved within the time bound. A higher number of agents makes the small network intractable with very high occupancy rates, which prevent agents from reaching their destinations. For all the networks, increasing the number of agents causes higher occupancy rates and lower success rates, as expected. Having more agents in the network means more potential conflicts to be solved, many of them being unsolvable within the given time bound. The success rate drops below 0.5 when the occupancy of the network is 25% or higher in the small and medium networks. For the large network, there are worse success rates for lower occupancy rates. The topology of the network creates a bottleneck in some resources that connect

---

[1] Results obtained on an Intel Core i7 2.9 GHz CPU computer with 16 GB of RAM.

Table 1. Results for the three types of networks.

Network	k	%O	Soft deadline				Medium deadline				Hard deadline			
			S	SOC	MK	T	S	SOC	MK	T	S	SOC	MK	T
SMALL	2	10.0	1.0	122.1	75.8	184.5	0.9	120.2	77.1	147.6	1.0	120.9	76.9	94.7
	3	15.0	0.9	174.1	84.2	500.2	0.8	167.5	86.6	581.5	0.9	170.9	86.3	1494.5
	4	20.0	0.8	235.1	98.1	1722.4	0.7	226.7	90.5	3186.1	0.8	222.3	89.1	3143.4
	5	25.0	0.5	256.8	93.3	2437.0	0.5	261.5	92.5	2430.5	0.6	279.8	97.3	6310.1
	6	30.0	0.3	289.5	89.6	2464.9	0.2	302.2	101.1	6784.7	0.3	292.0	98.7	10046.5
MEDIUM	2	7.2	1.0	115.6	74.2	122.2	0.9	116.2	74.8	105.7	0.9	121.7	77.6	81.5
	3	10.9	0.9	163.4	79.8	830.8	0.9	165.9	80.7	1056.1	0.9	169.5	80.5	1644.6
	4	14.5	0.9	209.9	83.1	1281.1	0.8	209.8	85.3	1365.9	0.9	209.1	81.9	1640.2
	5	18.1	0.7	256.8	84.6	3092.4	0.8	240.9	84.6	4122.2	0.8	242.9	81.3	2955.7
	6	21.8	0.5	297.6	91.6	7713.5	0.6	283.3	92.3	4579.2	0.7	271.6	81.9	5395.1
	7	25.4	0.3	293.8	79.6	8366.5	0.4	308.3	81.0	7828.9	0.5	300.6	86.7	10867.0
	8	29.0	0.2	359.6	97.8	10634.9	0.1	355.6	84.6	6660.3	0.2	330.7	88.7	8672.1
	9	32.7	0.07	326.5	106.5	11896.5	0.1	356.1	87.7	13187.9	0.09	324.0	79.5	23325.1
	10	36.3	0.05	390.5	89.0	28865.7	0.08	365.3	93.1	14941.0	0.1	378.5	90.3	23050.8
LARGE	2	3.4	0.9	148.1	95.5	90.1	1.0	153.5	96.4	235.6	0.9	163.8	102.7	189.4
	3	5.2	0.9	226.5	111.2	244.7	0.9	226.9	109.0	477.4	0.9	221.0	106.8	680.37
	4	6.9	0.9	282.7	111.8	990.2	0.9	300.6	117.1	1697.6	0.9	292.4	115.2	2321.1
	5	8.7	0.8	344.7	119.4	2909.1	0.8	349.3	120.8	4069.4	0.8	337.1	118.0	1751.0
	6	10.4	0.6	401.3	125.8	5492.0	0.7	404.9	122.1	7108.1	0.7	408.3	124.0	4687.2
	7	12.1	0.5	446.7	118.2	8220.7	0.5	484.4	126.8	9653.6	0.4	452.6	122.1	6645.8
	8	13.9	0.2	497.5	123.5	10284.9	0.2	511.7	129.2	14845.7	0.3	503.5	135.5	10484.7
	9	15.6	0.1	509.1	117.9	26109.0	0.2	487.4	117.8	17595.5	0.2	508.9	116.1	14108.9
	10	17.3	0.1	555.2	121.5	13578.3	0.08	585.1	118.4	9409.1	0.07	601.6	131.3	14904.5

two main areas, which causes a high number of conflicts. Regarding the deadlines, there is no apparent relationship between the type of deadline and the success rate. Looser deadlines have a less constrained search space, and the algorithm might exceed the given time while looking for a solution.

6   Conclusions and Future Work

In this paper we introduced an approach for solving TRTP problems as MAPF problems using CBS. We consider specific problem's features: the search is performed in a DVG, which allows representing implicitly the physical characteristics of railway networks and exclusive resources related to the railway safety system; continuous time, deadlines, and actions with duration; agents with arbitrary length; direction change maneuvers; and abstract goal definition that may involve solving the platforming problem.

We evaluated the approach on three different scenarios, varying the size of the network, the number of agents, and the deadline tightness. The results show that the higher the occupancy rate is, the lower the success rate is, given that a higher number of agents results in a higher number of potential conflicts.

We would like to consider the full complexity inherent to a real TRTP, which would involve dealing with sub-goal sequences in the initial route timetable, vehicle coupling and decoupling maneuvers, resource sharing, deposit operations, and additional metrics to consider the platforming occupation time or the robustness of timetables. We would also like to evaluate it in real-world scenarios.

Acknowledgements. This work was funded by research projects TIN2017-88476-C2-2-R, RTC-2017-6753-4 of Spanish Ministerio de Economía, Industria y Competitividad/FEDER UE, and the Madrid government under the Multiannual Agreement with UC3M in the line of Excellence of University Professors (EPUC3M17), V PRICIT (Regional Programme of Research and Technological Innovation). This work was developed in cooperation with Goal Systems S.L. (www.goalsystems.com) whose working team provided expert knowledge of railway management and its properties. Special thanks to the technical staff for making this cooperation possible.

References

1. Andreychuk, A., Yakovlev, K., Atzmon, D., Stern, R.: Multi-agent pathfinding with continuous time. In: Proceedings of IJCAI-19, pp. 39–45 (2019)
2. Atzmon, D., Diei, A., Rave, D.: Multi-train path finding. In: Proceedings of SOCS-19, pp. 125–129 (2019)
3. Cacchiani, V., Furini, F., Kidd, M.: Approaches to a real-world train timetabling problem in a railway node. Omega **58**, 97–110 (2015)
4. Dewilde, T., Sels, P., Cattrysse, D., Vansteenwegen, P.: Robust railway station planning: an interaction between routing, timetabling and platforming. J. Rail Transp. Plan. Manag. **3**, 68–77 (2013)
5. Felner, A., et al.: Search-based optimal solvers for the multi-agent pathfinding problem: summary and challenges. In: Proceedings of SOCS-17, pp. 29–37 (2017)
6. Flórez, J., Torralba, A., Borrajo, D., Linares López, C., Olaya, A., Sáenz, J.: Combining linear programming and automated planning to solve intermodal transportation problems. Eur. J. Oper. Res. **227**, 216–226 (2013)
7. Higgins, A., Kozan, E., Ferreira, L.: Heuristic techniques for single line train scheduling. J. Heuristics **3**, 43–62 (1997)
8. Li, J., Surynek, P., Felner, A., Ma, H., Kumar, T.S., Koeing, S.: Multi-agent path finding for large agents. In: Proceedings of AAAI-19, pp. 7627–7634 (2019)
9. Ma, H., Wagner, G., Felner, A., Li, J., Kumar, T., Koenig, S.: Multi-agent path finding with deadlines. In: Proceedings of IJCAI-18, pp. 417–423 (2018)
10. Montigel, M.: Representation of track topologies with double vertex graphs. In: Computers in Railway, vol. 2 (1992)
11. Murali, P., Ordóñez, F., Dessouky, M.: Modeling strategies for effectively routing freight trains through complex networks. Transp. Res. Part C Emerg. Technol. **70**, 197–213 (2016)
12. Pouryousef, H., Lautala, P., Watkins, D.: Development of hybrid optimization of train schedules model for n-track rail corridors. Transp. Res. Part C Emerg. Technol. **67**, 169–192 (2016)
13. Qi, J., Yang, L., Gao, Y., Li, S., Gao, Z.: Integrated multi-track station layout design and train scheduling models on railway corridors. Transp. Res. Part C Emerg. Technol. **69**, 91–119 (2016)
14. Rodríguez, J.: A constraint programming model for real-time train scheduling at junctions. Transp. Res. Part B Methodol. **41**, 231–245 (2007)
15. Sharon, G., Stern, R., Felner, A., Sturtevant, N.: Conflict-based search for optimal multi-agent pathfinding. Artif. Intell. **219**, 40–66 (2015)

Citizen Centric Optimal Electric Vehicle Charging Stations Locations in a Full City: Case of Malaga

Christian Cintrano[1]([✉]) [iD], Jamal Toutouh[1,2] [iD], and Enrique Alba[1] [iD]

[1] University of Malaga, Bulevar Louis Pasteur 35, 29010 Malaga, Spain
{cintrano,jamal,eat}@lcc.uma.es
[2] Massachusetts Institute of Technology, CSAIL, Cambridge, MA, USA
toutouh@mit.edu

Abstract. This article presents the problem of locating electric vehicle (EV) charging stations in a city by defining the `Electric Vehicle Charging Stations Locations (EV-CSL)` problem. The idea is to minimize the distance the citizens have to travel to charge their vehicles. `EV-CSL` takes into account the maximum number of charging stations to install and the electric power requirements. Two metaheuristics are applied to address the relying optimization problem: a genetic algorithm (GA) and a variable neighborhood search (VNS). The experimental analysis over a realistic scenario of Malaga city, Spain, shows that the metaheuristics are able to find competitive solutions which dramatically improve the actual installation of the stations in Malaga. GA provided statistically the best results.

Keywords: Electric vehicle · Charging station location · Metaheuristics

1 Introduction

Road transportation is one of the main sources of air pollutants in our cities [12]. Reducing the road vehicles' emissions would have an important impact on tackling global warming [17] and improving inhabitants' health [11]. An extended use of electric vehicle (EV) transportation will reduce the emission of pollutants. However, at the time of this research, the EV adoption is limited by several factors. One of the main factors is the need for a specific charging infrastructure for EV, which present two main issues [9]: *a)* charging times determine the number of vehicles that can be charged over the time; and *b)* charging stations have high energy consumption requirements, which limits the number of stations that can be installed in a given area. Improving the availability of charging stations will lead to increasing the adoption of this type of green transportation [9].

Smart cities provide a series of tools for advanced knowledge and decision-making support [2,3,8,12]. In this line, this work focuses on providing a solution

© Springer Nature Switzerland AG 2021
E. Alba et al. (Eds.): CAEPIA 2021, LNAI 12882, pp. 247–257, 2021.
https://doi.org/10.1007/978-3-030-85713-4_24

to efficiently allocate EV charging stations to ease EV uptake by the citizens. The proposed approach takes into account the distance the users have to travel to charge their EV and the power electric substations installed in the city to provide electric power to the different urban areas. These electric substations produce a limited energy, which determines the maximum EV charging stations to be allocated in a given area. Thus, we have defined an optimization problem named Electric Vehicle Charging Stations Locations (EV-CSL).

Finding the best locations of EV charging stations is attracting the attention of the research community. In Brandstätter et al. [1] the authors presented an ad-hoc heuristic for solving the EV-CSL problem. The main drawback of their approach is that it does not take into account the energy constraints of the substations. Other research studies only considered the aspects related to the installation of the EV charging points [10], i.e., installation price, maintenance, etc., leaving quality of service (QoS) and users aside of the problem.

The problem of finding the optimal locations for the EV charging stations for a full city can be defined as a variant of a p-median problem [5,14], which have been proven to be an NP-Hard optimization problem. The large search space makes impractical the use of traditional optimization methods (e.g., enumeration techniques or dynamic programming). Thus, heuristic and metaheuristics are useful methods to perform the search using bounded computational resources [4]. Here, two metaheuristic algorithms have been applied to address EV-CSL: a genetic algorithm (GA) [19] and a variable neighborhood search (VNS) [15].

To evaluate the proposed approach, a realistic scenario of the whole city of Malaga (Spain) has been modeled by taking into account real data (i.e., open data provided by the municipality of the city, road maps from Open Street Maps [16], and electric substations locations). In turn, the computed results are compared against the current solution provided by the municipality (actual locations of the charging stations), as a baseline solution.

The main contributions of our work are:

- Providing the mathematical formulation of EV-CSL.
- Modeling a realistic instance based on real data of the city of Malaga to address EV-CSL focusing on citizens' needs and electricity supply constraints.
- Implementing and applying two metaheuristics to EV-CSL: a GA and a VNS.
- Studying the solutions computed by the proposed algorithms to analyze their performance when addressing this problem and comparing them with the actual solution deployed in Malaga.

The rest of this article is organised as follows: the following section defines the EV-CSL addressed in this research. Section 3 introduces the main aspects of the metaheuristics applied and implemented. Section 4 describes the real-world scenario defined to tackle the EV-CSL problem and the main experimental settings. The experimental analysis is reported in Sect. 5. Finally, Sect. 6 presents the conclusions and formulates the main lines for future work.

2   Efficient Full City EV Charging Station Locations

The `Electric Vehicle Charging Stations Locations` (EV-CSL) problem is
defined to provide potential locations of EV charging stations for a full city given
a maximum number of charging stations (Ms) to provide the best QoS possible.
In this study, as a preliminary approach, the QoS is given by the distance between
the citizens' homes and the EV charging station. The mathematical formulation
of `EV-CSL` is defined considering the following:

– A maximum number of electric car charging station defined by Ms.
– A set $S = \{s_1, \ldots, s_M\}$ of potential street segments for charging stations. For
  this version of the problem, each street segment of S can be the location of
  one charging station.
– A set $C = \{c_1, \ldots, c_N\}$ of client locations. Following a usual approach in the
  related literature, nearby locations are grouped in clusters, assuming a similar
  behavior between elements in each cluster. The number of users to serve at
  each location c is u_c. The distance from client c to the charging station $s \in S$
  is $dc_{c,s}$, and the maximum distance between any client in C and its assigned
  charging station (in meters) is Dc.
– A set $E = \{e_1, \ldots, e_T\}$ of electrical substations that serve as electric power
  source for the charging stations. The distance from the electrical substation e
  to the charging station in $s \in S$ is $de_{e,s}$, and the maximum distance between
  substation e in E and its assigned charging station s (in meters) is De. As the
  substations have electric power restrictions, the number of charging stations
  that can be fed by a substation e is limited by mp_e.

Equations 1–7 describe the model, using the following variables: $x_{c,s}$ is 1 if the
client c is assigned to the station located in s and 0 otherwise, and $y_{e,s}$ is 1
if the electrical substation e is feeding the charging station located in s and 0
otherwise.

$$\min \sum_{c \in C,\ s \in S} x_{c,s} d_{c,s} u_c \tag{1}$$

subject to

$$\sum_{s \in S} x_{c,s} = 1 \qquad\qquad\qquad \forall\, c \in C \tag{2}$$

$$\sum_{c \in C,\ s \in S} x_{c,s} = |C| \tag{3}$$

$$dc_{c,s} x_{c,s} \leq Dc \qquad\qquad\qquad \forall\, c \in C,\ s \in S \tag{4}$$

$$de_{e,s} y_{e,s} \leq De \qquad\qquad\qquad \forall\, e \in E,\ s \in S \tag{5}$$

$$\sum_{s \in S} y_{e,s} \leq mp_{e,s} \qquad\qquad\qquad \forall\, e \in E \tag{6}$$

$$|S_o| = Ms \qquad\qquad S_o = \{s_o \backslash \forall s_o \in S, \sum_{c \in C} x_{c,s_o} > 0\} \tag{7}$$

As the QoS provided is measured in terms of distance between the clients and the charging stations, a single objective is provided in Eq. 1: minimizing the distance between the clients and the assigned charging stations. Regarding the problem constraints, all the clients are assigned to a unique charging station (Eq. 2); all the clients are served for any charging station, i.e., there are not potential clients without a charging station assigned (Eq. 3); the maximum distance between the charging station and the client assigned should be lower than Dc (Eq. 4); the maximum distance between the electric substation and the fed charging station should be lower De (Eq. 5); the number of charging stations that are fed by a given electric substation should be lower or equal than pm_e (Eq. 6); and the number of charging stations located should be lower than the maximum number of charging stations to be located Ms.

3   Metaheuristics for Efficient EV-CSL

This section summarizes the applied metaheuristics to address EV-CSL in the city of Malaga and introduces the main implementation details.

3.1   Algorithms

Genetic Algorithm: It was originally presented by John Holland inspired by the evolution of species in Nature [19]. A basic pseudocode is showed in Algorithm 1. GA is an iterative method. In each iteration, the algorithm generates λ new solutions (new population). A new solution is generated from several parent solutions (two parents this case, p_1 and p_2) selected from the previous population. The selected solutions are mixed (crossover) between them to generate a new one, which is probabilistically disturbed (mutated). At the end of an iteration, the new solutions replace others from the previous population following some kind of strategy. Finally, the algorithm returns the best solution found.

Variable Neighbourhood Search: It is based on the concept of neighbourhood [15]. The pseudocode is showed in Algorithm 2. Each solution has a defined neighbourhood, i.e., a set of solutions with closest facilities to it. The current solution x is modified according to these neighbourhoods ($next()$ indicates the number of modifications) and improved by a local search. In this version, a number K of consecutive non-improvements is allowed before finishing the algorithm. The VNS applied in the proposed approach is based on the version defined in [6].

Algorithm 1. GA	Algorithm 2. VNS
1: $pop \leftarrow generatepopulaion()$	1: $x \leftarrow generation()$
2: $i \leftarrow 1$	2: $x \leftarrow localsearch(x)$
3: **while** non stop condition **do**	3: $r \leftarrow true$
4: $pop' \leftarrow \emptyset$	4: **while** r & non stop condition **do**
5: **for** $l \in \{1..\lambda\}$ **do**	5: $r \leftarrow false$
6: $p_1, p_2 \leftarrow select(pop)$	6: $j \leftarrow 1$
7: $x \leftarrow crossover(p_1, p_2)$	7: **while** $\neg r$ & $j \leq K$ **do**
8: $x' \leftarrow mutation(x)$	8: $i \leftarrow 1$
9: $pop' \leftarrow x'$	9: **while** $\neg r$ & $i \leq k_{max}$ **do**
10: **end for**	10: $k \leftarrow next(i, k_{max})$
11: $pop \leftarrow replacement(pop, pop')$	11: $x' \leftarrow shake(x, k)$
12: $i \leftarrow i + 1$	12: $x' \leftarrow localsearch2(x')$
13: **end while**	13: $x \leftarrow acceptation(x, x')$
14: **return** pop	14: **if** $x = x'$ **then** $r \leftarrow true$
	15: **else** $r \leftarrow false$
	16: **end if**
	17: $i \leftarrow i + 1$
	18: **end while**
	19: $j \leftarrow j + 1$
	20: **end while**
	21: **end while**
	22: **return** x

3.2   Implementation Details

The solution encoding and the fitness function evaluation are defined in this section. Other details about the applied algorithms (i.e., GA and VNS variation operators) are presented in the parameter settings section (see Sect. 5).

Solution Encoding: The applied solution encoding considers a vector S^o of S_M binary elements, i.e., $S^o = \langle s_0^o, ..., s_{S_M}^o \rangle$, being S_M the number of road segments that are potential locations for the EV charging stations (in the modeled scenario $S_M = 33,550$, see Sect. 4.1). Thus, if in the road segment i there is an EV charging station $s_i^o = 1$, otherwise $s_i^o = 0$.

Fitness Function: The fitness function evaluates the QoS provided by installing EV charging stations in the locations represent by the solution S^o. In this approach, the QoS is given by the distance that the users have to travel from their homes to the charging station. Thus, the EV-CSL problem is defined as a minimization problem in which the objective function is the average distance the citizens travel from their homes (in EV-CSL are known as neighborhood centers that groups a set of buildings) to the EV charging station. The objective function is defied according to Eq. 1.

4   Experimental Settings

This section describes the main aspects of the experiments carried out to address EV-CSL by using GAs and VNSs. It presents the real-world scenario/instance defined to evaluate the proposed approach. It summarizes the implementation and computational platform. It describes the experiments performed by using irace to configure the main parameters of the applied algorithms.

4.1   Scenarios

The EV-CSL is addressed over the city of Malaga, as case study. This realistic scenario consists of 567,953 citizens in 363 neighborhoods. The road map is defied by using the data of Open Street Maps Based. The map includes total of 33,550 road segments as tentative locations for the charging stations (i.e., $S_M = 33{,}550$). Finally, the scenario includes the main data of the actual 14 electrical substations, i.e., locations, maximum energy flow capacity, etc. (see Fig. 1). The maximum energy flow capacity limits the number of charging stations that can be located in a given area. Thus, it is not realistic to place as many charging stations as we want in any place because a fast charge of a medium-class EV station consumes more than a whole building of apartments. The different colors in Fig. 1 show the areas of the city covered by each substation.

Different instances have been defined by changing the maximum number of EV charging stations to be installed, i.e., M_s. To compare among the different

Street segment
Neighborhood center
Power electric substation location

Fig. 1. Road map of Malaga, Spain. The edges represent each possible street segment associated with a substation.

methods, five instances are use with $M_s \in \{10, 20, 30, 40, 50\}$. Besides, to compare the provided solutions against the actual one provided by the municipality of Malaga (baseline), another instance was defined with $M_s = 45$ because at the time of this research Malaga has 45 EV charging stations.

4.2 Implementation and Hardware Platform

The computation platform used in this work consists of a cluster of 144 cores, equipped with three Intel Xeon CPU (E5-2670 v3) at 2.30 GHz and 64 GB memory. We have carried out 30 runs of each experiment. The stop condition for both algorithms is the computational time, in this case, they run for 60 CPU seconds. After that, the algorithms report the best solution found in each of the runs. The algorithms were implemented by using C++, the source code can be found in https://github.com/NEO-Research-Group/EV-CSL.

4.3 Parameter Settings

GAs and VNSs can use parameters and operators: crossover, mutation, local searches, etc. We have implemented several alternatives for these operators. To get the best parameter setting of the algorithms for our problem, a preliminary parameter setting study was performed. Using a reduced scenario, i.e., the northwest area of Malaga, and irace [13] tool to obtain the best configuration of our algorithms. The two best configurations returned by irace are the ones used in the experimental analysis, trying to avoid possible overfitting in the process carried out by irace. Table 1 shows the configurations of the GA and the VNS.

5 Experimental Analysis

This section presents the main results of the experiments carried out by performing 30 independent runs of each algorithm variation and each of the instances (i.e., $M_s \in \{10, 20, 30, 40, 45, 50\}$).

Table 1. Two best parameter configurations found by irace for GA and VNS.

Parameter	GA-1	GA-2	Parameter	VNS-1	VNS-2
population	30	50	Neighbour. model	Quadr. [3]	Closest [3]
λ	12	6	Neighbour. Size	17	6
selection	Worse one	Better one	shake	Random	Random
crossover	None	CUPCAP [4]	next	None	None
mutation	Random	Random	localsearch	None	IALT$_{L=20}$ [7]
mut. prob.	0.65	0.76	localsearch2	FI [18]	FI [18]
replacement	(μ, λ)	$(\mu + \lambda)$	k_{max}	44	34
			K	85	59
			accept	Elitist	Elitist

5.1   Optimization Results Comparison

Figure 2 and Table 2 presents the results of each algorithm for the six instances addressed in terms of fitness value (i.e., average distance that users have to travel to get the assigned charging station) of the best solution found. The blue line represents the fitness value obtained for the solution that represents the actual location of the EV charging stations in Malaga (baseline solution). Comparing the four metaheuristic alternatives, GA-2 provides the best (lowest) results for all the instances. In turn, GA-2 provides the most robust method because it shows the lowest variability among the different runs.

According to Wilcoxon Signed Ranks with Bonferroni correction, GA-2 is the best method and GA-1 provides the worst results, for all the instances. This remarks the importance of finding the proper configuration of the GA. For instances $M_s = 10$ and $M_s = 20$, VNS-1 and VNS-2 do not show statistical difference. VNS-2 provides statistically the second best results the rest of instances.

As it can be seen in Fig. 2, all the proposed algorithms improve the baseline QoS (distance) when installing only 20 stations. In turn, GA-2 is able to improve the baseline using only 10 stations.

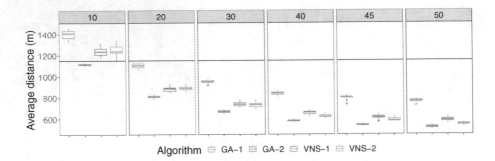

Fig. 2. Fitness value (average distance) of each algorithm for the different instances. The blue line represents the fitness value of baseline solution. (Color figure online)

Table 2. Experimental results for each algorithm in each instance ($\times 10^2$).

M_s	Algorithm	Mean ± SD	Min	Median	Max
10	GA-1	14.08 ± 0.38	13.25	14.14	14.63
10	GA-2	**11.21 ± 0.075**	**11.03**	**11.12**	**11.31**
10	VNS-1	12.44 ± 0.40	11.73	12.42	13.14
10	VNS-2	12.52 ± 0.46	11.54	12.41	13.43
20	GA-1	11.03 ± 0.20	10.60	11.06	11.42
20	GA-2	**8.08 ± 0.11**	**7.86**	**8.07**	**8.34**
20	VNS-1	8.80 ± 0.22	8.44	8.84	9.31
20	VNS-2	8.89 ± 0.20	8.52	8.89	9.31

(*continued*)

Table 2. (*continued*)

M_s	Algorithm	Mean ± SD	Min	Median	Max
30	GA-1	9.51 ± 0.14	9.19	9.50	9.79
30	GA-2	**6.68 ± 0.11**	**6.48**	**6.70**	**6.87**
30	VNS-1	7.36 ± 0.19	7.04	7.36	7.74
30	VNS-2	7.28 ± 0.21	6.92	7.33	7.80
40	GA-1	8.40 ± 0.15	8.06	8.40	8.69
40	GA-2	**5.80 ± 0.08**	**5.62**	**5.81**	**5.96**
40	VNS-1	6.55 ± 0.16	6.16	6.59	6.84
40	VNS-2	6.23 ± 0.14	5.98	6.21	6.51
45	GA-1	7.99 ± 0.17	7.35	8.02	8.26
45	GA-2	**5.42 ± 0.08**	**5.26**	**5.43**	**5.58**
45	VNS-1	6.12 ± 0.16	5.73	6.14	6.46
45	VNS-2	5.88 ± 0.16	5.66	5.84	6.27
50	GA-1	7.66 ± 0.13	7.27	7.67	7.93
50	GA-2	**5.20 ± 0.10**	**5.00**	**5.18**	**5.40**
50	VNS-1	5.86 ± 0.16	5.54	5.87	6.23
50	VNS-2	5.49 ± 0.10	5.23	5.47	5.71

5.2 Improvement on Travel Distance over the Real Layout of Stations

To better illustrate the improvement offered by our algorithms versus the actual stations locations in the city of Malaga (a.k.a. baseline solution), we have compare the solutions found by installing the same number of stations ($M_s = 45$) in terms of average distance that the EV users have to travel to charge their cars.

Figure 3 shows the proportion of solutions for each algorithm (y-axis) obtained less than the percentage of improvement defined in the x-axis, i.e., the percentage of computed solutions that achieved at most that percentage of

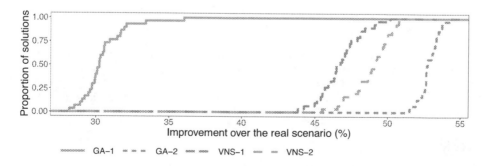

Fig. 3. Empirical cumulative distribution of the percentage of improvement of our solutions in each algorithm, compared to the baseline solution.

improvement. GA-1 lags far behind the other algorithms by only over 30% in the 75% of its solutions. The two versions of VNS offer improvements between 40–50%. The best algorithm is GA-2, being also the most stable (less steep curve) with a 52% of improvement in more than the 70% of its solutions. In general, it is interesting to note that the algorithms using the second-best configurations found by irace offer the most significant improvements. This result underlines the importance of take into account the overfitting when we configuring machine learning techniques.

6   Conclusion

This article presented a definition of the EV-CSL optimization problem. The optimization problem takes into account the QoS provided (in terms of distance customers have to travel to get the charging station) and the energy limitations of the different electric substations around the city. Two different metaheuristic algorithms, both parameterized using irace, have been proposed and implemented to address the problem: GA and VNS.

A realistic scenario based on city of Malaga has been defined by using real data (i.e., road maps, inhabitants' home location, electric substations location, etc.) Different instances have been defined by locating a different number of charging stations (from 10 to 50).

The main results of the experimental evaluation indicate that the proposed metaheuristics were able find competitive solutions. The solutions provided by the proposed methodology were able to improve the actual QoS provided in Malaga with 45 stations installing only 20. In general, a variation of GA provided the best results for the different instances. When comparing the actual solution in the city with the ones provided by the four metaheuristic variations analyzed here, metaheuristic dramatically improve the QoS.

The main lines for future work are related to extending the proposed problem model to consider the number of parking slots in each station and the charging time, exploring other optimization methods, and defining a multi-objective variation of the problem by including other objectives, such as the installation costs. In addition, we are working to improve the proposed model to include in the QoS the idea that the vehicles can be charged when the citizens are working or doing other activities.

Acknowledgment. This research was partially funded by the University of Málaga, Andalucía Tech, the Junta de Andalucía UMA18-FEDERJA-003 and the project TAILOR Grant #952215, H2020-ICT-2019-3. J. Toutouh research was partially funded by European Union's Horizon 2020 research and innovation program under the Marie Skłodowska-Curie grant agreement No 799078.

References

1. Brandstätter, G., Kahr, M., Leitner, M.: Determining optimal locations for charging stations of electric car-sharing systems under stochastic demand. Transp. Res. Part B Methodol. **104**, 17–35 (2017)

2. Camero, A., Alba, E.: Smart city and information technology: a review. Cities **93**, 84–94 (2019)
3. Cintrano, C., Chicano, F., Alba, E.: Using metaheuristics for the location of bicycle stations. Expert Syst. Appl. **161**, 113684 (2020)
4. Colmenar, J., Martí, R., Duarte, A.: Multi-objective memetic optimization for the bi-objective obnoxious p-median problem. Knowl.-Based Syst. **144**, 88–101 (2018)
5. Dantrakul, S., Likasiri, C., Pongvuthithum, R.: Applied p-median and p-center algorithms for facility location problems. Expert Syst. Appl. **41**(8), 3596–3604 (2014)
6. Drezner, Z., Brimberg, J., Mladenović, N., Salhi, S.: New heuristic algorithms for solving the planar p-median problem. Comput. Oper. Res. **62**, 296–304 (2015)
7. Drezner, Z., Brimberg, J., Mladenović, N., Salhi, S.: New local searches for solving the multi-source Weber problem. Ann. Oper. Res. **246**(1–2), 181–203 (2016). https://doi.org/10.1007/s10479-015-1797-5
8. Fabbiani, E., Nesmachnow, S., Toutouh, J., Tchernykh, A., Avetisyan, A., Radchenko, G.: Analysis of mobility patterns for public transportation and bus stops relocation. Program. Comput. Softw. **44**(6), 508–525 (2018). https://doi.org/10.1134/S0361768819010031
9. Haustein, S., Jensen, A.F.: Factors of electric vehicle adoption: a comparison of conventional and electric car users based on an extended theory of planned behavior. Int. J. Sustain. Transp. **12**(7), 484–496 (2018)
10. Huang, Y., Kockelman, K.M.: Electric vehicle charging station locations: elastic demand, station congestion, and network equilibrium. Transp. Res. Part D: Transp. Environ. **78**, 102179 (2020)
11. Lebrusán, I., Toutouh, J.: Car restriction policies for better urban health: a low emission zone in Madrid, Spain. Air Qua. Atmos. Health **14**, 333–342 (2020). https://doi.org/10.1007/s11869-020-00938-z
12. Lebrusán, I., Toutouh, J.: Using smart city tools to evaluate the effectiveness of a low emissions zone in Spain: Madrid central. Smart Cities **3**(2), 456–478 (2020)
13. López-Ibáñez, M., Dubois-Lacoste, J., Cáceres, L.P., Birattari, M., Stützle, T.: The irace package: iterated racing for automatic algorithm configuration. Oper. Res. Perspect. **3**, 43–58 (2016)
14. Megiddot, N., Supowits, K.J.: On the complexity of some common geometric location problems. SIAM J. Comput. **13**(1), 182–196 (1984)
15. Mladenović, N., Hansen, P.: Variable neighborhood search. Comput. Oper. Res. **24**(11), 1097–1100 (1997)
16. OpenStreetMap Contributors: Planet dump (2017). https://planet.osm.org. https://www.openstreetmap.org
17. Paraschiv, S., Paraschiv, L.S.: Analysis of traffic and industrial source contributions to ambient air pollution with nitrogen dioxide in two urban areas in Romania. Energy Procedia **157**, 1553–1560 (2019). Technologies and Materials for Renewable Energy, Environment and Sustainability (TMREES)
18. Whitaker, R.A.: A fast algorithm for the greedy interchange for large-scale clustering and median location problems. INFOR: Inf. Syst. Oper. Res. **21**(2), 95–108 (1983)
19. Whitley, D.: A genetic algorithm tutorial. Stat. Comput. **4**(2), 65–85 (1994). https://doi.org/10.1007/BF00175354

Modeling Administrative Discretion Using Goal-Directed Answer Set Programming

Joaquín Arias$^{(\boxtimes)}$ ⓘ, Mar Moreno-Rebato ⓘ, Jose A. Rodriguez-García ⓘ,
and Sascha Ossowski ⓘ

CETINIA, Universidad Rey Juan Carlos, Madrid, Spain
{joaquin.arias,mar.rebato,joseantonio.rodriguez,sascha.ossowski}@urjc.es

Abstract. Automated legal reasoning and its application in smart contract is getting interest. In this context, ethical and legal concerns make it necessary for automated reasoners to *justify* in human-understandable terms the advice given. Logic Programming, specially Answer Set Programming, has a rich semantics and has been used to very concisely express complex knowledge. However, modelling vague concepts such as *ambiguity* and *discretion* cannot be expressed in top-down execution models based on Prolog, and in bottom-up execution models based on ASP the justifications are incomplete and/or not scalable. We propose to use s(CASP), a top-down execution model for predicate ASP, to model ambiguity and discretion following a set of patterns. We have implemented a framework, called s(LAW), to model, reason, and justify the applicable legislation and validate it by translating (and benchmarking) the criteria for the admission of students in public centers established by the "Comunidad de Madrid".

Keywords: Answer Set Programming · Goal-directed · Ambiguity · Administrative discretion

1 Introduction

The formal representation of a legal text to automatize reasoning about them is well known in literature. For deterministic rules there are several proposals, often based on logic-based programming languages [12,14].

This topic is recently gaining much attention thanks to the interest in the so-called smart contracts, and to autonomous decisions by public administrations [3,10,15]. A smart contract is a program that represents the legal terms of a contract and is deployed on a block-chain platform to automatically execute, control and document the events described in the contract.

This work has been partially supported by the Spanish Ministry of Science, Innovation and Universities, co-funded by EU FEDER Funds, through project grant InEDGEMobility RTI2018-095390-B-C33 (MCIU/AEI/FEDER, UE).

ⓒ Springer Nature Switzerland AG 2021
E. Alba et al. (Eds.): CAEPIA 2021, LNAI 12882, pp. 258–267, 2021.
https://doi.org/10.1007/978-3-030-85713-4_25

However, none of the existing proposals are able to represent the ambiguity and/or administrative discretion present in contracts and/or applicable legislation, e.g., *force majeure*. Force majeure is a law term that must be understood as referring to abnormal and unforeseeable circumstances which were outside the control of the party by whom it is pleaded and the consequences of which could not have been avoided in spite of the exercise of all due care (see judgment Court of Justice of European Union, case Tomas Vilkas, C-640/15, 25 January 2017). In the procedure for awarding school places in centers supported with public funds in the "Comunidad de Madrid" (CM), in Spain, the proximity of a school to a family's home or work address plays an important role. This proximity is determined based on existing educational districts, except in cases of force majeure, but these cases are not defined a priory.

In this work we present a framework, called s(LAW), that allows for modeling legal rules involving ambiguity, and supports reasoning and inferring conclusions based on them. Additionally, thanks to the goal-directed execution of s(CASP), the underlying system used to implement our proposal, s(LAW) provides justification of the resulting conclusions (in natural language).

To evaluate the expressiveness of our proposal we have translated the procedure for awarding school places for the "Educación Secundaria Obligatoria" (ESO) of centers supported with public funds in the CM. The Spanish Organic Law on Education[1] regulates, in article 84, the criteria for the admission of students in public centers and private subsidized centers and, in its second paragraph of this article 84, indicates adjudication criteria. However, since Spain is a politically decentralized country, it is the autonomous communities (and, therefore, their educational administrations) that have powers to develop these aspects of basic state legislation. The CM, in use of its powers in educational matters, establishes the framework and general procedure for the admission of students to educational centers supported with public funds for the ESO.[2] The case presented in this paper is, therefore, a real case, based on the regulations currently in force in the CM.

2   Goal-Directed Answer Set Programming

Our proposal relies on Answer Set Programming (ASP) [7] for coding contracts and legal rules. More specifically, we use s(CASP) [1], a goal-directed implementation of ASP that features predicates, constraints among non-ground variables, and uninterpreted functions.

---

[1] Organic Law 2/2006, May 3, last modified by Organic Law 3/2020, December 29.

[2] Decree 29/2013, of April 11, modified by Decree 11/2019, of March 5, of the Governing Council, on freedom of choice respecting school centers; Order 1240/2013, of April 17, of the Department of Education, Youth and Sports of Community of Madrid, modified by Order 1534/2019, of May 17, of the Department of Education and Research Community of Madrid; Resolution of July 31, 2013, of the General Directorate for the Improvement of the Quality of Education (regarding bilingual education); and Joint Resolution of the Deputy Department of Educational Policy and Educational Organization, of February 18, 2021 (https://bit.ly/3dAX22d).

The top-down query-driven execution strategy of s(CASP) has three major advantages w.r.t. traditional ASP system: (a) it does not require to ground the programs; (b) its execution starts with a query and the evaluation only explores the parts of the knowledge base relevant to the query; and (c) s(CASP) returns partial stable models (the relevant subsets of the ASP stable models needed to support the query) and their corresponding justification (proof tree). Thus, our proposal automates commonsense reasoning and is scalable whereas ground based ASP systems do not (Sect. 5).

Additionally, s(CASP) provides a mechanism to present justifications in natural language using a generic translation, and the possibility of customizing them with directives that provide explanation patterns in natural language. Both plain text and user-friendly, expandable HTML can be generated. These patterns can be used with the program text itself, thereby making it easier for experts without a programming background to understand both the program and the results, i.e., partial model and justification, of its execution.

3   Administrative and Judicial Discretion Reasoner

This work makes two main contributions: (i) a set of patterns to translate legal rules into ASP, and natural language patterns to generate readable justifications; (ii) a framework to model, reason, and justify conclusions based on the evidence provided by the user and the applicable legislation, representing ambiguity, discretion and/or incomplete information (key concepts in legal cases).

3.1   Patterns to Translate Law into ASP

The translation of legal rules into logic predicates has been considered a straightforward task for many years. However, the translation of ambiguity and/or discretion concepts required the help of an expert in law and/or in the field of application, in order to specify only one interpretation and/or decision.

Let us use the encoding of the procedure for the adjudication of schools places in the CM (Fig. 1) to explain the following patterns:

Requirement For Applying. These are the most common constructions in legal articles. There are two patterns:

- Disjunction of requirements, e.g., "s/he obtains a school place if one of the following common requirements are met". Which is translated by separating each requirement in different clauses, see Fig. 1 lines 9, 12, and 19:
- Conjunction of requirements, e.g., "In addition, some of the specific requirements must be met". Which is translated to a single clause where the comma ',' means *and*, see Fig. 1 lines 5–7:

Exceptions For Applying. As we mentioned before, a legal article is a default rule subject to possible exceptions. In s(CASP) the exceptions can be encoded using negation as failure. For example, Fig. 1 lines 2–4 shows the translation of "It will be possible to obtain a school place if the requirement is met and there is no exception" and then, the compiler of s(CASP) would generate its dual, i.e., not exception, by collecting and checking that no exceptions hold:

```
1  not exception :- not exception_1, ..., not exception_n.
```

where `not exception_i` is a new predicate name that identified the dual of the ith exception. For the sake of brevity let us omit the explanation of how the compiler generates the dual for each exception (see [1,9] for details). Fig. 1 lines 46–57 shows the translation of the unique exception defined in our running example: "Students coming from non-bilingual public schools, who apply for a place in English language bilingual schools and who wish to study in the Bilingual Section, need to accredit a level of English in the four skills equivalent to level B1 for $1^{st}/2^{nd}$ ESO, and to level B2 for $3^{rd}/4^{th}$ ESO".

Ambiguity. Ambiguity occurs when some aspects of the law can be interpreted in different ways. For example, "proximity to the family or work address" is a specific and defined requirement based on the distribution by educational districts. However, in case of *force majeure*, students from a education district may be reassigned to a school from another district. Figure 1 lines 34–44 encode this scenario allowing evaluation without having to determine a priori the force majeure circumstances necessary to justify the reassignment of students. This pattern generates a model where `force_majeure` is assumed to hold and another model where there is *no* evidence that `force_majeure` holds.

Discretion To Act. The discretion to act introduces different possible interpretations of the law and/or the contract that we intent to model by generating multiple models. Implementations based on Prolog compute a single, canonical model, and therefore, bypass this non determinism by selecting one interpretation. The discretion to act can be considered as a ground or an exception following the previous patterns. For example, Fig. 1 lines 59–79 shows the translation of the discretion to act rule: "The School Council may add another complementary criterion". The resulting encoding uses predicates in which the variable `CC` can be instantiated with different values. This feature allows us to reuse some of the clauses without repeating them, i.e., the clauses in lines 59–79 are generic, while clauses 81–88 specify the ground and exceptions of the criteria added by a particular school. Clauses in lines 66–71 generate two possible models if the discretion to act is exercised according to the purpose/intention of the law and it is not unlawful. In one model the complementary criterion is applied and in the other it does not. Then, clauses in lines 86–88 state the cases in which the discretion to act has a purpose and/or is unlawful.

Unknown Information. The use of default negation may introduce unexpected results in the absence of information (positive and/or negative). Therefore, in many cases the desirable behavior should capture the absence of information by generating different models depending on the relevant information. For example, it may be unclear whether the documents we have to certify that we are a `large_family` are valid or not, so we avoid introducing that information and the reasoner would reason assuming both scenarios. To state that some information is certain we would use the predicate `evidence/1`, e.g., `evidence(large_family)` means that s/he has the condition of large family. Additionally, s(LAW) would provide *strong* negation, denoted with '`-`', to specify that we have evidences

```
1    %% Obtain a school place if...
2    obtain_place :-
3        met_requirement,
4        not exception.
5    met_requirement :-
6        met_common_requirement,
7        met_specific_requirement.
8    %% Common requirements:
9    met_common_requirement :-
10       large_family.
11
12   met_common_requirement :-
13       recipient_social_benefits.
14   recipient_social_benefits :-
15       renta_minima_insercion.
16   recipient_social_benefits :-
17       ingreso_minimo_vital.
18
19   met_common_requirement :-
20       disability_status.
21   disability_status :-
22       disabled_parent.
23   disability_status :-
24       disabled_sibling.
25   %% Specific requirements:
26   met_specific_requirement :-
27       sibling_enroll_center.
28   met_specific_requirement :-
29       legal_guardian_work_center.
30
31   met_specific_requirement :-
32       relative_former_student.
33
34   met_specific_requirement :-
35       school_proximity.
36   school_proximity :-
37       same_education_district.
38   school_proximity :-
39       not same_education_district,
40       force_majeure.    % Ambiguity
41   force_majeure :-
42       not n_force_majeure.
43   n_force_majeure :-
44       not force_majeure.

45   %% Exceptions:
46   exception :-
47       come_non_bilingual,
48       want_bilingual_section(Course),
49       not accredit_english_level(Course).
50   accredit_english_level('1st ESO') :-
51       b1_certificate.
52   accredit_english_level('2nd ESO') :-
53       b1_certificate.
54   accredit_english_level('3rd ESO') :-
55       b2_certificate.
56   accredit_english_level('4th ESO') :-
57       b2_certificate.
58   %% Discretion To Act:
59   obtain_place :-
60       not met_requirement,
61       met_complementary_criterion(CC).
62   obtain_place :-
63       met_requirement, exception,
64       met_complementary_criterion(CC).
65
66   met_complementary_criterion(CC) :-
67       school_criteria(CC),
68       purpose(CC), not unlawful(CC),
69       not n_met_complementary_criterion(CC).
70   n_nmet_complementary_criterion(CC) :-
71       not met_complementary_criterion(CC).
72   purpose(CC) :-
73       promote_diversity(CC).
74   unlawful(CC) :-
75       sex_discrimination(CC).
76   unlawful(CC) :-
77       race_discrimination(CC).
78   unlawful(CC) :-
79       religion_discrimination(CC).
80
81   school_criteria(foreign_student) :-
82       foreign_student.
83   school_criteria(specific_etnia) :-
84       specific_etnia.
85
86   promote_diversity(foreign_student).
87   promote_diversity(specific_etnia).
88   race_discrimination(specific_etnia).
```

Fig. 1. Translation of the procedure for awarding school places under s(LAW).

supporting the falsehood of some information, e.g., -evidence(large_family) means that s/he does not have the condition of large family.

3.2   Description of s(LAW)

s(LAW), built on top of s(CASP), is composed by three modules: the first contains the *articles*, the second contains *explanations* to generate readable justifications, and the third one contains the *evidences*. In our running example:

```
 1   s/he may obtain a school place, because
 2       a common requirement is met, because
 3           s/he is part of a large family.
 4       a specific requirement is met, because
 5           s/he has siblings enrolled in the center.
 6       there is no evidence that an exception applies, because
 7           s/he came from a non-bilingual public school, and
 8           s/he wish to study 2nd ESO in the Bilingual Section, and
 9           s/he accredit required level of English for 2nd ESO, because
10               in the four skills certificate level b1.
```

Fig. 3. Justification in Natural Language for the evaluation of `student01.pl`.

ArticleESO.pl. Contains the legislation rules in Fig. 1 following the patterns described in Sect. 3.1.

ArticleESO.pre.pl. Contains the natural language patterns for the predicates that are relevant to provide readable justifications of the conclusions inferred by s(LAW). The directive `#pred` defines the natural language patterns, e.g.:

```
1   #pred obtain_place :: 's/he may obtain a school place'.
```

Additionally, to facilitate the understanding of the code we can obtain a readable code (in natural language) by invoking `scasp --code --human`.

StudentXX.pl. Figure 2 shows the encoding of the module `student01.pl` corresponding to one student. This last module encodes the evidences of a student and links them with the previous modules `ArticleESO.pl` and `ArticleESO.pred.pl` (lines 1–2). The predicates `evidences/1` and `-evidence/1` (explained in Sect. 3.1) are used to specify the known information (positive or negative evidences). For the sake of brevity, let us handle as *unknown* the evidences corresponding to: `large_family`, `renta_minima_insercion`, `sibling_enroll_center`, `same_education_district`, `b1_certificate`, `foreign_student`, and `specific_etnia`. Figure 2 lines 7–13 provide the known information corresponding to this student. Additionally, we consider that the students, coming from non-bilingual public schools, apply for a place in English language bilingual schools and wish to study in the Bilingual Section (Fig. 2 lines 4–5).

```
 1   #include('ArticleESO.pl').
 2   #include('ArticleESO.pred.pl').
 3
 4   come_non_bilingual.
 5   want_bilingual_section('2nd ESO').
 6
 7   evidence(large_family).
 8   evidence(renta_minima_insercion).
 9   evidence(sibling_enroll_center).
10   evidence(same_education_district).
11   evidence(b1_certificate).
12   -evidence(foreign_student).
13   -evidence(specific_etnia).
```

Fig. 2. File `student01.pl`.

4 Reasoning and Deduction with Real Use-Cases

The modules of s(LAW) are implemented under s(CASP) version 0.21.04.04 (https://gitlab.software.imdea.org/ciao-lang/sCASP), that runs under Ciao

Table 1. Case of different students evaluated using s(LAW).
Note: '+' is a positive evidence, '−' is a negative evidence, '?' means unkown.

	st_1	st_2	st_3	st_4	st_5	st_6
large_family	+	+	+	−	−	−
renta_minima_insercion	+	+	+	?	−	−
sibling_enroll_center	+	+	−	+	−	−
same_education_district	+	+	−	+	−	−
b1_certificate	+	−	+	?	−	−
foreign_student	−	−	−	−	+	−
specific_etnia	−	−	−	−	−	+
?- obtain_place	yes	no	yes	yes	yes	no

Prolog version 1.19-480. (http://ciao-lang.org/). The benchmarks used in this section are available at http://platon.etsii.urjc.es/~jarias/papers/slaw-caepia21 and were run on a MacOS 11.2.3 laptop with an Intel Core i7 at 2.6 GHz.

A priori Deduction: Consider we run our reasoner s(LAW) in the interactive mode to reason about six different students by invoking:

```
1   scasp -i --tree --human --short studentXX.pl
```

where **XX** corresponds to the 'id' of each student (from 1 to 6). Then, we ask the queries to obtain conclusions from the reasoner. Table 1 shows the data corresponding to the candidates and the conclusion generated by s(LAW) for the query ?- obtain_place. Students 1, 3, 4, and 5 obtain a place at the school while students 2 and 6 do not.

- Student 1: Fig. 2 contains the information corresponding to this student. Since s/he meets common and specific requirements and avoids the exception (having level b1 in English), the evaluation returns the partial model:

    { obtain_place, large_family, sibling_enroll_center, come_non_bilingual,
    want_bilingual_section(2nd ESO), b1_certificate }

   and the corresponding justification shown in Fig. 3.
- Student 2: meets common and specific requirements but has to be rejected because s/he does not accredit level b1 in English.
- Student 3: meets common requirements, avoids the exception and by assuming force_majeure s/he also meets a specific requirement (school proximity). Note that s/he does not live in the same education district.
- Student 4: in this use-case there is absence of information regarding the "renta minima de insercion" and the English certificate (marked with ?). The partial model returned assumes that the truth values for these pieces of information are true. Therefore, based on that assumption the student would obtain a place.

```
1     there is no evidence that s/he may obtain a school place, because
2        there is no evidence that a common requirement is met, because
3           there is no evidence that s/he is part of a large family, and
4           there is no evidence that s/he is a recipient of the RMI, and
5           there is no evidence that a parent or sibling has disability status.
6        there is no evidence that the criterion foreign_student is met, because
7           there is no evidence that s/he meets the criteria foreign_student, because
8              there is no evidence that s/he is a foreign student.
9        there is no evidence that the criterion specific_etnia is met, because
10          s/he meets the criteria specific_etnia, because
11             s/he belongs to a specific etnia.
12          specific_etnia follows the purpose of the procedure, because
13             specific_etnia promotes the diversity.
14          specific_etnia is illegal, because
15             specific_etnia discriminates based on race.
```

Fig. 4. Justification in Natural Language for the evaluation of `student06.pl`.

– Student 5: now we consider that the school added a complementary criterion for foreign students and therefore, since the student is a foreigner, s/he obtains a place.
– Student 6: in this use-case the complementary criterion `specific_etnia` cannot be applied because it discriminates by race and therefore, it is unlawful. Therefore, the student does not obtain a place.

A posteriori Deduction. The main advantage of s(LAW) is its ability to generate justifications not only for positive but also for negative information. This ability allows us to analyze the reason for a specific inference and/or to determine which are the requirements needed to obtain a specific conclusion:

– For student 3, the query `?- not force_majeure, obtain_place` avoids the assumption of force majeure and the student does not obtain a place.
– For student 4, the query `?- not obtain_place` returns the partial models (with the assumptions) for which this student does not obtain a place.
– For student 6, Fig. 4 shows the justification of the query `?- not obtain_place` so we can analyze more in detail why this student is rejected. While the complementary criteria for student 5 (`foreign_student`) is similar to `specific_etnia`, the justification tree shows that this student does not obtain a place because the complementary criterion is illegal (Fig. 4 lines 14–15).

Additionally, we can collect the partial models, in which the school place is or is not obtained, together with their justification and analyze "Epistemic Specifications" [6], that is, what is true in all/some models, which partial models share certain assumptions, etc. This reasoning makes it possible to detect the missing information that would change the decision from "not obtained" (or "obtained" under some assumptions) to "obtained". Note that, by introducing the new evidences, the resulting justification of s(LAW) provides an explanation in which these evidences are used to support the decision.

5   Related Work

Most ASP systems follow bottom-up executions that require a grounding phase where the variables of the program are replaced with their possible values. During the grounding phase, links between variables are lost and therefore an explanation framework for these systems must face many challenges to provide a concise justification of why a specific answer set satisfies the rules (and which rules). The most relevant approaches are: off-line and on-line justifications [11]; Causal Graph Justification [2]; and Labeled ABA-Based Answer Set Justification (LABAS) [13]. However, these approaches are applied to grounded versions of the programs, i.e., non-ground programs have to be grounded, and they may produce unwieldy justifications when the non-ground program has uninterpreted functions, consults large databases and/or requires the representation of dense domains [1].

On the other hand, systems that follow a top-down execution can trace which rules have been used to obtain the answers more easily. One such system is ErgoAI (https://coherentknowledge.com), based on XSB [16], that generates justification trees for programs with variables. ErgoAI has been applied to analyze streams of financial regulatory and policy compliance in near real-time providing explanations in English that are fully detailed and interactively navigable. However, default negation in ErgoAI is based on the well-founded semantics [5] and therefore ErgoAI is not a framework that allows the representation of ambiguity and/or administrative discretion.

Finally, we would like to emphasize that explainable AI techniques for black-box AI tools, most of them based on machine learning, are not able to explain how variation in the input data changes the resulting decision [4].

6   Conclusions

In this paper we have shown that using goal-directed answer set programming, s(LAW) is capable of modeling discretion and ambiguity. The deduction based on s(LAW) allows: the consideration of different conclusions (multiple models) which can be analyzed by humans thanks to the justification generated in natural language; and the reasoning about the set of these conclusions/models. To the best of our knowledge, s(LAW) is the only system that exhibits the property of modelling vague concepts.[3]

Our future work unfolds among two major lines. The first is to complete the modeling of the legislation by tabulation for each of the criteria used in the procedure for adjudication of school places in centers supported with public funds. And, second, the use of this tabulation of criteria to check (by employing the underlying constraint solver of s(SCASP)) whether automated decisions can be made when the regulation includes ambiguity, administrative discretion and unknown information.

---

[3] On January 14th, 2021, Dr. Robert Kowalski explained how they bypassed in [14] the representation of vague concepts such as *without undue delay* [8, 1:20:15, 1:26:00].

References

1. Arias, J., Carro, M., Salazar, E., Marple, K., Gupta, G.: Constraint answer set programming without grounding. Theory Pract. Logic Program. **18**(3–4), 337–354 (2018). https://doi.org/10.1017/S1471068418000285
2. Cabalar, P., Fandinno, J., Fink, M.: Causal graph justifications of logic programs. Theory Pract. Logic Program. **14**(4–5), 603–618 (2014). https://doi.org/10.1017/S1471068414000234
3. Cobbe, J.: Administrative law and the machines of government: judicial review of automated public-sector decision-making. Legal Stud. **39**(4), 636–655 (2019)
4. DARPA: Explainable Artificial Intelligence (XAI). Defense Advanced Research Projects Agency (2017). https://www.darpa.mil/program/explainable-artificial-intelligence
5. Gelder, A.V., Ross, K., Schlipf, J.: The well-founded semantics for general logic programs. J. ACM **38**, 620–650 (1991). https://doi.org/10.1145/116825.116838
6. Gelfond, M.: Logic programming and reasoning with incomplete information. Ann. Math. Artif. Intell. **12**(1), 89–116 (1994)
7. Gelfond, M., Lifschitz, V.: The stable model semantics for logic programming. In: 5th International Conference on Logic Programming, pp. 1070–1080 (1988). http://www.cse.unsw.edu.au/~cs4415/2010/resources/stable.pdf, https://bit.ly/3fGDie6
8. Kowalski, R.A.: Logical English = Logic + English + Computing, Hack-Reason Opening Ceremony, January 2021. https://utdallas.app.box.com/s/ngsyloscj5sk24uh3axexxz451o74z0u. Accessed 19 Apr 2021
9. Marple, K., Salazar, E., Gupta, G.: computing stable models of normal logic programs without grounding. arXiv 1709.00501 (2017). http://arxiv.org/abs/1709.00501
10. Cerrillo i Martínez, A.: El derecho para una inteligencia artificial centrada en el ser humano y al servicio de las instituciones: Presentación del monográfico. IDP: Revista de Internet, Derecho y Politica (30) (2019)
11. Pontelli, E., Son, T.C., El-Khatib, O.: Justifications for logic programs under answer set semantics. Theory Pract. Logic Program. **9**(1), 1–56 (2009). https://doi.org/10.1017/S1471068408003633
12. Ramakrishna, S., Górski, Ł, Paschke, A.: A dialogue between a lawyer and computer scientist: the evaluation of knowledge transformation from legal text to computer-readable format. Appl. Artif. Intell. **30**(3), 216–232 (2016)
13. Schulz, C., Toni, F.: Justifying answer sets using argumentation. Theory Pract. Logic Program. **16**(1), 59–110 (2016). https://doi.org/10.1017/S1471068414000702
14. Sergot, M.J., Sadri, F., Kowalski, R.A., Kriwaczek, F., Hammond, P., Cory, H.T.: The British nationality act as a logic program. Commun. ACM **29**(5), 370–386 (1986)
15. Solé, J.P.: Inteligencia artificial, derecho administrativo y reserva de humanidad: algoritmos y procedimiento administrativo debido tecnológico. Revista general de Derecho administrativo **50** (2019)
16. Swift, T., Warren, D.S.: XSB: extending prolog with tabled logic programming. Theory Pract. Logic Program. **12**(1–2), 157–187 (2012). https://doi.org/10.1017/S1471068411000500

Author Index

Printed in the United States
by Baker & Taylor Publisher Services